ENGLISH
SKILLS
WITH
READINGS

Carlos A. B [handwritten]

English 095 Writing
Patrick Sullivan

W9-CYS-158

OTHER BOOKS BY JOHN LANGAN

English Skills
College Writing Skills
College Writing Skills with Readings
Sentence Skills (Forms A, B, and C)
Reading and Study Skills (Forms A and B)

ENGLISH SKILLS WITH READINGS

THIRD EDITION

JOHN LANGAN

Atlantic Community College

McGRAW-HILL, INC.

New York   St. Louis   San Francisco   Auckland
Bogotá   Caracas   Lisbon   London   Madrid
Mexico City   Milan   Montreal   New Delhi
San Juan   Singapore   Sydney   Tokyo   Toronto

ENGLISH SKILLS WITH READINGS

Copyright ©1995, 1991, 1988 by McGraw-Hill, Inc. All rights reserved.
Printed in the United States of America. Except as permitted under the
United States Copyright Act of 1976, no part of this publication may be
reproduced or distributed in any form or by any means, or stored in a data
base or retrieval system, without the prior written permission of the
publisher.

Acknowledgments for the readings appear on page 570, and on this page by reference.

 This book is printed on recycled, acid-free paper containing 10% postconsumer waste.

1 2 3 4 5 6 7 8 9 0   DOC   DOC   9 0 9 8 7 6 5 4

ISBN 0-07-036418-4

This book was set in Times Roman by Monotype Composition Company.
The editors were Tim Julet and Susan Gamer;
the designer was Rafael Hernandez;
the production supervisor was Richard A. Ausburn.
R. R. Donnelley & Sons Company was printer and binder.

Library of Congress Cataloging-in-Publication Data

Langan, John, (date).
    English skills with readings / John Langan. — 3d ed.
       p.   cm.
    Includes index.
    ISBN 0-07-036418-4
     1. English language—Rhetoric.   2. College readers.   I. Title.
PE1408.L3182   1995
808'.0427—dc20   94-17411

ABOUT
THE AUTHOR

John Langan has taught reading and writing at Atlantic Community College near Atlantic City, New Jersey, for over twenty years. The author of a popular series of college textbooks on both subjects, he enjoys the challenge of developing materials that teach skills in an especially clear and lively way. Before teaching, he earned advanced degrees in writing at Rutgers University and in reading at Glassboro State College. He also spent a year writing fiction that, he says, "is now at the back of a drawer waiting to be discovered and acclaimed posthumously." While in school, he supported himself by working as a truck driver, machinist, battery assembler, hospital attendant, and apple packer. He presently lives with his wife, Judith Nadell, near Philadelphia. Among his everyday pleasures are running, working on his Macintosh computer, and watching Philadelphia sports teams on TV. He also loves to read: newspapers at breakfast, magazines at lunch, and a chapter or two of a recent book ("preferably an autobiography") at night.

TO MY WIFE,
JUDITH NADELL

CONTENTS

READINGS LISTED BY RHETORICAL MODE

Note: Some selections are listed more than once because they illustrate more than one rhetorical method of development.

TO
THE
INSTRUCTOR

English Skills with Readings will help students learn and apply the basic principles of effective composition. It will also help them master essential reading skills. This nuts-and-bolts book is based on a number of assumptions about the writing and reading process:

■ First of all, *English Skills with Readings* assumes that four principles in particular are keys to effective writing: unity, support, coherence, and sentence skills. These four principles are highlighted on the inside front cover and reinforced throughout the book. Part One focuses on the first three principles; Part Four treats sentence skills fully. The rest of the book shows how the four principles apply in different types of paragraph development (Part Two), in traditional five-paragraph essays (Part Three), and in both paragraphs and essays (Part Five).

■ The book reflects the belief that, in addition to the four principles, there are other important factors in writing effectively. After a brief introductory chapter, the second chapter of the book discusses prewriting, rewriting, and editing. Besides encouraging students to see writing as a process, the chapter also asks students to examine their attitude about writing, to write on what they know about or can learn about, to consider keeping a writing journal, and to include outlining as part of the writing process.

■ *English Skills with Readings* assumes that the best way to begin writing is with personal experience. After students have learned to support a point by providing material from their own experience, they are ready to develop an idea by drawing on their own reasoning abilities and on information in notes, articles, and books. Students are asked to write on both experiential and objective topics in Parts Two and Three. And the reading selections in Part Five generate a variety of first- and third-person assignments.

- The book also assumes that beginning writers are more likely to learn composing skills through lively, engaging, and realistic models than through materials remote from the common experiences that are part of everyday life. For example, when a writer argues that proms should be banned, or catalogs ways to harass an instructor, or talks about why some teenagers take drugs, students are more apt to remember and follow the writing principles that may be involved. After reading vigorous papers composed by other students and some of the stimulating selections by professionals in Part Five, students will understand better the power that good writing can have. They will then be more likely to aim for similar honesty, realism, and detail in their own work.

- Another premise of *English Skills with Readings* is that mastery of the paragraph should precede work on the several-paragraph essay. Thus Part One illustrates the basic principles of composition using paragraph models, and the assignments in Part Two aim at developing the ability to support ideas within a variety of paragraph forms. The essential principles of paragraph writing are then applied to the traditional five-paragraph essays in Part Three. Finally, in Part Five, each reading selection is followed by two paragraph assignments and one essay assignment.

- Another assumption is that, since no two people will use an English text in exactly the same way, the material should be organized in a highly accessible manner. Because each of the five parts of the book deals with a distinct area, instructors can turn quickly and easily to the skills they want to present. At the same time, ideas for sequencing material are provided by three boxes titled "Some Suggestions on What to Do Next"; these boxes appear in the opening chapters of the book. And a detailed syllabus is provided in the Instructor's Manual.

- Finally, an assumption central to this book is that reading and writing are closely connected skills—so that practicing one helps the other, and neglecting one hurts the other. Part Five enables students to work on becoming better readers as well as better writers. An introductory section to Part Five offers a series of tips on effective reading, and ten questions after each of the selections provide practice in key reading comprehension skills. A set of discussion questions also follows each selection, serving to deepen students' understanding of the content and to make them aware of basic matters having to do with structure, style, and tone. Last, there are three writing assignments for each selection, along with guidelines to help students think about and get started with the assignments.

DIFFERENCES BETWEEN THIS BOOK
AND *ENGLISH SKILLS*

■ Parts One to Three are essentially the same as the three rhetoric sections of *English Skills*. There are three omissions: the research assignment (typically "Writing Assignment 4") has been omitted from the sequence of writing assignments that follow each type of paragraph development in Part Two; the "Additional Paragraph Assignments" have been removed from the end of Part Two; and an article titled "A Suicide at Twelve—Why, Steve?" has been taken out of Part Three.

■ There is also an addition: an extra writing assignment appears at the end of each chapter in Part Three. Titled "Writing about a Reading Selection," this assignment asks students to read one of the professional essays in Part Five illustrating a certain rhetorical mode. (For example, in the chapter on comparison and contrast, students are asked to read "People Need People," which develops its point through the use of contrast.) They are then asked to write a paragraph using the mode of development in question.

■ Part Four of *English Skills*, "Special Skills," has been omitted to help create space for the fifteen readings. Note, however, that some of the content of "Key Study Skills" can be found in the selection "Power Learning"; and information that originally appeared in "Writing a Résumé and Job Application Letter" now appears (in a somewhat different form) in the selection "Finding a Career and a Job: A No-Nonsense Guide."

■ Part Five of *English Skills*, "Sentence Skills"—which becomes Part Four in *English Skills with Readings*— has been reduced somewhat, again to create space for the readings. Material omitted includes the diagnostic and achievement tests, "Sentence Sense," and five of the ten editing tests.

■ As the title indicates, what is most different in this book is the inclusion of fifteen reading selections by professional writers, along with detailed reading and writing apparatus following each selection.

THE READINGS

■ The fifteen selections have been chosen for their content as much as for rhetorical mode. They are organized thematically into three groups: "Goals and Values," "Education and Self-Improvement," and "Human Groups and Society." Some reflect important contemporary concerns: for instance, "Let's Really Reform Our Schools," "Television Changed My Family Forever," and "What It Means to Be Young Today." Some provide information many students may find helpful; examples are "Power Learning," "Finding a Career and a Job: A No-Nonsense Guide," and "How to Think Clearly." Some recount profoundly human experiences: "The Tryout," "Adolescent Confusion," and "A Drunken Ride, A Tragic Aftermath." All the selections should capture the interest of a wide range of students. (A list on pages xiii–xiv presents the readings by rhetorical mode.)

- Each reading begins with a preview that supplies background information where needed and stimulates interest in the piece.

- The ten reading comprehension questions that follow each selection give students practice in five key skills: summarizing (by choosing an alternative title), determining the main idea, recognizing key supporting details, making inferences, and understanding vocabulary in context. Reading educators agree that these are among the most crucial comprehension skills. A special chart at the back of the book enables students to track their progress as they practice these skills.

- Discussion questions following the reading comprehension questions deal with matters of content as well as aspects of structure, style, and tone. Through the questions on structure in particular, students will see that professional authors practice some of the same basic composing techniques (such as the use of transitions and emphatic order to achieve coherence) that they have been asked to practice in their own writing.

When assigning a selection, instructors may find it helpful to ask students to read the preview as well as to answer the reading comprehension and discussion questions that follow the selection. Answers can then be gone over quickly in class. Through these activities, a writing instructor can contribute to the improvement of his or her students' reading skills.

NOTES ON THIS EDITION

With pleasure and gratitude, I have watched the audience for *English Skills with Readings* expand each year. Instructors continue to say that the four bases really do help students learn to write effectively. And they continue to comment that students find the model passages, activities, assignments, and readings in the book especially interesting and worthwhile.

At the same time, more and more instructors have said that the book would benefit from an earlier emphasis on the writing process. In this edition, therefore, I have expanded my treatment of prewriting and other important factors in writing and relocated those materials as the second chapter of the book. Instructors who are more comfortable with the previous format of the text can easily skip the second chapter and move directly to the next chapter and its treatment of the first two steps in effective writing. The material skipped can then be worked into a course a bit at a time.

Here is an overview of what is in this new edition:

- The first chapter, "Getting Started," now introduces students to the basic principles of effective writing in more detail. Almost immediately, students read and discuss a model paragraph; they are then asked to write a paragraph of their own. This "baseline" paragraph provides the instructor and the student with a standard of comparison that can be used to measure progress in writing during the semester.

- The second chapter, "Important Factors in Writing," includes material that made up Part Two in earlier editions of the book. Some of that material has been revised, and there are new sections on keeping a journal and prewriting in the form of diagramming or "mapping."

- "Introduction to Paragraph Development"—the chapter that begins Part Two—has been expanded to include writing for a specific purpose and audience, using peer review, and using a personal checklist.

- Part Four, "Sentence Skills," has been enlarged to include two new chapters— "Pronoun Types" and "Adjectives and Adverbs."

- Many smaller changes appear throughout the book. For example, there is a new introduction to "Transitions" in Part One; the chapter on run-ons in Part Four now includes subordination as a method of correction; two rhetorical chapters in Part Two ("Explaining a Process" and "Examining Cause and Effect") and three sentence-skills chapters in Part Four ("Misplaced Modifiers," "Dangling Modifiers," and "Faulty Parallelism") have been resequenced.

- Finally, three new selections are now part of the fifteen selections in Part Five: "Old before Her Time," by Katherine Barrett; "Television Changed My Family Forever," by Linda Ellerbee; and "Let's Really Reform Our Schools," by Anita Garland. All three selections deal with themes that should engage the interest of students and make for rewarding writing assignments.

SUPPLEMENTS

A newly designed Instructor's Manual includes, whenever possible, separate answer sheets for each skill. Instructors can easily copy the appropriate sheets and pass them out to students for self-teaching. The manual and a computer disk of mastery tests (now in both IBM and Macintosh formats) are both available from the local McGraw-Hill representative or by writing to the College English Editor, 43d Floor, McGraw-Hill, Inc., 1221 Avenue of the Americas, New York, New York 10020.

ACKNOWLEDGMENTS

Reviewers who have provided assistance include Deborah Barberhousse, Horry-Georgetown Technical College; Barbara Colavecchio, Community College of Rhode Island; Julie Draus, Charles County Community College; Jim Farber, Vernon Regional Junior College; Noreen Fiacco, Eastern Nazarene College; Karen Gleeman, Normandale Community College; Judy Harvey, Wilmington College; Mary Joan Hoff, Valencia Community College; Bernita Howton, Consumnes River College; Gloria John, Catonsville Community College; Kay Jones, Mississippi Gulf Coast Community College; Alice Lyon, Community College of Rhode Island; Marilyn Mechtenburg, Glendale Community College; Maureen O'Brien, Springfield Technical College; Zira Piltch, Iona College; Ann Pope Stone, Santa Monica College; Ed Sams, Gavilan College; Louisa Strock, Northwest Technical College; Debra Watson, Mississippi Gulf Coast Community College; Lisa Wernsman-Mehlig, Rock Valley College; Paige Wilson, Pasadena City College; and David Winspar, Springfield Technical Community College.

I am also grateful for help provided by Janet M. Goldstein, Carole Mohr, and Amy K. Fisher. And, as always, I owe thanks to Susan Gamer, my editing supervisor at McGraw-Hill. Her pursuit of consistency, correctness, and quality is a model for people in publishing everywhere.

John Langan

ENGLISH
SKILLS
WITH
READINGS

PART ONE

BASIC PRINCIPLES OF EFFECTIVE WRITING

PREVIEW

Part One begins by introducing you to this book and to paragraph form. As you work through the brief activities in the first chapter, "Getting Started," you will gain a quick understanding of the book's purpose, the way it is organized, and how it will help you develop your writing skills. After presenting a series of important general factors that will help you create good papers, Part One then describes four basic steps that can make you an effective writer. The four steps are:

1 Make a point.
2 Support the point with specific evidence.
3 Organize and connect the specific evidence.
4 Write clear, error-free sentences.

Explanations, examples, and activities are provided to help you master the first three steps. (You will be referred to Part Four of the book for a detailed treatment of the fourth step.) After seeing how these steps can help you write a competent paper, you will learn how they lead to four standards, or "bases," of effective writing: unity, support, coherence, and sentence skills. You will then practice evaluating a number of papers in terms of these four bases.

GETTING
STARTED

This chapter will

- Introduce you to the basic principles of effective writing
- Ask you to write a simple paragraph
- Explain how the book is organized
- Suggest a sequence for using the book

English Skills grows out of experiences I had when learning how to write. My early memories of writing in school are not pleasant. In the middle grades I remember getting back paper after paper on which the only comment was ''Handwriting very poor.'' In high school, the night before a book report was due, I recall working anxiously at a card table in my bedroom. I was nervous and sweaty because I felt so out of my element, like a person who knows only how to open a can of soup being asked to cook a five-course meal. The act of writing was hard enough, and my feeling that I wasn't any good at it made me hate the process all the more.

Luckily, in college I had an instructor who changed my negative attitude about writing. During my first semester in composition, I realized that my instructor repeatedly asked two questions of any paper I wrote: ''What is your point?'' and ''What is your support for that point?'' I learned that sound writing consists basically of making a point and then providing evidence to support or develop that point. As I understood, practiced, and mastered these and other principles, I began to write effective papers. By the end of the semester, much of my uneasiness and bad feelings about writing had disappeared. I knew that competent writing is a skill that I or anyone can learn with practice. It is a nuts-and-bolts process consisting of a number of principles and skills that can be studied and mastered. Further, I learned that while there is no alternative to the work required for competent writing, there is satisfaction to be gained through such work. I no longer feared or hated writing, for I knew I could work at it and be good at it.

English Skills explains in a clear and direct way the basic principles and skills you must learn to write effectively. And it provides a number of practice materials so that you can work on these skills enough to make them habits. This chapter will introduce the most basic principles of effective writing. The chapter will also show you how the rest of the book is organized and how it can help you become an effective writer.

AN INTRODUCTION TO WRITING

Point and Support:
An Important Difference between Writing and Talking

In everyday conversation, you make all kinds of points, or assertions. You say, for example, ''I hate my job''; ''Sue's a really generous person''; or ''That exam was unfair.'' The points that you make concern such personal matters as well as, at times, larger issues: ''A lot of doctors are arrogant''; ''The death penalty should exist for certain crimes''; ''Tobacco and marijuana are equally dangerous.''

The people you are talking with do not always challenge you to give reasons for your statements. They may know why you feel as you do, or they may already agree with you, or they simply may not want to put you on the spot; and so they do not always ask ''Why?'' But the people who *read* what you write may not know you, agree with you, or feel in any way obliged to you. If you want to communicate effectively with readers, you must provide solid evidence for any point you make. An important difference, then, between writing and talking is this: *In writing, any idea that you advance must be supported with specific reasons or details.*

Think of your readers as reasonable people. They will not take your views on faith, but they *are* willing to accept what you say as long as you support it. Therefore, remember to support any statement that you make with specific evidence.

Point and Support in a Paragraph

A *paragraph* is a short paper of 150 words or more. It usually consists of an opening point called a *topic sentence* followed by a series of specifics, in the form of sentences, that support the point. Most of the writing featured in this book will be paragraphs.

A Sample Paragraph: Below is a paragraph on why the writer plans not to go out with Tony anymore.

Good-Bye, Tony

I have decided not to go out with Tony anymore. First of all, he was late for our first date. He said that he would be at my house by 8:30, but he did not arrive until 9:20. Second, he was bossy. He told me that it would be too late to go to the new Steve Martin movie I wanted to see, and that we would go to a horror classic, The Night of the Living Dead, instead. I told him that I didn't like gruesome movies, but he said that I could shut my eyes during the gory parts. Only because it was a first date did I let him have his way. Finally, he was abrupt. After the movie, rather than suggesting a hamburger or a drink, he drove right out to a back road near Oakcrest High School and started necking with me. What he did a half hour later angered me most of all. He cut his finger on a pin I was wearing and immediately said we had to go right home. He was afraid the scratch would get infected if he didn't put Bactine and a Band-Aid on it. When he dropped me off, I said, ''Good-bye, Tony,'' in a friendly enough way, but in my head I thought, ''Good-bye forever, Tony.''

Notice what the details in this paragraph have done. They have provided you, the reader, with a basis for understanding why the writer made the decision she did. Through specific evidence, the writer has explained and communicated her point successfully. The evidence that supports the point in a paragraph often consists of a series of reasons introduced by signal words (*First of all, Second,* and the like) and followed by examples and details that support the reasons. That is true of the sample paragraph above: three reasons are provided, followed by examples and details that back up those reasons.

Activity 1

Complete the following outline of the sample paragraph. Summarize in a few words the details that develop each reason, rather than writing the details out in full.

Point: _____

_____

Reason 1: _____

Details that develop reason 1: _____

_____

_____

Reason 2: _____

Details that develop reason 2: _____

_____

_____

Reason 3: _____

Details that develop reason 3: _____

_____

_____

Activity 2

See if you can complete the statements below.

1. An important difference between writing and talking is that in writing we absolutely must _____ any statement we make.

2. A _____ is a collection of specifics that support a point.

Writing a Paragraph: An excellent way to get a feel for the paragraph is to write one. Your instructor may ask you to do that now. The only guidelines you need to follow are the ones described here. There is an advantage to writing a paragraph right away, at a point where you have had almost no instruction. This first paragraph will give a quick sense of your needs as a writer and will provide a baseline — a standard of comparison that you and your instructor can use to measure your writing progress during the semester.

Activity

Here, then, is your topic: write a paragraph on the best or worst job you have ever had. Provide three reasons why your job was the best or the worst, and give plenty of details to develop each of your three reasons. Note that the sample paragraph, "Good-Bye, Tony," has the same format your paragraph should have: the author (1) states a point in her first sentence, (2) gives three reasons to support the point, (3) clearly introduces each reason with signal words (*First of all, Second,* and *Finally*), and then (4) provides details that develop each of the three reasons. Write your paragraph on a separate sheet of paper.

AN INTRODUCTION TO THIS BOOK

How the Book Is Organized

English Skills with Readings is divided into five parts. Each part will be discussed briefly below. Brief questions appear as well, not to test you but simply to introduce you to the central ideas in the text and the organization of the book. Your instructor may ask you to write in the answers or just to note the answers in your head.

Part One (Pages 1–118):   A good way to get a quick sense of any part of a book is to look at the table of contents. Turn back to the contents at the start of this book (pages vii – xi) and answer the following questions:

■   What is the title of Part One? _____

■   "Getting Started" is the opening chapter of Part One. What is the title of the *next* chapter in Part One, and what are the first seven subheads after the title?

   Title _____

   Subhead _____

   Subhead _____

   Subhead _____

   Subhead _____

   Subhead _____

   Subhead _____

   Subhead _____

These seven headings refer to important general factors that will help you become an effective writer.

■   The title of the third chapter in Part One is "The First and Second Steps in Writing." According to the subheads, what are the first and second steps in writing?

   _____

   _____

■   The title of the fourth chapter in Part One is "The Third and Fourth Steps in Writing." According to the subheads, what are the third and fourth steps in writing?

   _____

   _____

Part One describes three of the four steps in writing. The fourth step, which includes all the skills involved in writing clear, error-free sentences, has been placed in a later part of the book, where these sentence skills can be treated in detail and can be easily referred to as needed. Use the table of contents (pages vii–xi) to answer the following question:

■   In what part of the book are sentence skills treated?

_____

■   The title of the final chapter in Part One is "Four Bases for Evaluating Writing." Look at the contents (pages vii–xi) again and fill in the first four subheads following the title.

Subhead _____

Subhead _____

Subhead _____

Subhead _____

Inside Front Cover: Turn now to the inside front cover. You will see there a

(*fill in the missing word*) _____ of the four bases of effective writing. These four standards can be used as a guide for every paper that you write. They are summarized on the inside front cover for easy reference. If you follow them, you are almost sure to write effective papers.

Part Two (Pages 119–206):   The title of Part Two is _____.

Part Two, as the title explains, is concerned with different ways to develop paragraphs. Read the preview on page 120 and record here how many types of

paragraph development are presented: _____.

Turn to the first method of paragraph development, "Providing Examples," on page 127. You will see that the chapter opens with a brief introduction followed by several paragraphs written by students. Then you will see a series of six (*fill

in the missing word*) _____ to help you evaluate the example paragraphs in terms of unity, support, and coherence. Finally, some writing topics that can be developed by means of examples are presented. The same format is used for each of the other methods of paragraph development in Part Two.

Part Three (Pages 207–228):   The title of Part Three is _____

_____.

As the preview on page 208 notes, in Part Two you were asked to write single paragraphs; in Part Three, you are asked to write papers of more than one (*fill

in the missing word*) _____.

Part Four (Pages 229–431): The title of Part Four is _____

_____.

    Part Four is the largest part of the book. It gives you practice in skills needed to write clear and effective sentences. You will note from the table of contents (pages vii–xi) that it contains the skills themselves and editing activities. The skills are grouped into four sections: ''Grammar,'' ''Mechanics,'' (*fill in the missing word*) ''_____,'' and ''Word Use.''

Part Five (Pages 433–570): The title of Part Five is _____

_____.

    Part Five contains a series of fifteen reading selections, along with activities that will help you improve both reading and writing skills. Turn to the first selection, "The Tryout," on page 440. You will see that the selection begins with a short preview that gives you background information on the piece. Following the selection there are ten comprehension (*fill in the missing word*)

_____ to help you practice important reading skills. Then, after a series of discussion questions that have to do with both reading and writing, there are several writing assignments.

Inside Back Cover: On the inside back cover is an alphabetical list of (*fill in the missing words*) _____.
Your instructor may use these symbols in marking your papers. In addition, you can use the page numbers in the list for quick reference to a specific sentence skill.

Charts in the Book: In addition to the guides on the inside front and back covers, several charts have been provided in the book to help you take responsibility for your own learning.

■ What are the names of the charts on pages 576–581?

_____

_____

_____

_____

_____

_____

How to Use the Book

Here is a suggested sequence for using this book if you are working on your own.

1 After completing this introduction, read the next four chapters in Part One and work through as many of the activities as you need to master the ideas in these chapters. Your instructor may give you answer sheets so that you can check your answers. At that point, you will have covered all the basic theory needed to write effective papers.

2 Turn to Part Four and do the introductory projects. These projects will help you identify the sentence skills you need to review. Study those skills one or two at a time while you continue to work on other parts of the book.

3 What you do next depends on course requirements, individual needs, or both. You will want to practice at least several different kinds of paragraph development in Part Two. If your time is limited, be sure to include ''Providing Examples,'' ''Explaining a Process,'' ''Comparing or Contrasting,'' and ''Arguing a Position.'' After that, you could logically go on to write one or more of the several-paragraph essays described in Part Three.

4 Read at least one of the fifteen selections in Part Five every week, always being sure to work through the two sets of questions that follow each reading.

AS YOU BEGIN . . .

English Skills with Readings will help you learn, practice, and apply the writing skills you need to communicate clearly and effectively. But the starting point must be your determination to do the work needed to become an independent writer. If you decide — *and only you can decide* — that you want to learn to write effectively, this book will help you reach that goal.

IMPORTANT
FACTORS
IN WRITING

This chapter will discuss the importance of

- **Your attitude about writing**
- **Writing for a specific purpose and audience**
- **Knowing or discovering your subject**
- **Keeping a journal**
- **Prewriting**
- **Outlining**
- **Revising, editing, and proofreading**

The preceding chapter introduced you to the paragraph form, and the chapters that follow in Part One will explain the basic steps in writing a paragraph and basic standards for evaluating a paragraph. The purpose of this chapter is to describe a number of important general factors that will help you create good papers. These factors are (1) having the right attitude about writing, (2) writing for a specific purpose and audience, (3) knowing or discovering your subject, (4) keeping a journal, (5) prewriting, (6), outlining, and (7) revising, editing, and proofreading.

Your Attitude about Writing

One way to wreck your chances of learning how to write competently is to believe that writing is a natural gift. People with this attitude think that they are the only ones for whom writing is unbearably difficult. They feel that everyone else finds writing easy or at least tolerable. Such people typically say, "I'm not any good at writing" or "English was not one of my good subjects." They imply that they simply do not have a talent for writing, while others do. As a result of this attitude, they do not do their best when they write, or — even worse — they hardly try at all. Their self-defeating attitude becomes a reality; their writing fails chiefly because they have brainwashed themselves into thinking that they don't have the "natural talent" needed to write. Until their attitude changes, they probably will not learn how to write effectively.

A realistic attitude about writing, rather than the mistaken notion that writing is a "natural gift," should build on two crucial ideas.

1   *Writing is hard work for almost everyone.* It is difficult to do the intense and active thinking that clear writing demands. (Perhaps television has made us all so passive that the active thinking necessary in both writing and reading now seems doubly hard.) It is frightening to sit down before a blank sheet of paper and know that an hour later, nothing on it may be worth keeping. It is frustrating to discover how much of a challenge it is to transfer thoughts and feelings from one's head onto a sheet of paper. It is upsetting to find that an apparently simple writing subject often turns out to be complicated. But writing is not an automatic process; we will not get something for nothing; and we cannot expect something for nothing. Competent writing results only from plain hard work — determination, sweat, and head-on battle.

2   *Writing is a skill.* Writing is a skill, like driving, typing, or cooking. Like any skill, it can be learned — if you decide that you are going to learn it, and if you then really work at it. This book will give you the extensive practice needed to develop your writing skills.

Activity

Answering these questions will help you evaluate your attitude about writing.

1.   How much practice were you given in writing compositions in high school?

     _____ Much   _____ Some   _____ Little

2.   How much feedback on your compositions (positive or negative comments) did your teachers give you?

     _____ Much   _____ Some   _____ Little

3. How did your teachers seem to regard your writing?

    _____ Good   _____ Fair   _____ Poor

4. Do you feel that some people simply have a gift for writing and others do not?

    _____ Yes   _____ Sometimes   _____ No

5. When do you start writing a paper?

    _____ Several days before it is due

    _____ About a day before it is due

    _____ At the last possible minute

Many people who answer *Little* to questions 1 and 2 also answer *Poor* to question 3, *Yes* to question 4, and *At the last possible minute* to question 5. On the other hand, people who answer *Much* or *Some* to questions 1 and 2 also tend to give more favorable responses to the other questions. The point is that people with little practice in writing often have understandably negative feelings about their ability to write. They need not have such feelings, however, because writing is a skill that they can learn with practice.

Writing for a Specific Purpose and Audience

The three most common purposes of writing are to inform, to entertain, and to persuade. Most of the writing you will do in this book will involve some form of persuasion. You will advance a point or topic sentence and then support it in a variety of ways. To some extent, also, you will write papers to inform — to provide readers with information about a particular subject.

Your audience will be primarily your instructor, and sometimes other students as well. Your instructor is really a symbol of the larger audience you should see yourself as writing for — an educated, adult audience that expects you to present your ideas in a clear, direct, organized way. If you can learn to write to persuade or inform such a general audience, you will have accomplished a great deal.

It will also be helpful for you to write some papers for a more specific audience. By so doing, you will develop an ability to choose words and adopt a tone of voice that is just right for a given purpose and a given group of people. For example, Part Two of this book includes assignments asking you to write with a very specific purpose in mind, and for a very specific audience.

Knowing or Discovering Your Subject

KNOWING YOUR SUBJECT

Whenever possible, try to write on a subject that interests you. You will then find it easier to put more time into your work. Even more important, try to write on a subject that you already know something about. If you do not have direct experience with the subject, you should at least have indirect experience — knowledge gained through thinking, prewriting (to be explained on pages 17–25), reading, or talking about the subject.

If you are asked to write on a topic about which you have no experience or knowledge, you should do whatever research (particularly in the library) is required to gain the information you need. Without direct or indirect experience, or the information you gain through research, you will not be able to provide the specific evidence needed to develop whatever point you are trying to make. Your writing will be starved for specifics.

DISCOVERING YOUR SUBJECT

At times you will not know your subject when you begin to write. Instead, you will discover it in the actual process of writing. For example, when a student named Gene sat down to write a paper about a memorable job (see page 33), he thought for a while that his topic was going to be an especially depressing moment on that job. As he began to accumulate details, however, he realized that his topic was really the job itself and all the drawbacks it entailed. When he began to write, Gene only *thought* he knew the focus of his paper. In fact, he *discovered his subject in the course of writing*.

Another student, Rhonda, talking afterwards about a paper she wrote, explained that at first her topic was how she relaxed with her children. But as she accumulated details, she realized after a page of writing that the words *relax* and *children* simply did not go together. Her details were really examples of how she *enjoyed* her children, not how she *relaxed* with them. She sensed that the real focus of her writing should be what she did by herself to relax, and then she thought suddenly that the best time of her week was Thursdays after school. ''A light clicked on in my head,'' she explained. ''I knew I had my paper.'' Then it was a matter of detailing exactly what she did to relax on Thursday evenings. Her paper, ''How I Relax,'' is on page 73.

The moral of these examples is that sometimes you must write a bit in order to find out just what you want to write. Writing can help you think about and explore your topic and decide just what direction your paper will finally take. The techniques presented in ''Prewriting'' – the section starting on page 17 – will suggest specific ways to discover and develop a subject.

One related feature of the writing process bears mention. Do not feel that you must proceed in a linear fashion when you write. That is, do not assume that the writing process is a railroad track going straight from your central point to supporting detail 1 to supporting detail 2 to supporting detail 3 to your concluding paragraph. Instead, as you draft the paper, proceed in whatever way seems most comfortable. You may want to start by writing the closing section or by developing your third supporting detail.

Do whatever is easiest; as you get material down on the page, it will make what you have left to do a bit easier. And sometimes, of course, as you work on one section, it may happen that a new focal point for your paper will emerge. That's fine: if your writing tells you that it wants to be something else, then revise or start over as needed to take advantage of that discovery. Your goal is to wind up with a paper that solidly makes and supports a point. Be ready and open to change direction and to make whatever adjustments are needed to reach your goal.

Activity 1

Answer the following questions.

1. What are three ways of gaining the knowledge you need to write about a subject?   a. _____   b. _____   c. _____

2. A student begins to write a paper about her favorite vacation. After writing for a half hour, she realizes that the most vivid details coming to her are of her worst vacation. What has happened in the process of writing?

    _____

    _____

    _____

3. Suppose you want to write a paper on different kinds of drivers. You think you can discuss slowpoke drivers, high-speed drivers, and sensible-speed drivers. You feel you have the most details about high-speed drivers. Should you start with that type of driver, or should you start with one of the other two types? _____

    _____

    _____

Activity 2

Write for five minutes about the house, dormitory, or apartment where you live. Simply write down whatever details come to you. Don't worry about being neat; just pile up as many details as you can.

Afterward, go through the material. Try to find a potential focus within all those details. Do the details suggest a simple point that you could make about the place where you live? If so, you've seen a small example of how writing about a topic can be an excellent way of discovering a point about that topic.

Keeping a Journal

Because writing is a skill, it makes sense that the more you practice writing, the better you will write. One excellent way to get practice in writing is to keep a daily or almost daily journal.

At some point during the day — perhaps in a study period after your last class, perhaps before dinner, or perhaps before going to bed — spend fifteen minutes or so writing in your journal. Keep in mind that you do not have to prepare what to write or be in the mood or worry about making mistakes; just write down whatever words come out. As a minimum, you should complete at least one page in each writing session.

You may want to use a notebook that you can easily carry with you for on-the-spot writing. Or you may decide to write on looseleaf paper that can be transferred later to a journal folder or binder on your desk. No matter how you proceed, be sure to date all your entries.

The content of your journal should be some of the specific happenings, thoughts, and feelings of the day. Your starting point may be a comment by an instructor, a classmate, or a family member; a gesture or action that has amused, angered, confused, or depressed you; something you have read or seen on television – anything, really, that has caught your attention and that you have decided to explore a bit in writing. Some journal entries may focus on a single subject; others may wander from one topic to another.

Your instructor may ask you to make journal entries a set number of times a week, for a set number of weeks. He or she may ask you to turn in your journal every so often for review and feedback. If you are keeping the journal on your own, try to make entries three to five times a week, every week of the semester.

Your journal can serve as a sourcebook of ideas for possible papers. More important, keeping a journal will help you develop the habit of thinking on paper, and it can help you make writing a familiar part of your life.

Following is an excerpt from one student's journal. (Sentence-skills mistakes have been corrected to improve readability.) As you read, look for a general point and supporting material that could be the basis for an interesting paper.

October 6

Today a woman came into our department at the store and wanted to know if we had any scrap lumber ten feet long. Ten feet! "Lady," I said, "anything we have that's ten feet long sure as heck isn't scrap." When the boss heard me say that, he almost canned me. My boss is a company man, down to his toe tips. He wants to make a big impression on his bosses, and he'll run us around like mad all night to make himself look good. He's the most ambitious man I've ever met. If I don't transfer out of Hardware soon, I'm going to go crazy on this job. I'm not ready to quit, though. The time is not right. I want to be here for a year and have another job lined up and have other things right before I quit. It's good the boss wasn't around tonight when another customer wanted me to carry a bookcase he had bought out to his car. He didn't ask me to help him — he <u>expected</u> me to help him. I hate that kind of "You're my servant" attitude, and I told him that carrying stuff out to cars wasn't my job. Ordinarily I go out of my way to give people a hand, but not guys like him. . . .

■ If the writer of this journal was looking for an idea for an essay, he could probably find several in this single entry. For example, he might write a narrative supporting the point that "In my sales job I have to deal with some irritating customers." See if you can find another idea in this entry that might be the basis for an interesting paragraph. Write your point in the space below.

_____

■ Take fifteen minutes to prepare a journal entry right now on this day in your life. On a separate sheet of paper, just start writing about anything that you have seen, said, heard, thought, or felt, and let your thoughts take you where they may.

Prewriting

If you are like many people, you may sometimes have trouble getting started writing. A mental block may develop when you sit down before a blank sheet of paper. You may not be able to think of a topic or an interesting slant on a topic. Or you may have trouble coming up with interesting and relevant details to support your topic. Even after starting a paper, you may hit snags — moments when you wonder "Where do I go next?"

The following pages describe five techniques that will help you think about and develop a topic and get words down on paper: (1) brainstorming, (2) freewriting, (3) making a list, (4) diagramming, and (5) making a scratch outline. These techniques, which are often called *prewriting techniques,* are a central part of the writing process.

TECHNIQUE 1: BRAINSTORMING

In *brainstorming*, you generate ideas and details by asking as many questions as you can think of about your subject. Such questions include *What? When? Why? How? Where?* and *Who?*

Following is an example of how one student, Sal, used brainstorming to generate material for a paper. Sal felt that he could write about a painful moment he had experienced, but he was having trouble getting started. So he asked himself a series of brainstorming questions about the experience. As a result, he accumulated a series of details that provided the basis for the paper he finally wrote.

Here are the questions Sal asked and the answers he wrote:

Questions	Answers
<u>Where</u> did the experience happen?	In my girlfriend's dorm room at Penn State.
<u>When</u> did it happen?	A week before Thanksgiving.
<u>Who</u> was involved?	My girlfriend, her roommate (briefly), and I.
<u>What</u> happened?	I discovered my girlfriend was dating someone else.
<u>Why</u> was the experience so painful?	Bonnie and I were engaged. She had never mentioned Blake. My surprise visit turned into a terrible surprise for me.
<u>How</u> did Bonnie react?	She was nervous and tried to avoid answering my questions.
<u>How</u> did I react?	I felt sick and angry. I wanted to do something violent. I wanted to tear up the poster with Blake's name on it. I wanted to slam the door, but I walked out quietly. My knees were shaking.

After brainstorming, Sal's next step was to prepare a scratch outline. He then prepared several drafts of the paper. The effective paragraph that eventually resulted from Sal's prewriting techniques appears on page 192.

Activity

To get a sense of brainstorming, use a sheet of paper to ask yourself a series of questions about a pleasant diner you have visited. See how many details you can accumulate about that diner in ten minutes.

TECHNIQUE 2: FREEWRITING

When you do not know what to write about a subject or when you are blocked in writing, freewriting sometimes helps. In *freewriting,* you write on your topic for ten minutes. You do not worry about spelling, punctuation, erasing mistakes, or finding exact words. You just write without stopping. If you get stuck for words, you write ''I am looking for something to say'' or repeat words until something comes. There is no need to feel inhibited, since mistakes do not count and you do not have to hand in your paper.

Freewriting will limber up your writing muscles and make you familiar with the act of writing. It is a way to break through mental blocks about writing and the fear of making errors. As you do not have to worry about making mistakes, you can concentrate on discovering what you want to say about a subject. Your initial ideas and impressions will often become clearer after you have gotten them down on paper. Through continued practice in freewriting, you will develop the habit of thinking as you write. And you will learn a technique that is a helpful way to get started on almost any paper that you write.

Here is the freewriting that one student did to accumulate details for a paper on why he stopped smoking:

> I was way overdue to stop smoking cigarettes and I finally did. I had a friend who went to the hospital with lung cancer. No one can say that he's going to recover. He's in Eagleville Hospital. When I heard about him, it was the last straw for me. Smoking is a life-and-death matter. My friend is the one who brought this message home to me. Smoking is a life-and-death matter just like the ads say. When I think about it, I hated the fact that I was helping corporations make a lot of money all the while that I smoked. The corporations produced all this slick advertising and I felt I was one of the puppets who listened to it. I marched to their tune. I didn't want to make wealthy corporations even richer, and I hated it every time I gave over hard-earned dollars for a carton of cigarettes. Cigarettes were a very expensive habit. I can hardly say how much a year I had to put out for them. You could see I smoked as you walked through my house. There were ashtrays in the living room, dining room, bathroom, and kitchen. My wife said there was a smell of smoke in the house. I couldn't tell. I had a nose so clogged that I couldn't smell much at all. Cigarettes were a bum trip that I am not going to take any longer.

The writer's next step was to use the freewriting as the basis for a scratch outline. The effective paper that eventually resulted from the author's freewriting, a scratch outline, and a good deal of rewriting appears on page 144.

Activity

To get a sense of freewriting, use a sheet of paper to freewrite about your everyday worries. See how many ideas and details you can accumulate in ten minutes.

TECHNIQUE 3: MAKING A LIST

Another way to get started is to make a list of as many different items as you can think of concerning your topic. Do not worry about repeating yourself, about sorting out major details from minor ones, or about spelling or punctuating correctly. Simply make a list of everything about your subject that occurs to you. Your aim is to generate details and to accumulate as much raw material for writing as possible.

Following is a list prepared by one student, Linda, who was gathering details for a paper on abuse of public parks. Her first stage in doing the paper was simply to make a list of thoughts and details that occurred to her about the topic. Here is her list:

Messy picnickers (most common)
Noisy radios
Graffiti on buildings and fences
Frisbee games that disturb others
Dumping car ashtrays
Stealing park property
Nude sunbathing
Destroying flowers
Damaging fountains and statues
Litter
Muggings

Notice that Linda puts in parentheses a note to herself that messy picnickers are the most common type of park abusers. Very often as you make a list, ideas about how to develop a paper will occur to you. Jot them down.

Making a list is an excellent way to get started. Often you can then go on to make a scratch outline and write the first draft of your paper. A scratch outline for Linda's list is shown on page 22.

Activity

To get a sense of making a list, use a sheet of paper to list specific problems you will face this semester. See how many ideas and details you can accumulate in ten minutes.

TECHNIQUE 4: DIAGRAMMING

Diagramming, also known as *mapping* or *clustering,* is another prewriting activity that can help you generate ideas and details about a topic. In diagramming, you use lines, boxes, arrows, and circles to show relationships among the ideas and details that come to you.

Diagramming is helpful to people who like to do their thinking in a visual way. Whether you use a diagram, and just how you proceed with it, is up to you.

Here is the diagram that one student, Mel, prepared for a paper on differences between his job as he imagined it and as it turned out to be. The diagram, with its clear picture of relationships, was especially helpful for the comparison-contrast paper that Mel was doing. His final essay appears on page 158.

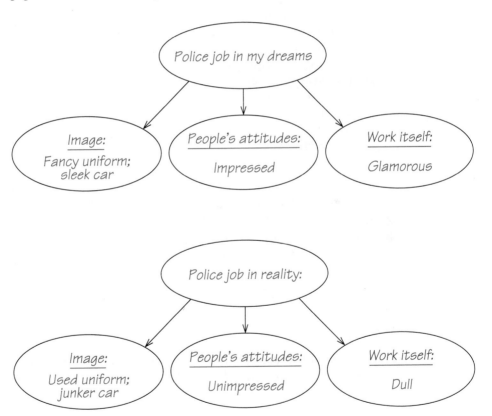

Activity

To get a sense of diagramming, use a sheet of paper to make a diagram of differences between two instructors or two jobs. See how many ideas and details you can accumulate in ten minutes.

TECHNIQUE 5: PREPARING A SCRATCH OUTLINE

A scratch outline can often be the *single most helpful technique* for writing a good paper. It is an excellent complement to the prewriting techniques already mentioned: brainstorming, freewriting, making a list, and diagramming. In a scratch outline, you think carefully about the exact point you are making, about the exact items you will use to support that point, and about the exact order in which you will arrange those items. The scratch outline is a plan or blueprint that will help you achieve a unified, supported, and organized composition.

Here is the scratch outline that Linda prepared from her general list about abuse of parks:

> Some people abuse public parks.
> 1. Cleaning out cars
>   a. Ashtrays
>   b. Litter bags
> 2. Defacing park property
> 3. Stealing park property
>   a. Flowers, trees, shrubs
>   b. Park sod
> 4. Not cleaning up after picnics
>   a. Paper trash
>   b. Bottles and cans

This scratch outline enabled Linda to think about her paper — to decide exactly which items to include and in what order. Without writing more than one sentence, she has taken a giant step toward a paper that is unified (she has left out items that are not related); supported (she has added items that develop her point); and organized (she has arranged the items in a logical way — here, in emphatic order). The effective paragraph that eventually resulted from Linda's list and scratch outline is on page 51 (paragraph A).

Activity

To get a sense of preparing a scratch outline, make an outline of reasons why you did well or did not do well in high school. See how many ideas and details you can accumulate in ten minutes.

USING ALL FIVE TECHNIQUES

Very often a scratch outline follows brainstorming, freewriting, diagramming, and making a list. At other times, the scratch outline may be substituted for the other four techniques. Also, you may use several techniques almost simultaneously when writing a paper. You may, for example, ask questions while making a list; you may diagram and outline the list as you write it; you may ask yourself questions and then freewrite answers to them. The five techniques are all ways to help you go about the process of writing a paper.

Activity 1

Answer the following questions.

1. Which of the prewriting techniques do you already practice?

   _____ Brainstorming

   _____ Making a list

   _____ Freewriting

   _____ Making a scratch outline

   _____ Diagramming

2. Which prewriting technique involves asking questions about your topic?

   _____

3. Which prewriting technique shows in a visual way the relationship between ideas and details?

   _____

4. Which prewriting technique involves writing quickly about your topic without being concerned about grammar or spelling?

   _____

5. Which prewriting technique is almost always part of doing an essay?

   _____

6. Which techniques do you think will work best for you?

   _____

Activity 2

Following are examples of how the five prewriting techniques could be used to develop the topic "Inconsiderate Drivers." Identify each technique by writing B (for *brainstorming*), F (for *freewriting*), D (for the *diagram*), L (for the *list*), or SO (for the *scratch outline*) in the answer space.

_____   High beams on
Weave in and out at high speeds
Treat street like a trash can
Open car door onto street without looking
Stop on street looking for an address
Don't use turn signals
High speeds in low-speed zones
Don't take turns merging
Use horn when they don't need to
Don't give walkers the right of way

_____   What is one example of an inconsiderate driver?

A person who suddenly turns without using a signal to let the drivers behind know in advance.

When does this happen?

At city intersections or on smaller country roads.

Why is this dangerous?

You have to be alert to slow down yourself to avoid rear-ending the car in front.

What is another example of inconsideration on the road?

Drivers who come toward you at night with their high beams on.

_____   Some people are inconsiderate drivers.
1. In city:
   a. Stop in middle of street
   b. Turn without signaling
2. On highway:
   a. Leave high beams on
   b. Stay in passing lane
   c. Cheat during a merge
3. Both in city and on highway: Throw trash out the windows

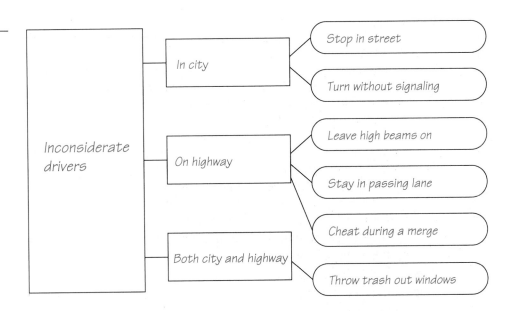

I was driving home last night after class and had three people try to blind me by coming at me with their high beams on. I had to zap them all with my high beams. Rude drivers make me crazy. The worst are the ones that use the road as a trash can. People who throw butts and cups and hamburger wrappings and other stuff out the car windows should be tossed into a trash dumpster. If word got around that this was the punishment maybe they would wise up. Other people do dumb things as well. I hate the person who will just stop in the middle of the street and try to figure out directions or look for a house address. Why don't they pull over to the side of the street? That hardly seems like too much to ask. Instead, they stop all traffic while doing their own thing. Then there are the people who keep what they want to do a secret. They're not going to tell you they plan to make a right- or left-hand turn. Instead, you've got to figure it out yourself when they suddenly slow down in front of you.

Outlining

As already mentioned, often the best way to write an effective paragraph is to outline it first. (At times, you may have to do a fair amount of writing first to discover your topic, but a stage will come when outlining, or reoutlining, will help.) Outlining is an organizational skill that will develop your ability to think clearly and logically. An outline lets you work on, and see, the bare bones of a paper, without the distraction of a clutter of words and sentences. Outlining provides a quick check on whether your paper is *unified.* It suggests right at the start whether your paper will be adequately *supported.* And it shows you how to plan a paper that is *well organized.*

The following series of exercises will help develop the outlining skills that are so important to writing an effective paper.

Activity 1

One key to effective outlining is the ability to distinguish between major ideas and the details that fit under those ideas. This exercise will develop your ability to generalize from a list of details and to determine a major thought. In each case on the opposite page, write in the heading that accurately describes the list provided. Note the two examples below.

Examples   <u>Signs of a cold</u>

Headache
Runny nose
Fever
Chills

<u>Fuels</u>

Wood
Oil
Gas
Kerosene

1. _____
    Vanilla fudge
    Strawberry
    Chocolate
    Butter almond

2. _____
    Lincoln
    Reagan
    Jefferson
    Roosevelt

3. _____
    Birthday
    Get well
    Anniversary
    Graduation

4. _____
    Anacin
    Bufferin
    Alka-Seltzer
    Tylenol

5. _____
    Robbery
    Murder
    Assault
    Kidnapping

6. _____
    Loafers
    Moccasins
    Sneakers
    Sandals

7. _____
    Russian
    Oil and vinegar
    Blue cheese
    French

8. _____
    Washing dishes
    Taking out trash
    Preparing meals
    Dusting

9. _____
    Cash
    Check
    Money order
    Credit card

10. _____
    Writing
    Speaking
    Listening
    Reading

Activity 2

Major and minor ideas are mixed together in the two paragraphs outlined below. Put the ideas in logical order by filling in the outlines.

1. **Topic sentence:** People can be classified by how they treat their cars.

    Seldom wax or vacuum car

    Keep every mechanical item in top shape

    Protective owners

    Deliberately ignore needed maintenance

    Indifferent owners

    Wash and polish car every week

    Accelerate too quickly and brake too hard

    Abusive owners

    Inspect and service car only when required by state law

    a. _____

    (1) _____

    (2) _____

    b. _____

    (1) _____

    (2) _____

    c. _____

    (1) _____

    (2) _____

2. **Topic sentence:** Living with an elderly parent has many benefits.

    Advantages for elderly person

    Live-in baby-sitter

    Learn about the past

    Advantages for adult children

    Serve useful role in family

    Help with household tasks

    Advantages for grandchildren

    Stay active and interested in young people

    More attention from adults

    a. _____

    (1) _____

    (2) _____

    b. _____

    (1) _____

    (2) _____

    c. _____

    (1) _____

    (2) _____

Activity 3

Again, major and minor ideas are mixed together. In addition, in each outline one of the three major ideas is missing and must be added. Put the ideas in logical order by filling in the outlines that follow and adding a third major idea.

1. **Topic sentence:** Extending the school day would have several advantages.

Help children academically

Parents know children are safe at the school

More time to spend on basics

Less pressure to cover subjects quickly

More time for extras like art, music, and sports

Help working parents

More convenient to pick up children at 4 or 5 P.M.

Teachers' salaries would be raised

a. _____

   (1) _____

   (2) _____

b. _____

   (1) _____

   (2) _____

c. _____

   (1) _____

   (2) _____

2. **Topic sentence:** Living in a mobile home has many disadvantages.

Cost of site rental can go up every year

Tiny baths and bedrooms

Few closets or storage areas

Crowded conditions in park

Lack of space

Noise from neighbors

Resale value low compared with houses

No privacy outside in tiny yards

a. _____

   (1) _____

   (2) _____

b. _____

   (1) _____

   (2) _____

c. _____

   (1) _____

   (2) _____

Activity 4

Read the following two paragraphs. Then outline each one in the space provided. Write out the topic sentence in each case and summarize in a few words the primary and secondary supporting material that fits under the topic sentence.

1. Why I'm a Stay-at-Home Baseball Fan

I'd much rather stay at home and watch ball games on television than go to the ball park. First of all, it's cheaper to watch a game at home. I don't have to spend $8 for a ticket and another $5 for a parking space. If I want some refreshments, I can have what's already in the refrigerator instead of shelling out another $3.50 for a limp, lukewarm hot dog and a watery Coke. Also, it's more comfortable at home. I avoid a bumper-to-bumper drive to the ball park and pushy crowds who want to go through the same gate I do. I can lie quietly on my living-room sofa instead of sitting on a hard stadium seat with noisy people all around me. Most of all, watching a game on television is more informative. Not only do I see all the plays which I might miss from my $8 seat, but I see some of them two and three times on instant replay. In addition, I get each play explained to me in glorious detail. If I were at the ball park, I wouldn't know that the pitch our third baseman hit was a high and inside slider or that his grand-slam home run was a record-setting seventh in his career. So I'll let the other fans spend their money, put up with traffic, crowds, and hard seats, and guess at the plays. I'll take my baseball lying down--at home.

Topic sentence: _____

_____

a. _____

   (1) _____

   (2) _____

b. _____

   (1) _____

   (2) _____

c. _____

   (1) _____

   (2) _____

2.   Why Teenagers Take Drugs

There are several reasons why teenagers take drugs. First of all, it is easy for young people to get drugs. Drugs are available almost anywhere, from a school cafeteria to a movie line to a football game. Teens don't have to risk traveling to the slums or dealing with shady types on street corners. It is also easy to get drugs because today's teens have spending money, which comes from allowances or earnings from part-time jobs. Teens can use their money to buy the luxuries they want--records, makeup, clothes, or drugs. Second, teens take drugs because the adolescent years are filled with psychological problems. For a teenager, one of these problems is facing the pressure of making important life decisions, such as choosing a career path. Another problem is establishing a sense of self. The teen years are the time when young people must become more independent from their parents and form their own values. The enormous mental pressures of these years can make some people turn to drugs. A final, and perhaps most important, reason why teenagers take drugs is peer pressure to conform. Teens often become very close to special friends, for one thing, and they will share a friend's interests, even if one of them is drugs. Teenagers also attend parties and other social events where it's all-important to be one of the crowd, to be "cool." Even the most mature teenager might be tempted to use drugs rather than risk being an outcast. For all these reasons, drugs are a major problem facing teenagers.

Topic sentence: _____

_____

a.   _____

  (1) _____

  (2) _____

b.   _____

  (1) _____

  (2) _____

c.   _____

  (1) _____

  (2) _____

Revising, Editing, and Proofreading

Writing an effective paper is almost never done all at once. Rather, it is a step-by-step process in which you take your paper through a series of stages—from prewriting to final draft.

In the first stage, you get your initial ideas and impressions about the subject down on paper; *you accumulate raw material.* You do this through brainstorming, freewriting, and making lists and scratch outlines.

In the second stage, *you shape, add to, and perhaps subtract from your raw material* as you take your paper through a series of two or three or four rough drafts. You work to make clear the single point of your paper, to develop fully the specific evidence needed to support that point, and to organize and connect the specific evidence. For example, perhaps in the second draft you will concentrate on adding details that will further support the main idea of your paper. At the same time you also may eliminate details that, you realize, do not truly back up your main point. And perhaps in the next draft, you will work on reorganizing the details and adding connections between sentences so that your material will hold together.

In the last stage, you *edit* and *proofread.* You *edit* the next-to-final draft—that is, you check it carefully for sentence skills—grammar, mechanics, punctuation, and usage. Then you *proofread* the final copy of the paper for any mistakes in typing or handwriting. Editing and proofreading are important steps that some people neglect, often because they have worked so hard (or so little) on the previous stages.

Ideally, you should have enough time to set your paper aside for a while, so that you can check it later from a fresh point of view. Remember that locating and correcting sentence-skills mistakes can turn an average paper into a better one and a good paper into an excellent one. A later section of this book will give you practice in editing and proofreading in the form of a series of editing tests (pages 426–431).

Practice in Seeing the Entire Writing Process

This section will show you the stages that can be involved in writing an effective paper. You will see what one student, Gene, does in preparing a paper about his worst job.

There is no single sequence that all people follow in writing a composition. However, the different stages in composing that Gene goes through in writing his paper should give you some idea of what to expect. As you'll see, Gene does not just sit down and proceed neatly from start to middle to finish. Writing seldom works like that.

STAGE 1:
THINKING AND PREWRITING ABOUT YOUR TOPIC

In retrospect, here is what Gene says about his initial writing topic and his reaction to it:

> "The assignment was to write about a memorable job. I rejected several ideas; I wanted something I had strong feelings about. Then I thought of a job that I had really hated, working in an apple plant. I remembered a moment when I thought I was at the end of the world. It was a cold winter morning about 5 A.M. I had just loaded apple juice all night and was now cleaning one of the apple vats. The vat was an old gasoline truck body. I was inside it, slipping on its rounded stainless steel floor. It was dark in there, the only light coming from a porthole entrance that I had used to crawl in. Apple juice residue was dripping onto my head, and I was using Ajax and a scrub brush to clean off the residue. I felt incredibly depressed. I didn't have a girlfriend then, and my parents were always fighting, and I was incredibly lonely. I felt I was at the bottom of the barrel in my life, and I was never going to get out.
>
> "All this is what I wanted to write about, I thought, and I scribbled down a lot of the details I just mentioned. After I had over two pages of material, I began to think, 'This is too large a topic. It involves a whole terrible phase in my life. I need to narrow my topic down.' Then I decided to focus on the job itself and what I didn't like about it. I felt I was on my way."

STAGE 2: MAKING A LIST

At this point Gene makes up an initial list of details about the job. The list is shown below:

Apple factory job—worst one I ever had

Boss was a madman
Working conditions were poor
Went to work at 5 P.M., got back at 7 A.M.
Lifted cartons of apple juice for ten hours
Slept, ate, and worked--no social life
Gas money to and from work
Loaded onto wooden skids in a truck
Short breaks but breakneck pace
No real companions at work
Cold outside
Floors of trucks cold metal
Had to clean apple vats

■ Comments and Activity

Fill in the missing words: Gene is fortunate enough to know almost from the start what the _____ in his paper will be. Most of his work can thus go into developing details to support the point. Details seldom come automatically; they must be dug for, and Gene's sketchy list of unpleasant aspects of the job is an early stage in the development of his subject. Making a

_____ is an excellent way to get started.

Note that, in his list, Gene is not concerned about ordering the details in any way, or about deciding whether any detail really fits, or even about repeating himself. He is just doing first things first: getting raw material down on paper. In the second stage, Gene will also concentrate on accumulating raw material and will start to give attention to shaping that material.

STAGE 3: ADDITIONAL PREWRITING

After making a list, Gene continues on to a partial draft of the paper.

Note: To keep Gene's drafts as readable as possible, his spelling and sentence-skills mistakes have been corrected. Ordinarily, a number of such mistakes might be present, and editing a paper for them would be a part of the writing process.

> I hated my job in the apple factory. I hated it because the work was hard. I loaded cartons of apple juice onto wooden skids in tractor trailers. Two parts to job: ten hours on line; two hours cleaning. I hated the job because the working conditions were bad and the pay was poor.

Why were working conditions bad?	Why was pay poor?
Outside weather cold	Two dollars an hour (minimum wage at the time)
Usually zero degrees	
Floor of tractor trailer was cold steel	Quarter more for working the second shift
Breaks were limited-- 10 minutes every $2\frac{1}{2}$ hours	Only money was in overtime--when you got time-and-a-half
$\frac{1}{2}$ hour for lunch	No double time
	I would work twenty hours Friday through Saturday to get as much overtime as possible

1 Work hard
3 Working conditions were poor
    (temperature outside, cleaning of the vats)
2 Money poor

■ Comments and Activity

Fill in the missing words: The second stage of Gene's paper combines freewriting, brainstorming, and a scratch _____. Gene uses all these techniques as he continues to draw out and accumulate _____.
At the same time, he has also realized how to organize his details. He decides to focus *not* on his unpleasant boss but on the job itself. In a rough scratch outline, he lists his three reasons (hard work, bad working conditions, poor wages) for hating the job. He then tentatively decides on working conditions as the worst part of the job and numbers the reasons 1, 2, 3—the order in which he might develop them. Keep in mind that as you accumulate and develop details, you should, like Gene, be thinking of a way to _____ them.

STAGE 4: WRITING A DRAFT

Gene puts his work aside for the day and then continues writing the next morning. He now moves to a fuller draft:

> Working in an apple plant was the worst job I ever had. The work was physically hard. For ~~a long time~~ ten hours a night, I stacked cartons in a tractor trailer. The cartons rolled down a metal track. ~~Each carton was very heavy Each carton was heavy with with cans or bottles of apple juice.~~ Each carton contained twelve thirty-two-ounce cans or bottles of apple juice, and they were heavy. ~~At the same time, I had to keep a mental count of all the cartons I had loaded.~~ The pay for the job was another bad feature. I was getting the minimum wage at that time plus a quarter extra for night shift. I worked ~~long hours~~ over sixty hours a week. I still did not take home much ~~money~~ more than $100. Working conditions were poor at the plant. During work we were limited to ~~short breaks~~ two ten-minute breaks and unpaid lunch. . . . The truck-loading dock had zero temperatures. . . . Lonely on the job . . . no interests with other loaders . . . worked by myself at the end of the shift . . . cleaned up the apple vats.

■ Comments and Activity

Fill in the missing words: At this stage, Gene has enough details to write the initial draft of his paper. Notice that he continues to accumulate specific supporting details as he writes the draft. For example, he crosses out and replaces "long hours" with the more specific _____; he crosses out and replaces "short breaks" with the more specific _____. He also works to improve some of his sentences (for instance, he writes three different versions of the sentence beginning with the words _____). In addition, he crosses out and eliminates a sentence about a _____ because he realizes it does not develop his first supporting point, that the work was physically hard.

Toward the end of the paper, Gene either can't find the right words to say what he wants to say or he doesn't quite know yet what he wants to say. So he freewrites (shown by the ellipses . . .), putting down on paper all the impressions that come into his head. He knows that the technique of _____ may help him move closer to the right thought and the right words.

In a second and a third draft, Gene continues to work on and improve his paper. He then edits his next-to-final draft carefully, and the result is the final draft that follows.

STAGE 5: WRITING THE FINAL VERSION

Thanks to the work done during the earlier stages, Gene can now progress to a final draft of the paper:

My Job in an Apple Plant

Working in an apple plant was the worst job I ever had. First of all, the work was physically hard. For ten hours a night, I took cartons that rolled down a metal track and stacked them onto wooden skids in a tractor trailer. Each carton contained twelve thirty-two-ounce cans or bottles of apple juice, and they were heavy. The second bad feature of the job was the pay. I was getting the minimum wage at that time, two dollars an hour, plus the minimum of a quarter extra for working the night shift. Even after working over sixty hours a week, I still did not take home much more than $100. The worst feature of the apple plant job was the working conditions. During work we were limited to two ten-minute breaks and an unpaid half hour for lunch. Most of my time was spent outside on the truck-loading dock in near-zero-degree temperatures. And I was very lonely on the job, since I had no interests in common with the other truck loaders. I felt this isolation especially when the production line shut down for the night, and I worked by myself for two hours cleaning the apple vats. The vats were an ugly place to be on a cold morning, and the job was a bitter one to have.

■ **Comments and Activity**

Fill in the missing words: Notice the many improvements that Gene has made as a result of his second and third drafts. He has added transitional words that mark clearly the three supporting points of his paper. The transitional words are "first of all," "_____," and "_____." He has sharpened his details, improved the phrasing of his sentences, and found the words needed to complete the last section of his paper. He has also edited and proofread his paper carefully, checking the spelling of words he was unsure about and correcting several sentence-skills mistakes.

Almost every effective writer, like Gene, is engaged in a continuing process of moving toward a completely realized paper. The final version is seldom, almost never, attained all at once. Instead, it is the end result of a series of _____. All too often, people stop writing when they are only partway through the writing process; they turn in a paper that is really only an early draft. They have the mistaken notion that a paper is something you should be able to do "all at once." But for almost everyone, writing means hard work and lots of _____. Be sure, then, to take your paper through the entire series of drafts that you probably will need to write an effective composition.

Activity 1

Answering the questions below will help you evaluate your attitude about revising, editing, and proofreading.

1. When do you typically start to work on a paper?

    _____ Several nights before it's due

    _____ Night before it's due

    _____ Day it's due

2. How many drafts do you typically write when doing a paper?

    _____ One _____ Two _____ Three _____ Four or more

3. How would you describe your editing (checking the next-to-final draft for sentence-skills mistakes)?

    _____ Do little or no editing

    _____ Look quickly for and correct obvious errors

    _____ Consult a sentence-skills handbook and a dictionary about all possible errors

4. How would you describe your proofreading (checking the final draft for typing or handwriting errors)?

    _____ Do not look at paper again after the last word is written

    _____ May glance quickly through the paper

    _____ Read paper over carefully to find mistakes

5. Do you ever get back papers marked for obvious errors?

    _____ Frequently _____ Sometimes _____ Almost never _____ Never

Activity 2

Listed in the box below are five different stages in the process of composing a paragraph titled ''Dangerous Places'':

1. Prewriting (list)
2. Prewriting (list, brainstorming, and outline)
3. First draft
4. Second draft
5. Final draft

The five stages appear in scrambled order below and on the next page. Write the number 1 in the blank space in front of the first stage of development and number the remaining stages in sequence.

_____   There are some places where I never feel safe. For example, bus stations. The people there look ~~strange look~~ tired and scared. The security guards there make me feel ~~something bad is going to happen~~ a fight is going to start. I'm also afraid in parking lots. ~~Late at night, I don't like walking in the lot After class, I don't like the parking lot.~~ When I leave my night class or the shopping mall late the walk to the car is scary. ~~Most parking lots have large lights which make me feel at least a little better.~~ I feel least safe in our laundry room . . . It is a depressing place . . . bars on the windows . . . pipes making noises . . . cement steps the only way out. . . .

_____   Dangerous Places
Highways
Cars—especially parking lots
Feel frightened in our laundry room
Big crowds—concerts, movies
Closed-in places
Bus and train stations
Airplane
Elevators and escalators

_____   Dangerous Places

There are some places where I never feel completely safe. For example, I never feel safe in bus stations. The people in bus stations often look tired and scared as they keep one hand protectively on their luggage. The security guards roaming around bus stations add to my feeling that a fight is about to break out, that someone is going to be mugged, or that someone will force me into a dark corner. I also feel unsafe in large, dark parking lots. When I leave my night class a little late, or I am one of the few leaving the mall at 10 P.M., I dread the walk to my car. I am afraid that someone may be lurking behind another car, ready to mug me. And I fear that my car will not start, leaving me stuck in the dark parking lot. The place where I feel least safe is the basement laundry room in our apartment building. No matter what time I do my laundry, I seem to be the only person there. The windows are barred, and the only exit is a steep flight of cement steps. While I'm folding the clothes, I feel trapped. If anyone unfriendly came down those steps, I would have nowhere to go. The pipes in the room make sudden gurgles, clanks, and hisses, adding to my uneasiness. Places like bus stations, dark parking lots, and our laundry room give me the shivers.

_____   There are some places where I never feel completely safe. For example, I never feel safe in bus stations. The people in bus stations often look tired and scared as they hang on to their luggage. The security guards add to my feeling that a fight is about to start. I also feel unsafe in large, dark parking lots. When I leave my night class a little late or I leave the mall at 10 P.M., the walk to the car is scary. I'm afraid that someone may be behind a car. Also that my car won't start. The place where I feel least safe is the basement laundry room in our apartment building. No matter when I do the laundry, I'm the only person there. The windows are barred and there are steep steps. I feel trapped when I fold the clothes. The pipes in the room make frightening noises such as hisses and clanks. Places like bus stations, parking lots, and our laundry room give me the shivers.

_____   Some places seem dangerous and unsafe to me. For example, last night I stayed till 10:15 after night class and walked out to parking lot alone. Very scary. Also, other places I go to every day, such as places in my apartment building. Also frightened by big crowds and lonely bus stations.

Why was the parking lot scary?	What places in my building scare me?
Dark	Laundry room (especially)
Only a few cars	Elevators
No one else in lot	Lobby at night sometimes
Could be someone behind a car	Outside walkway at night
Cold	

2   Parking lots
3   Laundry room
1   Bus stations

Activity 3

The author of ''Dangerous Places'' in Activity 2 made a number of editing changes between the second draft and the final draft. Compare the two drafts and identify five of the changes in the spaces provided below.

1. _____

2. _____

3. _____

4. _____

5. _____

A Review of the Chapter

Fill in the missing words in the following summary of this chapter.

Having the Right Attitude: Some people feel that in order to be a good writer, writing must come easily. This idea is false and can interfere with the ability to make progress in writing. A more realistic and productive attitude includes the understanding that, for most people, writing is _____ . In addition, it helps to realize that, like driving or typing, writing is a _____ that can be learned with lots of _____ .

Writing for a Specific Purpose and Audience: The three most common purposes of writing are to _____ , to _____ , and to _____ . In this book, you will have a lot of practice in writing to persuade people and some practice in writing to provide information.

   Your main audience in class is your _____ . But he or she is really a symbol for a general audience of well-educated adults. Writing for this audience should be clear and well organized.

   This book will also give you practice in writing for a specific audience. That practice will help you develop the knack of choosing the words and tone of voice that suit specific purposes and people.

Knowing or Discovering Your Subject: It is best to write about a subject that _____ you and that you know something about, either directly or indirectly. When you must write on a topic about which you have little or no background, you should do _____ to gain the necessary knowledge. The library is one good place to do that.

   There are times, however, when you won't know your exact subject until after you have written for a while. Writing will help you think about and explore your material. On occasion you will write for a page or two and discover that it will make sense to change the _____ of your paper.

   As you work on a paper, remember that it is not necessary to write a paper straight through from _____ to end. You should proceed in whatever way seems easiest, including starting at the middle or even the end. Make whatever adjustments are needed to reach your goal of a paper that makes and _____ a point.

Prewriting: There are five prewriting techniques. One technique, called

_____ , is a process of generating ideas by asking questions about your subject. Such questions include *What? When?* and *Why?*

Freewriting is a second prewriting technique. It involves writing on your topic for ten minutes without _____ or worrying about being correct. In this process, your thoughts about your paper often become clearer.

Making a _____ is a third excellent prewriting technique for getting started on a paper. The goal is to generate many possible details for your paper and maybe even ways of developing that paper.

Diagramming, also known as _____ or _____ , is a fourth prewriting activity. Here you use lines, boxes, arrows, and circles to show relationships among the ideas and details that come to you.

Fifth, perhaps the most helpful technique for writing a good paper is preparing a scratch outline. It is an excellent follow-up to the other prewriting techniques. Sometimes you may even skip the other techniques and concentrate on this one. In a scratch outline, you think about the specific point you will make in your

paper, the exact _____ that will support that point, and the exact

_____ in which you will arrange those items.

Outlining: Often the best way to write an effective paragraph is to

_____ it. Outlining develops your ability to think clearly and logically. It helps you to see and work with the fundamental ideas of a paper, and it helps you to focus on producing a paper that is unified, well supported, and well organized.

Revising, Editing, and Proofreading: Writing a paper is usually a step-by-step process. It begins with prewriting, during which you accumulate raw material. In the second stage, you shape your paper by writing and revising it several times. Finally, you edit and proofread. Editing involves checking your paper for mistakes

in sentence _____ . Proofreading involves checking the final copy

of your paper for mistakes in _____ or _____ .

THE FIRST
AND SECOND
STEPS
IN WRITING

This chapter will show you how to

- **Begin a paper by making a point of some kind**
- **Provide specific evidence to support that point**
- **Write a simple paragraph**

The four basic steps in writing an effective paragraph are as follows:

1   Make a point.
2   Support the point with specific evidence.
3   Organize and connect the specific evidence.
4   Write clear, error-free sentences.

This chapter will present the first two steps, and the chapter that follows (see page 72) will present the last two.

Step 1: Make a Point

Your first step in writing is to decide what point you want to make and to write that point in a single sentence. The point is commonly known as a *topic sentence*. As a guide to yourself and to the reader, put that point in the first sentence of your paragraph. Everything else in the paragraph should then develop and support in specific ways the single point given in the first sentence.

Activity

Read the two paragraphs below, written by students on the topic ''Cheating in Everyday Life.'' Which paragraph starts with a clear, single point and goes on to support that point? Which paragraph fails to start with a clear point and rambles on in many directions, introducing a number of ideas but developing none of them?

Paragraph A

Cheating

Cheating has always been a part of life, and it will be so in the future. An obvious situation is that students have many ways of cheating in school. This habit can continue after school is over and become part of their daily lives. There are steps that can be taken to prevent cheating, but many teachers do not seem to care. Maybe they are so burned out by their jobs that they do not want to bother. The honest student is often the one hurt by the cheating of others. Cheating at work occurs also. This cheating may be more dangerous, because employers watch out for it more. Businesses have had to close down because cheating by employees took away a good deal of their profits. A news story recently concerned a waiter who was fired for taking a steak home from the restaurant where he worked, but his taking the steak may have been justified. Cheating in the sense of being unfaithful to a loved one is a different story because emotions are involved. People will probably never stop cheating unless there is a heavy penalty to be paid.

Paragraph B

Everyday Cheating

Cheating is common in everyday life. For one thing, cheating at school is common. Many students will borrow a friend's homework and copy it in their own handwriting. During a test, students will use a tiny sheet of answers stored in their pockets or sit near a friend to copy answers. People also cheat on the job. They use the postal meter at work for personal mail or take home office supplies such as tape, paper, or pens. Some people who are not closely supervised or who are out on the road may cheat an employer by taking dozens of breaks or using work time for personal chores. Finally, many people cheat when they deal with large businesses. For instance, few customers will report an incorrect bill in their favor. Visitors in a hotel may take home towels, and restaurant patrons may take home silverware. A customer in a store may change price tags because "This is how much the shirt cost last month." For many people, daily cheating is an acceptable way to behave.

Complete the following statement: Paragraph _____ is effective because it makes a clear, single point in the first sentence and goes on in the remaining sentences to support that single point.

Paragraph B starts with a single idea — that people cheat in everyday life — and then supports that idea with several different examples. But paragraph A does not begin by making a definite point. Instead, we get two broad, obvious statements — that cheating "has always been a part of life" and "will be so in the future." Because the author has not focused on a clear, single point, what happens in this paragraph is inevitable.

The line of thought in paragraph A swerves about like a car without a steering wheel. In the second sentence, we read that ". . . students have many ways of cheating in school," and we think for a moment that this will be the author's point: he or she will give us supporting details about different ways students cheat in school. But the next sentence makes another point: that after school is over, students may continue to cheat as "part of their daily lives." We therefore expect the author to give us details backing up the idea that students who cheat continue to cheat after they leave or finish school. However, the next sentence makes two additional points: "There are steps that can be taken to prevent cheating, but many teachers do not seem to care." These are two more ideas that could be — but are not — the focus of the paragraph. By now we are not really surprised at what happens in the following sentences. Several more points are made: "The honest student is often the one hurt by the cheating of others," cheating at work "may be more dangerous," an employee who stole a steak "may have been justified," and cheating by being unfaithful is different "because emotions are involved." No single idea is developed; the result is confusion.

Step 2: Support the Point with Specific Evidence

The first essential step in writing effectively is to start with a clearly stated point. The second basic step is to support that point with specific evidence. Following are the two examples of supported points that you've already read.

Point 1

I've decided not to go out with Tony anymore.

Support for Point 1

1. Late for our date
2. Bossy
3. Abrupt

Point 2

Cheating is common in everyday life.

Support for Point 2

1. At school
   a. Copying homework
   b. Cheating on tests
2. At work
   a. Using postage meter
   b. Stealing office supplies
   c. Taking breaks and doing errands on company time
3. With large businesses
   a. Not reporting error on bill
   b. Stealing towels and silverware
   c. Switching price tags

The supporting evidence is needed so that we can *see and understand for ourselves* that each writer's point is sound. By providing us with particulars about Tony's actions, the first writer shows why she has decided not to go out with him anymore. We can see that she has made a sound point. Likewise, the author of "Everyday Cheating" has supplied specific supporting examples of how cheating is common in everyday life. That paragraph, too, has provided the evidence that is needed for us to understand and agree with the writer's point.

Activity

Both of the paragraphs that follow resulted from an assignment to ''Write a paper that details your reasons for being in college.'' Both writers make the point that they have various reasons for attending college. Which paragraph then goes on to provide plenty of specific evidence to back up its point? Which paragraph is vague and repetitive and lacks the concrete details needed to show us exactly why the author decided to attend college?

Hint: Imagine that you were asked to make a short film based on each paragraph. Which one suggests specific pictures, locations, words, and scenes you could shoot?

Paragraph A

Reasons for Going to College

I decided to attend college for various reasons. One reason is self-respect. For a long time now, I have felt little self-respect. I spent a lot of time doing nothing, just hanging around or getting into trouble, and eventually I began to feel bad about it. Going to college is a way to start feeling better about myself. By accomplishing things, I will improve my self-image. Another reason for going to college is that things happened in my life that made me think about a change. For one thing, I lost the part-time job I had. When I lost the job, I realized I would have to do something in life, so I thought about school. I was in a rut and needed to get out of it but did not know how. But when something happens out of your control, then you have to make some kind of decision. The most important reason for college, though, is to fulfill my dream. I know I need an education, and I want to take the courses I need to reach the position that I think I can handle. Only by qualifying yourself can you get what you want. Going to college will help me fulfill this goal. These are the main reasons why I am attending college.

Paragraph B

Why I'm in School

There are several reasons I'm in school. First of all, my father's attitude made me want to succeed in school. One night last year, after I had come in at 3 A.M., my father said, ''Mickey, you're a bum. When I look at my son, all I see is a good-for-nothing bum.'' I was angry, but I knew my father was right in a way. I had spent the last two years working odd jobs at a pizza parlor and luncheonette, taking ''uppers'' and ''downers'' with my friends. That night, though, I decided I would prove my father wrong. I would go to college and be a success. Another reason I'm in college is my girlfriend's encouragement. Marie has already been in school for a year, and she is doing well in her computer courses. Marie helped me fill out my application and register for courses. She even lent me sixty-five dollars for textbooks. On her day off, she lets me use her car so I don't have to take the college bus. The main reason I am in college is to fulfill a personal goal: I want to finish something for the first time in my life. For example, I quit high school in the eleventh grade. Then I enrolled in a government job-training program, but I dropped out after six months. I tried to get a high school equivalency diploma, but I started missing classes and eventually gave up. Now I am in a special program where I will earn my high school degree by completing a series of five courses. I am determined to accomplish this goal and to then go on and work for a degree in hotel management.

Complete the following statement: Paragraph _____ provides clear, vividly detailed reasons why the writer decided to attend college.

Paragraph B is the one that solidly backs up its point. The writer gives us specific reasons he is in school. On the basis of such evidence, we can clearly understand his opening point. The writer of paragraph A offers only vague, general reasons for being in school. We do not get specific examples of how the writer was "getting into trouble," what events occurred that forced the decision, or even what kind of job he or she wants to qualify for. We sense that the feeling expressed is sincere; but without the benefit of particular examples, we cannot really see why the writer decided to attend college.

THE IMPORTANCE OF SPECIFIC DETAILS

The point that opens a paper is a general statement. The evidence that supports a point is made up of specific details, reasons, examples, and facts.

Specific details have two key functions. First of all, details *excite the reader's interest.* They make writing a pleasure to read, for we all enjoy learning particulars about other people—what they do and think and feel. Second, details *support and explain a writer's point;* they give the evidence needed for us to see and understand a general idea. For example, the writer of "Good-Bye, Tony" provides details that make vividly clear her decision not to see Tony anymore. She specifies the exact time Tony was supposed to arrive (8:30) and when he actually arrived (9:20). She mentions the kind of film she wanted to see (a new Steve Martin movie) and the one that Tony took her to instead (*The Night of the Living Dead*). She tells us what she may have wanted to do after the movie (have a hamburger or a drink) and what Tony did instead (went necking); she even specifies the exact location of the place Tony took her (a back road near Oakcrest High School). She explains precisely what happened next (Tony "cut his finger on a pin I was wearing") and even mentions by name (Bactine and a Band-Aid) the treatments he planned to use.

The writer of "Why I'm in School" provides equally vivid details. He gives clear reasons for being in school (his father's attitude, his girlfriend's encouragement, and his wish to fulfill a personal goal) and backs up each reason with specific details. His details give us many sharp pictures. For instance, we hear the exact words his father spoke: "Mickey, you're a bum." He tells us exactly how he was spending his time ("working odd jobs at a pizza parlor and luncheonette, taking 'uppers' and 'downers' with my friends"). He describes how his girlfriend helped him (filling out the college application, lending money and her car). Finally, instead of stating generally that "you have to make some kind of decision," as the writer of "Reasons for Going to College" does, he specifies that he has a strong desire to finish college because he dropped out of many schools and programs in the past: high school, a job-training program, and a high school equivalency course.

In both "Good-Bye, Tony" and "Why I'm in School," then, the vivid, exact details capture our interest and enable us to share in the writer's experience. We see people's actions and hear their words; the details provide pictures that make each of us feel "I am there." The particulars also allow us to understand each writer's point clearly. We are shown exactly why the first writer has decided not to see Tony anymore and exactly why the second writer is attending college.

Activity

Each of the five points below is followed by two selections. Write S (for *specific*) in the space next to the selection that provides specific support for the point. Write NS (for *not specific*) in the space next to the selection that lacks supporting details.

1. My two-year-old son was in a stubborn mood today.

   _____ a. When I asked him to do something, he gave me nothing but trouble. He seemed determined to make things difficult for me, for he had his mind made up.

   _____ b. When I asked him to stop playing in the yard and come indoors, he looked me square in the eye and shouted "No!" and then spelled it out, "N . . . O!"

2. The prices in the amusement park were outrageously high.

   _____ a. The food seemed to cost twice as much as it would in a supermarket and was sometimes of poor quality. The rides also cost a lot, and so I had to tell the children that they were limited to a certain number of them.

   _____ b. The cost of the log flume, a ride that lasts roughly 3 minutes, was $4.75 a person. Then I had to pay $1.50 for an 8-ounce cup of Coke and $3.25 for a hot dog.

3. My brother-in-law is accident-prone.

    _____ a. Once he tried to open a tube of Krazy Glue with his teeth. When the cap came loose, glue squirted out and sealed his lips shut. They had to be pried open in a hospital emergency room.

    _____ b. Even when he does seemingly simple jobs, he seems to get into trouble. This can lead to hilarious, but sometimes dangerous, results. Things never seem to go right for him, and he often needs the help of others to get out of one predicament or another.

4. The so-called "bargains" at the yard sale were junk.

    _____ a. The tables at the yard sale were filled with useless stuff no one could possibly want. They were the kinds of things that should be thrown away, not sold.

    _____ b. The "bargains" at the yard sale included two headless dolls, blankets filled with holes, scorched pot holders, and a plastic Christmas tree with several branches missing.

5. The key to success in college is organization.

    _____ a. Knowing what you're doing, when you have to do it, and so on is a big help for a student. A system is crucial in achieving an ordered approach to study. Otherwise, things become very disorganized, and it is not long before grades will begin to drop.

    _____ b. Organized students never forget paper or exam dates, which are marked on a calendar above their desks. And instead of having to cram for exams, they study their clear, neat classroom and textbook notes on a daily basis.

Comments: The specific support for the first point is answer *b.* The writer does not just tell us that the little boy was stubborn but provides an example that shows us. In particular, the detail of the son's spelling out "N . . . O!" makes his stubbornness vividly real for the reader. For the second point, answer *b* gives specific prices ($4.75 for a ride, $1.50 for a Coke, and $3.25 for a hot dog) to support the idea that the amusement park was expensive. For the third point, answer *a* vividly backs up the idea that the brother-in-law is accident-prone by detailing an accident with Krazy Glue. The fourth point is supported by answer *b,* which lists specific examples of useless items that were offered for sale—from headless dolls to a broken plastic Christmas tree. We cannot help agreeing with the writer's point that the items were not bargains but junk. The fifth point is backed up by answer *b,* which identifies two specific strategies of organized students: they mark important dates on calendars above their desks, and they take careful notes and study them on a daily basis.

In each of the five cases, then, specific evidence is presented to enable us to *see for ourselves* that the writer's point is valid.

THE IMPORTANCE OF ADEQUATE DETAILS

One of the most common and most serious problems in students' writing is inadequate development. You must provide *enough* specific details to support fully a point you are making. You could not, for example, submit a paragraph about how your brother-in-law is accident-prone and provide only a short example. You would have to add several other examples or provide an extended example of your brother-in-law's ill luck. Without such additional support, your paragraph would be underdeveloped.

At times, students try to disguise an undersupported point by using repetition and wordy generalities. You saw this, for example, in the paragraph titled ''Reasons for Going to College'' on page 47. Be prepared to do the plain hard work needed to ensure that each of your paragraphs has full and solid support.

Activity

The following paragraphs were written on the same topic, and each has a clear opening point. Which one is adequately developed? Which one has only several particulars and uses mostly vague, general, wordy sentences to conceal the fact that it is starved for specific details?

Paragraph A

Abuse of Public Parks

Some people abuse public parks. Instead of using the park for recreation, they go there, for instance, to clean their cars. Park caretakers regularly have to pick up the contents of dumped ashtrays and car litter bags. Certain juveniles visit parks with cans of spray paint to deface buildings, fences, fountains, and statues. Other offenders are those who dig up and cart away park flowers, shrubs, and trees. One couple were even arrested for stealing park sod, which they were using to fill in their back lawn. Perhaps the most widespread offenders are the people who use park tables and benches and fireplaces but do not clean up afterward. Picnic tables are littered with trash, including crumpled bags, paper plates smeared with catsup, and paper cups half-filled with stale soda. On the ground are empty beer bottles, dented soda cans, and sharp metal pop tops. Parks are made for people, and yet--ironically--their worst enemy is ''people pollution.''

Paragraph B

Mistreatment of Public Parks

Some people mistreat public parks. Their behavior is evident in many ways, and the catalog of abuses could go on almost without stopping. Different kinds of debris are left by people who have used the park as a place for attending to their automobiles. They are not the only individuals who mistreat public parks, which should be used with respect for the common good of all. Many young people come to the park and abuse it, and their offenses can occur in any season of the year. The reason for their inconsiderate behavior is best known only to themselves. Other visitors have a lack of personal cleanliness in their personal habits when they come to the park, and the park suffers because of it. Such people seem to have the attitude that someone else should clean up after them. It is an undeniable fact that people are the most dangerous thing that parks must contend with.

Complete the following statement: Paragraph _____ provides an adequate number of specific details to support its point.

Paragraph A offers a series of well-detailed examples of how people abuse parks. Paragraph B, on the other hand, is underdeveloped. Paragraph B speaks only of "different kinds of debris," while paragraph A refers specifically to "dumped ashtrays and car litter bags"; paragraph B talks in a general way of young people abusing the park, while paragraph A supplies such particulars as "cans of spray paint" and defacing "buildings, fences, fountains, and statues." And there is no equivalent in paragraph B for the specifics in paragraph A about people who steal park property and litter park grounds. In summary, paragraph B lacks the full, detailed support needed to develop its opening point convincingly.

■ Review Activity

To check your understanding of the chapter so far, see if you can answer the following questions.

1. It has been observed: "To write well, the first thing you must do is decide what nail you want to drive home." What is meant by *nail*?

   _____

2. How do you drive home the nail in a paper?

   _____

3. What are the two reasons for using specific details in your writing?

   a.   _____

   b.   _____

Practice in Making and Supporting a Point

You now know the two most important steps in competent writing: (1) making a point and (2) supporting that point with specific evidence. The purpose of this section is to expand and strengthen your understanding of these two basic steps.

You will first work through a series of activities on *making* a point:

1 Identifying Common Errors in Topic Sentences
2 Understanding the Two Parts of a Topic Sentence
3 Writing a Topic Sentence: I
4 Writing a Topic Sentence: II

You will then sharpen your understanding of specific details by working through a series of activities on *supporting* a point:

5 Making Words and Phrases Specific
6 Making Sentences Specific
7 Providing Specific Evidence
8 Identifying Adequate Supporting Evidence
9 Adding Details to Complete a Paragraph

Finally, you will practice writing a paragraph of your own:

10 Writing a Simple Paragraph

1   IDENTIFYING COMMON ERRORS IN TOPIC SENTENCES

When writing a point, or topic sentence, people sometimes make mistakes that undermine their chances of producing an effective paper. One mistake is to substitute an announcement of the topic for a true topic sentence. Other mistakes include writing statements that are too broad or too narrow. On the following page are examples of all three errors, along with contrasting examples of effective topic sentences.

Announcement

My Ford Escort is the concern of this paragraph.

The statement above is a simple announcement of a subject, rather than a topic sentence in which an idea is expressed about the subject.

Statement That Is Too Broad

Many people have problems with their cars.

The statement above is too broad to be supported adequately with specific details in a single paragraph.

Statement That Is Too Narrow

My car is a Ford Escort.

The statement above is too narrow to be expanded into a paragraph. Such a narrow statement is sometimes called a *dead-end statement* because there is no place to go with it. It is a simple fact that does not need or call for any support.

Effective Topic Sentence

I hate my Ford Escort.

The statement above expresses an opinion that could be supported in a paragraph. The writer could offer a series of specific supporting reasons, examples, and details to make it clear why he or she hates the car.

Here are additional examples:

Announcements

The subject of this paper will be my apartment.

I want to talk about increases in the divorce rate.

Statements That Are Too Broad

The places where people live have definite effects on their lives.

Many people have trouble getting along with others.

Statements That Are Too Narrow

I have no hot water in my apartment at night.

Almost one of every two marriages ends in divorce.

Effective Topic Sentences

My apartment is a terrible place to live.

The divorce rate is increasing for several reasons.

Activity 1

In each pair of sentences below, write A beside the sentence that only *announces* a topic. Write OK beside the sentence that *presents an idea* about the topic.

1. _____ a. This paper will deal with flunking math.

 _____ b. I flunked math last semester for several reasons.

2. _____ a. I am going to write about my job as a gas station attendant.

 _____ b. Working as a gas station attendant was the worst job I ever had.

3. _____ a. Obscene phone calls are the subject of this paragraph.

 _____ b. People should know what to do when they receive an obscene phone call.

4. _____ a. In several ways, my college library is inconvenient to use.

 _____ b. This paragraph will deal with the college library.

5. _____ a. My paper will discuss the topic of procrastinating.

 _____ b. The following steps will help you stop procrastinating.

Activity 2

In each pair of sentences below, write TN beside the statement that is *too narrow* to be developed into a paragraph. (Such a narrow statement is also known as a *dead-end sentence.*) Write OK beside the statement in each pair that calls for support or development of some kind.

1. _____ a. I do push-ups and sit-ups each morning.

 _____ b. Exercising every morning has had positive effects on my health.

2. _____ a. José works nine hours a day and then goes to school three hours a night.

 _____ b. José is an ambitious man.

3. _____ a. I started college after being away from school for seven years.

 _____ b. Several of my fears about returning to school have proved to be groundless.

4. _____ a. Parts of Walt Disney's *Bambi* make it a frightening movie for children.

 _____ b. Last summer I visited Disneyland in Anaheim, California.

5. _____ a. My brother was depressed yesterday for several reasons.

 _____ b. Yesterday my brother had to pay fifty-two dollars for a motor tune-up.

Activity 3

In each pair of sentences below, write TB beside the statement that is *too broad* to be supported adequately in a short paper. Write OK beside the statement that makes a limited point.

1. _____ a. Professional football is a dangerous sport.

   _____ b. Professional sports are violent.

2. _____ a. Married life is the best way of living.

   _____ b. Teenage marriages often end in divorce for several reasons.

3. _____ a. Aspirin can have several harmful side effects.

   _____ b. Drugs are dangerous.

4. _____ a. I've always done poorly in school.

   _____ b. I flunked math last semester for several reasons.

5. _____ a. Computers are changing our society.

   _____ b. Using computers to teach schoolchildren is a mistake.

2 UNDERSTANDING THE TWO PARTS OF A TOPIC SENTENCE

As stated earlier, the point that opens a paragraph is often called a *topic sentence.* When you look closely at a point, or topic sentence, you can see that it is made up of two parts:

1 The *limited topic*

2 The writer's *attitude* about the limited topic

The writer's attitude or point of view or idea is usually expressed in a *key word* or *words.* All the details in a paragraph should support the idea expressed in the key words. In each of the topic sentences below, a single line appears under the topic and a double line under the idea about the topic (expressed in a key word or words):

My girlfriend is very aggressive.

Highway accidents are often caused by absentmindedness.

The kitchen is the most widely used room in my house.

Voting should be required by law in the United States.

My pickup truck is the most reliable vehicle I have ever owned.

In the first sentence, the topic is *girlfriend,* and the key word that expresses the writer's idea about his topic is that his girlfriend is *aggressive.* In the second sentence, the topic is *highway accidents,* and the key word that determines the focus of the paragraph is that such accidents are often caused by *absentmindedness.* Notice each topic and key word or words in the other three sentences as well.

Activity

For each point below, draw a single line under the topic and a double line under the idea about the topic.

1. Billboards should be abolished.
2. My boss is an ambitious man.
3. The middle child is often a neglected member of the family.
4. The apartment needed repairs.
5. Television commercials are often insulting.
6. My parents have rigid racial attitudes.
7. The language in many movies today is offensive.
8. Homeowners today are more energy-conscious than ever before.
9. My friend Debbie, who is only nineteen, is extremely old-fashioned.
10. Looking for a job can be a degrading experience.
11. Certain regulations in the school cafeteria should be strictly enforced.
12. My car is a temperamental machine.
13. Living in a one-room apartment has its drawbacks.
14. The city's traffic-light system has both values and drawbacks.
15. Consumers' complaints can often have positive results.

3   WRITING A TOPIC SENTENCE: I

Activity

The activity on the following pages will give you practice in writing an accurate point, or topic sentence—one that is neither too broad nor too narrow for the supporting material in a paragraph. Sometimes you will construct your topic sentence after you have decided what details you want to discuss. An added value of this activity is that it shows you how to write a topic sentence that will exactly match the details you have developed.

1. *Topic sentence:* _____

   _____

   a. Some are caused by careless people tossing matches out of car windows.
   b. A few are started when lightning strikes a tree.
   c. Some result from campers who fail to douse cooking fires.
   d. The majority of forest fires are deliberately set by arsonists.

2. *Topic sentence:* _____

   _____

   a. We had to wait a half hour even though we had reserved a table.
   b. Our appetizers and main courses all arrived at the same time.
   c. The busboy ignored our requests for more water.
   d. The wrong desserts were delivered to us.

3. *Topic sentence:* _____

   _____

   a. My phone goes dead at certain times of the day.
   b. When I talk long distance, I hear conversations in the background.
   c. The line to the phone service center is busy for hours.
   d. My telephone bill includes three calls I never made.

4. *Topic sentence:* _____

   _____

   a. The crowd scenes were crudely spliced from another film.
   b. Mountains and other background scenery were just painted cardboard cutouts.
   c. The ''sync'' was off, so that you heard voices even when the actors' lips were not moving.
   d. The so-called monster was just a spider that had been filmed through a magnifying lens.

5. | *Topic sentence:* _____
    _____

    a. In early grades we had spelling bees, and I would be among the first ones sitting down.
    b. In sixth-grade English, my teacher kept me busy diagramming sentences on the board.
    c. In tenth grade we had to recite poems, and I always forgot my lines.
    d. In my senior year, my compositions had more red correction marks than anyone else's.

4   WRITING A TOPIC SENTENCE: II

Often you will start with a general topic or a general idea of what you want to write about. You may, for example, want to write a paragraph about some aspect of school life. To come up with a point about school life, begin by limiting your topic. One way to do this is to make a list of all the limited topics you can think of that fit under the general topic.

Activity

On the following pages are five general topics and a series of limited topics that fit under them. Make a point out of one of the limited topics in each group.

Hint: To create a topic sentence, ask yourself, "What point do I want to make about _____ (*my limited topic*)?"

Example   Recreation

- Movies
- Dancing
- TV shows
- Reading
- Sports parks

Your point: *Sports parks today have some truly exciting games.* _____

1. Your school

    - Instructor
    - Cafeteria
    - Specific class
    - Particular room or building
    - Particular policy (attendance, grading, etc.)
    - Classmate

    Your point: _____

2. Job

    - Pay
    - Boss
    - Working conditions
    - Duties
    - Coworkers
    - Customers or clients

    Your point: _____

3. Money

    - Budgets
    - Credit cards
    - Dealing with a bank
    - School expenses
    - Ways to get it
    - Ways to save it

    Your point: _____

4. Cars

    - First car
    - Driver's test
    - Road conditions
    - Accident
    - Mandatory speed limit
    - Safety problems

    Your point: _____

5. Sports

- A team's chances
- At your school
- Women's teams
- Recreational versus spectator
- Favorite team
- Outstanding athlete

Your point: _____

5   MAKING WORDS AND PHRASES SPECIFIC

To be an effective writer, you must use specific, rather than general, words. Specific words create pictures in the reader's mind. They help capture interest and make your meaning clear.

Activity

This activity will give you practice at replacing vague, indefinite words with sharp, specific words. Insert three or more specific words to replace the general word or words underlined in each sentence. Make changes in the wording of a sentence as necessary.

Example   My bathroom cabinet contains many drugs.

My bathroom cabinet contains aspirin, antibiotics, tranquilizers,

and codeine cough medicine.

1. At the shopping center, we visited several stores.

    _____

    _____

2. Sunday is my day to take care of chores.

    _____

    _____

3. Lola enjoys various activities in her spare time.

    _____

    _____

4. I spent most of my afternoon doing <u>homework</u>.

   _____

   _____

5. We returned home from vacation to discover that <u>several pests</u> had invaded the house.

   _____

   _____

6 MAKING SENTENCES SPECIFIC

Again, you will practice replacing vague, indefinite writing with lively, image-filled writing that captures your reader's interest and makes your meaning clear. Compare the following sentences:

General	*Specific*
The boy came down the street.	Jerry ran down Woodlawn Avenue.
A bird appeared on the grass.	A blue jay swooped down on the frost-covered lawn.
She stopped the car.	Wanda slammed on the brakes of her Escort.

The specific sentences create clear pictures in your reader's mind. The details *show* readers exactly what has happened.

Here are four ways to make your words and sentences specific:

1 Use exact names.

She loves her *motorbike.*
Lola loves her *Honda.*

2 Use lively verbs.

The garbage truck *went* down Front Street.
The garbage truck *rumbled* down Front Street.

3 Use descriptive words (modifiers) before nouns.

A girl peeked out the window.
A *chubby, six-year-old* girl peeked out the *dirty kitchen* window.

4 Use words that relate to the five senses: sight, hearing, taste, smell, and touch.

That woman is a karate expert.
That *tiny, silver-haired* woman is a karate expert. (*Sight*)

When the dryer stopped, a signal sounded.
When the *whooshing* dryer stopped, a *loud buzzer* sounded. (*Hearing*)

Lola offered me an orange slice.
Lola offered me a *sweet, juicy* orange slice. (*Taste*)

The real estate agent opened the door of the closet.
The real estate agent opened the door of the *cedar-scented* closet. (*Smell*)

I pulled the blanket around me to fight off the wind.
I pulled the *scratchy* blanket around me to fight off the *chilling* wind. (*Touch*)

Activity

With the help of the methods described above, add specific details to any eight of the ten sentences that follow. Use separate paper.

Examples   The person got out of the car.

The elderly man painfully lifted himself out of the white Buick station wagon.

The fans enjoyed the victory.
Many of the fifty thousand fans stood, waved blankets, and cheered wildly when Barnes scored the winning touchdown.

1. The lunch was not very good.
2. The animal ran away.
3. An accident occurred.
4. The instructor came into the room.
5. The machine did not work.
6. The crowd grew restless.
7. I relaxed.
8. The room was cluttered.
9. The child threw the object.
10. The driver was angry.

7 PROVIDING SPECIFIC EVIDENCE

Activity

Provide three details that logically support each of the following points, or topic sentences. Your details can be drawn from your own experience, or they can be invented. In each case, the details should show in a specific way what the point expresses in only a general way. State your details briefly in several words rather than in complete sentences.

Example Steve had several ways of passing time during the dull lecture.

> *Shielded his eyes with his hand and dozed awhile.*
>
> *Read the sports magazine he had brought to class.*
>
> *Made an elaborate drawing on a page of his notebook.*

1. I could tell I was coming down with flu.

    _____

    _____

    _____

2. The food at the cafeteria was terrible yesterday.

    _____

    _____

    _____

3. I had car problems recently.

    _____

    _____

    _____

4. When your money gets tight, there are several ways to economize.

    _____

    _____

    _____

5. Some people have dangerous driving habits.

    _____

    _____

    _____

8   IDENTIFYING ADEQUATE SUPPORTING EVIDENCE

Activity

Two of the following paragraphs provide sufficient details to support their topic sentences convincingly. Write AD, for *adequate development*, beside those paragraphs. There are also three paragraphs that, for the most part, use vague, general, or wordy sentences as a substitute for concrete details. Write U, for *underdeveloped,* beside those paragraphs.

_____ 1.   My Husband's Stubbornness

My husband's worst problem is his stubbornness. He simply will not let any kind of weakness show. If he isn't feeling well, he refuses to admit it. He will keep on doing whatever he is doing and will wait until the symptoms get almost unbearable before he will even hint that anything is the matter with him. Then things are so far along that he has to spend more time recovering than he would if he had a different attitude. He also hates to be wrong. If he is wrong, he will be the last to admit it. This happened once when we went shopping, and he spent an endless amount of time going from one place to the next. He insisted that one of them had a fantastic sale on things he wanted. We never found a sale, but the fact that this situation happened will not change his attitude. Finally, he never listens to anyone else's suggestions on a car trip. He always knows he's on the right road, and the results have led to a lot of time wasted getting back in the right direction. Every time one of these incidents happens, it only means it is going to happen again in the future.

_____ 2.   Dangerous Games

Because they feel compelled to show off in front of their friends, some teenagers play dangerous games. In one incident, police found a group of boys performing a dangerous stunt with their cars. The boys would perch on the hoods of cars going thirty-five or forty miles an hour. Then the driver would brake sharply, and the boy who flew the farthest off the car would win. Teenagers also drive their cars with the lights off and pass each other on hills or curves as ways of challenging each other. Water, as well as cars, seems to tempt young people to invent dangerous contests. Some students dared each other to swim through a narrow pipe under a four-lane highway. The pipe carried water from a stream to a pond, and the swimmer would have to hold his or her breath for several minutes before coming out on the other side. Another contest involved diving off the rocky sides of a quarry. Because large stones sat under the water in certain places, any dive could result in a broken neck. But the students would egg each other on to go "rock diving." Playing deadly games like these is a horrifying phase of growing up for some teenagers.

———— 3.

Attitudes about Food

Attitudes about food that we form as children are not easily changed. In some families, food is love. Not all families are like this, but some children grow up with this attitude. Some families think of food as something precious and not to be wasted. The attitudes children pick up about food are hard to change in adulthood. Some families celebrate with food. If a child learns an attitude, it is hard to break this later. Someone once said: "As the twig is bent, so grows the tree." Children are very impressionable, and they can't really think for themselves when they are small. Children learn from the parent figures in their lives, and later from their peers. Some families have healthy attitudes about food. It is important for adults to teach their children these healthy attitudes. Otherwise, the children may have weight problems when they are adults.

———— 4.

Qualities in a Friend

There are several qualities I look for in a friend. A friend should give support and security. A friend should also be fun to be around. Friends can have faults, like anyone else, and sometimes it is hard to overlook them. But a friend can't be dropped because he or she has faults. A friend should stick by you, even in bad times. There is a saying that "a friend in need is a friend indeed." I believe this means that there are good friends and fair-weather friends. The second type is not a true friend. He or she is the kind of person who runs when there's trouble. Friends don't always last a lifetime. Someone you believed to be your best friend may lose contact with you if you move to a different area or go around with a different group of people. A friend should be generous and understanding. A friend does not have to be exactly like you. Sometimes friends are opposites, but they still like each other and get along. Since I am a very quiet person, I can't say that I have many friends. But these are the qualities I believe a friend should have.

———— 5.

A Dangerous Place

We play touch football on a dangerous field. First of all, the grass on the field is seldom mowed. The result is that we have to run through tangled weeds that wrap around our ankles like trip wires. The tall grass also hides some gaping holes lurking beneath. The best players know the exact positions of all the holes and manage to detour around them like soldiers zigzagging across a minefield. Most of us, though, endure at least one sprained ankle per game. Another danger is the old baseball infield that we use as the last twenty yards of our gridiron. This area is covered with stones and broken glass. No matter how often we clean it up, we can never keep pace with the broken bottles hurled on the field by the teenagers we call the "night shift." These people apparently hold drinking parties every night in the abandoned dugout and enjoy throwing the empties out on the field. During every game, we try to avoid falling on especially big chunks of Budweiser bottles. Finally, encircling the entire field is an old, rusty chain-link fence full of tears and holes. Being slammed into the fence during the play can mean a painful stabbing by the jagged wires. All these dangers have made us less afraid of opposing teams than of the field where we play.

9   ADDING DETAILS TO COMPLETE A PARAGRAPH

Activity

Each of the following paragraphs needs specific details to back up its supporting points. In the spaces provided, add a sentence or two of realistic details for each supporting point. The more specific you are, the more convincing your details are likely to be.

1.

A Pushover Instructor

We knew after the first few classes that the instructor was a pushover. First of all, he didn't seem able to control the class.

_____

_____

In addition, he made some course requirements easier when a few

students complained. _____

_____

_____

_____

Finally, he gave the easiest quiz we had ever taken. _____

_____

_____

_____

2.

Helping a Parent in College

There are several ways a family can help a parent who is attending college. First, family members can take over some of the household chores that the parent usually does. _____

_____

_____

_____

Also, family members can make sure that the student has some quiet study time. _____

_____

_____

_____

Third, families can take an interest in the student's problems and accomplishments. _____

_____

_____

_____

10   WRITING A SIMPLE PARAGRAPH

You know now that an effective paragraph does two essential things: (1) it makes a point, and (2) it provides specific details to support that point. You have considered a number of paragraphs that were effective because they followed these two basic steps or ineffective because they failed to follow them.

You are ready, then, to write a simple paragraph of your own. Choose one of the three assignments below, and follow carefully the guidelines provided.

■ Assignment 1

Turn back to the activity on page 64 and select the point for which you have the best supporting details. Develop the point into a paragraph by following these steps:

a If necessary, rewrite the point so that the first sentence is more specific or suits your purpose more exactly. For example, you might want to rewrite the second point so that it includes a specific time and place: "Dinner at the Union Building Cafeteria was terrible yesterday."

b Provide several sentences of information to develop each of your three supporting details fully. Make sure that all the information in your paragraph truly supports your point. As an aid, use the paragraph form on page 579.

c Use the words *First of all, Second,* and *Finally* to introduce each of your three supporting details.

d Conclude your paragraph with a sentence that refers to your opening point. This last sentence "rounds off" the paragraph and lets the reader know that your discussion is complete. For example, the second paragraph about cheating on page 44 begins with "Cheating is common in everyday life." It closes with a statement that refers to, and echoes, the opening point: "For many people, daily cheating is an acceptable way to behave."

e Supply a title based on the point. For instance, the fourth point might have the title "Ways to Economize."

Use the following list to check your paragraph for each of the above items:

Yes	No	
____	____	Do you begin with a point?
____	____	Do you provide relevant, specific details that support the point?
____	____	Do you use the words *First of all, Second,* and *Finally* to introduce each of your three supporting details?
____	____	Do you have a closing sentence?
____	____	Do you have a title based on the point?
____	____	Are your sentences clear and free from obvious errors?

■ Assignment 2

In this chapter you have read two paragraphs (page 47) on reasons for being in college. For this assignment, write a paragraph describing your own reasons for being in college. You might want to look first at the following list of common reasons students give for going to school. Use the ones that apply to you (making them as specific as possible) or supply your own. Select three of your most important reasons for being in school and generate specific supporting details for each reason.

Before starting, reread paragraph B on page 47. *You must provide comparable specific details of your own.* Make your paragraph truly personal; do not fall back on vague generalities like those in paragraph A on page 47. Use the checklist for Assignment 1 as a guideline as you work on the paragraph.

Apply
in
My Case   ***Reasons Students Go to College***

_____ ■ To have some fun before getting a job

_____ ■ To prepare for a specific career

_____ ■ To please their families

_____ ■ To educate and enrich themselves

_____ ■ To be with friends who are going to college

_____ ■ To take advantage of an opportunity they didn't have before

_____ ■ To find a husband or wife

_____ ■ To see if college has anything to offer them

_____ ■ To do more with their lives than they've done so far

_____ ■ To take advantage of Veterans' Administration benefits or other special funding

_____ ■ To earn the status that they feel comes with a college degree

_____ ■ To get a new start in life

■ Assignment 3

Write a paragraph about stress in your life. Choose three of the following areas of stress and provide specific examples and details to develop each area.

Stress at school

Stress at work

Stress at home

Stress with a friend or friends

Use the checklist for Assignment 1 as a guideline while working on the paragraph.

Some Suggestions on What to Do Next

1   Work through the next chapter in Part One: ''The Third and Fourth Steps in Writing'' (page 72).

2   Read ''Providing Examples'' (page 127) in Part Two and do the first writing assignment.

3   Work through ''Using the Dictionary'' (page 376) and ''Improving Spelling'' (page 384) in Part Four.

4   Do the introductory projects in Part Five and begin working on the sentence skills you need to review.

THE THIRD
AND FOURTH
STEPS
IN WRITING

This chapter will show you how to

- **Organize specific evidence in a paper by using a clear method of organization**
- **Connect the specific evidence by using transitions and other connecting words**
- **Write clear, error-free sentences by referring to the rules in Part Four of this book**

The third and fourth steps in effective writing are

3   Organize and connect the specific evidence
4   Write clear, error-free sentences

You know from the previous chapter that the first two steps in writing an effective paragraph are stating a point and supporting it with specific evidence. The third step is organizing and connecting the specific evidence. Most of this chapter will deal with the chief ways to organize and connect the supporting information in a paper. The chapter will then look briefly at the sentence skills that make up the fourth step in writing a successful paper.

Step 3: Organize and Connect the Specific Evidence

At the same time that you are generating the specific details needed to support a point, you should be thinking about ways to organize and connect those details. All the details in your paper must cohere, or stick together; when they do, your reader is able to move smoothly and clearly from one bit of supporting information to the next. This chapter will discuss the following ways to organize and connect supporting details: (1) common methods of organization, (2) transitions, and (3) other connecting words.

COMMON METHODS OF ORGANIZATION: TIME ORDER AND EMPHATIC ORDER

Time order and emphatic order are common methods used to organize the supporting material in a paper. You will learn more specialized methods of development in Part Two of the book.

Time order simply means that details are listed as they occur in time. *First* this is done; *next* this; *then* this; *after* that, this; and so on. Here is a paragraph that organizes its details through time order:

How I Relax

The way I relax when I get home from school on Thursday night is, first of all, to put my three children to bed. Next, I run hot water in the tub and put in lots of perfumed bubble bath. As the bubbles rise, I undress and get into the tub. The water is relaxing to my tired muscles, and the bubbles are tingly on my skin. I lie back and put my feet on the water spigots, with everything but my hair under the water. I like to stick my big toe up the spigot and spray water over the tub. After about ten minutes of soaking, I wash myself with scented soap, get out and dry myself off, and put on my nightgown. Then I go downstairs and make myself two ham, lettuce, and tomato sandwiches on white bread and pour myself a tall glass of iced tea with plenty of sugar and ice cubes. I carry these into the living room and turn on the television. To get comfortable, I sit on the couch with a pillow behind me and my legs under me. I enjoy watching the Tonight Show or a late movie. The time is very peaceful after a long, hard day of housecleaning, cooking, washing, and attending night class.

Fill in the missing words: "How I Relax" uses the following words to help show time order: _____, _____, _____, _____, and _____.

Emphatic order is sometimes described as "save-the-best-till-last" order. It means that the most interesting or important detail is placed in the last part of a paper. (In cases where all the details seem equal in importance, the writer should impose a personal order that seems logical or appropriate to the details in question.) The last position in a paper is the most emphatic position because the reader is most likely to remember the last thing read. *Finally, last of all,* and *most important* are typical words showing emphasis. The following paragraph organizes its details through emphatic order.

The National Enquirer

There are several reasons why the National Enquirer is so popular. First of all, the paper is heavily advertised on television. In the ads, attractive-looking people say, with a smile, "I want to know!" as they scan the pages of the Enquirer. The ads reassure people that it's all right to want to read stories such as "Grace Kelly's Ghost Haunts Her Family" or "Burt's Secret Affair with Schoolgirl." In addition, the paper is easily available. In supermarkets, convenience stores, and drugstores, the Enquirer is always placed in racks close to the cash register. As customers wait in line, they can't help being attracted by the paper's glaring headlines. Then, on impulse, customers will add the paper to their other purchases. Most of all, people read the Enquirer because of a love of gossip. We find other people's lives fascinating, especially if those people are rich and famous. We want to see and read about their homes; their clothes; their friends, lovers, and families. We also take a kind of mean delight in their problems and mistakes, perhaps because we're jealous of them. It's hard to resist buying a paper that promises to show "Liz's Fabulous Jewels," "The Husband Barbra Dumped," or even--though we may feel ashamed of our interest-- "Michael's Secret Love." The Enquirer knows how to get us interested and make us buy.

Fill in the missing words: The paragraph lists a total of _____ different reasons people read the *National Enquirer.* The writer of the paragraph feels that the most important reason is _____.

He or she signals this reason by using the emphasis words _____.

Some paragraphs use a *combination of time order and emphatic order.* For example, "Good-Bye, Tony" on page 5 includes time order: it moves from the time Tony arrived to the end of the evening. In addition, the writer uses emphatic order, ending with her most important reason (signaled by the words "most of all") for not wanting to see Tony anymore.

TRANSITIONS

Transitions are signal words that help readers follow the direction of the writer's thought. They show the relationship between ideas, connecting one thought with the next. They can be compared to signs on the road that guide travelers.

To see the value of transitions, look at the following pairs of examples. Put a check beside the example in each pair that is easier and clearer to read and understand.

1. _____ a. Our landlord recently repainted our apartment. He replaced our faulty air conditioner.

   _____ b. Our landlord recently repainted our apartment. Also, he replaced our faulty air conditioner.

2. _____ a. I carefully inserted a disk into the computer. I turned on the power button.

   _____ b. I carefully inserted a disk into the computer. Then I turned on the power button.

3. _____ a. Moviegoers usually dislike film monsters. Filmgoers pitied King Kong and even shed tears at his death.

   _____ b. Moviegoers usually dislike film monsters. However, filmgoers pitied King Kong and even shed tears at his death.

You should have checked the second example in each pair. The transitional words in those sentences—*Also, Then,* and *However*—make the relationship between the sentences clear. Like all effective transitions, they help connect the writer's thoughts.

In the following box are common transitional words and phrases, grouped according to the kind of signal they give readers. Note that certain words provide more than one kind of signal. In the paragraphs you write, you will most often use addition signals: words like *first of all, also, another,* and *finally* will help you move from one supporting reason or detail to the next.

Transitions

Addition signals: first of all, for one thing, second, the third reason, also, next, another, and, in addition, moreover, furthermore, finally, last of all

Time signals: first, then, next, after, as, before, while, meanwhile, now, during, finally

Space signals: next to, across, on the opposite side, to the left, to the right, in front, in back, above, below, behind, nearby

Change-of-direction signals: but, however, yet, in contrast, otherwise, still, on the contrary, on the other hand

Illustration signals: for example, for instance, specifically, as an illustration, once, such as

Conclusion signals: therefore, consequently, thus, then, as a result, in summary, to conclude, last of all, finally

Activity

1. Underline the three *addition* signals in the following selection:

> I am opposed to state-supported lotteries for a number of reasons. First of all, by supporting lotteries, states are supporting gambling. I don't see anything morally wrong with gambling, but it is a known cause of suffering for many people who do it to excess. The state should be concerned with relieving suffering, not causing it. Another objection I have to the state lotteries is the kind of advertising they do on television. The commercials promote the lotteries as an easy way to get rich. In fact, the odds against getting rich are astronomical. Last, the lotteries take advantage of the people who can least afford them. Studies have shown that people with lower incomes are more likely to play the lottery than people with higher incomes. This is the harshest reality of the lotteries: the state is encouraging people of limited means not to save their money but to throw it away on a state-supported pipe dream.

2. Underline the four *time* signals in the following selection:

It is often easy to spot bad drivers on the road because they usually make more than one mistake: they make their mistakes in series. First, for example, you notice that a man is tailgating you. Then, almost as soon as you notice, he has passed you in a no-passing zone. That's two mistakes already in a matter of seconds. Next, almost invariably, you see him speed down the road and pass someone else. Finally, as you watch in disbelief, glad that he's out of your way, he speeds through a red light or cuts across oncoming traffic in a wild left turn.

3. Underline the three *space* signals in the following selection:

Standing in the burned-out shell of my living room was a shocking experience. Above my head were charred beams, all that remained of our ceiling. In front of me, where our television and stereo had once stood, were twisted pieces of metal and chunks of blackened glass. Strangely, some items seemed little damaged by the fire. For example, I could see the TV tuner knob and a dusty CD under the rubble. I walked through the gritty ashes until I came to what was left of our sofa. Behind the sofa had been a wall of family photographs. Now, the wall and the pictures were gone. I found only a water-logged scrap of my wedding picture.

4. Underline the four *change-of-direction* signals in the following selection:

In some ways, train travel is superior to air travel. People always marvel at the speed with which airplanes can zip from one end of the country to another. Trains, on the other hand, definitely take longer. But sometimes longer can be better. Traveling across the country by train allows you to experience the trip more completely. You get to see the cities and towns, mountains and prairies that too often pass by unnoticed when you fly. Another advantage of train travel is comfort. Traveling by plane means wedging yourself into a narrow seat with your knees bumping the back of the seat in front of you and being handed a "snack" consisting of a bag of ten roasted peanuts. In contrast, the seats on most trains are spacious and comfortable, permitting even the most long-legged traveler to stretch out and watch the scenery just outside the window. And when train travelers grow hungry, they can get up and stroll to the dining car, where they can order anything from a simple snack to a gourmet meal. There's no question that train travel is definitely slow and old-fashioned compared with air travel. However, in many ways it is much more civilized.

5. Underline the three *illustration* signals in the following selection:

> Status symbols are all around us. The cars we drive, for instance, say something about who we are and how successful we have been. The auto makers depend on this perception of automobiles, designing their commercials to show older, well-established people driving Cadillacs and young, fun-loving people driving to the beach in sports cars. Television, too, has become something of a status symbol. Specifically, schoolchildren are often rated by their classmates according to whether or not their family has a cable television hookup. Another example of a status symbol is the video cassette recorder. This device, not so long ago considered a novelty, is now considered as common as the television set itself. Being without a VCR today is like having a car without whitewalls in the fifties.

6. Underline the *conclusion* signal in the following selection:

> A hundred years ago, miners used to bring caged canaries down into the mines with them to act as warning signals. If the bird died, the miner knew that the oxygen was running out. The smaller animal would be affected much more quickly than the miners. In the same way, animals are acting as warning signals to us today. Baby birds die before they can hatch because pesticides in the environment cause the adults to lay eggs with paper-thin shells. Fish die when lakes are contaminated with acid rain or poisonous mercury. The dangers in our environment will eventually affect all life on earth, including humans. Therefore, we must pay attention to these early warning signals. If we don't, we will be as foolish as a miner who ignored a dead canary--and we will die.

OTHER CONNECTING WORDS

In addition to transitions, there are three other kinds of connecting words that help tie together the specific evidence in a paper: repeated words, pronouns, and synonyms. Each will be discussed in turn.

Repeated Words

Many of us have been taught by English instructors — correctly so — not to repeat ourselves in our writing. On the other hand, repeating key words can help tie a flow of thought together. In the selection that follows, the word *retirement* is repeated to remind readers of the key idea on which the discussion is centered. Underline the word the five times it appears.

> Oddly enough, retirement can pose more problems for the spouse than for the retired person. For a person who has been accustomed to a demanding job, retirement can mean frustration and a feeling of

uselessness. This feeling will put pressure on the spouse to provide challenges at home equal to those of the workplace. Often, these tasks will disrupt the spouse's well-established routine. Another problem arising from retirement is filling up all those empty hours. The spouse may find himself or herself in the role of social director or tour guide, expected to come up with a new form of amusement every day. Without sufficient challenges or leisure activities, a person can become irritable and take out the resulting boredom and frustration of retirement on the marriage partner. It is no wonder that many of these partners wish their spouses would come out of retirement and do something--anything--just to get out of the house.

Pronouns

Pronouns (*he, she, it, you, they, this, that,* and others) are another way to connect ideas as you develop a paper. Using pronouns to take the place of other words or ideas can help you avoid needless repetition. (Be sure, though, to use pronouns with care in order to avoid the unclear or inconsistent pronoun references described on pages 294–301 of this book.) Underline the eight pronouns in the passage below, noting at the same time the words that the pronouns refer to.

> A professor of nutrition at a major university recently advised his students that they could do better on their examinations by eating lots of sweets. He told them that the sugar in cakes and candy would stimulate their brains to work more efficiently, and that if the sugar was eaten for only a month or two, it would not do them any harm.

Synonyms

Using synonyms — words that are alike in meaning — can also help move the reader clearly from one thought to the next. In addition, the use of synonyms increases variety and interest by avoiding needless repetition of the same words. Underline the three words used as synonyms for *fallacies* in the following selection.

> There are many fallacies about suicide. One false idea is that a person who talks about suicide never follows through. The truth is that about three out of every four people who commit suicide notify one or more other persons ahead of time. Another misconception is that a person who commits suicide is poor or downtrodden. Actually, poverty appears to be a deterrent to suicide rather than a predisposing factor. A third myth about suicide is that people bent on suicide will eventually take their lives one way or another, whether or not the most obvious means of suicide is removed from their reach. In fact, since an attempt at suicide is a kind of cry for help, removing a convenient means of taking one's life, such as a gun, shows people bent on suicide that someone cares enough about them to try to prevent it.

Activity

Read the selection below and then answer the questions about it that follow.

My Worst Experience of the Week

[1]The registration process at State College was a nightmare. [2]The night before registration officially began, I went to bed anxious about the whole matter, and nothing that happened the next day served to ease my tension. [3]First, even though I had paid my registration fee early last spring, the people at the bursar's office had no record of my payment. [4]And for some bizarre reason, they wouldn't accept the receipt I had. [5]Consequently, I had to stand in line for two hours, waiting for someone to give me a slip of paper which stated that I had, in fact, paid my registration fee. [6]The need for this new receipt seemed ludicrous to me since, all along, I had proof that I had paid. [7]I was next told that I had to see my adviser in the Law and Justice Department and that the department was in Corridor C of the Triad Building. [8]I had no idea what or where the Triad was. [9]But, finally, I found my way to the ugly, gray-white building. [10]Then I began looking for Corridor C. [11]When I found it, everyone there was a member of the Communications Department. [12]No one seemed to know where Law and Justice had gone. [13]Finally, one instructor said she thought Law and Justice was in Corridor A. [14]"And where is Corridor A?" I asked. [15]"I don't know," the teacher answered. [16]"I'm new here." [17]She saw the bewildered look on my face and said sympathetically, "You're not the only one who's confused." [18]I nodded and walked numbly away. [19]I felt as if I were fated to spend the rest of the semester trying to complete the registration process, and I wondered if I would ever become an official college student.

Questions

1. How many times is the key idea *registration* repeated? _____

2. Write here the pronoun that is used for *people at the bursar's office* (sentence 4): _____; *Corridor C* (sentence 11): _____; *instructor* (sentence 17): _____.

3. Write here the words that are used as a synonym for *receipt* (sentence 5):

   _____;

   the words that are used as a synonym for *Triad* (sentence 9):

   _____;

   the word that is used as a synonym for *instructor* (sentence 15):

   _____.

Step 4: Write Clear, Error-Free Sentences

The fourth step in writing an effective paper is to follow the agreed-upon rules, or conventions, of written English. These conventions — or, as they are called in this book, *sentence skills* — must be followed if your sentences are to be clear and error-free. Here are some of the most important of these skills.

1 Write complete sentences rather than fragments.

2 Do not write run-on sentences.

3 Use verb forms and tenses correctly and consistently.

4 Make sure that subjects and verbs agree.

5 Use pronoun forms and types correctly.

6 Use adjectives and adverbs correctly.

7 Eliminate faulty modifiers and faulty parallelism.

8 Use correct paper format.

9 Use capital letters where needed.

10 Use numbers and abbreviations correctly.

11 Use the following punctuation marks correctly: apostrophe, quotation marks, comma, colon, semicolon, dash, hyphen, parentheses.

12 Use the dictionary as necessary.

13 Eliminate spelling errors.

14 Use words accurately by developing your vocabulary and distinguishing between commonly confused words.

15 Choose words effectively to avoid slang, clichés, and wordiness.

16 Vary your sentences.

17 Edit and proofread to eliminate careless errors.

Sentence skills are explained in detail, and activities are provided, in Part Four, where they can be referred to easily as needed. Introductory projects will help you determine which skills you need to work on. Your instructor will also identify such skills in marking your papers and may use the correction symbols shown on the inside back cover. Note that the correction symbols, and also the checklist of sentence skills on the inside front cover, include page references, so that you can turn quickly to those skills that give you problems.

■ **Review Activity**

Complete the following statements.

1. The four steps in writing a paper are:

   a. _____

   b. _____

   c. _____

   d. _____

2. *Time order* means _____

   _____

3. *Emphatic order* means _____

   _____

4. _____ are signal words that help readers follow the direction of a writer's thought.

5. In addition to transitions, three other kinds of connecting words that help link sentences and ideas are repeated words, _____, and _____.

Practice in Organizing and Connecting Specific Evidence

You now know the third step in effective writing: organizing the specific evidence used to support the main point of a paper. You also know that the fourth step — writing clear, error-free sentences—is treated in detail in Part Four of the book. This section will expand and strengthen your understanding of the third step in writing.

   You will work through the following series of activities:

1 Organizing through Time Order
2 Organizing through Emphatic Order
3 Organizing through a Combination of Time Order and Emphatic Order
4 Identifying Transitions
5 Providing Transitions
6 Identifying Transitions and Other Connecting Words

1   ORGANIZING THROUGH TIME ORDER

Activity

Use time order to organize the scrambled list of sentences below. Write the number 1 beside the point that all the other sentences support. Then number each supporting sentence as it occurs in time.

_____   The table is right near the garbage pail.

_____   So you reluctantly select a gluelike tuna-fish sandwich, a crushed apple pie, and watery hot coffee.

_____   You sit at the edge of the table, away from the garbage pail, and gulp down your meal.

_____   Trying to eat in the cafeteria is an unpleasant experience.

_____   Suddenly you spot a free table in the corner.

_____   With a last swallow of the lukewarm coffee, you get up and leave the cafeteria as rapidly as possible.

_____   Flies are flitting in and out of the pail.

_____   By the time it is your turn, the few things that are almost good are gone.

_____   There does not seem to be a free table anywhere.

_____   Unfortunately, there is a line in the cafeteria.

_____   The hoagies, coconut-custard pie, and iced tea have all disappeared.

_____   You hold your tray and look for a place to sit down.

_____   You have a class in a few minutes, and so you run in to grab something to eat quickly.

2   ORGANIZING THROUGH EMPHATIC ORDER

Activity

Use emphatic order (order of importance) to arrange the scrambled list of sentences on the following page. Write the number 1 beside the point that all the other sentences support. Then number each supporting sentence, starting with what seems the least important detail and ending with the most important detail.

——— The people here are all around my age and seem to be genuinely friendly and interested in me.

——— The place where I live has several important advantages.

——— The schools in this neighborhood have a good reputation, so I feel that my daughter is getting a good education.

——— The best thing of all about this area, though, is the school system.

——— Therefore, I don't have to put up with public transportation or worry about how much it's going to cost to park each day.

——— The school also has an extended day-care program, so I know my daughter is in good hands until I come home from work.

——— First of all, I like the people who live in the other apartments near mine.

——— Another positive aspect of this area is that it's close to where I work.

——— That's more than I can say for the last place I lived, where people stayed behind locked doors.

——— The office where I'm a receptionist is only a six-block walk from my house.

——— In addition, I save a lot of wear and tear on my car.

3   ORGANIZING THROUGH A COMBINATION OF TIME ORDER AND EMPHATIC ORDER

Activity

Use a combination of time and emphatic order to arrange the scrambled list of sentences below. Write the number 1 beside the point that all the other sentences support. Then number each supporting sentence. Paying close attention to transitional words and phrases will help you organize and connect the supporting sentences.

——— I did not see the spider but visited my friend in the hospital, where he suffered through a week of nausea and dizziness because of the poison.

——— We were listening to the radio when we discovered that nature was calling.

_____   As I got back into the car, I sensed, rather than felt or saw, a presence on my left hand.

_____   After my two experiences, I suspect that my fear of spiders will be with me until I die.

_____   The first experience was when my best friend received a bite from a black widow spider.

_____   I looked down at my hand, but I could not see anything because it was so dark.

_____   I had two experiences when I was sixteen that are the cause of my *arachniphobia,* or terrible and uncontrollable fear of spiders.

_____   We stopped the car at the side of the road, walked into the woods a few feet, and watered the leaves.

_____   My friend then entered the car, putting on the dashboard light, and I almost passed out with horror.

_____   I saw the bandage on his hand and the puffy swelling when the bandage was removed.

_____   Then it flew off my hand and into the dark bushes nearby.

_____   I sat in the car for an hour afterward, shaking and sweating and constantly rubbing the fingers of my hand to reassure myself that the spider was no longer there.

_____   But my more dramatic experience with spiders happened one evening when another friend and I were driving around in his car.

_____   Almost completely covering my fingers was a monstrous brown spider, with white stripes running down each of a seemingly endless number of long, furry legs.

_____   Most of all, I saw the ugly red scab on his hand and the yellow pus that continued oozing from under the scab for several weeks.

_____   I imagined my entire hand soon disappearing as the behemoth relentlessly devoured it.

_____   At the same time I cried out ''Arghh!'' and flicked my hand violently back and forth to shake off the spider.

_____   For a long, horrible second it clung stickily, as if intertwined for good among the fingers of my hand.

4 IDENTIFYING TRANSITIONS

Activity

Locate the major transitions used in the following two selections. Then write the transitions in the spaces provided. Mostly you will find addition words such as *another* and *also.* You will also find several change-of-direction words such as *but* and *however.*

1.

Watching TV Football

Watching a football game on television may seem like the easiest thing in the world. However, like the game of football itself, watching a game correctly is far more complicated than it appears. First is the matter of the company. The ideal number of people depends on the size of your living room. Also, at least one of your companions should be rooting for the opposite team. There's nothing like a little rivalry to increase the enjoyment of a football game. Next, you must attend to the refreshments. Make sure to have on hand plenty of everyone's favorite drinks, along with the essential chips, dips, and pretzels. You may even want something more substantial on hand, like sandwiches or pizza. If you do, make everyone wait until the moment of kickoff before eating. Waiting will make everything taste much better. Finally, there is one last piece of equipment you should have on hand: a football. The purpose of this object is not to send lamps hurtling from tables or to smash the television screen, but to toss around--outside-- during halftime. If your team happens to be getting trounced, you may decide not to wait until halftime.

a. _____

b. _____

c. _____

d. _____

e. _____

2.   Avoidance Tactics

Getting down to studying for an exam or writing a paper is hard, and so it is tempting for students to use one of the following five avoidance tactics in order to put the work aside. For one thing, students may say to themselves, "I can't do it." They adopt a defeatist attitude at the start and give up without a struggle. They could get help with their work by using such college services as tutoring programs and skills labs. However, they refuse even to try. A second avoidance technique is to say, "I'm too busy." Students may take on an extra job, become heavily involved in social activities, or allow family problems to become so time-consuming that they cannot concentrate on their studies. Yet if college really matters to a student, he or she will make sure that there is enough time to do the required work. Another avoidance technique is expressed by the phrase "I'm too tired." Typically, sleepiness occurs when it is time to study or go to class and then vanishes when the school pressure is off. This sleepiness is a sign of work avoidance. A fourth excuse is to say, "I'll do it later." Putting things off until the last minute is practically a guarantee of poor grades on tests and papers. When everything else--watching TV, calling a friend, or even cleaning the oven-- seems more urgent than studying, a student may simply be escaping academic work. Last, some students avoid work by saying to themselves, "I'm here, and that's what counts." Such students live under the dangerous delusion that, since they possess a college ID, a parking sticker, and textbooks, the course work will somehow take care of itself. But once a student has a college ID in a pocket, he or she has only just begun. Doing the necessary studying, writing, and reading will bring real results: good grades, genuine learning, and a sense of accomplishment.

a. _____

b. _____

c. _____

d. _____

e. _____

f. _____

g. _____

h. _____

5 PROVIDING TRANSITIONS

Activity

In the spaces provided, add logical transitions to tie together the sentences and ideas in the following paragraphs. Use the words in the boxes that precede each paragraph.

1.

however	a second	last of all
for one thing	also	on the other hand

Why School May Frighten a Young Child

Schools may be frightening to young children for a number of reasons.

_____, the regimented environment may be a new and disturbing experience. At home children may have been able to do what they

wanted when they wanted to do it. In school, _____, they are given a set time for talking, working, playing, eating, and even going to the

toilet. _____ source of anxiety may be the public method of discipline that some teachers use. Whereas at home children are scolded in private, in school they may be held up to embarrassment and ridicule in front of their peers. "Bonnie," the teacher may say, "why are you the only one in the class who didn't do your homework?" Or, "David, why are you the only

one who can't work quietly at your seat?" Children may _____ be frightened by the loss of personal attention. Their little discomforts or mishaps, such as tripping on the stairs, may bring instant sympathy from a parent; in school, there is often no one to notice, or the teacher is frequently too busy to care and just says, "Go do your work. You'll be all right."

_____, a child may be scared by the competitive environment of the school. At home, one hopes, such competition for attention is

minimal. In school, _____, children may vie for the teacher's approving glance or tone of voice, or for stars on a paper, or for favored seats in the front row. For these and other reasons, it is not surprising that children may have difficulty adjusting to school.

2.

for example	finally	first of all
but	such as	as a result
	another	

Job Burnout

Job burnout has several causes. _____, successful workers may be given more to do just because they do their jobs well. Soon they become overloaded and must work even harder just to keep up with the pace. The work load becomes impossible, and exhaustion sets in.

_____ cause of burnout is conflicting demands. Many career women, _____, find themselves trapped between one set of expectations in the workplace and another at home. They are expected to perform competently for eight hours a day and then come home to cook a gourmet meal or help a child or spouse with a problem. _____, certain occupations entail a high risk of burnout. People in the service professions, _____ nurses, social workers, and teachers, begin their careers filled with idealism and commitment. _____ the long hours, heavy case loads or enrollments, and miles of red tape become overwhelming, and the rewards--the few people they can help--are all too few.

_____, burnout for these people is almost inevitable.

6 IDENTIFYING TRANSITIONS AND OTHER CONNECTING WORDS

Activity

The selections on the following page use transitions, repeated words, synonyms, and pronouns to help tie ideas together. The connecting words you are to identify have been underlined. In the space provided, write T for *transition,* RW for *repeated word,* S for *synonym,* or P for *pronoun.*

_____ 1. I decided to pick up a drop-add form from the registrar's office. However, I changed my mind when I saw the long line of students waiting there.

_____ 2. We absorb radiation from many sources in our environment. Our color television sets and microwave ovens, among other things, give off low-level radiation.

_____ 3. I checked my car's tires, oil, water, and belts before the trip. But the ungrateful machine blew a gasket about fifty miles from home.

_____ 4. At the turn of the century, bananas were still an oddity in America. Some people even attempted to eat them with the skins on.

_____ 5. Many researchers believe that people have weight set-points their bodies try to maintain. This may explain why many dieters return to their original weight.

_____ 6. Women's clothes, in general, use less material than men's clothes. Yet women's garments are usually more expensive than men's.

_____ 7. In England, drivers use the left-hand side of the road. Consequently, steering wheels are on the right-hand side of their cars.

_____ 8. At the end of the rock concert, thousands of fans held up Bic lighters in the darkened arena. The sea of lights signaled that the fans wanted an encore.

_____ 9. The temperance movement in this country sought to ban alcohol. Drinking liquor, movement leaders said, led to violence, poverty, prostitution, and insanity.

_____ 10. Crawling babies will often investigate new objects by putting them in their mouths. Therefore, parents should be alert for any pins, tacks, or other dangerous items on floors and carpets.

_____ 11. One technique that advertisers use is to have a celebrity endorse a product. The consumer then associates the star qualities of the celebrity with the product.

_____ 12. Canning vegetables is easy and economical. It can also be very dangerous.

_____ 13. For me, apathy quickly sets in when the weather becomes hot and humid. This listlessness disappears when the humidity decreases.

_____ 14. Establishing credit is important for a woman. A good credit history is often necessary when applying for a loan or charge account.

_____ 15. The restaurant table must have had uneven legs. Every time we tried to eat, it wobbled like a seesaw.

Some Suggestions on What to Do Next

1 Work through the final chapter in Part One: ''Four Bases for Evaluating Writing.''

2 Read ''Explaining a Process'' (page 136) in Part Two and do the first writing assignment.

3 Read ''Vocabulary Development'' (page 392) in Part Four.

4 Continue your review of sentence skills in Part Four. If you plan to make a general review of all the skills, here is an appropriate sequence to follow: (1) Paper Format, (2) Capital Letters, (3) Subjects and Verbs, (4) Sentence Fragments, (5) Run-Ons, (6) Standard English Verbs, (7) Irregular Verbs, (8) Subject-Verb Agreement, (9) Apostrophe, (10) Comma, (11) Quotation Marks, (12) Sentence Variety.

FOUR BASES
FOR EVALUATING
WRITING

This chapter will show you how to evaluate a paper for

- **Unity**
- **Support**
- **Coherence**
- **Sentence skills**

In the preceding two chapters, you learned four essential steps in writing an effective paper. The box below shows how these steps lead to four bases, or standards, you can use in evaluating a paper.

Four Steps ⎯⎯⎯⎯⎯⎯⎯⎯⎯→ *Four Bases*

1 If you make one point and stick to that point,   your writing will have *unity*.

2 If you back up the point with specific evidence,   your writing will have *support*.

3 If you organize and connect the specific evidence,   your writing will have *coherence*.

4 If you write clear, error-free sentences,   your writing will reflect effective *sentence skills*.

This chapter will discuss the four bases of unity, support, coherence, and sentence skills and will show how these four bases can be used to evaluate writing.

Base 1: Unity

Activity

The following two paragraphs were written by students on the topic ''Why Students Drop Out of College.'' Read them and decide which one makes its point more clearly and effectively, and why.

Paragraph A

Why Students Drop Out

Students drop out of college for many reasons. First of all, some students are bored in school. These students may enter college expecting nonstop fun or a series of fascinating courses. When they find out that college is often routine, they quickly lose interest. They do not want to take dull required courses or spend their nights studying, and so they drop out. Students also drop out of college because the work is harder than they thought it would be. These students may have made decent grades in high school simply by showing up for class. In college, however, they may have to prepare for two-hour exams, write fifteen-page term papers, or make detailed presentations to a class. The hard work comes as a shock, and students give up. Perhaps the most common reason students drop out is that they are having personal or emotional problems. Younger students, especially, may be attending college at an age when they are also feeling confused, lonely, or depressed. These students may have problems with roommates, family, boyfriends, or girlfriends. They become too unhappy to deal with both hard academic work and emotional troubles. For many types of students, dropping out seems to be the only solution they can imagine.

Paragraph B

Student Dropouts

There are three main reasons students drop out of college. Some students, for one thing, are not really sure they want to be in school and lack the desire to do the work. When exams come up, or when a course requires a difficult project or term paper, these students will not do the required studying or research. Eventually, they may drop out because their grades are so poor they are about to flunk out anyway. Such students sometimes come back to school later with a completely different attitude about school. Other students drop out for financial reasons. The pressures of paying tuition, buying textbooks, and possibly having to support themselves can be overwhelming. These students can often be helped by the school because financial aid is available, and some schools offer work-study programs.

Finally, students drop out because they have personal problems. They cannot concentrate on their courses because they are unhappy at home, they are lonely, or they are having trouble with boyfriends or girlfriends. Instructors should suggest that such troubled students see counselors or join support groups. If instructors would take a more personal interest in their students, more students would make it through troubled times.

Fill in the blanks: Paragraph _____ makes its point more clearly and effectively

because _____

_____

_____ .

UNDERSTANDING UNITY

Paragraph A is more effective because it is *unified.* All the details in this paragraph are *on target;* they support and develop the single point expressed in the first sentence — that there are many reasons students drop out of college. On the other hand, paragraph B contains some details irrelevant to the opening point — that there are three main reasons students drop out. These details should be omitted in the interest of paragraph unity. Go back to paragraph B and cross out the sections that are off target — the sections that do not support the opening idea.

You should have crossed out the following sections: "Such students sometimes . . . attitude about school"; "These students can often . . . work-study programs"; and "Instructors should suggest . . . through troubled times."

The difference between these two paragraphs leads us to the first base, or standard, of effective writing: *unity.* To achieve unity is to have all the details in your paper related to the single point expressed in the topic sentence, the first sentence. Each time you think of something to put in, ask yourself whether it relates to your main point. If it does not, leave it out. For example, if you were writing about a certain job as the worst job you ever had and then spent a couple of sentences talking about the interesting people that you met there, you would be missing the first and most essential base of good writing. (The pages ahead will consider the other three bases that you must touch in order to "score" in your writing.)

CHECKING FOR UNITY

To check a paper for unity, ask yourself these questions:

1   Is there a clear opening statement of the point of the paper?
2   Is all the material on target in support of the opening point?

Base 2: Support

Activity

The following student paragraphs were written on the topic "A Quality of Some Person You Know." Both are unified, but one communicates more clearly and effectively. Which one, and why?

Paragraph A

My Quick-Tempered Father

My father is easily angered by normal everyday mistakes. One day my father told me to wash the car and cut the grass. I did not hear exactly what he said, and so I asked him to repeat it. Then he went into a hysterical mood and shouted, "Can't you hear?" Another time he asked my mother to go to the store and buy groceries with a fifty-dollar bill, and he told her to spend no more than twenty dollars. She spent twenty-two dollars. As soon as he found out, he immediately took the change from her and told her not to go anywhere else for him; he did not speak to her the rest of the day. My father even gives my older brothers a hard time with his irritable moods. One day he told them to be home from their dates by midnight; they came home at 12:15. He informed them that they were grounded for three weeks. To my father, making a simple mistake is like committing a crime.

Paragraph B

My Generous Grandfather

My grandfather is the most generous person I know. He has given up a life of his own in order to give his grandchildren everything they want. Not only has he given up many years of his life to raise his children properly, but he is now sacrificing many more years to his grandchildren. His generosity is also evident in his relationship with his neighbors, friends, and the members of his church. He has been responsible for many good deeds and has always been there to help all the people around him in times of trouble. Everyone knows that he will gladly lend a helping hand. He is so generous that you almost have to feel sorry for him. If one day he suddenly became selfish, it would be earthshaking. That's my grandfather.

Fill in the blanks: Paragraph _____ makes its point more clearly and effectively

because _____

_____

_____ .

UNDERSTANDING SUPPORT

Paragraph A is more effective, for it offers specific examples that show us the writer's father in action. We see for ourselves why the writer describes the father as quick-tempered. The second writer, on the other hand, gives us no specific evidence. This writer tells us repeatedly that the grandfather is generous but never shows us examples of that generosity. Just how, for instance, did the grandfather sacrifice his life for his children and grandchildren? Did he hold two jobs so that his son could go to college, or so that his daughter could have her own car? Does he give up time with his wife and friends to travel every day to his daughter's house to baby-sit, go to the store, and help with the dishes? Does he wear threadbare suits and coats and eat Hamburger Helper and other inexpensive meals (with no desserts) so that he can give money to his children and toys to his grandchildren? We want to see and judge for ourselves whether the writer is making a valid point about the grandfather, but without specific details we cannot do so. In fact, we have almost no picture of him at all.

Consideration of these two paragraphs leads us to the second base of effective writing: *support.* After realizing the importance of specific supporting details, one student writer revised a paper she had done on a restaurant job as the worst job she ever had. In the revised paper, instead of talking about ''unsanitary conditions in the kitchen,'' she referred to such specifics as ''green mold on the bacon'' and ''ants in the potato salad.'' All your papers should include many vivid details!

CHECKING FOR SUPPORT

To check a paper for support, ask yourself these questions:

1   Is there *specific* evidence to support the opening point?
2   Is there *enough* specific evidence?

Base 3: Coherence

Activity

The following two paragraphs were written on the topic ''The Best or Worst Job You Ever Had.'' Both are unified and both are supported. However, one communicates more clearly and effectively. Which one, and why?

Paragraph A

Pantry Helper

My worst job was as a pantry helper in one of San Diego's well-known restaurants. I had an assistant from three to six in the afternoon who did little but stand around and eat the whole time she was there. She kept an ear open for the sound of the back door opening, which was a sure sign the boss was coming in. The boss would testily say to me, ''You've got a lot of things to do here, Alice. Try to get a move on.'' I would come in at two o'clock to relieve the woman on the morning shift. If her day was busy, that meant I would have to prepare salads, slice meat and cheese, and so on. Orders for sandwiches and cold platters would come in and have to be prepared. The worst thing about the job was that the heat in the kitchen, combined with my nerves, would give me an upset stomach by seven o'clock almost every night. I might be going to the storeroom to get some supplies, and one of the waitresses would tell me she wanted a bacon, lettuce, and tomato sandwich on white toast. I would put the toast in and head for the supply room, and a waitress would holler out that her customer was in a hurry. Green flies would come in through the torn screen in the kitchen window and sting me. I was getting paid only $3.60 an hour. At five o'clock when the dinner rush began, I would be dead tired. Roaches scurried in all directions whenever I moved a box or picked up a head of lettuce to cut.

Paragraph B

My Worst Job

The worst job I ever had was as a waiter at the Westside Inn. First of all, many of the people I waited on were rude. When a baked potato was hard inside or a salad was flat or their steak wasn't just the way they wanted it, they blamed me, rather than the kitchen. Or they would ask me to light their cigarettes, or chase flies from their tables, or even take their children to the bathroom. Also, I had to contend with not only the customers but the kitchen staff as well. The cooks and busboys were often undependable and surly. If I didn't treat them just right, I would wind up having to apologize to customers because their meals came late or their water glasses weren't filled. Another reason I didn't like the job was that I was always moving. Because of the constant line at the door, as soon as one group left, another would take its place. I usually had only a twenty-minute lunch break and a ten-minute break in almost nine hours of work. I think I could have put up with the job if I had been able to pause and rest more often. The last and most important reason I hated the job was my boss. She played favorites with the waiters and waitresses, giving some the best-tipping repeat customers and preferences on holidays. She would hover around during my break to make sure I didn't take a second more than the allotted time. And even when I helped out by working through a break, she never had an appreciative word but would just tell me not to be late for work the next day.

Fill in the blanks: Paragraph _____ makes its point more clearly and effectively

because _____

_____

_____ .

UNDERSTANDING COHERENCE

Paragraph B is more effective because the material is organized clearly and logically. Using emphatic order, the writer gives us a list of four reasons why the job was so bad: rude customers, unreliable kitchen staff, constant motion, and — most of all — an unfair boss. Further, the writer includes transitional words that act as signposts, making movement from one idea to the next easy to follow. The major transitions are *First of all, Also, Another reason,* and *The last and most important reason.*

While paragraph A is unified and supported, the writer does not have any clear and consistent way of organizing the material. Partly, emphatic order is used, but this is not made clear by transitions or by saving the most important reason for last. Partly, time order is used, but it moves inconsistently from two to seven to five o'clock.

These two paragraphs lead us to the third base of effective writing: *coherence.* The supporting ideas and sentences in a composition must be organized so that they cohere or "stick together." As has already been mentioned, key techniques for tying material together are a clear method of organization (such as time order or emphatic order), transitions, and other connecting words.

CHECKING FOR COHERENCE

To check a paper for coherence, ask yourself these questions:

1   Does the paper have a clear method of organization?

2   Are transitions and other connecting words used to tie together the material?

Base 4: Sentence Skills

Activity

Two versions of a paragraph are given below. Both are unified, supported, and organized, but one version communicates more clearly and effectively. Which one, and why?

Paragraph A

Falling Asleep Anywhere

[1]There are times when people are so tired that they fall asleep almost anywhere. [2]For example, there is a lot of sleeping on the bus or train on the way home from work in the evenings. [3]A man will be reading the newspaper, and seconds later it appears as if he is trying to eat it. [4]Or he will fall asleep on the shoulder of the stranger sitting next to him. [5]Another place where unplanned naps go on is the lecture hall. [6]In some classes, a student will start snoring so loudly that the professor has to ask another student to shake the sleeper awake. [7]A more embarrassing situation occurs when a student leans on one elbow and starts drifting off to sleep. [8]The weight of the head pushes the elbow off the desk, and this momentum carries the rest of the body along. [9]The student wakes up on the floor with no memory of getting there. [10]The worst time to fall asleep is when driving a car. [11]Police reports are full of accidents that occur when people lose consciousness and go off the road.[12] If the drivers are lucky, they are not seriously hurt. [13]One woman's car, for instance, went into the river. [14]She woke up in four feet of water and thought it was raining. [15]When people are really tired, nothing will stop them from falling asleep--no matter where they are.

Paragraph B

Falling Asleep Anywhere

[1]There are times when people are so tired that they fall asleep almost anywhere. [2]For example, on the bus or train on the way home from work. [3]A man will be reading the newspaper, seconds later it appears as if he is trying to eat it. [4]Or he will fall asleep on the shoulder of the stranger sitting next to him. [5]Another place where unplanned naps go on are in the lecture hall. [6]In some classes, a student will start snoring so loudly that the professor has to ask another student to shake the sleeper awake. [7]A more embarrassing situation occurs when a student leans on one elbow and starting to drift off to sleep. [8]The weight of the head push the elbow off the desk, and this momentum carries the rest of the body along. [9]The student wakes up on the floor with no memory of getting there. [10]The worst time to fall asleep is when

driving a car. [11]Police reports are full of accidents that occur when people conk out and go off the road. [12]If the drivers are lucky they are not seriously hurt. [13]One womans car, for instance went into the river. [14]She woke up in four feet of water. [15]And thought it was raining. [16]When people are really tired, nothing will stop them from falling asleep--no matter where they are.

Fill in the blanks: Paragraph _____ makes its point more clearly and effectively

because _____

_____

_____ .

UNDERSTANDING SENTENCE SKILLS

Paragraph A is more effective because it incorporates *sentence skills,* the fourth base of competent writing. See now if you can identify the ten sentence-skills mistakes in paragraph B. Do this, first of all, by going back and underlining the ten spots in paragraph B that differ in wording or punctuation from paragraph A. Then try to identify the ten sentence-skills mistakes by circling what you feel is the correct answer in each of the ten statements below.

Note: Comparing paragraph B with the correct version may help you guess correct answers even if you are not familiar with the names of certain skills.

1. In word group 2, there is a
   a. missing comma
   b. missing apostrophe
   c. sentence fragment
   d. dangling modifier

2. In word group 3, there is a
   a. run-on
   b. sentence fragment
   c. mistake in subject-verb agreement
   d. mistake involving an irregular verb

3. In word group 5, there is a
   a. sentence fragment
   b. spelling error
   c. run-on
   d. mistake in subject-verb agreement

4. In word group 7, there is a
   a. misplaced modifier
   b. dangling modifier
   c. mistake in parallelism
   d. run-on

5. In word group 8, there is a
   a. nonstandard English verb
   b. run-on
   c. comma mistake
   d. missing capital letter

6. In word group 11, there is a
   a. mistake involving an irregular verb
   b. sentence fragment
   c. slang phrase
   d. mistake in subject-verb agreement

7. In word group 12, there is a
   a. missing apostrophe
   b. missing comma
   c. mistake involving an irregular verb
   d. sentence fragment

8. In word group 13, there is a
   a. mistake in parallelism
   b. mistake involving an irregular verb
   c. missing apostrophe
   d. missing capital letter

9. In word group 13, there is a
   a. missing comma around an interrupter
   b. dangling modifier
   c. run-on
   d. cliché

10. In word group 15, there is a
    a. missing quotation mark
    b. mistake involving an irregular verb
    c. sentence fragment
    d. mistake in pronoun point of view

You should have chosen the following answers:

1. c	3. d	5. a	7. b	9. a
2. a	4. c	6. c	8. c	10. c

Part Four of this book explains these and other sentence skills. You should review all the skills carefully. Doing so will ensure that you know the most important rules of grammar, punctuation, and usage — rules needed to write clear, error-free sentences.

CHECKING FOR SENTENCE SKILLS

Sentence skills are summarized in the chart on the following page and on the inside front cover of the book.

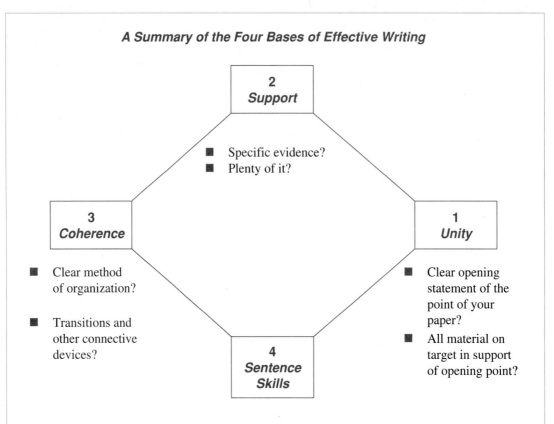

A Summary of the Four Bases of Effective Writing

2 Support

- Specific evidence?
- Plenty of it?

3 Coherence

- Clear method of organization?
- Transitions and other connective devices?

1 Unity

- Clear opening statement of the point of your paper?
- All material on target in support of opening point?

4 Sentence Skills

- Fragments eliminated? (page 236)
- Run-ons eliminated? (253)
- Correct verb forms? (268, 277, 285)
- Subject and verb agreement? (285)
- Faulty parallelism and faulty modifiers eliminated? (313, 317, 322)
- Faulty pronouns eliminated? (294)
- Capital letters used correctly? (331)
- Punctuation marks where needed?
  - (a) Apostrophe (344)
  - (b) Quotation marks (353)
  - (c) Comma (361)
  - (d) Colon; semicolon (372; 373)
  - (e) Dash; hyphen (373; 374)
  - (f) Parentheses (375)
- Correct paper format? (326)
- Needless words eliminated? (412)
- Correct word choices? (408)
- Possible spelling errors checked? (377, 384, 396)
- Careless errors eliminated through proofreading? (32, 426)
- Sentences varied? (416)

Practice in Using the Four Bases

You are now familiar with four bases, or standards, of effective writing: unity, support, coherence, and sentence skills. In this closing section, you will expand and strengthen your understanding of the four bases as you work through the following activities:

1   Evaluating Scratch Outlines for Unity
2   Evaluating Paragraphs for Unity
3   Evaluating Paragraphs for Support
4   Evaluating Paragraphs for Coherence
5   Revising Paragraphs for Coherence
6   Evaluating Paragraphs for All Four Bases:
    Unity, Support, Coherence, and Sentence Skills

1   EVALUATING SCRATCH OUTLINES FOR UNITY

The best time to check a paper for unity is when it is in outline form. A scratch outline, as explained on page 22, is one of the best techniques for getting started with a paper.

Look at the following scratch outline that one student prepared and then corrected for unity:

I had a depressing weekend.

1. Hay fever bothered me
2. Had to pay seventy-seven-dollar car bill
3. ~~Felt bad~~
4. Boyfriend and I had a fight
5. ~~Did poorly in my math test today as a result~~
6. My mother yelled at me unfairly

Four reasons support the opening statement that the writer was depressed over the weekend. The writer crossed out ''Felt bad'' because it was not a specific reason for her depression. (Saying that she felt bad is only another way of saying that she was depressed.) She also crossed out the item about the day's math test because the point she is supporting is that she was depressed over the weekend.

Activity

Cross out the items that do not support the opening point in each outline. These items must be omitted in order to achieve paragraph unity.

1. The cost of raising a child keeps increasing.
   a. School taxes get higher every year.
   b. A pair of children's shoes will probably cost $200 by the year 2000.
   c. Overpopulation is a worldwide problem.
   d. Providing nutritious food is more costly because of inflated prices.
   e. Children should work at age sixteen.

2. My father's compulsive gambling hurt our family life.
   a. We were always short of money for bills.
   b. Luckily, my father didn't drink.
   c. My father ignored his children to spend time at the racetrack.
   d. Gamblers' Anonymous can help compulsive gamblers.
   e. My mother and father argued constantly.

3. There are several ways to get better mileage in your car.
   a. Check air pressure in tires regularly.
   b. Drive at the fifty-five-mile-per-hour speed limit.
   c. Orange and yellow cars are the most visible.
   d. Avoid jackrabbit starts at stop signs and traffic lights.
   e. Always have duplicate ignition and trunk keys.

4. My swimming instructor helped me overcome my terror of the water.
   a. He talked with me about my fears.
   b. I was never good at sports.
   c. He showed me how to hold my head under water and not panic.
   d. I held on to a floating board until I was confident enough to give it up.
   e. My instructor was on the swimming team at his college.

5. Fred Wilkes is the best candidate for state governor.
   a. He has fifteen years' experience in the state senate.
   b. His son is a professional football player.
   c. He has helped stop air and water pollution in the state.
   d. His opponent has been divorced.
   e. He has brought new industries and jobs to the state.

2   EVALUATING PARAGRAPHS FOR UNITY

Activity

Each of the following five paragraphs contains sentences that are off target — sentences that do not support the opening point — and so the paragraphs are not unified. In the interest of paragraph unity, such sentences must be omitted.

Cross out the irrelevant sentences and write the numbers of those sentences in the spaces provided. The number of spaces will tell you the number of irrelevant sentences in each paragraph.

1.   A Kindergarten Failure

[1]In kindergarten I experienced the fear of failure that haunts many schoolchildren. [2]My moment of panic occurred on my last day in kindergarten at Charles Foos Public School in Riverside, California. [3]My family lived in California for three years before we moved to Omaha, Nebraska, where my father was a personnel manager for Mutual of Omaha. [4]Our teacher began reading a list of names of all those students who were to line up at the door in order to visit the first-grade classroom. [5]Our teacher was a pleasant-faced woman who had resumed her career after raising her own children. [6]She called off every name but mine, and I was left sitting alone in the class while everyone else left, the teacher included. [7]I sat there in absolute horror. [8]I imagined that I was the first kid in human history who had flunked things like crayons, sandbox, and sliding board. [9]Without getting the teacher's permission, I got up and walked to the bathroom and threw up into a sink. [10]Only when I ran home in tears to my mother did I get an explanation of what had happened. [11]Since I was to go to a parochial school in the fall, I had not been taken with the other children to meet the first-grade teacher at the public school. [12]My moment of terror and shame had been only a misunderstanding.

The numbers of the irrelevant sentences: _____   _____

2.   How to Prevent Cheating

[1]Instructors should take steps to prevent students from cheating on exams. [2]To begin with, instructors should stop reusing old tests. [3]A test that has been used even once is soon known on the student grapevine. [4]Students will check with their friends to find out, for example, what was on Dr. Thompson's biology final last term. [5]They may even manage to find a copy of the test itself, "accidentally" not turned in by a former student of Dr. Thompson's. [6]Instructors should also take some commonsense precautions at test time. [7]They should make students separate themselves--by at least one seat--during an exam, and they should watch the class closely. [8]The best place for the instructor to sit is in the rear of the room, so that a student is never sure if the instructor is looking at him or her. [9]Last of all, instructors must make it clear to students that there will be stiff penalties for cheating. [10]One of the problems with our school systems is a lack of discipline. [11]Instructors never used to give in to students' demands or put up with bad behavior, as they do today. [12]Anyone caught cheating should immediately receive a zero for the exam. [13]A person even suspected of cheating should be forced to take an alternative exam in the instructor's office. [14]Because cheating is unfair to honest students, it should not be tolerated.

The numbers of the irrelevant sentences: _____   _____

3.   A Dangerous Cook

[1]When my friend Tom sets to work in the kitchen, disaster often results. [2]Once he tried to make toasted cheese sandwiches for us by putting slices of cheese in the toaster along with the bread; he ruined the toaster. [3]Unfortunately, the toaster was a fairly new one that I had just bought for him three weeks before, on his birthday. [4]On another occasion, he had cut up some fresh beans and put them in a pot to steam. [5]I was really looking forward to the beans, for I eat nothing but canned vegetables in my dormitory. [6]I, frankly, am not much of a cook either. [7]The water in the Teflon pan steamed away while Tom was on the telephone, and both the beans and the Teflon coating in the pan were ruined. [8]Finally, another time Tom made spaghetti for us, and the noodles stuck so tightly together that we had to cut off slices with a knife and fork. [9]In addition, the meatballs were burned on the outside but almost raw inside. [10]The tomato sauce, on the other hand, turned out well. [11]For some reason, Tom is very good at making meat and vegetable sauces. [12]Because of Tom's kitchen mishaps, I never eat at his place without an Alka-Seltzer in my pocket, or without money in case we have to go out to eat.

The numbers of the irrelevant sentences:

_____   _____   _____   _____   _____

4.   Why Adults Visit Amusement Parks

[1]Adults visit amusement parks for several reasons. [2]For one thing, an amusement park is a place where it is acceptable to "pig out" on junk food. [3]At the park, everyone is drinking soda and eating popcorn, ice cream, or hot dogs. [4]No one seems to be on a diet, and so buying all the junk food you can eat is a guilt-free experience. [5]Parks should provide stands where healthier food, such as salads or cold chicken, would be sold. [6]Another reason people visit amusement parks is to prove themselves. [7]They want to visit the park that has the newest, scariest ride in order to say that they went on the Parachute Drop, the seven-story Elevator, the Water Chute, or the Death Slide. [8]Going on a scary ride is a way to feel courageous and adventurous without taking much of a risk. [9]Some rides, however, can be dangerous. [10]Rides that are not properly inspected or maintained have killed people all over the country. [11]A final reason people visit amusement parks is to escape from everyday pressures. [12]When people are poised at the top of a gigantic roller coaster, they are not thinking of bills, work, or personal problems. [13]A scary ride empties the mind of all worries--except making it to the bottom alive. [14]Adults at an amusement park may claim they have come for their children, but they are there for themselves as well.

The numbers of the irrelevant sentences: _____   _____   _____

5.   My Color Television

[1]My color television has given me nothing but heartburn. [2]I was able to buy it a little over a year ago because I had my relatives give me money for my birthday instead of a lot of clothes that wouldn't fit. [3]My first dose of stomach acid came when I bought the set. [4]I let a salesclerk fool me into buying a discontinued model. [5]I realized this a day later, when I saw newspaper advertisements for the set at seventy-five dollars less than I had paid. [6]The set worked so beautifully when I first got it home that I would keep it on until stations signed off for the night. [7]Fortunately, I didn't get any channels showing all-night movies, or I would never have gotten to bed. [8]Then I started developing a problem with the set that involved static noise. [9]For some reason, when certain shows switched into a commercial, a loud buzz would sound for a few seconds. [10]Gradually, this sound began to appear during a show, and to get rid of it, I had to click the dial to another channel and click it back. [11]Sometimes this technique would not work, and I had to pick up the set and shake it to remove the buzzing sound. [12]I actually began to build up my arm muscles shaking my set; I could feel the new muscles working whenever I shot a basketball. [13]When neither of these methods removed the static noise, I would sit popping Tums and wait for the sound to go away. [14]Eventually I wound up slamming the set with my hand again, and it stopped working altogether. [15]My trip to the repair shop cost me $62. [16]The set is working well now, but I keep expecting more trouble.

The numbers of the irrelevant sentences: _____ _____ _____ _____

3   EVALUATING PARAGRAPHS FOR SUPPORT

Activity

The five paragraphs that follow lack sufficient supporting details. Identify the spot or spots where more specific details are needed in each paragraph.

1.   Chicken: Our Best Friend

[1]Chicken is the best-selling meat today for a number of good reasons. [2]First of all, its reasonable cost puts it within everyone's reach. [3]Chicken is popular, too, because it can be prepared in so many different ways. [4]It can, for example, be cooked by itself, in spaghetti sauce, or with noodles and gravy. [5]It can be baked, boiled, broiled, or fried. [6]Chicken is also convenient. [7]Last and most important, chicken has a high nutritional value. [8]Four ounces of chicken contain twenty-eight grams of protein, which is almost half the recommended daily dietary allowance.

Fill in the blanks: The first spot where supporting details are needed occurs after sentence number _____ . The second spot occurs after sentence number

_____ .

2.

A Car Accident

[1]I was on my way home from work when my terrible car accident took place. [2]As I drove my car around the curve of the expressway exit, I saw a number of cars ahead of me, backed up because of a red light at the main road. [3]I slowly came to a stop behind a dozen or more cars. [4]In my rear-view mirror, I then noticed a car coming up behind me that did not slow down or stop. [5]I had a horrible, helpless feeling as I realized the car would hit me. [6]I knew there was nothing I could do to signal the driver in time, nor was there any way I could get away from the car. [7]Minutes after the collision, I picked up my glasses, which were on the seat beside me. [8]My lip was bleeding, and I got out a tissue to wipe it. [9]The police arrived quickly, along with an ambulance for the driver of the car that hit me. [10]My car was so damaged that it had to be towed away. [11]Today, eight years after the accident, I still relive the details of the experience whenever a car gets too close behind me.

Fill in the blank: The point where details are clearly needed occurs after sentence number _____ .

3.

Tips on Bringing Up Children

[1]In some ways, children should be treated as mature people. [2]For one thing, adults should not use baby talk with children. [3]Using real words with children helps them develop language skills more quickly. [4]Baby talk makes children feel patronized, frustrated, and confused, for they want to understand and communicate with adults by learning their speech. [5]So animals should be called cows and dogs, not ''moo-moos'' and ''bow-wows.'' [6]Second, parents should be consistent when disciplining children. [7]For example, if a parent tells a child, ''You cannot have dessert unless you put away your toys,'' it is important that the parent follow through on the warning. [8]By being consistent, parents will teach children responsibility and give them a stable center around which to grow. [9]Finally, and most important, children should be allowed and encouraged to make simple decisions. [10]Parents will thus be helping their children prepare for the complex decisions that they will have to deal with in later life.

Fill in the blank: The spot where supporting details are needed occurs after sentence number _____ .

4. Telephone Answering Machines

[1]Telephone answering machines are beginning to annoy me. [2]First of all, I am so surprised when a machine answers the phone that I become tongue-tied or flustered. [3]As the metallic voice says, "Please leave your message when you hear the tone," my mind goes blank. [4]I don't like to hang up, but I know I'll sound like a fool when the owner plays back the message: "Uh, uh, Dr. Spencer, uh, I wanted to make an appointment, uh, wait a minute, for the fifth, no the second, uh, I'm not sure. . . ." [5]Another problem I have with the machines is that they can malfunction. [6]I sometimes call big catalog companies to place orders, and the order is taken by a recording machine. [7]Just as I'm trying to say, "Two blouses, number B107, size 10," the machine clicks off. [8]When I call back, another mix-up will occur. [9]Above all, I dislike the so-called funny tapes that some people now use to answer their phones. [10]One of my coworkers recently bought an answering machine and uses one of these tapes. [11]Answering machines seem to be spreading all over the country, but I would rather talk to a human voice anytime.

Fill in the blanks: The first spot where supporting details are needed occurs after sentence number _____. The second spot occurs after sentence number

_____ .

5. Being on TV

[1]People act a little strangely when a television camera comes their way. [2]Some people behave as if a crazy puppet-master is pulling their strings. [3]Their arms jerk wildly about, and they begin jumping up and down for no apparent reason. [4]Often they accompany their body movements with loud screams, squeals, and yelps. [5]Another group of people engage in an activity known as the cover-up. [6]They will be calmly watching a sports game or other televised event when they realize the camera is focused on them. [7]The camera operator can't resist zooming in for a close-up of these people. [8]Then there are those who practice their funny faces on the unsuspecting public. [9]They take advantage of the television time to show off their talents, hoping to get that big break that will carry them to stardom. [10]Finally, there are those who pretend they are above reacting for the camera.[11]They wipe all expression from their faces and appear to be interested in something else. [12]Yet if the camera stays on them long enough, they will slyly check to see if they are still being watched. [13]Everybody's behavior seems to be slightly strange in front of a TV camera.

Fill in the blanks: The first spot where supporting details are needed occurs after sentence number _____ . The second spot occurs after sentence number

_____ .

4 EVALUATING PARAGRAPHS FOR COHERENCE

Activity

Answer the questions about coherence that follow each of the two paragraphs below.

1.

Why I Bought a Handgun

¹I bought a handgun to keep in my house for several reasons. ²Most important, I have had a frightening experience with an obscene phone caller. ³For several weeks, a man has called me once or twice a day, sometimes as late as three in the morning. ⁴As soon as I pick up the phone, he whispers something obscene or threatens me by saying, "I'll get you." ⁵I decided to buy a gun because crime is increasing in my neighborhood. ⁶One neighbor's house was burglarized while she was at work; the thieves not only stole her appliances but also threw paint around her living room and slashed her furniture. ⁷Not long after this incident, an elderly woman from the apartment house on the corner was mugged on her way to the supermarket. ⁸The man grabbed her purse and threw her to the ground, breaking her hip. ⁹I started thinking about buying a gun about a year ago when I was listening to the news one night. ¹⁰It seemed that every news story involved violence of some kind--rapes, murders, muggings, and robberies. ¹¹I wondered if some of the victims in the stories would still be alive if they had been able to frighten off the criminal with a gun. ¹²As time passed, I became more convinced that I should keep a gun in the house.

a. What words show emphasis in sentence 2? _____

b. What is the number of the sentence to which the transition *In addition* could be added? _____

c. In sentence 8, to whom does the pronoun *her* refer? _____

d. How many times is the key word *gun* repeated in the paragraph? _____

e. The paragraph should use emphatic order. Write a 1 before the reason that is slightly less important than the other two, a 2 before the second-most-important reason, and a 3 before the most important reason.

_____ Obscene phone caller

_____ Crime increase in neighborhood

_____ News stories about crime victims

2.   Joining a Health Club

[1]You should do some investigating before you decide to join a health club. [2]Make sure that the contract you sign is accurate. [3]Check the agreement to be certain that the fees listed are correct, that the penalties for breaking the contract are specified, and that no hidden charges are included. [4]As soon as you begin thinking about joining a health club, make a list of your needs and requirements. [5]Decide if you want (or will ever use) facilities such as a swimming pool, jogging track, steam room, weight machines, racquet-ball courts, or a bar and lounge. [6]Your requirements will determine what kind of club you should join and where you will truly get your money's worth. [7]After you have decided what type of exercise club is best for you, visit some local clubs and check out the facilities. [8]Make sure that the equipment is in good order, that the changing rooms and exercise areas are clean, and that there are enough instructors for everyone. [9]Talk to some of the members to see if they are satisfied with the club and its management. [10]Ask them if they have had any problems with contracts, the club's hours, or lack of equipment. [11]Once you have found the best club, you are ready to sign a membership contract.

a. What is the number of the sentence to which the word *Also* could be added? _____

b. To whom does the pronoun *them* in sentence 10 refer? _____

c. What is a synonym for *contract* in sentence 3? _____

d. What is the number of a sentence to which the words *For example* could be added? _____

e. The paragraph should use time order. Put a 1 before the step that should come first, a 2 before the intermediate step, and a 3 before the final step.

_____ Make sure the contract is accurate.

_____ Make a list of your needs and requirements.

_____ Visit some local clubs to check facilities.

5 REVISING PARAGRAPHS FOR COHERENCE

The two paragraphs in this section begin with a clear point, but the supporting material that follows the point is not coherent. Read each paragraph and the comments that follow it on how to organize and connect the supporting material. Then do the activity provided in each case.

Paragraph 1

A Difficult Period

Since I arrived in the Bay Area in midsummer, I have had the most difficult period of my life. I had to look for an apartment. I found only one place that I could afford, but the landlord said I could not move in until it was painted. When I first arrived in San Francisco, my thoughts were to stay with my father and stepmother. I had to set out looking for a job so that I could afford my own place, for I soon realized that my stepmother was not at all happy having me live with them. A three-week search led to a job shampooing rugs for a housecleaning company. I painted the apartment myself, and at least that problem was ended. I was in a hurry to get settled because I was starting school at the University of San Francisco in September. A transportation problem developed because my stepmother insisted that I return my father's bike, which I was using at first to get to school. I had to rely on a bus that often arrived late, with the result that I missed some classes and was late for others. I had already had a problem with registration in early September. My counselor had made a mistake with my classes, and I had to register all over again. This meant that I was one week late for class. Now I'm riding to school with a classmate and no longer have to depend on the bus. My life is starting to order itself, but I must admit that at first I thought it was hopeless to stay here.

Comments on Paragraph 1:   The writer of this paragraph has provided a good deal of specific evidence to support the opening point. The evidence, however, needs to be organized. Before starting the paragraph, the writer should have decided to arrange the details by using time order. He or she could then have listed in a scratch outline the exact sequence of events that made for such a difficult period.

Activity 1

Here is a list of the various events described by the writer of paragraph 1. Number the events in the correct time sequence by writing a 1 in front of the first event that occurred, a 2 in front of the second event, and so on.

Since I arrived in the Bay Area in midsummer, I have had the most difficult period of my life.

_____ I had to search for an apartment I could afford.

_____ I had to find a job so that I could afford my own place.

_____ My stepmother objected to my living with her and my father.

_____ I had to paint the apartment before I could move in.

_____ I had to find an alternative to unreliable bus transportation.

_____ I had to reregister for my college courses because of a counselor's mistake.

Your instructor may now have you rewrite the paragraph on separate paper. If so, be sure to use time signals such as *first, next, then, during, when, after,* and *now* to help guide your reader from one event to the next.

Paragraph 2

Childhood Cruelty

When I was in grade school, my classmates and I found a number of excuses for being cruel to a boy named Andy Poppovian. Sometimes Andy gave off a strong body odor, and we knew that several days had passed since he had taken a bath. Andy was very slow in speaking, as well as very careless in personal hygiene. The teacher would call on him during a math or grammar drill. He would sit there silently for so long before answering that she sometimes said, "Are you awake, Andy?" Andy had long fingernails that he never seemed to cut, with black dirt caked under them. We called him "Poppy," or we accented the first syllable in his name and mispronounced the rest of it and said to him, "How are you today, POP-o-van?" His name was funny. Other times we called him "Popeye," and we would shout at him, "Where's your spinach today, Popeye?" Andy always had sand in the corners of his eyes. When we played tag games at recess, Andy was always "it" or the first one who was caught. He was so physically slow that five guys could dance around him and he wouldn't be able to touch any of them. Even when we tried to hold a regular conversation with him about sports or a teacher, he was so slow in responding to a question that we got bored talking with him. Andy's hair was always uncombed, and it was often full of white flakes of dandruff. Only when Andy died suddenly of spinal meningitis in seventh grade did some of us begin to realize and regret our cruelty toward him.

Comments on Paragraph 2:   The writer of this paragraph provides a number of specifics that support the opening point. However, the supporting material has not been organized clearly. Before writing this paragraph, the author should have (1) decided to arrange the supporting evidence by using emphatic order and (2) listed in a scratch outline the reasons for the cruelty to Andy Poppovian and the supporting details for each reason. The writer could also have determined which reason to use in the emphatic final position of the paper.

Activity 2

Create a clear outline for paragraph 2 by filling in the scheme below. The outline is partially completed.

> When I was in grade school, my classmates and I found a number of excuses for being cruel to a boy named Andy Poppovian.

Reason   1. *Physically slow* _____

Details   a. _____

               b. *Five guys could dance around him.* _____

Reason   2. _____

Details   a. _____

               b. *Sand in eyes* _____

               c. _____

               d. _____

Reason   3. *Funny name* _____

Details   a. _____

               b. _____

Reason   4. _____

Details   a. _____

               b. *In regular conversation* _____

Your instructor may have you rewrite the paragraph on separate paper. If so, be sure to introduce each of the four reasons with transitions such as *First, Second, Another reason,* and *Finally.* You may also want to use repeated words, pronouns, and synonyms to help tie your sentences together.

6   EVALUATING PARAGRAPHS FOR ALL FOUR BASES: UNITY, SUPPORT, COHERENCE, AND SENTENCE SKILLS

Activity

In this activity, you will evaluate paragraphs in terms of all four bases: unity, support, coherence, and sentence skills. Evaluative comments follow each paragraph below. Circle the letter of the statement that best applies in each case.

1.

Ponderosa Steak House

There are a number of advantages to eating at Ponderosa Steak House. The first advantage is that the meals are moderate in price. Another reason is that the surroundings are clean, and the people are pleasant. Also, I have a variety of dinners to choose from. The last and main advantage is that I don't have to plan and prepare the meal.

a. The paragraph is not unified.
b. The paragraph is not adequately supported.
c. The paragraph is not well organized.
d. The paragraph does not show a command of sentence skills.
e. The paragraph is well written in terms of the four bases.

2.

A Frustrating Moment

A frustrating moment happened to me several days ago. When I was shopping. I had picked up a tube of crest toothpaste and a jar of noxema skin cream. After the cashier rang up the purchases, which came to $4.15. I handed her $10. Then got back my change, which was only $0.85. I told the cashier that she had made a mistake. Giving me change for $5 instead of $10. But she insist that I had only gave her $5, I became very upset and insist that she return the rest of my change. She refused to do so instead she asked me to step aside so she could wait on the next customer. I stood very rigid, trying not to lose my temper. I simply said to her, I'm not going to leave here, Miss, without my change for $10. Giving in at this point a bell was rung and the manager was summoned. After the situation was explain to him, he ask the cashier to ring off her register to check for the change. After doing so, the cashier was $5 over her sale receipts. Only then did the manager return my change and apologize for the cashier mistake.

a. The paragraph is not unified.
b. The paragraph is not adequately supported.
c. The paragraph is not well organized.
d. The paragraph does not show a command of sentence skills.
e. The paragraph is well written in terms of the four bases.

3.   Asking Girls Out

There are several reasons I have trouble asking girls to go out with me. I have asked some girls out and have been turned down. This is one reason that I can't talk to them. At one time I was very shy and quiet, and people sometimes didn't even know I was present. I can talk to girls now as friends, but as soon as I want to ask them out, I usually start to become quiet, and a little bit of shyness comes out. When I get the nerve up finally, the girl will turn me down, and I swear that I will never ask another one out again. I feel sure I will get a refusal, and I have no confidence in myself. Also, my friends mock me, though they aren't any better than I am. It can become discouraging when your friends get on you. Sometimes I just stand there and wait to hear what line the girl will use. The one they use a lot is "We like you as a friend, Ted, and it's better that way." Sometimes I want to have the line put on a tape recorder, so they won't have to waste their breath on me. All my past experiences with girls have been just as bad. One girl used me to make her old boyfriend jealous. Then when she succeeded, she started going out with him again. I had a bad experience when I took a girl to the prom. I spent a lot of money on her. Two days later, she told me that she was going steady with another guy. I feel that when I meet a girl I have to be sure I can trust her. I don't want her to turn on me.

a. The paragraph is not unified.
b. The paragraph is not adequately supported.
c. The paragraph is not well organized.
d. The paragraph does not show a command of sentence skills.
e. The paragraph is well written in terms of the four bases.

4.   A Change in My Writing

A technique in my present English class has corrected a writing problem that I've always had. In past English courses, I had major problems with commas in the wrong places, bad spelling, capitalizing the wrong words, sentence fragments, and run-on sentences. I never had any big problems with unity, support, or coherence, but the sentence skills were another matter. They were like little bugs that always appeared to infest my writing. My present instructor asked me to rewrite papers, just concentrating on sentence skills. I thought that the instructor was crazy because I didn't feel that rewriting would do any good. I soon became certain that my instructor was out of his mind, for he made me rewrite my first paper four times. It was very frustrating, for I became tired of doing the same paper over and over. I wanted to belt my instructor against the wall when I'd show him each new draft and he'd find skills mistakes and say "Rewrite." Finally, my papers began to improve and the sentence skills began to fall into place. I was able to see them and correct them before turning in a paper, whereas I couldn't before. Why or how this happened I don't know, but I think that rewriting helped a lot. It took me most of the semester, but I stuck it out and the work paid off.

a. The paragraph is not unified.
b. The paragraph is not adequately supported.
c. The paragraph is not well organized.
d. The paragraph does not show a command of sentence skills.
e. The paragraph is well written in terms of the four bases.

5.

Luck and Me

I am a very lucky young man, which has not been the case with the rest of my family. Sometimes when I get depressed, which is too frequently, it's hard to see just how lucky I am. I'm lucky that I'm living in a country that is free. I'm allowed to worship the way I want to, and that is very important to me. Without a belief in God a person cannot live with any real certainty in life. My family cares about me, though maybe not as much as I would like. My relationship with my girlfriend is a source of good fortune for me. She gives me security and that's something I need a lot. Even with these positive realities in my life, I still seem to find time for insecurity, worry, and, worst of all, depression. At times in my life I have had bouts of terrible luck. But overall, I'm a very lucky guy. I plan to further develop the positive aspects of my life and try to eliminate the negative ones.

a. The paragraph is not unified.
b. The paragraph is not adequately supported.
c. The paragraph is not well organized.
d. The paragraph does not show a command of sentence skills.
e. The paragraph is well written in terms of the four bases.

Some Suggestions on What to Do Next

1 Read ''Providing Examples'' (page 127) or ''Narrating an Event'' (page 190) in Part Two and do the writing assignments given. Then go on to the other types of paragraph development in Part Two.

2 When you have mastered the different types of paragraph development, you may want to work through ''Writing the Essay'' in Part Three and do one or more of the writing assignments.

3 Continue review of sentence skills in Part Four.

PART TWO

PARAGRAPH DEVELOPMENT

PREVIEW

Part Two introduces you to paragraph development and gives you practice in the following common types of paragraph development:

Providing Examples
Explaining a Process
Examining Cause and Effect
Comparing or Contrasting
Defining a Term
Dividing and Classifying
Describing a Scene or Person
Narrating an Event
Arguing a Position

After a brief explanation of each type of paragraph development, student paragraphs illustrating each type are presented, followed by questions about those paragraphs. The questions relate to the standards of effective writing described in Part One. You are then asked to write your own paragraph. In each case, writing assignments progress from personal-experience topics to more formal and objective topics. The final assignment, ''Writing about a Reading Selection,'' asks you first to read one of the professional essays in Part Five that illustrates a particular type of development. At times, topic sentences are suggested, so that you can concentrate on (1) making sure your evidence is on target in support of your opening idea, (2) providing plenty of specific supporting details to back up your point, and (3) organizing your supporting material clearly.

INTRODUCTION TO PARAGRAPH DEVELOPMENT

Nine Patterns of Paragraph Development

Traditionally, all writing has been divided into the following forms:

- Exposition
  - Examples   Comparison or contrast
  - Process   Definition
  - Cause and effect   Division and classification
- Description
- Narration
- Argumentation or persuasion

In *exposition,* the writer provides information about and explains a particular subject. Patterns of development in exposition include (1) giving examples, (2) detailing the process of doing or making something, (3) analyzing causes or effects, (4) comparing or contrasting, (5) defining a term or concept, and (6) dividing something into parts or grouping it into categories. In this part of the book, each of the six patterns of exposition is presented in a separate chapter.

There are also individual chapters devoted to (7) description, (8) narration, and (9) argument. A *description* is a verbal picture of a person, place, or thing. In a *narration*, a writer tells the story of something that happened. *Argumentation* or *persuasion* is an attempt to prove a point or defend an opinion.

You will have a chance, then, to learn how nine different patterns can help organize material in your papers. Each of the nine patterns has its own internal logic and provides its own special strategies for imposing order on your ideas.

As you practice each pattern, you should keep the following two points in mind:

■ In each paragraph that you write, one pattern will predominate, but very often one or more additional patterns may also be involved. For instance, ''Good-Bye, Tony'' — a paragraph you have already read (page 5) — presents a series of causes leading to an effect: that the writer will not go out with Tony again. But the writer also presents examples to explain each of the causes (Tony was late, he was bossy, he was abrupt). And there is an element of narration, as the writer presents examples that occur from the beginning to the end of the date.

■ More important, a paragraph you write in almost any pattern will probably involve some form of argumentation. You will advance a point and then go on to support your point. To convince the reader that your thesis is valid, you may use a series of examples, or narration, or description, or some other pattern of organization. Among the paragraphs you will read in Part Two, one writer supports the point that a certain pet shop is depressing by providing a number of descriptive details. Another writer labels a certain experience in his life as a ''heartbreak'' and then uses a narrative to demonstrate the truth of his statement. A third writer advances the opinion that good horror movies can be easily distinguished from bad horror movies and then supplies comparative information about both to support her claim. Much of your writing, in short, will have the purpose of persuading your reader that the idea you have advanced is valid.

Writer, Purpose, and Audience

As was noted in ''Important Factors in Writing'' in Part One, the purpose of most writing is to inform, entertain, or persuade; in this book, most of your writing will involve some form of persuasion or information. The audience for your writing is primarily your instructors and sometimes other students—who are really a symbol for any general audience of educated adults. Sometimes, however, you must write for more specific audiences; therefore, it is important to develop the skills of choosing appropriate words, and adopting an appropriate tone of voice, for a particular purpose and particular readers.

This part of the book, then, includes assignments that ask you to write with a very specific purpose in mind and for a very specific audience. You will be asked, for example, to imagine yourself as a TV critic addressing parents at a school, as a graduate of a local high school advising a counselor there about a drug problem, as an aide at a day-care center preparing instructions for children, as an apartment tenant complaining to a landlord about neighbors, or as a client of a video dating service introducing himself or herself to potential dates. Through these and other assignments, you will learn how to adjust your style and tone of voice to a given writing situation.

Tools for Paragraph Development

USING PART TWO: THE PROGRESSION IN EACH CHAPTER

After each type of essay development is explained, student papers illustrating that type are presented, followed by questions about the papers. The questions relate to unity, support, and coherence — the principles of effective writing explained earlier in the book. You are then asked to write your own essay. In most cases, the first assignment is fairly structured and provides a good deal of guidance for the writing process. The other assignments offer a wide choice of writing topics. One assignment requires writing with a specific purpose and for a specific audience, and one assignment relates to the reading selections in Part Five.

USING PEER REVIEW

In addition to having your instructor as an audience for your writing, you will benefit by having another student in your class as an audience. On the day a paper is due, or on a day when you are writing papers in class, your instructor may ask you to pair up with another student. That student will read your paper, and you will read his or her paper.

Ideally, read the other paper aloud while your peer listens. If that is not practical, read it in a whisper while your peer looks on. As you read, both you and your peer should look and listen for spots where the paper does not read smoothly and clearly. Check or circle the trouble spots where your reading snags.

Your peer should then read your paper, marking possible trouble spots while doing so. Then each of you should do the following three things.

1 Identification

On a separate sheet of paper, write at the top the title and author of the paper you have read. Underneath that, write your name as the reader of the paper.

2 Scratch Outline

"X-ray" the paper for its inner logic by making up a scratch outline. The scratch outline need be no more than twenty words or so, but it should show clearly the logical foundation on which the paper is built. It should identify and summarize the overall point of the paper and the three areas of support for the main point.

Your outline can look as follows.

Point: _____
Support:

(1) _____

(2) _____

(3) _____

For example, here is a scratch outline of the paper on a new puppy in the house on page 143:

Point: _A new puppy can have drastic effects in a house._

Support:

(1) _Keeps family awake at night_

(2) _Destroys possessions_

(3) _Causes arguments_

3   Comments

Under the outline, write the heading "Comments." Here is what you should comment on:

- Look at the spots where your reading of the paper snagged: Are words missing or misspelled? Is there a lack of parallel structure? Are there mistakes with punctuation? Is the meaning of a sentence confused? Try to figure out what the problems are and suggest ways of fixing them.
- Are there spots in the paper where you see problems with *unity, support,* or *organization*? If so, offer comments. For example, you might say, "More details are needed in the first supporting paragraph," or "Some of the details in the last supporting paragraph don't really back up your point."
- Finally, make note of something you really liked about the paper, such as good use of transitions or an especially realistic or vivid specific detail.

After you have completed your evaluation of the paper, give it to your peer. Your instructor may provide you with the option of rewriting a paper in light of this feedback. Whether or not you rewrite, be sure to hand in the peer evaluation form with your paper.

USING A PERSONAL CHECKLIST

After you have completed a paper, there are three ways you should check it yourself. You should *always* do the first two checks, which take only a couple of minutes. Ideally, you should take the time to do the detailed final check as well.

1   Read the paper *out loud.* If it does not sound right — that is, if it does not read smoothly and clearly — then make the changes needed to ensure that it does.

2   Make sure you can answer clearly and concisely two basic questions: "What is the point of my essay? What are the three distinct bits of support for my point?"

3   Last, evaluate your paper in terms of the detailed checklist given on the following page. The checklist is also reproduced on the inside front cover of this book.

Checklist of the Four Bases in Effective Writing

Use the questions below as a guide in both writing and evaluating a paper. Numbers in parentheses refer to the pages that explain each skill.

Base 1: Unity

- Clear opening statement of the point of your paper? (44–45; 53–56)
- All material on target in support of opening point? (93–94; 103–107)

Base 2: Support

- *Specific* evidence? (46–50; 61–64; 95–96)
- Plenty of it? (51–52; 65–68; 107–109)

Base 3: Coherence

- Clear method of organization? (73–75; 82–87; 97–98; 111–114)
- Transitions and other connective devices? (75–80; 88–90)

Base 4: Sentence Skills

- Fragments eliminated? (236)
- Run-ons eliminated? (253)
- Correct verb forms? (268; 277; 285)
- Subject and verb agreement? (285)
- Faulty modifiers and faulty parallelism eliminated? (313; 317; 322)
- Faulty pronouns eliminated? (294)
- Capital letters used correctly? (331)
- Punctuation marks where needed?
  - a Apostrophe (344)
  - b Quotation marks (353)
  - c Comma (361)
  - d Colon; semicolon (372; 373)
  - e Dash; hyphen (373; 374)
  - f Parentheses (375)
- Correct paper format? (326)
- Needless words eliminated? (412)
- Correct word choices? (408)
- Possible spelling errors checked? (377; 384; 396)
- Careless errors removed through editing and through proofreading? (32; 426)
- Sentences varied? (416)

PROVIDING EXAMPLES

In our daily conversations, we often provide *examples* — that is, details, particulars, specific instances — to explain statements that we make. In the box below are several statements and supporting examples:

Statement	**Examples**
The A&P was crowded today.	There were at least four carts waiting at each of the checkout counters, and it took me forty-five minutes to get through a line.
The corduroy shirt I bought is poorly made.	When I washed it, the colors began to fade, one button cracked and another fell off, a shoulder seam opened, and the sleeves shrank almost two inches.
My son Peter is unreliable.	If I depend on him to turn off a pot of beans in ten minutes, the family is likely to eat burned beans. If I ask him to turn down the thermostat before he goes to bed, the heat is likely to stay on all night.

In each case, the examples help us *see for ourselves* the truth of the statement that has been made. In paragraphs, too, explanatory examples help the audience fully understand a point. Lively, specific examples also add interest to a paper.

In this chapter, you will be asked to provide a series of examples to support a topic sentence. Providing examples to support a point is one of the most common and simplest methods of paragraph development. First read the paragraphs ahead; they all use examples to develop their points. Then answer the questions that follow.

PARAGRAPHS TO CONSIDER

Inconsiderate Drivers

[1]Some people are inconsiderate drivers. [2]In the city, they will at times stop right in the middle of the street while looking for a certain home or landmark. [3]If they had any consideration for the cars behind them, they would pull over to the curb first. [4]Other drivers will suddenly slow down unexpectedly at a city intersection to make a right or left turn. [5]The least they could do is use their turn signals to let those behind them know in advance of their intention. [6]On the highway, a common example of inconsiderateness is night drivers who fail to turn off their high beams, creating glare for cars approaching in the other direction. [7]Other rude highway drivers move to the second or passing lane and then stay there, making it impossible for cars behind to go around them. [8]Yet other drivers who act as if they have special privileges are those who do not wait their turn in bottleneck situations where the cars in two lanes must merge alternately into one lane. [9]Perhaps the most inconsiderate drivers are those who throw trash out their windows, creating litter that takes away some of the pleasure of driving and that must be paid for with everyone's tax dollars.

The Cruelty of Children

[1]Children can be very cruel. [2]For one thing, they start very early to use words that wound. [3]Three-year-olds in nursery school, for example, call each other "dum-dum" or "weirdo," and slightly older children use nicknames like "fatty" or "four-eyes" to tease their schoolmates. [4]Children who are just a bit older learn facts about other kids from their parents, and use those facts to make someone break down and cry. [5]Children also attack each other physically. [6]For instance, whenever a group of grade-schoolers come home from school, there is a lot of pushing, tripping, punching, and pinching. [7]An argument may end in shoving and hair-pulling. [8]But far worse than harsh words or physical violence is the emotional hurt that children can cause their classmates by their cruelty. [9]By junior high school days, for example, young teenagers start to shut out the people they do not like. [10]They ignore the kids whose looks, clothes, interests, or finances differ from their own. [11]Popular kids form groups, and the unpopular ones are left to face social isolation, loneliness, and depression. [12]Many adults think that childhood is an ideal time, but terribly cruel things can happen then.

An Egotistical Neighbor

[1]I have an egotistical neighbor named Alice. [2]If I tell Alice how beautiful I think the dress she is wearing is, she will take the time to tell me the name of the store where she bought it, the type of material that was used in making it, and the price. [3]Alice is also egotistical when it comes to her children. [4]Because they are hers, she thinks they just have to be the best children on the block. [5]I am wasting my time by trying to tell her I have seen her kids expose themselves on the street or take things from parked cars. [6]I do not think parents should praise their children too much. [7]Kids have learned how to be good at home and simply awful when they are not at home. [8]Finally, Alice is quick to describe the furnishings of her home for someone who is meeting her for the first time. [9]She tells how much she paid for the paneling in her dining room. [10]She mentions that she has two color television sets and that they were bought at an expensive furniture store. [11]She lets the person know that the stereo set in her living room cost more than a thousand dollars, and that she has such a large collection of recordings that she would not be able to play them all in one week. [12]Poor Alice is so self-centered that she never realizes how boring she can be.

■ Questions

About Unity

1. Which two sentences in ''An Egotistical Neighbor'' are irrelevant to the point that Alice is egotistical? (*Write the sentence numbers here.*) _____ _____

About Support

2. In ''Inconsiderate Drivers,'' how many examples are given of inconsiderate drivers?

   _____ one   _____ two   _____ four   _____ six

3. After which sentence in ''The Cruelty of Children'' are specific details needed?

   _____

About Coherence

4. What are the three main transition words used in ''The Cruelty of Children''?

   a. _____

   b. _____

   c. _____

5. What are the two main transition words in ''An Egotistical Neighbor''?

    a. _____

    b. _____

6. Which two paragraphs clearly use emphatic order to organize their details, saving for last what the writers regard as their most important examples?

    _____

    _____

WRITING AN EXAMPLES PARAGRAPH

■ Writing Assignment 1

The assignment here is to complete an unfinished paragraph (opposite page), which has as its topic sentence, ''My husband Roger is a selfish person.'' Provide the supporting details needed to fill out the examples of Roger's selfishness. The first example has been done for you.

How to Proceed: To do this assignment, first jot down on separate paper a couple of answers for each of the following questions.

a What specific vacations did the family go on because Roger wanted to go? Give places, length of stay, time of year. What vacations has the family never gone on (for example, to visit the wife's relatives), even though the wife wanted to?

b What specific items has Roger bought for himself (rather than for the whole family's use) with leftover budget money?

c What chores and duties involved in the everyday caring for the children has Roger never done?

Note: Your instructor may ask you to work with one or two other students in generating the details needed to develop the three examples in the paragraph. Each group may then be asked to read their details aloud, with the class deciding which details are the most effective for each example.

Here and in general in your writing, try to generate *more* supporting material than you need. You are then in a position to choose the most convincing details for your paper. Now take your best details, reshape them as needed, and use them to complete the paragraph about Roger.

A Selfish Person

My husband Roger is a selfish person. For one thing, he refuses to move out of the city, even though it is a bad place to raise the children. *We inherited some money when my parents died, and it might be enough for a down payment on a small house in a nearby town. But Roger says he would miss his buddies in the neighborhood.* Also, when we go on vacation, we always go where Roger wants to go.

_____

_____

_____

_____

Another example of Roger's selfishness is that he always spends any budget money that is left over. _____

_____

_____

_____

_____

Finally, Roger leaves all the work of caring for the children to me. _____

_____

_____

_____

_____

■ Writing Assignment 2

Write a paragraph about one quality of a person you know well. The person might be a member of your family, a friend, a roommate, a boss or supervisor, a neighbor, an instructor, or someone else. Listed on the next page are some descriptive words that can be applied to people. They are only suggestions; you can write about any other specific quality.

Honest	Hardworking	Jealous
Bad-tempered	Supportive	Materialistic
Ambitious	Suspicious	Sarcastic
Bigoted	Open-minded	Self-centered
Considerate	Lazy	Spineless
Argumentative	Independent	Good-humored
Softhearted	Stubborn	Cooperative
Energetic	Flirtatious	Disciplined
Patient	Irresponsible	Sentimental
Reliable	Stingy	Defensive
Generous	Trustworthy	Dishonest
Persistent	Aggressive	Insensitive
Shy	Courageous	Unpretentious
Sloppy	Compulsive	Neat

How to Proceed

a   Begin by prewriting. Make a list of examples that will support your topic sentence. For example, if you decide to write about your brother's irresponsibility, jot down several examples of times when he showed this quality. Part of your list might look like this:

Lost rent money
Forgot to return borrowed textbooks
Didn't show up for big family dinner
Left dog alone in the apartment for two days
Left my bike out in the rain
Missed conference with instructor

Another way to get started is to ask yourself questions about your topic and write down the answers. Again, if you were writing about your brother's irresponsibility, you might ask yourself questions such as these:

How has Bill been irresponsible?
What are examples of times he has shown this quality?
What happened on these occasions?
Who was involved?
What were the results of his actions?

The answers to these questions should serve as an excellent source of details for the paragraph.

b Then prepare a scratch outline made up of the strongest examples from the prewriting material you generated above. Note that as you make this outline, you should group related details together. For example, the items in the list about the irresponsible brother might be categorized as follows:

At apartment
Lost rent money
Left dog alone in apartment

At home
Missed family dinner
Left bike in rain

At school
Didn't return textbooks
Missed conference

c Next, write out your topic sentence. This first sentence should tell the name of the person you are writing about, your relationship to the person, and the specific quality you are focusing on. For example, you might write, "Linda is a flirtatious girl I know at school," or "Stubbornness is Uncle Carl's outstanding characteristic."

Do not make the mistake of beginning with more than one quality ("I have a cousin named Alan who is softhearted and generous") or with a general quality ("My boss is a good person"). Focus on *one specific quality.*

d Develop your examples with specific details. Remember that you don't want to *tell* us about the person; rather, you want to *show* the person to us by detailing words, actions, or both. You might want to go back and reread the examples provided in "An Egotistical Neighbor."

e As you are writing drafts of your paragraph, ask yourself repeatedly: "Do my examples truly show that my subject has a certain quality?" Your aims in this assignment are twofold: (1) to provide *truly specific* details for the quality in question and (2) to provide *enough* specific details so that you solidly support your point.

f When you are satisfied that you have provided effective examples, edit your paragraph carefully for the sentence-skills mistakes listed on the inside front cover. In addition, make sure you can answer *Yes* to the questions on unity, support, and coherence.

■ Writing Assignment 3

Write a paragraph that uses examples to develop one of the following statements or a related statement of your own.

1. _____ is a distracting place to try to study.
2. The daily life of a student is filled with conflicts.
3. Abundant evidence exists that the United States has become a health-conscious nation.
4. Despite modern appliances, many household chores are still drudgery.
5. One of my instructors, _____, has some good (*or* unusual) teaching techniques.
6. Wasted electricity is all around us.
7. Life in the United States is faster-paced than ever before.
8. Violence on television is widespread.
9. Women today (*or* men today) are wearing some ridiculous fashions.
10. Some students here at _____ do not care about learning (*or* are overly concerned about grades).

Be sure to choose examples that truly support your point. They should be relevant facts, statistics, personal experiences, or incidents you have heard or read about. Organize your paragraph by grouping several examples that support your point. Save the most vivid, convincing, or important example for last.

■ Writing Assignment 4

Imagine that you are a television critic and are still living near the high school you attended. The principal is planning a special parents' evening and would like you to make a speech on the topic "Television and the Responsible Parent." You accept the invitation and decide to organize your talk around this thesis: "There are three television programs that represent worthwhile viewing for families." Write a one-paragraph summary of your talk.

To make an outline for your speech, think of three programs you would recommend for viewing by all members of a family. Write down the titles of the programs, and then list under each the specific features that made you choose that show.

■ Writing Assignment 5

Writing about a Reading Selection: Read Packard's selection ''What It Means to Be Young Today'' on pages 543–547. Then write a paragraph in which you cite a series of examples in order to agree or disagree with one of the findings in Packard's article.

You might, for instance, advance a topic sentence such as the following:

I agree with Packard's point that children today are lonely a good deal of the time.

a. Example 1

b. Example 2

c. Example 3

The children you cite can be from your own family or from the families of relatives, friends, neighbors, or other people that you know.

Alternatively, you might write a paragraph in which you disagree with one of Packard's findings, again citing a series of examples to back up your assertion. For instance:

I disagree with Packard's statement that most children today have little or no contact with adults.

a. Example 1

b. Example 2

c. Example 3

To get started, read through the article again and jot down examples you can think of that support or refute Packard's points. Eventually, you'll realize that there is one point in particular for which you'll have a good deal of evidence. Write down all the examples you can generate for that point. Then select the best examples, decide in which order you want to present them (you'll want to end with the most compelling one), and go on to prepare the first draft of your paper.

The hints on ''How to Proceed'' on pages 132–133 may be helpful as you work on your paragraph.

EXPLAINING
A PROCESS

Every day we perform many activities that are processes — that is, series of steps carried out in a definite order. Many of these processes are familiar and automatic: for example, tying shoelaces, changing bed linen, using a vending machine, and starting a car. We are thus seldom aware of the sequence of steps making up each activity. In other cases, such as when we are asked for directions to a particular place or when we try to read and follow the directions for a new table game, we may be painfully conscious of the whole series of steps involved in the process.

In this section, you will be asked to write a process paragraph — one that explains clearly how to do or make something. To prepare for this assignment, you should first read the student process papers below and then respond to the questions that follow.

Note: In process writing, where you are often giving instruction, the pronoun *you* can appropriately be used. Two of the model paragraphs here use *you* — as indeed does much of this book, which gives instruction on how to write effectively. As a general rule, though, do not use *you* in your writing.

PARAGRAPHS TO CONSIDER

Sneaking into the House at Night

[1]The first step I take is bringing my key along with me. [2]Obviously, I don't want to have to knock on the door at 1:30 in the morning and rouse my parents out of bed. [3]Second, I make it a point to stay out past midnight. [4]If I come in before then, my father is still up. [5]I find it hard to face his disapproving look after a night out. [6]All I need in my life right now is for him to make me feel guilty. [7]Trying to make it as a college student is as much as I'm ready to handle. [8]Next, I am careful to be very quiet upon entering the house. [9]This involves lifting the front door up slightly as I open it, so that it does not creak. [10]It also means treating the floor and steps to the second floor like a minefield, stepping carefully over the spots that squeak. [11]Finally, I stop briefly in the bathroom without turning on the light and then tiptoe to my room, put my clothes in a pile on a chair, and slip quietly into bed. [12]With my careful method of sneaking into the house at night, I have avoided some major hassles with my parents.

How to Harass an Instructor

[1]You can use a number of time-proven techniques to harass an instructor. [2]First of all, show up late for class, so that you can interrupt the beginning of the instructor's presentation. [3]Saunter in nonchalantly and try to find a seat by a friend. [4]In a normal tone of voice, speak some words of greeting to your friends as you sit down, and scrape your chair as loudly as possible while you make yourself comfortable in it. [5]Then just sit there and do anything but pay attention. [6]When the instructor sees that you are not involved in the class, he or she may pop a quick question, probably hoping to embarrass you. [7]You should then say, in a loud voice, "I DON'T KNOW THE ANSWER." [8]This declaration of ignorance will throw the instructor off guard. [9]If the instructor then asks you why you don't know the answer, say "I don't even know what page we're on" or "I thought the assignment was boring, so I didn't do it." [10]Give the impression that there is no sane reason why you should be expected to know the answer. [11]After the instructor calls on someone else, get up loudly from your seat, walk to the front of the classroom, and demand to be excused for an emergency meeting in the washroom. [12]Stay at least fifteen minutes and take your time coming back. [13]If the instructor asks you where you've been when you reenter the room, simply ignore the question and go to your seat. [14]Flop into your chair, slouching back and extending your legs as far out as possible. [15]When the instructor informs you of the assignment that the class is working on, heave an exaggerated sigh and very slowly open up your book and start turning the pages. [16]As soon as he or she stops looking at you, rest your elbows on the desk, hold your pencil between your fingertips, and gaze off into space. [17]The instructor will look at you and wonder whether it wouldn't have been better to go into business instead of education.

Driving around a Traffic Circle

[1]If you want to drive around one of our country's treacherous traffic circles and live to tell about it, there are a number of steps to follow. [2]To begin, you must prepare yourself mentally as you approach the circle. [3]Do not give in to panic or begin to quiver with terror. [4]Instead, try repeating to yourself, in a calm tone of voice, "Other drivers do not want to kill me. [5]They are sane people. [6]We will all go around the circle in an orderly way." [7]Next, as you actually begin to negotiate the circle, you should practice the technique of looking in all directions at once. [8]Every second, check your rearview mirror, left mirror, right mirror, and then turn your head quickly to cover any blind spots. [9]Following this, you must deal with the flow of traffic merging onto the circle from other roads. [10]Try to maintain your speed at all costs. [11]Do not slow down to read road signs or stop to allow another car to enter the circle. [12]This will merely create a massive pileup behind you. [13]Finally, the trickiest part of traffic-circle driving is exiting from the circle. [14]At some point, you must stop going around and make a move, usually across two lanes of traffic, toward a side road. [15]You can use your directional signals, although these will have little effect on the other drivers. [16]The best way to exit is to check your rearview mirror until you spot a timid-looking driver slightly behind you in the next lane. [17]This person will slow down as you cut into his or her lane and make a successful dash for the exit. [18]Never cut across in front of a Cadillac driver smoking a thick cigar or in front of an eighteen-year-old in a Trans Am. [19]Such people will speed up, not slow down. [20]These instructions, then, should enable you to enter a traffic circle and come out in one piece on the other side.

■ Questions

About Unity

1. Which paragraph lacks a topic sentence?

   _____

2. Which two sentences in "Sneaking into the House at Night" should be eliminated in the interest of paragraph unity? (*Write the sentence numbers here.*) _____   _____

About Support

3. After which sentence in "How to Harass an Instructor" are supporting details needed? _____

4. Summarize the four steps in the process of driving around a traffic circle.

   a. _____

   b. _____

   c. _____

   d. _____

About Coherence

5. Do these paragraphs use time order or emphatic order?

   _____

6. List the four main transition words in ''Sneaking into the House at Night.''

   a. _____   c. _____

   b. _____   d. _____

WRITING A PROCESS PARAGRAPH

■ Writing Assignment 1

Choose one of the topics below to write about in a process paper.

How to change a car or bike tire
How to bathe a dog or cat
How to get rid of house or garden pests such as mice, roaches, or wasps
How to fall asleep (if you need to and can't)
How to play a simple game like checkers, tic-tac-toe, or an easy card game
How to load a van
How to learn a song
How to live on a limited budget
How to shorten a skirt or pants
How to plant a garden
How to take care of plants
How to fix a leaky faucet, a clogged drain, or the like
How to build a campfire
How to make your house look lived in when you are away
How to study for an important exam
How to paint a ceiling
How to conduct a yard or garage sale
How to wash dishes efficiently, clean a bathroom, do laundry, or the like

How to Proceed

a Begin by prewriting. Freewrite for ten minutes on the topic you have chosen. Do not worry about spelling, grammar, organization, or other matters of correct form. Just write whatever comes into your head regarding the topic. Keep writing for more than ten minutes if added details about the topic occur to you. This freewriting will give you a base of raw material that you can draw on in the next phase of your work on the paragraph. After freewriting, you should have a sense of whether there is enough material available for you to write a process paragraph about the topic. If so, continue as explained below. If not, choose another topic and freewrite about *it* for ten minutes.

b Write a clear, direct topic sentence about the process you are going to describe. In your topic sentence, you can (1) say that it is important for your audience to know about the process (''Knowing how to study effectively for a major exam can mean the difference between passing and failing a course''), or (2) state your opinion of the process (''My technique for building a campfire is almost foolproof'').

c List all the steps you can think of that may be part of the process. Don't worry, at this point, about how each step fits or whether certain steps overlap. Here, for example, is the list prepared by the author of ''Sneaking into the House at Night'':

Quiet on stairs	Lift up front door
Come in after Dad's asleep	Late dances on Saturday night
House is freezing at night	Don't turn on bathroom light
Bring key	Avoid squeaky spots on floor
Know which steps to avoid	Get into bed quietly

d Number your items in time order; strike out items that do not fit in the list; add others that come to mind. Thus:

~~Quiet on stairs~~
2 Come in after Dad's asleep
~~House is freezing at night~~
1 Bring key
5 Know which steps to avoid
3 Lift up front door
~~Late dances on Saturday night~~
6 Don't turn on bathroom light
4 Avoid squeaky spots on floor
8 Get into bed quietly
7 *Undress quietly*

e Use your list as a guide to write the first rough draft of your paper. As you write, try to think of additional details that will support your opening sentence. Do not expect to finish your paper in one draft. You should, in fact, be ready to write a series of lists and drafts as you work toward the goals of unity, support, and coherence.

f Be sure that the point of view in your paragraph is consistent. For example, if you begin to write "How *I* got rid of mice" (first person), do not switch suddenly to "*You* must buy the right traps" (second person). Write your paragraph either from the first-person point of view (*I-we*) *or* from the second-person point of view (*you*). As noted at the beginning of this chapter, do not hesitate to use the second-person *you* point of view. A process paragraph in which you give instructions is one of the few situations in formal writing where the second-person *you* is acceptable.

g Be sure to use some transitions such as *first, next, also, then, after, now, during,* and *finally* so that your paper moves smoothly and clearly from one step in the process to the next.

h While working on your paper, refer to the checklist on the inside front cover to make sure you can answer *Yes* to the questions about unity, support, and coherence. Also, refer to the checklist when you edit the next-to-final draft of your paper for sentence-skills mistakes, including spelling.

▪ Writing Assignment 2

For this assignment, you will be working with more general topics than those in Writing Assignment 1. You will find, in many cases, that you must invent your own steps in a particular process. You will also have to make decisions about how many steps to include and what order to place them in.

How to break a bad habit such as smoking, overeating, or excess drinking
How to improve a course you have taken
How to make someone you know happy
How to go about meeting people
How to discipline a child
How to improve the place where you work
How to show appreciation to others
How to make someone forgive you
How to con an instructor
How to make yourself depressed
How to get over a broken relationship
How to procrastinate
How to flirt

■ **Writing Assignment 3**

Everyone is an expert at something. Write a process paragraph on some skill that you can perform very well. The skill might be, for example, "refereeing a game," "fishing for perch," "playing third base," "putting up a tent," "making an ice cream soda," "becoming a long-distance runner," or "fine-tuning a car engine." Write from the point of view that "This is how _____ should be done."

■ **Writing Assignment 4**

Option 1: You have a part-time job helping out in a day-care center. The director, who is pleased with your work and wants to give you more responsibility, has assigned you to be in charge of a group activity (for example, an exercise session, an alphabet lesson, or a valentine-making project). But before you actually begin the activity, the director wants to see a summary of how you would go about it. What advance preparation would be needed, and what exactly would you be doing throughout the time of the project? Write a paragraph explaining the steps you would follow in conducting the activity.

Option 2: Alternatively, write an explanation you might give to one of the children on how to do a simple classroom task — serving juice and cookies, getting ready for nap time, watering a plant, putting toys or other classroom materials away, or any other task you choose. Explain each step of the task in a way that a child would understand.

■ **Writing Assignment 5**

Writing about a Reading Selection: Read the selection titled "Power Learning" on pages 483–489. Then write a process paragraph or essay on how you could go about improving your study skills. Your topic sentence or thesis might be, "To become a better student, I will take the following steps to strengthen my time control, my classroom note-taking, and my textbook study."

To get started, read through "Power Learning" again and jot down a list of all the suggestions that will be helpful for you. Then pull out the five or six that seem most important. Next, put the steps into a sequence: put hints on time control first, hints on note-taking second, and hints on textbook study third. Then prepare a rough draft of your paper in which you present each step and explain briefly why it is valuable for you. Use transitions and synonyms such as *One step, Another way, A third study aid, Next, A fifth means,* and *Last* as you develop your ideas.

EXAMINING
CAUSE AND EFFECT

What caused Pat to drop out of school? Why are soap operas so popular? Why does our football team do so poorly each year? How has retirement affected Dad? What effects does divorce have on children? Every day we ask questions similar to these and look for answers. We realize that many actions do not occur without causes, and we realize also that a given action can have a series of effects — for good or bad. By examining the causes or effects of an action, we seek to understand and explain things that happen in our lives.

In this section, you will be asked to do some detective work by examining the causes of something or the effects of something. First read the three paragraphs that follow and answer the questions about them. Each of the three paragraphs supports its opening point by explaining a series of causes or a series of effects.

PARAGRAPHS TO CONSIDER

New Puppy in the House

[1]Buying a new puppy can have drastic effects on a quiet household. [2]For one thing, the puppy keeps the entire family awake for at least two solid weeks. [3]Every night when the puppy is placed in its box, it begins to howl, yip, and whine. [4]Even after the lights go out and the house quiets down, the puppy continues to moan. [5]Since it is impossible to sleep while listening to a heartbroken, trembling "Woo-wooo," the family soon begins to suffer the effects of loss of sleep. [6]Everyone becomes hostile, short-tempered, depressed, and irritable. [7]A second effect is that the puppy tortures the family by destroying its material possessions. [8]Every day something different is damaged. [9]Family members find chewed belts and shoes, gnawed table legs, and leaking sofa cushions. [10]In addition, the puppy usually ruins the wall-to-wall carpeting and makes the house smell like a public restroom at a big-city bus station. [11]Worst of all, though, the puppy causes family arguments. [12]Parents argue with children about who is supposed to feed and walk the dog. [13]Children argue among themselves about whose turn it is to play with the puppy. [14]Everyone argues about whose idea it was to get the puppy in the first place. [15]These continual arguments, along with the effects of sleeplessness and the loss of valued possessions, seriously disrupt a household. [16]Only when the puppy gets a bit older will the house be peaceful again.

My Car Accident

[1]Several factors caused my recent car accident. [2]First of all, because a heavy snow and freezing rain had fallen the day before, the road that I was driving on was hazardous. [3]The road had been plowed but was dangerously icy in spots where dense clusters of trees kept the early morning sun from hitting the road. [4]Second, despite the slick patches, I was stupidly going along at about fifty miles an hour instead of driving more cautiously. [5]I have a daredevil streak in my nature and sometimes feel I want to become a stock-car racer after I finish school, rather than an accountant as my parents want me to be. [6]Another factor contributing to my accident was a dirty green Chevy van that suddenly pulled onto the road from a small intersecting street about fifty yards ahead of me. [7]The road was a sheet of ice at that point, but I was forced to apply my brake and also swing my car into the next lane. [8]Unfortunately, the fourth and final cause of my accident now presented itself. [9]The rear of my Honda Civic was heavy because I had a barbell set in the backseat. [10]I was selling the fairly new weight-lifting set to someone at school, since the weights had failed to build up my muscles immediately and I had gotten tired of practicing with them. [11]The result of all the weight in the rear was that after I passed the van, my car spun completely around on the slick road. [12]For a few horrifying, helpless moments, I was sliding down the highway backwards at fifty miles an hour, with no control whatsoever over the car. [13]Then, abruptly, I slid off the road, thumping into a high plowed snowbank. [14]I felt stunned for a moment but then also relieved. [15]I saw a telephone pole about six feet to the right of me and realized that my accident could have been really disastrous.

Why I Stopped Smoking

[1]For one thing, I realized that my cigarette smoke bothered others, particularly my wife and children, irritating their eyes and causing them to cough and sneeze. [2]Also, cigarettes are a messy habit. [3]Our house was littered with ashtrays piled high with butts, matchsticks, and ashes, and the children were always knocking them over. [4]Cigarettes are expensive, and I estimated that the carton a week that I was smoking cost me about $950 a year. [5]Another reason I stopped was that the message about cigarettes being harmful to health finally got through to me. [6]A heavy smoker I know from work is in Eagleville Hospital now with lung cancer. [7]Cigarettes were also inconvenient. [8]Whenever I smoked, I would have to drink something to wet down my dry throat, and that meant I had to keep going to the bathroom all the time. [9]I sometimes seemed to spend whole weekends doing nothing but smoking, drinking, and going to the bathroom. [10]Most of all, I resolved to stop smoking because I felt exploited. [11]I hated the thought of wealthy, greedy corporations making money off my sweat and blood. [12]The rich may keep getting richer, but--at least as regards cigarettes--with no thanks to me.

■ Questions

About Unity

1. Which two sentences in "My Car Accident" are not on target in support of the opening idea and so should be omitted? (*Write the sentence numbers here.*) _____   _____

2. Which paragraph lacks a topic sentence?

   _____

About Support

3. How many causes are given to support the opening idea in "My Car Accident"?

   _____ one   _____ two   _____ three   _____ four

   In "Why I Stopped Smoking"?

   _____ one   _____ two   _____ three   _____ four   _____ five   _____ six

4. How many effects of bringing a new puppy into the home are given in "New Puppy in the House"?

   _____ one   _____ two   _____ three   _____ four

About Coherence

5. What are the five major transition words used in "Why I Stopped Smoking"?

   a. _____   c. _____   e. _____

   b. _____   d. _____

6. What words signal the most important effect in "New Puppy in the House"?

   _____

Activity 1

Complete the following outline of "Why I Stopped Smoking." The effect is that the author stopped smoking; the causes are what make up the paragraph. Summarize each in a few words. The first cause and details are given for you as an example.

Point

There are a number of reasons why I stopped smoking.

1. Reason: _Bothered others_

   Details: _Eye irritation, coughing, sneezing_

2. Reason: _____

   Details: _____

3. Reason: _____

   Details: _____

4. Reason: _____

   Details: _____

5. Reason: _____

   Details: _____

6. Reason: _____

   Details: _____

Activity 2

This exercise will help you tell the difference between *reasons* that back up a point and the supporting *details* that go with each one of the reasons. The scrambled list below contains both reasons and supporting details. Complete the outline following the list by writing the reasons in the lettered blanks (a, b, c, d) and the appropriate supporting details in the numbered blanks (1, 2, 3). Arrange the reasons in what *you feel* is their order of importance. Also, summarize the reasons and details in a few words rather than writing them out completely.

Point

There are a number of reasons why people enjoy eating at Burger Village.

Reasons and Details

An order is ready no more than three minutes or so after it is placed.

A hostess is present in the dining room to help parents with children.

The workers wear clean uniforms, and their hands are clean.

There are french fries in two sizes.

The hostess hands out moistened cloths to wash the children after they eat.

The waiting line moves quickly.

Customers can order hamburgers or fish, chicken, or ham sandwiches.

The hostess helps with the children's coats and gets a highchair for the baby.

The place is clean.

There are several flavors of milk shakes and several kinds of soft drinks, as well as coffee and hot chocolate.

Someone is always sweeping the floor, collecting trays, and wiping off tables.

The kitchen area is all clean and polished stainless steel.

The service is fast and convenient.

The hostess gives the children small cups to drink from and special hats.

There are a variety of items on the menu.

Orders come packaged in bags or boxes for easy carrying out.

Outline

a. _____

   (1) _____

   (2) _____

   (3) _____

b. _____

   (1) _____

   (2) _____

   (3) _____

c. _____

   (1) _____

   (2) _____

   (3) _____

d. _____

   (1) _____

   (2) _____

   (3) _____

WRITING A CAUSE-EFFECT PARAGRAPH

■ Writing Assignment 1

Listed below are topic sentences and brief outlines for three cause or effect paragraphs. Choose one of them to develop into a paragraph.

Option 1

Topic sentence: There are several reasons why some high school graduates are unable to read.
a. Failure of parents (cause)
b. Failure of schools (cause)
c. Failure of students themselves (cause)

Option 2

Topic sentence: Attending college has changed my personality in positive ways.
a. More confident (effect)
b. More knowledgeable (effect)
c. More assertive (effect)

Option 3

Topic sentence: Living with roommates (*or* family) makes attending college difficult.
a. Late night hours (cause)
b. More temptations to cut class (cause)
c. More distractions from studying (cause)

How to Proceed

a Begin by prewriting. On separate paper, make a list of details that might go under each of the supporting points. Provide more details than you can actually use. Here, for example, are some of the details generated by the writer of ''New Puppy in the House'' while working on the paragraph:

Whines and moans
Arguments about walking dog
Arguments about feeding dog
Purchase collar, leash, food
Chewed belts and shoes
Arguments about playing with dog
Loss of sleep

Visits to vet
Short tempers
Accidents on carpet
Chewed cushions and tables

b Decide which details you will use to develop the paragraph. Also, number the details in the order in which you will present them. Here is how the writer of ''New Puppy in the House'' made decisions about details:

2 Whines and moans
6 Arguments about walking dog
6 Arguments about feeding dog
~~Purchase collar, leash, food~~
4 Chewed belts and shoes
6 Arguments about playing with dog
1 Loss of sleep
~~Visits to vet~~
3 Short tempers
5 Accidents on carpet
4 Chewed cushions and tables

Notice that the writer has put the same number in front of certain details that go together. For example, there is a ''4'' in front of ''Chewed belts and shoes'' and also in front of ''Chewed cushions and tables.''

c As you are working on your paper, keep checking your material to make sure it is unified, supported, and coherent.

d Finally, edit the next-to-final draft of your paper for sentence-skills mistakes, including spelling.

■ Writing Assignment 2

Below are ten topic sentences for a cause or effect paper. In scratch outline form on separate paper, provide brief supporting points for five of the ten statements.

List the Causes

1. There are several reasons so many accidents occur on _____ (*name a local road, traffic circle, or intersection*).

2. _____ is (*or* is not) a good instructor (*or* employer), for several reasons.

3. _____ is a sport that cannot be appreciated on television.

4. _____ is the most difficult course I have ever taken.

5. For several reasons, many students live at home while going to school.

List the Effects

6. Watching too much TV can have a bad effect on students.

7. When I heard the news that _____, I was affected in various ways.

8. Conflicts between parents can have harmful effects on a child.

9. Breaking my bad habit of _____ has changed my life (*or* would change my life).

10. My fear of _____ has affected my everyday life.

Decide which of your outlines would be most promising to develop into a paragraph. Make sure that your causes or effects are logical ones that truly support the point in the topic sentence. Then follow the directions on ''How to Proceed'' in Writing Assignment 1.

■ Writing Assignment 3

Most of us criticize others readily, but we find it more difficult to give compliments. For this assignment, write a one-paragraph letter praising someone. The letter may be to a person you know (parent, relative, friend); to a public figure (actor, politician, leader, sports star, and so on); or to a company or organization (for example, the manufacturer of a product you own, a newspaper, a TV network, or a government agency).

To start, make a list of reasons why you admire the person or organization. Here are examples of reasons for praising an automobile manufacturer:

My car's dependability
Prompt action on a complaint
Well-thought-out design
Friendly dealer service

Here are reasons for admiring a parent:

Sacrifices you made
Patience with me
Your sense of humor
Your fairness
Your encouragement

Then follow the suggestions on ''How to Proceed'' in Writing Assignment 1.

■ Writing Assignment 4

Option 1:   Assume that there has been an alarming increase in drug abuse among the students at the high school you attended. What might be the causes of this increase? Spend some time thinking about several possible causes. Then, as a concerned member of the local community, write a letter to the high school guidance counselor explaining the reasons for the increased drug abuse. Your purpose in the letter is to provide helpful information that the counselor may be able to use in dealing with the problem.

Option 2:   Your roommate has been complaining that it's impossible to succeed in Mr. X's class because the class is too stressful. You volunteer to attend the class and see for yourself. Afterward, you decide to write a letter to the instructor, calling attention to the stressful conditions in the class and suggesting concrete ways that he or she could deal with these conditions. Write this letter, dealing with the causes and effects of stress in the class.

■ Writing Assignment 5

Writing about a Reading Selection: Read the selection titled "The Tryout" on pages 440–448. You'll see that Greg Talerico did not let his disability keep him from trying to do something he really cared about. What goal or dream do you have that you have not yet reached for? Write a paragraph explaining what has kept you from trying to reach your goal. Your topic sentence might be, "My secret dream is to _____, but there are three main reasons why I have not yet pursued it." Be sure to describe clearly the feelings and situations involved by using specific details. If you develop more than one reason, use signal words such as *One, Another,* and *Finally* to introduce each reason, and end with the most important one.

Alternatively, if you have worked toward achieving a special goal, write a paragraph describing your efforts. Include details about the difficulties and fears you had to confront and overcome.

COMPARING OR CONTRASTING

Comparison and contrast are two thought processes we constantly perform in everyday life. When we *compare* two things, we show how they are similar; when we *contrast* two things, we show how they are different. We might compare or contrast two brand-name products (for example, Levi's versus Wrangler jeans), two television shows, two cars, two instructors, two jobs, two friends, or two courses of action we could take in a given situation. The purpose of comparing or contrasting is to understand each of the two things more clearly and, at times, to make judgments about them.

In this section, you will be asked to write a paper of comparison or contrast. First, however, you must learn the two common methods of developing a comparison or contrast paragraph. Read the two paragraphs that follow and try to explain the difference in the two methods of development.

PARAGRAPHS TO CONSIDER

My Senior Prom

[1]My senior prom was nothing like what I had expected it to be. [2]From the start of my senior year, I had pictured getting dressed in a blue gown that my aunt would make and that would cost two hundred dollars in any store. [3]No one else would have a gown as attractive as mine. [4]I imagined my boyfriend coming to the door with a lovely blue corsage, and I pictured myself happily inhaling its perfume all evening long. [5]I saw us setting off for the evening in his brother's 1992 Lincoln Continental. [6]We would make a flourish as we swept in and out of a series of parties before the prom. [7]Our evening would be capped by a delicious shrimp dinner at the prom and by dancing closely together into the early morning hours. [8]The prom was held on May 16, 1992, at the Pony Club on the Black Horse Pike. [9]However, because of sickness in

her family, my aunt had no time to finish my gown and I had to buy an ugly pink one at the last minute for eighty dollars. [10]My corsage of yellow carnations looked terrible on my pink gown, and I do not remember its having any scent. [11]My boyfriend's brother was out of town, and I stepped outside to the stripped-down Chevy that he used at races on weekends. [12]We went to one party where I drank a lot of wine that made me sleepy and upset my stomach. [13]After we arrived at the prom, I did not have much more to eat than a roll and some celery sticks. [14]Worst of all, we left early without dancing because my boyfriend and I had had a fight several days before and at the time we did not really want to be with each other.

Computer versus Typewriter

[1]The Macintosh computer that I use at school is dramatically different from the family typewriter that I have at home. [2]First of all, the computer with its word processing program is easy to use. [3]On the screen in front of me, I can see an entire rough draft of a paragraph as I'm working on it. [4]When I'm using the typewriter, in contrast, all that I have to look at is the rough draft that's on a sheet of paper next to the typewriter. [5]I have to keep looking back and forth between that and the draft I'm typing out. [6]Second, the computer is quick. [7]In a moment or two I can easily delete sentences from the paragraph or insert new sentences into it. [8]I can move a sentence from one part of the paragraph to the next, and I can make corrections in spelling or wording with a few strokes on the keyboard. [9]But with the typewriter, there is no quick way to make a correction, delete a sentence, add a sentence, or move a sentence around. [10]Every time I want to make a change, I have to use an eraser or correction fluid, or I have to type a new draft of the paragraph. [11]Finally, the computer offers helpful options. [12]At any point I can give it a command to check my spelling in the paper that I'm writing. [13]I can also have it analyze my grammatical style and make suggestions for improvements. [14]I can ask it to count the number of words in my paper. [15]I can have it change my margins and spaces between lines, and I can order it to number the pages of my paper as it prints them out. [16]The typewriter, on the other hand, offers not a single one of these options. [17]With the computer, I feel that I'm on the cutting edge of technology; with the typewriter, I feel that I'm back in the Stone Age.

Complete this comment: The difference in the methods of contrast in the two

paragraphs is _____

_____

_____

_____ .

Compare your answer with the following explanation of the two methods of development used in comparison or contrast paragraphs.

METHODS OF DEVELOPMENT

There are two common methods of development in a comparison or contrast paper. Details can be presented in a *one-side-at-a-time* or a *point-by-point* format.

One Side at a Time

Look at the outline of "My Senior Prom":

    a. Expectations *(first half of paper)*
        (1) Gown (expensive, blue)
        (2) Corsage (lovely, fragrant blue)
        (3) Car (Lincoln Continental)
        (4) Partying (much)
        (5) Dinner (shrimp)
        (6) Dancing (all night)
    b. Reality *(second half of paper)*
        (1) Gown (cheap, pink)
        (2) Corsage (wrong color, no scent)
        (3) Car (stripped-down Chevy)
        (4) Partying (little)
        (5) Dinner (roll and celery sticks)
        (6) Dancing (didn't because of quarrel)

The first half of the paragraph explains fully one side of the contrast; the second half of the paragraph deals entirely with the other side. In using this method, be sure to follow the same order of points of contrast (or comparison) for each side.

Point by Point

Now look at the outline of "Computer versus Typewriter":

    a. Easy
        (1) Computer
        (2) Typewriter
    b. Quick
        (1) Computer
        (2) Typewriter
    c. Helpful options
        (1) Computer
        (2) Typewriter

The outline shows how the computer and the typewriter are contrasted point by point. First, the writer compares the ease of using the computer with the awkwardness of using the typewriter; next, the writer compares the speed of the computer with the slowness of the typewriter; finally, the writer compares the handy options on the computer with the lack of such options on the typewriter.

When you begin a comparison or contrast paper, you should decide right away whether you are going to use the one-side-at-a-time format or the point-by-point format. An outline is an essential step in helping you decide which format will be more workable for your topic.

Activity 1

Complete the partial outlines provided for the two paragraphs that follow.

1.   How My Parents' Divorce Changed Me

In the three years since my parents' divorce, I have changed from a spoiled brat to a reasonably normal college student. Before the divorce, I expected my mother to wait on me. She did my laundry, cooked and cleaned up after meals, and even straightened up my room. My only response was to complain if the meat was too well done or if the sweater I wanted to wear was not clean. In addition, I expected money for anything I wanted. Whether it was an expensive bowling ball or a new school jacket, I expected Mom to hand over the money. If she refused, I would get it from Dad. However, he left when I was fifteen, and things changed. When Mom got a full-time job to support us, I was the one with the free time to do housework. Now, I did the laundry, started the dinner, and cleaned not only my own room but the whole house. Fortunately, Mom was tolerant. She did not even complain when my first laundry project left us with streaky blue underwear. Also, I no longer asked her for money, since I knew there was none to spare. Instead, I got a part-time job on weekends to earn my own spending money. Today I have my own car that I am paying for, and I am putting myself through college. Things have been hard sometimes, but I am glad not to be that spoiled kid any more.

Topic sentence: In the three years since my parents' divorce, I have changed from a spoiled brat to a reasonably normal college student.

   a. Before the divorce

      (1)   _____

      (2)   _____

   b. After the divorce

      (1)   _____

      (2)   _____

Complete the following statement: Paragraph 1 uses a _____ method of development.

2.

Good and Bad Horror Movies

   A good horror movie is easily distinguished from a bad one. A good horror movie, first of all, has both male and female victims. Both sexes suffer terrible fates at the hands of monsters and maniacs. Therefore, everyone in the audience has a chance to identify with the victim. Bad horror movies, on the other hand, tend to concentrate on women, especially half-dressed ones. These movies are obviously prejudiced against half the human race. Second, a good horror movie inspires compassion for its characters. For example, the audience will feel sympathy for the Wolfman's victims and also for the Wolfman, who is shown to be a sad victim of fate. In contrast, a bad horror movie encourages feelings of aggression and violence in viewers. For instance, in the Halloween films, the murder scenes use the murderer's point of view. The effect is that the audience stalks the victims along with the killer and feels the same thrill he does. Finally, every good horror movie has a sense of humor. In Dracula, the Count says meaningfully at dinner, "I don't drink wine" as he stares at a young woman's juicy neck. Humor provides relief from the horror and makes the characters more human. A bad horror movie, though, is humorless and boring. One murder is piled on top of another, and the characters are just cardboard figures. Bad horror movies may provide cheap thrills, but the good ones touch our emotions and live forever.

Topic sentence: A good horror movie is easily distinguished from a bad one.

a. Kinds of victims

   (1) _____

   (2) _____

b. Effect on audience

   (1) _____

   (2) _____

c. Tone

   (1) _____

   (2) _____

Complete the following statement: Paragraph 2 uses a _____ method of development.

Activity 2

Write the number 1 beside the point that is supported by all the other scrambled sentences in the list below. Then number the rest of the sentences in a logical order. To do this, you will have to decide whether the sentences should be arranged according to a *one-side-at-a-time* order or *point-by-point* order.

A Change in Attitude

_____   Eventually I could not find a dress or pair of slacks in my wardrobe that I could wear while still continuing to breathe.

_____   In the evening when I got hungry, I made myself tomato, lettuce, and onion salad with vinegar dressing.

_____   I have kicked my chocolate habit, saved my clothes wardrobe, and enabled myself to breathe again.

_____   I also could seldom resist driving over to the nearby Snack Shack in the evening to get a large chocolate shake.

_____   For dessert at lunch I had an orange or other fruit.

_____   I gobbled chocolate bars during breaks at work, had chocolate cake for dessert at lunch, and ate chocolate-covered butter creams in the evening.

_____   At this point I began using willpower to control my urge for chocolate.

_____   As a result, the twelve pounds that I didn't want dropped off steadily and eventually disappeared.

_____   When the pounds began to multiply steadily, I tried to console myself.

_____   I have been able to lose weight by changing my attitude about chocolate.

_____   I said, "Well, that's only three pounds; I can lose that next week."

_____   Also, I made myself go and step on the bathroom scale whenever I got the urge to drive over to the Snack Shack.

_____   There was a time when I made chocolate a big part of my daily diet.

_____   Instead of eating chocolate bars on my break, I munched celery and carrots.

Complete the following statement: The sentences can be organized using

_____ order.

ADDITIONAL PARAGRAPHS TO CONSIDER

Read these additional paragraphs of comparison or contrast and then answer the questions that follow.

My Broken Dream

[1]When I became a police officer in my town, the job was not as I had dreamed it would be. [2]I began to dream about being a police officer at about age ten. [3]I could picture myself wearing a handsome blue uniform and having an impressive-looking badge on my chest. [4]I could also picture myself driving a powerful patrol car through town and seeing everyone stare at me with envy. [5]But most of all, I dreamed of wearing a gun and using all the equipment that "TV cops" use. [6]I just knew everyone would be proud of me. [7]I could almost hear the guys on the block saying, "Boy, Steve made it big. [8]Did you hear he's a cop?" [9]I dreamed of leading an exciting life, solving big crimes, and meeting lots of people. [10]I just knew that if I became a cop everyone in town would look up to me. [11]However, when I actually did become a police officer, I soon found out that it was not as I had dreamed it would be. [12]My first disappointment came when I was sworn in and handed a well-used, baggy uniform. [13]My disappointment continued when I was given a badge that looked like something pulled out of a Cracker Jack box. [14]I was assigned a beat-up old junker and told that it would be my patrol car. [15]It had a striking resemblance to a car that had lost a demolition derby at a stock-car raceway. [16]Disappointment seemed to continue. [17]I soon found out that I was not the envy of all my friends. [18]When I drove through town, they acted as if they had not seen me. [19]I was told I was crazy doing this kind of job by people I thought would look up to me. [20]My job was not as exciting as I had dreamed it would be either. [21]Instead of solving robberies and murders every day, I found that I spent a great deal of time comforting a local resident because a neighborhood dog had watered his favorite bush.

Two Views on Toys

[1]There is a vast difference between children and adults where presents are concerned. [2]First, there is the matter of taste. [3]Adults pride themselves on taste, while children ignore the matter of taste in favor of things that are fun. [4]Adults, especially grandparents, pick out tasteful toys that go unused, while children love the cheap playthings advertised on television. [5]Then, of course, there is the matter of money. [6]The new games on the market today are a case in point. [7]Have you ever tried to lure a child away from some expensive game in order to get him or her to play with an old-fashioned game or toy? [8]Finally, there is a difference between an adult's and a child's idea of what is educational. [9]Adults, filled with memories of their own childhoods, tend to be fond of the written word. [10]Today's children, on the other hand, concentrate on anything electronic. [11]These things mean much more to them

than to adults. [12]Next holiday season, examine the toys that adults choose for children. [13]Then look at the toys the children prefer. [14]You will see the difference.

Mike and Helen

[1]Like his wife Helen, Mike has a good sense of humor. [2]Also, they are both short, dark-haired, and slightly pudgy. [3]Both Mike and Helen can be charming when they want to be, and they seem to handle small crises in a calm, cool way. [4]A problem such as an overflowing washer, a stalled car, or a sick child is not a cause for panic; they seem to take such events in stride. [5]Unlike Helen, though, Mike tends to be disorganized. [6]He is late for appointments and unable to keep important documents--bank records, receipts, and insurance papers--where he can find them. [7]And unlike Helen, Mike tends to hold a grudge. [8]He is slow to forget a cruel remark, a careless joke, or an unfriendly slight. [9]Also, Mike enjoys swimming, camping, and tennis, unlike Helen, who is an indoors type.

■ Questions

About Unity

1. Which paragraph lacks a topic sentence?

    _____

2. Which paragraph has a topic sentence that is too broad?

    _____

About Support

3. Which paragraph contains virtually no specific details?

    _____

4. Which paragraph do you feel offers the most effective details?

    _____

About Coherence

5. What method of development (one side at a time or point by point) is used in ''My Broken Dream''?

    _____

    In ''Two Views on Toys''?

    _____

6. Which paragraph offers specific details but lacks a clear, consistent method of development?

    _____

WRITING A COMPARISON OR CONTRAST PARAGRAPH

■ Writing Assignment 1

Below are topic sentences and supporting points for three contrast paragraphs. Choose one of the three to develop into a paragraph.

Option 1

Topic sentence: I abused my body when I was twenty, but I treat myself much differently at the age of thirty.

a.   At twenty, I was a heavy smoker. . . .
Now, instead of smoking, I . . .

b.   At twenty, I had a highly irregular diet. . . .
Today, on the other hand, I eat . . .

c.   Finally, at twenty, I never exercised. . . .
Today, I work out regularly. . . .

Option 2

Topic sentence: Dating is still much easier for boys than it is for girls.

a.   A boy can take the initial step of asking for a date without seeming too aggressive. . . .
In contrast, a girl . . .

b.   The boy is usually in charge of deciding where to go and what to do. . . .
The girl, on the other hand, has to live with the choices. . . .

c.   At the end of the night, the boy knows the moves he is planning to make, if any. . . .
But the girl waits nervously to see what will happen. . . .

Option 3

Topic sentence: My sociology instructor teaches a class quite differently from my psychology instructor.

a.   For one thing, Ms. X demands many hours of homework each week. . . .
In contrast, Mr. Y does not believe in much work outside class. . . .

b. In addition, Ms. X gives difficult tests—with no study aids. . . .

Mr. Y's tests, on the other hand, are easy. . . .

c. Finally, Ms. X keeps every class strictly on the subject of the day. . . .

But Mr. Y will wander off onto any topic that snags his interest. . . .

How to Proceed

a Begin by prewriting. To develop some supporting details for the paragraph, freewrite for five minutes on the topic sentence you have chosen.

b Then add to the material you have written by asking yourself questions. If you were writing about how you treat your body differently at thirty, for example, you might ask yourself:

How many cigarettes did I smoke at twenty?

What have I substituted for cigarettes?

What kinds of food did I eat?

How regularly did I eat?

What foods do I eat today?

Why didn't I exercise at twenty?

What made me decide to start exercising?

What kind of exercises do I do?

How often do I exercise?

Write down whatever answers occur to you for these and other questions. As with the freewriting, do not worry at this stage about writing correctly. Instead, concentrate on getting down all the information you can think of that supports each point.

c Now go through all the material you have accumulated. Perhaps some of the details you have written down may help you think of even better details that would fit. If so, write them down.

d As you work on the drafts of your paper, use words such as *in contrast, but, on the other hand,* and *however* to tie your material together.

e Be sure to edit the next-to-final draft of your paper for sentence-skills mistakes, including spelling.

■ Writing Assignment 2

Write a comparison or contrast paragraph on one of the twenty topics below.

Two holidays	Two jobs
Two instructors	Two characters in the same
Two children	movie or TV show
Two kinds of eaters	Two commercials
Two drivers	Two methods of studying
Two coworkers	Two cartoon strips
Two members of a team	Two cars
(or two teams)	Two friends
Two singers or groups	Two crises
Two animals	Two employees
Two parties	Two magazines

How to Proceed

a You must begin by making two decisions: (1) what your topic will be and (2) whether you are going to do a comparison or a contrast paper. Many times, students choose to do essays centered on differences between two things. For example, you might write about how a math instructor you have in college differs from a math teacher you had in high school. You might discuss important differences between two coworkers or between two of your friends. You might contrast a factory job you had packing vegetables with a white-collar job you had as a salesperson in a clothing store.

b After you choose a tentative topic, write a simple topic sentence expressing it. Then see what kind of support you can generate for that topic. For instance, if you plan to contrast two cars, see if you can think of and jot down three distinct ways they differ. In other words, prepare a scratch outline. An outline is an excellent prewriting technique to use when doing any paragraph; it is almost indispensable when planning a comparison or contrast paragraph. For a model, look back at the outlines given on pages 26–31.

    Keep in mind that this planning stage is probably the *single most important phase* of work you will do on your paper. Without clear planning, you are not likely to write an effective paragraph.

c After you have decided on a topic and the main lines of support, you must decide whether to use a one-side-at-a-time or a point-by-point method of development. Both methods are explained and illustrated in this chapter.

d Now, freewrite for ten minutes on the topic you have chosen. Do not worry about punctuation, spelling, or other matters relating to correct form. Just get as many details as you can onto the page. You want a base of raw material that you can add to and select from as you now work on the first draft of your paper. After you do a first draft, try to put it aside for a day or at least several hours. You will then be ready to return with a fresh perspective on the material and build on what you have already done.

e Use transition words like *first, in addition, also, in contrast, another difference, on the other hand, but, however,* and *most important* to link points together.

f As you continue working on your paper, refer to the checklist on the inside front cover. Make sure that you can answer *Yes* to the questions about unity, support, and coherence.

g Finally, use the checklist on the inside front cover to edit the next-to-final draft of your paper for sentence-skills mistakes, including spelling.

■ Writing Assignment 3

Write a contrast paragraph on one of the fifteen topics below.

> Neighborhood stores versus a shopping mall
> Driving on an expressway versus driving on country roads
> *People* versus *Reader's Digest* (or any other two popular magazines)
> Camping in a tent versus camping in a recreational vehicle
> Working parents versus stay-at-home parents
> Last year's fashions versus this year's
> Used car versus new car
> Tapes versus CDs
> PG-rated movies versus R-rated movies
> News in a newspaper versus news on television
> Yesterday's toys versus today's
> Fresh food versus canned or frozen food
> Winning locker room after a game versus losing one
> Ad on television versus ad (for the same product) in a magazine
> Amateur sport versus professional sport

Follow the directions on "How to Proceed" given in Writing Assignment 2.

■ Writing Assignment 4

You are living in an apartment building in which new tenants are making life unpleasant for you. Write a letter of complaint to your landlord comparing and contrasting life before and after the tenants arrived. You might want to focus on one or more of the following:

Noise level

Trash

Safety hazards

Parking situation

■ Writing Assignment 5

Writing about a Reading Selection: Read the selection ''People Need People'' on pages 535–539. Then write a paragraph contrasting two times in your life: a time when you had few human contacts and a time when you had many.

To get started, you might make up two lists: (1) happy times when you had especially close connections with other people; (2) lonely times when you seemed to lack even a single person who cared about you. You might, for example, have felt particularly happy when you were with a group of close friends at some time in high school; you might have felt neglected during a time of trouble between your parents. Choose those two times for which you have the sharpest memory of details. Then freewrite for five or ten minutes about each of them, putting down on paper whatever comes into mind.

Next, decide whether to use a side-by-side or a point-by-point method of develoment. Both methods are explained and illustrated in this chapter. If you use a side-by-side method, you might use an outline like this:

Happy time: Sad time:
a. Situation (when and where)   a. Situation (when and where)
b. Your thoughts and feelings   b. Your thoughts and feelings
c. Why the time ended   c. Why the time ended

Once you have your outline, you should be ready to work on the first draft of your paper. You may also find it helpful to look over the general guidelines on pages 162–163 while writing your paragraph.

DEFINING
A TERM

In talking with other people, we at times offer informal definitions to explain just what we mean by particular terms. Suppose, for example, we say to a friend, "Ted is an anxious person." We might then expand on our idea of *anxious* by saying, "He's always worrying about the future. Yesterday he was talking about how many bills he'll probably have this year. Then he was worrying about what he would ever do if he got laid off." In a written definition, we make clear in a more complete and formal way our own personal understanding of a term. Such a definition typically starts with one meaning of a term. The meaning is then illustrated with a series of examples or a story.

In this section, you will be asked to write a paragraph in which you define a term. The three student papers below are all examples of definition paragraphs. Read them and then answer the questions that follow.

PARAGRAPHS TO CONSIDER

Luck

[1]Luck is putting $1.75 into a vending machine and getting the money back with your snacks. [2]It is a teacher's decision to give a retest on a test where you first scored thirty. [3]Luck refers to moments of good fortune that happen in everyday life. [4]It is not going to the dentist for two years and then going and finding out that you do not have any cavities. [5]It is calling up a plumber to fix a leak on a day when the plumber has no other work to do. [6]Luck is finding a used car for sale at a good price at exactly the time when your car rolls its last mile. [7]It is driving into a traffic bottleneck and choosing the lane that winds up moving most rapidly. [8]Luck is being late for work on a day when your boss arrives later than you do. [9]It is having a new checkout aisle at the supermarket open up just as your cart arrives. [10]The best kind of luck is winning a new color TV set on a chance for which you paid only a quarter.

Disillusionment

[1]Disillusionment is the feeling of having one of our most cherished beliefs stolen from us. [2]I learned about disillusionment firsthand the day Mr. Keller, our eighth-grade teacher, handed out the grades on our class biology projects. [3]I had worked hard to assemble what I thought was the best insect collection any school had ever seen. [4]For weeks, I had set up homemade traps around our house, in the woods, and in vacant lots. [5]At night, I would stretch a white sheet between two trees, shine a lantern on it, and collect the night-flying insects that gathered there. [6]With my own money, I had bought killing jars, insect pins, gummed labels, and display boxes. [7]I carefully arranged related insects together, with labels listing each scientific name and the place and date of capture. [8]Slowly and painfully, I wrote and typed the report that accompanied my project at the school science fair. [9]In contrast, my friend Eddie did almost nothing for his project. [10]He had his father, a doctor, build an impressive maze complete with live rats and a sign that read, "You are the trainer." [11]A person could lift a little plastic door, send a rat running through the maze, and then hit a button to release a pellet of rat food as a reward. [12]This exhibit turned out to be the most popular one at the fair. [13]I felt sure that our teacher would know that Eddie could not have built it, and I was certain that my hard work would be recognized and rewarded. [14]Then the grades were finally handed out, and I was crushed. [15]Eddie had gotten an A plus, but my grade was a B. [16]I suddenly realized that honesty and hard work don't always pay off in the end. [17]The idea that life is not fair, that sometimes it pays to cheat, hit me with such force that I felt sick. [18]I will never forget that moment.

A Mickey Mouse Course

[1]A Mickey Mouse course is any college course that is so easy that even Mickey or Minnie Mouse could achieve an A grade. [2]A student who is taking a heavy schedule, or who does not want four or five especially difficult courses, will try to sandwich in a Mickey Mouse course. [3]A student can find out about such a course by consulting other students, since word of a genuine Mickey Mouse course spreads like wildfire. [4]Or a student can study the college master schedule for telltale course titles like The Art of Pressing Wild Flowers, History of the Comic Book, or Watching Television Creatively. [5]In an advanced course such as microbiology, though, a student had better be prepared to spend a good deal of time during the semester on that course. [6]Students in a Mickey Mouse course can attend the classes while half-asleep, hung-over, or wearing stereo earphones or a blindfold; they will still pass. [7]The course exams (if there are any) would not challenge a five-year-old. [8]The course lectures usually consist of information that anyone with

common sense knows anyway. ^{9}Attendance may be required, but participation or involvement in the class is not. ^{10}The main requirement for passing is that a student's body is there, warming a seat in the classroom. ^{11}There are no difficult labs or special projects, and term papers are never mentioned. ^{12}Once safely registered for such a course, all the students have to do is sit back and watch the credits accumulate on their transcripts.

■ Questions

About Unity

1. Which paragraph places its topic sentence within the paragraph rather than, more appropriately, at the beginning?

   _____

2. Which sentence in "A Mickey Mouse Course" should be omitted in the interest of paragraph unity? (*Write the sentence number here.*) _____

About Support

3. Which two paragraphs develop their definitions through a series of short examples?

   _____

   _____

4. Which paragraph develops its definition through a single extended example?

   _____

About Coherence

5. Which paragraph uses emphatic order, saving its best detail for last?

   _____

6. Which paragraph uses time order to organize its details?

   _____

WRITING A DEFINITION PARAGRAPH

■ Writing Assignment 1

Following are a topic sentence and three supporting points for a paragraph that defines the term *TV addict*. Using separate paper, plan out and write the secondary supporting details and closing sentence needed to complete the paragraph. Refer to the suggestions bellow on ''How to Proceed.''

Topic sentence: Television addicts are people who will watch all the programs they can, for as long as they can, rather than do anything else.

a. TV addicts, first of all, will watch anything on the tube, no matter how bad it is. . . .

b. In addition, addicts watch TV more hours than normal people do. . . .

c. Finally, addicts feel that TV is more important than any other activities or events that might be going on. . . .

How to Proceed

a Begin by prewriting. Prepare examples for each of the three qualities of a TV addict. For each quality, you should have at least two or three sentences that provide either an extended example or shorter examples of this quality in action.

b To generate these details, ask yourself the following questions:

What are some examples of terrible shows that I (or people I know) watch just because the television is turned on?

What are some examples of how much I (or people I know) watch TV?

What are some other activities or events that I (or people I know) give up in order to watch TV?

Write down quickly whatever answers occur to you. Do not worry about writing correct sentences; just concentrate on getting down all the details about television addicts that you can think of.

c Draw from and add to this material as you work on the paragraph. Make sure that your paragraph is unified, supported, and coherent.

d Finally, edit the next-to-final draft of your paper for sentence-skills mistakes, including spelling.

■ Writing Assignment 2

Write an essay that defines one of the following terms. Each term refers to a certain kind of person.

Bigmouth	Clown	Good example
Charmer	Jellyfish	Hypocrite
Loser	Leader	Perfectionist
Lazybones	Nerd	Pack rat
Kibitzer	Good neighbor	Hard worker
Con artist	Optimist	Apple-polisher
Fair-weather friend	Pessimist	Fusspot
Team player		

How to Proceed

a   To write a topic sentence for your definition paragraph, your first step should be to *place the term in a class or category.* Then *describe what you feel are the special features that distinguish your term from all the other members of its class.*

   In the sample topic sentences below, underline the class, or category, that the term belongs to and double-underline the distinguishing details of that class, or category. One is done for you as an example.

A klutz is a <u>person</u> who <u>stumbles through life</u>.

A worrywart is a person who sees danger everywhere.

The class clown is a student who gets attention in the wrong way.

A clotheshorse is a person who needs new clothes to be happy.

b   In order to develop your definition, use one of the following methods:

   Examples. Give several examples that support your topic sentence.

   Extended example. Use one longer example to support your topic sentence.

   Contrast. Support your topic sentence by showing what your term is *not*. For instance, you may want to define a "fair-weather friend" by contrasting his or her actions with those of a true friend.

c   Once you have created a topic sentence and decided how to develop your paragraph, write a scratch outline. This step is especially important if you are using a contrast method of development.

d   Be sure you touch the four bases of unity, support, coherence, and sentence skills in your writing.

■ Writing Assignment 3

Write an essay that defines one of the abstract terms below.

Persistence	Responsibility	Fear
Rebellion	Insecurity	Arrogance
Sense of humor	Assertiveness	Conscience
Escape	Jealousy	Class
Danger	Nostalgia	Innocence
Curiosity	Gentleness	Freedom
Common sense	Depression	Violence
Family	Obsession	Shyness
Practicality	Self-control	

As a guide in writing your paper, use the suggestions on ''How to Proceed'' in Writing Assignment 2. Remember to place your term in a class, or category, and to describe what *you* feel are the distinguishing features of that term. Three examples follow.

Laziness is a quality that doesn't deserve its bad reputation.

Jealousy is the emotion that hurts the most.

Persistence is the quality of not giving up even during rough times.

■ Writing Assignment 4

Option 1:   At the place where you work, one employee has just quit, creating a new job opening. Since you have been working there for a while, your boss has asked you to write a job description of the position. That description, which is really a detailed definition of the job, will be sent to employment services. These services will be responsible for interviewing candidates. Choose any position you know about, and write a job description for it. First give the purpose of the job, and then list its duties and responsibilities. Finally, give the qualifications for the position.

Option 2:   Alternatively, imagine that a new worker has been hired, and your boss has asked you to explain ''team spirit'' to him or her. The purpose of your explanation will be to give the newcomer an idea of the teamwork that is expected in this workplace. Write a paragraph that defines in detail what your boss means by *team spirit.* Use examples or one extended example to illustrate your general statements.

■ **Writing Assignment 5**

Writing about a Reading Selection: Read the selection titled "What Good Families Are Doing Right" on pages 458–466. Then write a definition paragraph on the hallmarks of a *bad* family. Your topic sentence might be, "A bad family is one that is ————, ————, and ————."

To get started, you should first reread the features of a good family explained in the selection. Doing so will help you think about what qualities are found in a bad family. Prepare a list of as many bad qualities as you can think of. Then go through the list and decide upon the qualities that seem most characteristic of a bad family.

Next, spend some time thinking of and jotting down examples of each of these qualities. You'll note that the selection provides examples of the hallmarks of a good family; your goal will be to provide examples of the hallmarks of a bad family. Your examples can be drawn from your own experience or observation, or they can be hypothetical examples—examples that you invent but that you feel are realistic. Perhaps your examples will be composites of several bad families or of behaviors that may occur at different times in any family.

Finally, decide on the order in which to present these qualities, keeping in mind that you will want to end with the most telling quality. And remember that you will want to use transition words and synonyms such as *The first hallmark, Another quality, A third feature,* and so on.

You should now be ready to write the first draft of your paper.

DIVIDING
AND
CLASSIFYING

If you were doing the laundry, you would probably begin by separating the clothing into piles. You might put all the whites in one pile and all the colors in another. You might put all cottons in one pile, polyesters in another, silks in a third, and so on. Or you might divide and classify the laundry not according to color or fabrics but on the basis of use. You might put bath towels in one pile, bed sheets in another, personal garments in a third, and so on. Sorting clothes in various ways is just one small example of how we spend a great deal of time organizing our environment in one manner or another.

In this section, you will be asked to write a paragraph in which you divide or classify a subject according to a single principle. To prepare for this assignment, first read the division and classification paragraphs below and then work through the questions and the activity that follow.

PARAGRAPHS TO CONSIDER

Automobile Drivers

[1]One type of automobile driver is the slowpoke. [2]A woman who is a slowpoke, for instance, will drive forty miles per hour in a fifty-five-mile zone. [3]She will slow down and start signaling for a left-hand turn three blocks before making it. [4]Or her car will slow down while she is in avid conversation with other people in the car, or while she puzzles over street signs to get her bearings, or while she looks at displays and sale signs in shop windows, or as she struggles to open the wrapping of her Burger King Whopper. [5]A second type is the high-speed driver. [6]A man who is a high-speed driver, for

example, will limit his speed only when he suspects that the state police or radar traps are nearby. [7]The state police must develop a system to ensure that they begin to catch this kind of driver. [8]He typically speeds past cars on the left and right sides, weaving in and around them sharply, and he closely tailgates a car that holds him up until it shifts to another lane. [9]He races to get through yellow or just-red lights at highway and city intersections, and he speeds down city streets, oblivious to the possibility that children may run out from between parked cars or that someone may open a car door. [10]The final type is the sensible-speed driver who, road conditions being normal, maintains the posted speed limits and drives at a consistent and moderate rate. [11]If these drivers do change their rate, they do so because they are driving defensively. [12]They are speeding up to pass the driver in front, who is creeping along to look at the pumpkins on display at a roadside stand. [13]Or they are slowing down to allow the speed demon who has tried passing to get back in lane and out of the path of an oncoming truck.

Studying for a Test

[1]The time a student spends studying for a test can be divided into three distinct phases. [2]Phase 1, often called the "no problem" phase, runs from the day the test is announced to approximately forty-eight hours before the dreaded exam is passed out. [3]During phase 1, the student is carefree, smiling, and kind to helpless animals and small children. [4]When asked by classmates if he or she has studied for the test yet, the reply will be an assured "No problem." [5]During phase 1, no actual studying takes place. [6]Phase 2 is entered two days before the test. [7]For example, if the test is scheduled for 9 A.M. Friday, phase 2 begins at 9 A.M. Wednesday. [8]During phase 2, again, no actual studying takes place. [9]Phase 3, the final phase, is entered twelve hours before "zero hour." [10]This is the acute phase, characterized by sweaty palms, nervous twitches, and confused mental patterns. [11]For a test at nine o'clock on Friday morning, a student begins exhibiting these symptoms at approximately nine o'clock on Thursday night. [12]Phase 3 is also termed the "shock" phase, since the student is shocked to discover the imminent nature of the exam and the amount of material to be studied. [13]During this phase, the student will probably be unable to sleep and will mumble meaningless phrases like "$a^2 + c^2$." [14]This phase will not end until the exam is over. [15]If the cram session has worked, the student will fall gratefully asleep. [16]On waking up, he or she will be ready to go through the whole cycle again with the next test.

The Dangers of Tools

[1]Tools can be divided into three categories according to how badly people can injure themselves with them. [2]The first group of tools causes dark-purple bruises to appear on the user's feet, fingers, or arms. [3]Hammers are famous for this, as millions of cartoons and comic strips have shown. [4]Mallets and crowbars, too, can go a bit off target and thud onto a bit of exposed flesh. [5]But first-class bruises can also be caused by clamps, pliers, vise grips, and wrenches. [6]In a split second, any one of these tools can lash out and badly squeeze a stray finger. [7]Later, the victim will see blue-black blood forming under the fingernail. [8]The second type of tool usually attacks by cutting or tearing. [9]Saws seem to enjoy cutting through human flesh as well as wood. [10]Keeping a hand too close to the saw, or using a pair of knees as a sawhorse, will help the saw satisfy its urge. [11]Planes, chisels, and screwdrivers also cut into skin. [12]And the utility knife--the kind with a razor blade projecting from a metal handle--probably cuts more people than it does linoleum. [13]The most dangerous tools, however, are the mutilators, the ones that send people directly to the emergency room. [14]People were definitely not made to handle monster tools like chain saws, table saws, power drills, and power hammers. [15]Newspapers are filled with stories of shocking accidents people have had with power tools. [16]In summary, if people are not careful, tools can definitely be hazardous to their health.

■ **Questions**

About Unity

1. Which paragraph lacks a topic sentence? _____

2. Which sentence in "Automobile Drivers" should be omitted in the interest of paragraph unity? (*Write the sentence number here.*) _____

About Support

3. Which of the three phases in "Studying for a Test" lacks specific details?

   _____

4. After which sentence in "The Dangers of Tools" are supporting details needed? _____

About Coherence

5. Which paragraph uses time order to organize its details?

   _____

6. Which paragraph uses emphatic order to organize its details?

   _____

7. What words in the emphatic-order paragraph signal the most important detail?

   _____

Activity

This activity will sharpen your sense of the classifying process. In each of the following ten groups, cross out the one item that has not been classified on the same basis as the other three. Also, indicate in the space provided the single principle of classification used for the three items. Note the examples.

Examples   Water
   a.   Cold
   b.   ~~Lake~~
   c.   Hot
   d.   Lukewarm
   Unifying principle:
   Temperature

Household pests
   a.   ~~Mice~~
   b.   Ants
   c.   Roaches
   d.   Flies
   Unifying principle:
   Insects

1.   Eyes
   a.   Blue
   b.   Nearsighted
   c.   Brown
   d.   Hazel
   Unifying principle:
   _____

2.   Mattresses
   a.   Double
   b.   Twin
   c.   Queen
   d.   Firm
   Unifying principle:
   _____

3.   Zoo animals
   a.   Flamingo
   b.   Peacock
   c.   Polar bear
   d.   Ostrich
   Unifying principle:
   _____

4.   Vacation
   a.   Summer
   b.   Holiday
   c.   Seashore
   d.   Weekend
   Unifying principle:
   _____

5.   College classes
   a.   Enjoy
   b.   Dislike
   c.   Tolerate
   d.   Morning
   Unifying principle:
   _____

6.   Wallets
   a.   Leather
   b.   Plastic
   c.   Stolen
   d.   Fabric
   Unifying principle:
   _____

7. Newspaper
   a. Wrapping garbage
   b. Editorials
   c. Making paper planes
   d. Covering floor while
      painting
   Unifying principle:

   _____

8. Students
   a. Freshman
   b. Transfer
   c. Junior
   d. Sophomore
   Unifying principle:

   _____

9. Exercise
   a. Running
   b. Swimming
   c. Gymnastics
   d. Fatigue
   Unifying principle:

   _____

10. Leftovers
    a. Cold chicken
    b. Feed to dog
    c. Reheat
    d. Use in a stew
    Unifying principle:

    _____

WRITING A DIVISION AND CLASSIFICATION PARAGRAPH

■ Writing Assignment 1

Below are four possible division and classification writing assignments, along with possible divisions. Choose *one* of them to develop into a paragraph.

Option 1

Supermarket shoppers
a. Slow, careful shoppers
b. Average shoppers
c. Rushed, hurried shoppers

Option 2

Eaters
a. Super-conservative eaters
b. Typical eaters
c. Adventurous eaters

Option 3

Methods of housekeeping
a. Never clean
b. Clean regularly
c. Clean constantly

Option 4

Attitudes toward money
a. Tightfisted
b. Sometimes splurge
c. Spendthrift

How to Proceed

a Begin by prewriting. To develop some ideas for the paragraph, freewrite for five or ten minutes on your topic.

b To add to the material you have written, ask yourself questions. If you are writing about supermarket shoppers, for example, you might ask:

How do the three kinds of shoppers pick out the items they want?

How many aisles will each type of shopper visit?

Which shoppers bring lists, calculators, coupons, and so on?

How much time does it take each type of shopper to finish shopping?

Write down whatever answers occur to you for these and other questions. As with freewriting, do not worry at this stage about writing correctly. Instead, concentrate on getting down all the information you can think of that supports each of the three points.

c Now go through all the material you have accumulated. Perhaps some of the details you have written down may help you think of even better details that would fit. If so, write them down. Then make decisions about the exact information you will use to support each point. Number the details 1, 2, 3, and so on, in the order you will present them.

d As you work on the drafts of your paragraph, make sure that it touches the bases of unity, support, and coherence.

e Finally, edit the next-to-final draft of your paper for sentence-skills mistakes, including spelling.

■ Writing Assignment 2

Write a division and classification essay on one of the following subjects:

Instructors	Drivers
Sports fans	Mothers or fathers
Eating places	Women's or men's magazines
Attitudes toward life	Presents
Commercials	Neighbors
Employers	Rock, pop, or country singers
Jobs	Amusement parks or rides
Bars	Guests or company
Family get-togethers	Ways to get an A (or F) in a course
Shoes	Car accessories

How to Proceed

a The first step in writing a division and classification paragraph is to divide your tentative topic into three reasonably complete parts. *Always use a single principle of division when you form your three parts.* For example, if your topic was "Automobile Drivers" and you divided them into slow, moderate, and fast drivers, your single basis for division would be "rate of speed." It would be illogical, then, to have as a fourth type "teenage drivers" (the basis of such a division would be "age") or "female drivers" (the basis of such a division would be "sex"). You could probably classify automobile drivers on the basis of age or sex or another division, for almost any subject can be analyzed in more than one way. What is important, however, is that in any single paper you choose only one basis for division and stick to it. Be consistent.

In "Studying for a Test," the writer divides the process of studying into three time phases: from the time the test is announced to forty-eight hours before the test; the day and a half before the test; the final twelve hours before the test. In "The Dangers of Tools," the single basis for dividing tools into three categories is the kind of injury each type inflicts: bruises, cuts, and major injuries.

b To ensure a clear three-part division in your own paragraph, fill in the outline below before starting your paper and make sure you can answer *Yes* to the questions that follow. You should expect to do a fair amount of thinking before coming up with a logical plan for your paper.

Topic: _____
Three-part division of the topic:

(1) _____

(2) _____

(3) _____

Is there a single basis of division for the three parts? _____

Is the division reasonably complete? _____

c Refer to the checklist of the four bases on the inside front cover while writing the drafts of your paper. Make sure you can answer *Yes* to the questions about unity, support, coherence, and sentence skills. Also, use the checklist when you edit the next-to-final draft of your paper for sentence-skills mistakes, including spelling.

■ **Writing Assignment 3**

There are many ways you could classify the students around you. Choose one of your courses and write a division and classification paragraph on the students in that class. You might want to categorize the students according to one of the principles of division below:

Attitude toward the class	Attendance
Participation in the class	Level of confidence
Method of taking notes in class	Performance during oral reports,
Method of taking a test in class	speeches, presentations, lab sessions
Punctuality	

Of course, you may use any other principle of division that seems appropriate. Follow the steps listed in "How to Proceed" for Writing Assignment 2.

■ **Writing Assignment 4**

You are teaching a class in safe driving at a high school, and part of today's lecture is about types of drivers to avoid. For this part of your presentation, write a paragraph dividing the category "unsafe drivers" into three or more types according to their driving habits. For each type, include both a description and suggestions to your students on how to avoid an accident with this type of driver.

■ **Writing Assignment 5**

Writing about a Reading Selection: Read the selection titled "How to Think Clearly" on pages 514–518. Then write a paragraph in which you present the three of four kinds of distorted thinking that you yourself, and other college students, seem to use most often. Your topic sentence might be, "The illogical thinking that students resort to can be divided into three (*or* four) types."

To get started, you should go carefully through all twelve types of twisted logic described in "How to Think Clearly." As you read about each type, think about the ways that it may be used by students. Jot down examples of its use— drawing on both your own experiences and your observations of other students. You are likely to find that several cognitive distortions in particular will apply. These will be the basis for your paragraph.

As you work on your paper, use transitions and synonyms such as *One kind of twisted logic, Another type of distorted thinking,* and *The final and perhaps most common mental distortion.* In each case, explain the illogical thinking briefly, in you own words, and then give one or two examples of it.

DESCRIBING
A SCENE
OR PERSON

When you describe something or someone, you give your readers a picture in words. To make this "word picture" as vivid and real as possible, you must observe and record specific details that appeal to your readers' senses (sight, hearing, taste, smell, and touch). More than any other type of writing, a descriptive paragraph needs sharp, colorful details.

Here is a description in which only the sense of sight is used:

A rug covers the living-room floor.

In contrast, here is a description rich in sense impressions:

A thick, reddish-brown shag rug is laid wall to wall across the living-room floor. The long, curled fibers of the shag seem to whisper as you walk through them in your bare feet, and when you squeeze your toes into the deep covering, the soft fibers push back at you with a spongy resiliency.

Sense impressions include sight (*thick, reddish-brown shag rug; laid wall to wall; walk through them in your bare feet; squeeze your toes into the deep covering; push back*), hearing (*whisper*), and touch (*bare feet, soft fibers, spongy resiliency*). The sharp, vivid images provided by the sensory details give us a clear picture of the rug and enable us to share in the writer's experience.

In this section, you will be asked to describe a person, place, or thing for your readers through the use of words rich in sensory details. To help you prepare for the assignment, first read the three paragraphs ahead and then answer the questions that follow.

PARAGRAPHS TO CONSIDER

An Athlete's Room

[1]As I entered the bright, cheerful space, with its beige walls and practical, flat-pile carpet, I noticed a closet to my right with the door open. [2]On the shelf above the bunched-together clothes were a red baseball cap, a fielder's glove, and a battered brown gym bag. [3]Turning from the closet, I noticed a single bed with its wooden headboard against the far wall. [4]The bedspread was a brown, orange, and beige print of basketball, football, and baseball scenes. [5]A lamp shaped like a baseball and a copy of Sports Illustrated were on the top of a nightstand to the left of the bed. [6]A sports schedule and several yellowing newspaper clippings were tacked to the cork bulletin board on the wall above the nightstand. [7]A desk with a bookcase top stood against the left wall. [8]I walked toward it to examine it more closely. [9]As I ran my fingers over the items on the dusty shelves, I noticed some tarnished medals and faded ribbons for track accomplishments. [10]These lay next to a heavy gold trophy that read, "MVP: Pinewood Varsity Basketball." [11]I accidentally tipped an autograph-covered, slightly deflated basketball off one shelf, and the ball bounced with dull thuds across the width of the room. [12]Next to the desk was a window with brightly printed curtains that matched the bedspread. [13]Between the window and the left corner stood a dresser with one drawer half open, revealing a tangle of odd sweat socks and a few stretched-out T shirts emblazoned with team insignias. [14]As I turned to leave the room, I carefully picked my way around scattered pairs of worn-out sneakers.

A Depressing Place

[1]The pet shop in the mall is a depressing place. [2]A display window attracts passersby who stare at the prisoners penned inside. [3]In the right-hand side of the window, two puppies press their forepaws against the glass and attempt to lick the human hands that press from the outside. [4]A cardboard barrier separates the dogs from several black-and-white kittens piled together in the opposite end of the window. [5]Inside the shop, rows of wire cages line one wall from top to bottom. [6]At first, it is hard to tell whether a bird, hamster, gerbil, cat, or dog is locked inside each cage. [7]Only an occasional movement or clawing, shuffling sound tells visitors that living creatures are inside. [8]Running down the center of the store is a line of large wooden perches that look like coat racks. [9]When customers pass by, the parrots and mynas chained to these perches flutter their clipped wings in a useless attempt to escape. [10]At the end of this center aisle is a large plastic

tub of dirty, stagnant-looking water containing a few motionless turtles. [11]The shelves against the left-hand wall are packed with all kinds of pet-related items. [12]The smell inside the entire shop is an unpleasant mixture of strong chemical deodorizers, urine-soaked newspapers, and musty sawdust. [13]Because so many animals are crammed together, the normally pleasant, slightly milky smell of the puppies and kittens is sour and strong. [14]The droppings inside the uncleaned birdcages give off a dry, stinging odor. [15]Visitors hurry out of the shop, anxious to feel fresh air and sunlight. [16]The animals stay on.

Karla

[1]Karla, my brother's new girlfriend, is a catlike creature. [2]Her face, with its wide forehead, sharp cheekbones, and narrow, pointed chin, resembles a triangle. [3]Karla's skin is a soft, velvety brown. [4]Her large brown eyes slant upward at the corners, and she emphasizes their angle with a sweep of maroon eye shadow. [5]Karla's habit of looking sidelong out of the tail of her eye makes her look cautious, as if she were expecting something to sneak up on her. [6]Her nose is small and flat. [7]The sharply outlined depression under it leads the observer's eye to a pair of red-tinted lips. [8]With their slight upward tilt at the corners, Karla's lips make her seem self-satisfied and secretly pleased. [9]One reason Karla may be happy is that she was recently asked to be in a local beauty contest. [10]Karla's face is framed by a smooth layer of brown hair that always looks just combed. [11]Her long neck and slim body are perfectly in proportion with her face. [12]Karla manages to look elegant and sleek no matter how she is standing or sitting, for her body seems to be made up of graceful angles. [13]Her slender hands are tipped with long, polished nails. [14]Her narrow feet are long, too, but they appear delicate even in flat-soled running shoes. [15]Somehow, Karla would look perfect in a cat's jeweled collar.

■ **Questions**

About Unity

1. Which paragraph lacks a topic sentence?

   _____

2. Which sentence in the paragraph on Karla should be omitted in the interest of paragraph unity? (*Write the sentence number here.*) _____

About Support

3. Label as *sight, touch, hearing,* or *smell* all the sensory details in the following sentences taken from the three paragraphs. The first one is done for you as an example.

   a.   *touch*   *sight*   *sight*
      I accidentally tipped an autograph-covered, slightly deflated basketball off

      sight   *hearing*
      one shelf, and the ball bounced with dull thuds across the width of the

      sight
      room.

   b. Because so many animals are crammed together, the normally pleasant, slightly milky smell of the puppies and kittens is sour and strong.

   c. Her slender hands are tipped with long, polished nails.

   d. As I ran my fingers over the items on the dusty shelves, I noticed some tarnished medals and faded ribbons for track accomplishments.

4. After which sentence in ''A Depressing Place'' are specific details needed?

   _____

About Coherence

5. Spatial signals (*above, next to, to the right,* and so on) are often used to help organize details in descriptive paragraphs. List four space signals that appear in ''An Athlete's Room'':

   _____

   _____

   _____

   _____

6. The writer of ''Karla'' organizes the details by observing Karla in an orderly way. Which of Karla's features is described first? _____ Which is described last? _____ Check the method of spatial organization that best describes the paragraph:

   _____ Interior to exterior

   _____ Near to far

   _____ Top to bottom

WRITING A DESCRIPTIVE PARAGRAPH

■ Writing Assignment 1

Write a paragraph describing a special kind of room. Use as your topic sentence "I could tell by looking at the room that a _____ lived there." There are many kinds of people who could be the focus for such a paragraph. You can select any one of the following, or think of some other type of person.

Photographer	Music lover	Carpenter
Cook	TV addict	Baby
Student	Camper	Cat or dog lover
Musician	Grandparent	World traveler
Hunter	Cheerleader	Drug addict
Slob	Football player	Little boy or girl
Outdoors person	Actor	Alcoholic
Instructor	Prostitute	Roller skater

How to Proceed

a   Begin by prewriting. After choosing a topic, spend a few minutes making sure it will work. Prepare a list of all the details you can think of that support the topic. For example, the writer of "An Athlete's Room" made this list:

Sports trophy
Autographed basketball
Sports Illustrated
Baseball lamp
Sports schedule
Medals and ribbons
Sports print on bedspread, curtains
Sweat socks, T shirts
Baseball cap
Baseball glove
Gym bag
Sports clippings

If you don't have enough details, then choose another type of person, and check your new choice with a list of details before committing yourself to the topic.

b As you work on the paragraph, you should keep in mind all four bases of effective writing.

Base 1: Unity. Everything in the paragraph should support your point. For example, if you are writing about an athlete's room, all the details should serve to show that the person who lives in the room is an athlete. Other details should be omitted. Then, after your paragraph is finished, imagine omitting the key word in your topic sentence. Your details alone should make it clear to the reader what word should fit in that empty space.

Base 2: Support. Description depends on the use of *specific* rather than *general* descriptive words. For example:

General	Specific
Old sports trophies	Tarnished medals and faded ribbons for track accomplishments
Ugly turtle tub	Large plastic tub of dirty, stagnant-looking water containing a few motionless turtles
Unpleasant smell	Unpleasant mixture of strong chemical deodorizers, urine-soaked newspapers, and musty sawdust
Nice skin	Soft, velvety brown skin

Remember that you want your readers to experience the room vividly as they read. Your words should be as detailed as a clear photograph and should give your readers a real feel for the room as well. Use as many senses as possible in describing the room. Chiefly you will use sight, but to some extent you may be able to use touch, hearing, and smell as well.

Base 3: Coherence. Organize your descriptive paragraph by using spatial order. Spatial order means that you move from right to left or from larger items to smaller ones, just as a visitor's eye might move around a room. For instance, the writer of ''An Athlete's Room'' presents an orderly description in which the eye moves from right to left around the room. Here are transition words that will help you connect your sentences as you describe the room:

to the left	across from	on the opposite side
to the right	above	nearby
next to	below	

Such transitions will help prevent you—and your reader—from getting lost as the description proceeds.

Base 4: Sentence skills. In the later drafts of your paper, edit carefully for sentence-skills mistakes. Refer to the checklist of such skills on the inside front cover of the book.

■ Writing Assignment 2

Write a paragraph about a particular place that you can observe carefully or that you already know well. It might be one of the following or some other place:

Student lounge area	Hair salon
Car showroom	Doctor's or dentist's office
Gymnasium	Classroom
Fast-food restaurant	Bank
Inside of a car	Dressing room
Ladies' or men's room	Attic
Movie theater	Street market
Auto repair garage	Place where you work
Record shop	Porch

How to Proceed

a   Remember that, like all paragraphs, a descriptive paper must have an opening point. This point, or topic sentence, should state a dominant impression about the place you are describing. In a single short sentence, state the place you want to describe and the dominant impression you want to make. The sentence can be refined later. For now, you just want to find and express a workable topic. You might write, for example, a sentence like one of the following:

The student lounge was hectic.

The record shop was noisy.

The car's interior was very clean.

The dressing room in the department store was stifling.

The dentist's office was soothing.

The movie theater was freezing.

The gymnasium was tense.

The attic was gloomy.

The men's room was classy.

The office where I work was strangely quiet.

b   Now make a list of all the details you can think of that support the general impression. For example, the writer of ''A Depressing Place'' made the list shown on the next page:

A Depressing Place
Puppies behind glass
Unpleasant smell
Chained birds
Rows of cages
Dirty tub of turtles
Stuffy atmosphere
Kittens in window
Sounds of caged animals
Droppings and urine on newspapers

c   Organize your paper by using any one or a combination of the following methods.

In terms of physical order: That is, move from left to right, or far to near, or in some other consistent order

In terms of size: That is, begin with large features or objects and work down to smaller ones

In terms of a special order: Use a special order appropriate to the subject.

For instance, the writer of "A Depressing Place" organizes the paper in terms of physical order (from one side of the pet shop to the center to the other side).

d   Use as many senses as possible in describing a scene. Chiefly you will use sight, but to some extent you may be able to use touch, hearing, smell, and perhaps even taste as well. Remember that it is through the richness of your sense impressions that the reader will gain a picture of the scene.

e   As you are working on the drafts of your paper, refer to the checklist on the inside front cover. Make sure you can answer *Yes* to the questions about unity, support, coherence, and sentence skills.

■ Writing Assignment 3

Write a paragraph describing a person. Decide on a dominant impression you have about the person, and use only those details that will add to that impression. Here are some examples of people you might want to write about.

TV or movie personality	Coworker
Instructor	Clergyman
Employer	Police officer
Child	Store owner or manager
Older person	Bartender
Close friend	Joker
Enemy	Neighbor

Before you begin, you may want to look carefully at the paragraph on Karla given earlier in this chapter and at "How to Proceed" in Writing Assignment 2.

Here are some possible topic sentences. Your instructor may let you develop one of these or may require you to write your own.

Kate gives the impression of being permanently nervous.

The old man was as faded and brittle as a dying leaf.

The child was a cherubic little figure.

Our high school principal resembled a cartoon drawing.

The young woman seemed to belong to another era.

Our neighbor is a fussy person.

The rock singer seemed to be plugged in to some special kind of energy source.

The drug addict looked as lifeless as a corpse.

My friend Mike is a slow, deliberate person.

The owner of that grocery store seems burdened with troubles.

■ Writing Assignment 4

Option 1:   You have just subscribed to a video dating service. Clients of this service are required to make a three-minute presentation, which will be recorded on videotape. In this presentation, clients describe the kind of person they would like to date. Write a one-paragraph description for your video presentation. Begin by brainstorming for a few minutes on what your "ideal date" would be like. Then arrange the details you come up with into some or all of the following categories:

■ *Character and personality*   (Are his or her attitudes important to you? Do you prefer someone who's quiet or someone who's outgoing?)

■ *Interests*   (Should your date have some of the same interests as you? If so, which ones?)

■ *Personal habits*   (Do you care, for instance, if your date is a nonsmoker?)

■ *Physical qualities*   (How might your ideal date look and dress?)

Option 2:   Alternatively, write a similar presentation in which you describe *yourself.* Your aim is to present yourself as honestly as possible, so that interested members of the dating service will get a good sense of what you are like.

■ **Writing Assignment 5**

Writing about a Reading Selection: Read Ruth's selection titled ''The Steel Magnolias'' on pages 528–531. Then write a descriptive paragraph about a host or guest on a television talk show. Prepare for this assignment by watching a talk show and taking notes on the person you plan to write about. Write down a variety of details about the person's dress, mannerisms, and attitudes. Also include a few brief quotations. Clarify your notes right after the show, while the details are still clear in your mind. (If you have a VCR, you may want to record the show so that you can see parts of it more than once.)

Your topic sentence for this paragraph might be similar to one of these:

Oprah Winfrey is an enthusiastic and caring talk-show hostess.

On a recent David Letterman show, _____ went to great lengths to be the center of attention.

A recent segment of the *Tonight Show* revealed _____ to be

. . . very open and honest.
. . . different from his (or her) public image.
. . . an insecure person.

Your purpose is to give your reader a specific impression of your subject by presenting a variety of revealing details. To do so, use those details in your notes that illustrate the personality trait you decide to write about. You may want to review ''The Steel Magnolias'' to see the types of details Ruth uses and how they contribute to a general impression of each actress.

Before starting this paper, you may also find it helpful to look over the writing suggestions on pages 186–187.

NARRATING
AN EVENT

At times we make a statement clear by relating in detail something that has happened to us. In the story we tell, we present the details in the order in which they happened. A person might say, for example, ''I was embarrassed yesterday,'' and then go on to illustrate the statement with the following narrative:

> I was hurrying across campus to get to a class. It had rained heavily all morning, so I was hopscotching my way around puddles in the pathway. I called to two friends ahead to wait for me, and right before I caught up to them, I came to a large puddle that covered the entire path. I had to make a quick choice of either stepping into the puddle or trying to jump over it. I jumped, wanting to seem cool since my friends were watching, but didn't clear the puddle. Water splashed everywhere, drenching my shoe, sock, and pants cuff, and also spraying the pants of my friends as well. ''Well done, Dave!'' they said. I felt the more embarrassed because I had tried to look so casual.

The speaker's details have made his moment of embarrassment vivid and real for us, and we can see and understand just why he felt as he did.

In this section, you will be asked to tell a story that illustrates some point. The paragraphs below all present narrative experiences that support a point. Read them and then answer the questions that follow.

PARAGRAPHS TO CONSIDER

Heartbreak

¹Bonnie and I had gotten engaged in August, just before she left for college at Penn State. ²A week before Thanksgiving, I drove up to see her as a surprise. ³When I knocked on the door of her dorm room, she was indeed surprised but not in a pleasant way. ⁴She introduced me to her roommate, who looked uncomfortable and quickly left. ⁵I asked Bonnie how classes were going, and at the same time I tugged on the sleeve of my heavy sweater in order to pull it off. ⁶As I was pulling it off, a large poster caught my eye. ⁷It was decorated with paper flowers and yellow ribbon, and it said, "Bonnie and Blake." ⁸"What's going on?" I said. ⁹I stood there stunned and then felt an anger that grew rapidly. ¹⁰"Who is Blake?" I asked. ¹¹Bonnie laughed nervously and said, "What do you want to hear about--my classes or Blake?" ¹²I don't really remember what she then told me, except that Blake was a sophomore math major. ¹³I felt a terrible pain in the pit of my stomach, and I wanted to rest my head on someone's shoulder and cry. ¹⁴I wanted to tear down the sign and run out, but I did nothing. ¹⁵Clumsily I pulled on my sweater again. ¹⁶My knees felt weak, and I barely had control of my body. ¹⁷I opened the room door, and suddenly more than anything I wanted to slam the door shut so hard that the dorm walls would collapse. ¹⁸Instead, I managed to close the door quietly. ¹⁹I walked away understanding what was meant by a broken heart.

A Childhood Disappointment

¹The time I almost won a car when I was ten years old was probably the most disappointing moment of my childhood. ²One hot summer afternoon I was wandering around a local department store, waiting for my mother to finish shopping. ³Near the toy department, I was attracted to a crowd of people gathered around a bright blue car that was on display in the main aisle. ⁴A sign indicated that the car was the first prize in a sweepstakes celebrating the store's tenth anniversary. ⁵The sign also said that a person did not have to buy anything to fill out an entry form. ⁶White entry cards and shiny yellow pencils were scattered on a card table nearby, and the table was just low enough for me to write on, so I filled out a card. ⁷Then, feeling very much like an adult, I slipped my card into the slot of a heavy blue wooden box that rested on another table nearby. ⁸I then proceeded to the toy department, completely forgetting about the car. ⁹However, about a month later, just as I was walking into the house from my first day back at school, the telephone rang. ¹⁰When my mother answered it, a man asked to speak to a Michael Winchester. ¹¹My mother said, "There's a Michael Williams here, but not a Michael Winchester." ¹²He asked, "Is this 862-9715 at 29 Williams Street?" ¹³My mother said, "That's the right number, but this is 29 Winchester Street." ¹⁴She then asked him, "What is this all about?" and he explained to her about the sweepstakes contest. ¹⁵My mother then called me

to ask if I had ever filled out an application for a sweepstakes drawing. [16]I said that I had, and she told me to get on the phone. [17]The man by this time had realized that I had filled in my first name and street name on the line where my full name was to be. [18]He told me I could not qualify for the prize because I had filled out the application incorrectly. [19]For the rest of the day, I cried whenever I thought of how close I had come to winning the car. [20]I am probably fated for the rest of my life to think of the "almost" prize whenever I fill out any kind of contest form.

A Frustrating Job

[1]Working as a baby-sitter was the most frustrating job I ever had. [2]I discovered this fact when my sister asked me to stay with her two sons for the evening. [3]I figured I would get them dinner, let them watch a little TV, and then put them to bed early. [4]The rest of the night I planned to watch TV and collect an easy twenty dollars. [5]It turned out to be anything but easy. [6]First, right before we were about to sit down for a pizza dinner, Rickie let the parakeet out of its cage. [7]This bird is really intelligent and can repeat almost any phrase. [8]The dog started chasing it around the house, so I decided to catch it before the dog did. [9]Rickie and Jeff volunteered to help, following at my heels. [10]We had the bird cornered by the fireplace when Rickie jumped for it and knocked over the hamster cage. [11]Then the bird escaped again, and the hamsters began scurrying around their cage like crazy creatures. [12]The dog had disappeared by this point, so I decided to clean up the hamsters' cage and try to calm them down. [13]While I was doing this, Rickie and Jeff caught the parakeet and put it back in its cage. [14]It was time to return to the kitchen and eat cold pizza. [15]But upon entering the kitchen, I discovered why the dog had lost interest in the bird chase. [16]What was left of the pizza was lying on the floor, and tomato sauce was dripping from the dog's chin. [17]I cleaned up the mess and then served chicken noodle soup and ice cream to the boys. [18]Only at nine o'clock did I get the kids to bed. [19]I then returned downstairs to find that the dog had thrown up pizza on the living-room rug. [20]When I finished cleaning the rug, my sister returned. [21]I took the twenty dollars and told her that she should get someone else next time.

■ Questions

About Unity

1. Which paragraph lacks a topic sentence?

   _____

   Write a topic sentence for the paragraph:

   _____

   _____

   _____

2. Which sentence in ''A Frustrating Job'' should be omitted in the interest of paragraph unity? (*Write the sentence number here.*) _____

About Support

3. What is for you the best (most real and vivid) detail or image in the paragraph ''Heartbreak''?

_____

_____

What is the best detail or image in ''A Childhood Disappointment''?

_____

_____

What is the best detail or image in ''A Frustrating Job''?

_____

_____

4. Which two paragraphs provide details in the form of the actual words used by the participants?

_____

_____

About Coherence

5. Do the three paragraphs use time order or emphatic order to organize details?

_____

6. What are four transition words used in ''A Frustrating Job''?

   a. _____

   b. _____

   c. _____

   d. _____

WRITING A NARRATIVE PARAGRAPH

■ Writing Assignment 1

Write an essay about an experience in which a certain emotion was predominant. The emotion might be fear, pride, satisfaction, embarrassment, or any of the following:

Frustration	Sympathy	Shyness
Love	Bitterness	Disappointment
Sadness	Violence	Happiness
Terror	Surprise	Jealousy
Shock	Nostalgia	Anger
Relief	Loss	Hate
Envy	Silliness	Nervousness

The experience should be limited in time. Note that the three paragraphs presented in this chapter all detail experiences that occurred within relatively short periods. One writer describes a heartbreaking surprise he received the day he visited his girlfriend; another describes the disappointing loss of a prize; the third describes a frustrating night of baby-sitting.

A good way to re-create an event is to include some dialog, as the writers of two of the three paragraphs in this chapter have done. Repeating what you have said or what you have heard someone else say helps make the situation come alive. First, though, be sure to check the section on quotation marks on pages 353–360.

How to Proceed

a   Begin by prewriting. Think of an experience or event in your life in which you felt a certain emotion strongly. Then spend ten minutes freewriting about the experience. Do not worry at this point about such matters as spelling or grammar or putting things in the right order; instead, just try to get down all the details you can think of that seem related to the experience.

b   This preliminary writing will help you decide whether your topic is promising enough to develop further. If it is not, choose another emotion. If it is, do two things:

   ■   First, write your topic sentence, underlining the emotion you will focus on. For example, ''My first day in kindergarten was one of the scariest days of my life.''

   ■   Second, make up a list of all the details involved in the experience. Then arrange these details in time order.

c Using your list of details as a guide, prepare a rough draft of your paper. Use time signals such as *first, then, next, after, while, during,* and *finally* to help connect details as you move from the beginning to the middle to the end of your narrative.

d As you work on the drafts of your paper, refer to the checklist on the inside front cover to make sure that you can answer *Yes* to the questions about unity, support, and coherence. Also use the checklist to edit the next-to-final draft of your paper for sentence-skills mistakes, including spelling.

■ **Writing Assignment 2**

Write a paper that shows, through some experience you have had, the truth *or* falsity of a popular belief. You might write about any one of the following statements or some other popular saying.

Every person has a price.

Haste makes waste.

Don't count your chickens before they're hatched.

A bird in the hand is worth two in the bush.

It isn't what you know, it's who you know.

Borrowing can get you into trouble.

What you don't know won't hurt you.

Keeping a promise is easier said than done.

You never really know people until you see them in an emergency.

If you don't help yourself, nobody will.

An ounce of prevention is worth a pound of cure.

Hope for the best but expect the worst.

Never give advice to a friend.

You get what you pay for.

A stitch in time saves nine.

A fool and his money are soon parted.

There is an exception to every rule.

Nice guys finish last.

Absence makes the heart grow fonder.

Misery loves company.

Never put off till tomorrow what you can do today.

Beauty is only skin-deep.

Begin your narrative paragraph with a topic sentence that expresses your agreement or disagreement with a popular saying. For example, ''My sister learned recently that 'Keeping a promise is easier said than done.' '' Or '' 'Never give advice to a friend' is not always good advice, as I learned after helping a friend reunite with her boyfriend.''

Refer to the suggestions about ''How to Proceed'' on pages 194–195 when doing your paper. Remember that the purpose of your story is to *support* your topic sentence. Feel free to select carefully from and even add to your experience so that the details truly support the point of your story.

■ Writing Assignment 3

Write an account of a memorable personal experience. Make sure that your story has a point, expressed in the first sentence of the paper. If necessary, tailor your narrative to fit your purpose. Use time order to organize your details (*first* this happened; *then* this; *after* that, this; *next,* this; and so on). Concentrate on providing as many specific details as possible so that the reader can really share your experience. Try to make it as vivid for the reader as it was for you when you first experienced it.

You might want to use one of the topics below, or a topic of your own choosing. Regardless, remember that your story must illustrate or support a point stated in the first sentence of your paper.

The first time you felt grown-up

A major decision

A moment you knew you were happy

The occasion of your best or worst date

A time you took a foolish risk

An argument you will never forget

An incident that changed your life

A time when you did or did not do the right thing

Your best or worst holiday, birthday, or other special occasion

A time you learned a lesson or taught one to someone else

An occasion of triumph in sports or some other event

You may want to refer to the suggestions on ''How to Proceed'' in Writing Assignment 1.

■ **Writing Assignment 4**

Imagine that a younger brother or sister, or a young friend, has to make a difficult decision of some kind. Perhaps he or she must decide how to go about preparing for a job interview, whether or not to get help with a difficult class, or what to do about a coworker who is taking money from the cash register. Write a narration from your own experience (or that of someone you know) that will teach a younger person something about the decision he or she must make. In your paragraph, include a comment or two about the lesson your story teaches. You may narrate an experience about any problem young people face, including any of those already mentioned or those listed below.

Should he or she save a little from a weekly paycheck?

Should he or she live at home or move to an apartment with some friends?

How should he or she deal with a group of friends who are involved with drugs, stealing, or both?

■ **Writing Assignment 5**

Writing about a Reading Selection: Read Maya Angelou's article "Adolescent Confusion" on pages 470–472. Most teenagers are, at times, as impulsive and unthinking as Angelou was. Write a narrative about a time during your teenage years when you did something impulsively, with little regard for the possible consequences—something which you later regretted. You may have committed this act because you, like Angelou, wanted to know about something or because you were pressured into it by others.

ARGUING
A POSITION

Most of us know someone who enjoys a good argument. Such a person usually challenges any sweeping statement we might make. ''Why do you say that?'' he or she will ask. ''Give your reasons.'' Our questioner then listens carefully as we cite our reasons, waiting to see if we really do have solid evidence to support our point of view. Such a questioner may make us feel a bit nervous, but we may also feel grateful to him or her for helping us think through our opinions.

The ability to advance sound and compelling arguments is an important skill in everyday life. We can use persuasion to get an extension on a term paper, obtain a favor from a friend, or convince an employer that we are the right person for a job. Understanding persuasion based on clear, logical reasoning can also help us see through the sometimes faulty arguments advanced by advertisers, editors, politicians, and others who try to bring us over to their side.

In this section, you will be asked to argue a position and defend it with a series of solid reasons. You are in a general way doing the same thing — making a point and then supporting it—with all the paragraphs in the book. The difference here is that, in a more direct and formal manner, you will advance a point about which you feel strongly and seek to convince others to agree with you.

PARAGRAPHS TO CONSIDER

Let's Ban Proms

[1]While many students regard proms as peak events in high school life, I believe that high school proms should be banned. [2]One reason is that even before the prom takes place, it causes problems. [3]Teenagers are separated into "the ones who were asked" and "the ones who weren't." [4]Being one of those who weren't asked can be heartbreaking to a sensitive young person. [5]Another pre-prom problem is money. [6]The price of the various items needed can add up quickly to a lot of money. [7]The prom itself can be unpleasant and frustrating, too. [8]At the beginning of the evening, the girls enviously compare dresses while the boys sweat nervously inside their rented suits. [9]During the dance, the couples who have gotten together only to go to the prom have split up into miserable singles. [10]When the prom draws to a close, the popular teenagers drive off happily to other parties while the less-popular ones head home, as usual. [11]Perhaps the main reason proms should be banned, however, is the drinking and driving that go on after the prom is over. [12]Teenagers pile into their cars on their way to "after-proms" and pull out the bottles and cans stashed under the seat. [13]By the time the big night is finally over, at 4 or 5 A.M., students are trying to weave home without encountering the police or a roadside tree. [14]Some of them do not make it, and prom night turns into tragedy. [15]For all these reasons, proms have no place in our schools.

A Terrible Vacation

[1]Despite much advertising to the contrary, taking a cruise is a terrible way to spend a vacation. [2]For one thing, there is too much food. [3]You are force-fed seven times a day: breakfast, midmorning snack, lunch, afternoon punch and pastries, dinner, the midnight buffet, and the 1:30 A.M. pizza in the disco. [4]Also, the waiters will not take "no" for an answer when they bring the food to your table. [5]They think "no" means "give me a medium-sized portion." [6]Another problem with a cruise is that there is too little genuine exercise. [7]The swimming pool is the size of a large bathtub. [8]Three strokes bring you to the other side. [9]And if you want to jog around the deck, you will have to dodge flying Ping-Pong balls and leapfrog over the shuffleboard players as you go. [10]Finally, the shipboard activities are boring. [11]The big event of the afternoon is bingo, and at night, for excitement, there is the Kentucky Derby, complete with little wooden horses and a social director throwing dice to see which one wins. [12]Many people are opposed to gambling anyway, and these games can be offensive to them. [13]If you try to start a conversation on deck with one of the other passengers, you will find that most of them have sent their minds on vacation along with their bodies.

[14]All they are interested in is what kind of suntan lotion you are using or what you think will be served at the next meal. [15]You will soon give up and join them in the chief activity on board--staring at the ocean. [16]So the next time you look through your vacation folders, pick the mountains, the seashore-- anything but a cruise ship. [17]This way, your vacation will expand your mind and your muscles but not your waistline.

Living Alone

[1]Living alone is quite an experience. [2]People who live alone, for one thing, have to learn to do all kinds of tasks by themselves. [3]They must learn--even if they have had no experience--to change fuses, put up curtains and shades, temporarily dam an overflowing toilet, cook a meal, and defrost a refrigerator. [4]When there is no father, husband, mother, or wife to depend on, a person can't fall back on the excuse, "I don't know how to do that." [5]Those who live alone also need the strength to deal with people. [6]Alone, singles must face noisy neighbors, unresponsive landlords, dishonest repair people, and aggressive bill collectors. [7]Because there are no buffers between themselves and the outside world, people living alone have to handle every visitor--friendly or unfriendly--alone. [8]Finally, singles need a large dose of courage to cope with occasional panic and unavoidable loneliness. [9]That weird thump in the night is even more terrifying when there is no one in the next bed or the next room. [10]Frightening weather or unexpected bad news is doubly bad when the worry can't be shared. [11]Even when life is going well, little moments of sudden loneliness can send shivers through the heart. [12]Struggling through such bad times taps into reserves of courage that people may not have known they possessed. [13]Facing everyday tasks, confronting all types of people, and handling panic and loneliness can shape singles into brave, resourceful, and more independent people.

■ Questions

About Unity

1. The topic sentence in "Living Alone" is too broad. Circle the topic sentence below that states accurately what the paragraph is about.
   a. Living alone takes courage.
   b. Living alone can create feelings of loneliness.
   c. Living alone should be avoided.
2. Which sentence in "A Terrible Vacation" should be eliminated in the interest of paragraph unity? (*Write the sentence number here.*) _____

About Support

3. How many reasons are given to support the topic sentence in each paragraph?

    a. In "A Terrible Vacation" ____ one ____ two ____ three ____ four

    b. In "Let's Ban Proms" ____ one ____ two ____ three ____ four

    c. In "Living Alone" ____ one ____ two ____ three ____ four

4. After which sentence in "Let's Ban Proms" are more specific details needed?

    _____

About Coherence

5. Which paragraph uses a combination of time and emphatic order to organize its details?

    _____

6. What are the three main transition words in "Living Alone"?

    a. _____ b. _____ c. _____

Activity

Complete the outline below of "A Terrible Vacation." Summarize in a few words the primary and secondary supporting material that fits under the topic sentence. Two items have been done for you as examples.

Topic sentence: Despite much advertising to the contrary, taking a cruise is a terrible way to spend a vacation.

a. _____

    (1) _____

    (2) _____

b. _____

    (1) _____

    (2) *Little room for jogging* _____

c. _____

    (1) _____

    (2) *Dull conversations with other passengers* _____

    (3) _____

WRITING AN ARGUMENT PARAGRAPH

■ **Writing Assignment 1**

On separate paper, make up brief outlines for any four of the eight statements that follow. Note the example. Make sure that you have three separate and distinct reasons for each statement.

Example   Large cities should outlaw passenger cars.
  a.   Cut down on smog and pollution
  b.   Cut down on noise
  c.   Create more room for pedestrians

1. Condoms should (*or* should not) be made available in schools.

2. _____ (*name a specific sports team*) should win its league championship.

3. Television is one of the best (*or* worst) inventions of this century.

4. _____ are the best (*or* worst) pets.

5. All cigarette and alcohol advertising should be banned.

6. Teenagers make poor parents.

7. _____ is one public figure today who can be considered a hero.

8. This college needs a better _____ (cafeteria *or* library *or* student center *or* grading policy *or* attendance policy).

How to Proceed

a   Decide, perhaps through discussion with your instructor or classmates, which of your outlines would be most promising to develop into a paragraph. Make sure that your supporting points are logical ones that actually back up your topic sentence. Ask yourself in each case, ''Does this item truly support my topic sentence?''

b   Now do some prewriting. Prepare a list of all the details you can think of that might support your point. To begin with, prepare more details than you can actually use. Here, for example, are details generated by the writer of ''Let's Ban Proms'' while working on the paragraph:

Car accidents (most important)	Waste of school money
Drinking after prom	Going with someone you don't like
Competition over dates	License to stay out all night
Preparation for prom cuts into school hours	Separates popular from unpopular
Rejection of not being asked	Expenses
	Parents' interference

c   Decide which details you will use to develop your paragraph. Also, number the details in the order in which you will present them. (You may also want to make an outline of your paragraph at this point.) Because emphatic order (most important reason last) is the most effective way to organize an argument paragraph, be sure to save your most powerful reason for last. Here is how the writer of "Let's Ban Proms" made decisions about details:

8   Car accidents (most important)
7   Drinking after prom
3   Competition over dates
~~Preparation for prom cuts into school hours~~
1   Rejection of not being asked
~~Waste of school money~~
4   Going with someone you don't like
6   License to stay out all night
5   Separates popular from unpopular
2   Expenses
~~Parents' interference~~

d   Develop each reason with specific details. For example, in "Let's Ban Proms," notice how the writer explains how unpleasant the prom can be by describing boys "who sweat nervously" and one-night-only dates splitting up into "miserable singles." The writer also expands the idea of after-prom drinking by describing the "bottles and cans stashed under the seat" and the teenagers "trying to weave home."

e   As you write, imagine that your audience is a jury that will ultimately render a verdict on your argument. Have you presented a convincing case? If *you* were on the jury, would you be favorably impressed with this argument?

f   As you are working on the drafts of your paper, keep the four bases of unity, support, coherence, and sentence skills in mind.

g   Finally, edit the next-to-final draft of your paper for sentence-skills mistakes, including spelling.

■ Writing Assignment 2

Write a paragraph that uses reasons to develop a point of some kind. You may advance and defend a point of your own about which you feel strongly, or you could support any one of the following statements:

1. Junk food should be banned from school cafeterias.
2. Being young is better than being old.
3. Being old is better than being young.
4. Fall can be seen as the saddest season.
5. Many college instructors know their subjects, but some are poor teachers.

6. _____ is a sport that should be banned.

7. _____ is a subject that should be taught in every school.

8. Athletes at schools with national reputations in sports should be paid for their work.

9. _____ is the one material possession that is indispensable in everyday life.

10. A college diploma is (*or* is not) essential for an ambitious person.

Use the suggestions in "How to Proceed" on pages 202–203 as a guide in writing your paragraph.

■ Writing Assignment 3

Write a paragraph in which you take a stand on one of the controversial subjects below. As a lead-in to this writing project, your instructor might give the class a chance to "stand up for what they believe in." One side of the front of the room should be designated *strong agreement* and the other side *strong disagreement,* with the space between for varying intermediate degrees of agreement or disagreement. As the class stands in front of the room, the instructor will read one value statement at a time from the list below, and students will move to the appropriate spot depending on their degree of agreement or disagreement. Some time will be allowed for students, first, to discuss with those near them the reasons they are standing where they are, and second, to state to those on the other end of the scale the reasons for their position.

1. Students should not be required to attend high school.
2. Prostitution should be legalized.
3. Homosexuals and lesbians should not be allowed to teach in schools.
4. The death penalty should exist for certain crimes.
5. Abortion should be legal.
6. Federal prisons should be coed, and prisoners should be allowed to marry.
7. Parents of girls under eighteen should be informed if their daughters receive birth-control aids.
8. The government should set up centers where sick or aged persons can go voluntarily to commit suicide.
9. Any woman on welfare who has more than two illegitimate children should be sterilized.
10. Parents should never hit their children.

Begin your paragraph by writing a sentence that expresses your attitude toward one of these value statements—for example, "I feel that prostitution should be legalized."

Outline the reason or reasons you hold the opinion that you do. Your support may be based on your own experience, the experience of someone you know, or logic. For example, an outline of a paragraph based on one student's logic proceeded as follows:

I feel that prostitution should be legalized for the following reasons:

1. Prostitutes would then have to pay their fair share of income tax.
2. Government health centers would administer regular checkups and thus help prevent the spread of venereal disease.
3. Prostitutes would be able to work openly and independently and would not be subject to exploitation by others.
4. Most of all, prostitutes would no longer be so much regarded as social outcasts--an attitude that is psychologically damaging to those who may already have emotional problems.

Another outline, based on experience, proceeded as follows:

I do not feel that prostitution should be legalized, because of a woman I know who was once a prostitute.

1. The attention Linda received as a prostitute prevented her from seeing and working on her personal problems.
2. She became embittered toward all men, whom she always suspected of wanting to exploit her.
3. She developed a negative self-image and felt that no one could love her.

Use your outline as the basis for writing a paragraph. Be sure to refer to the suggestions on ''How to Proceed'' on pages 202–203.

■ Writing Assignment 4

You have finally met Mr. or Ms. Right—but your parents don't approve of him or her. Specifically, they are against your doing one of the following:

Continuing to see this person

Going steady

Moving in together

Getting married at the end of the school year

Write a letter to your parents explaining in a fully detailed way why you have made your choice. Do your best to convince them that it is a good choice.

■ Writing Assignment 5

Writing about a Reading Selection: Read Garland's selection titled "Let's Really Reform Our Schools" on pages 476–479. Then write a persuasive paragraph in which you agree or disagree with one of her suggested reforms. Your topic sentence may be something simple and direct, like these:

> I strongly agree with Garland's point that attendance should be voluntary in our high schools.

> I disagree with Garland's point that high school students should be required to wear uniforms.

Alternatively, you may want to develop your own paragraph calling for reform in some other area of American life. Your topic sentence might be like one of the following:

> We need to make radical changes in our treatment of homeless people.

> Strong new steps must be taken to control the sale of guns in our country.

> Major changes are needed to keep television from dominating the lives of our children.

PART THREE

ESSAY
DEVELOPMENT

PREVIEW

Part Three moves from the single-paragraph paper to the several-paragraph essay. The differences between a paragraph and an essay are explained and then illustrated with a paragraph that has been expanded into an essay. You are shown how to begin an essay, how to tie its supporting paragraphs together, and how to conclude it. Three student essays are presented, along with questions to increase your understanding of the essay form. Finally, directions on how to plan an essay are followed by a series of essay writing assignments.

WRITING
THE ESSAY

What Is an Essay?

DIFFERENCES BETWEEN AN ESSAY AND A PARAGRAPH

An essay is simply a paper of several paragraphs, rather than one paragraph, supporting a single point. In an essay, subjects can and should be treated more fully than they would be in a single-paragraph paper.

The main idea or point developed in an essay is called the *thesis statement* (rather than, as in a paragraph, the *topic sentence*). The thesis statement appears in the introductory paragraph, and it is then developed in the supporting paragraphs that follow. A short concluding paragraph closes the essay.

THE FORM OF AN ESSAY

The diagram on the next page shows the form of an essay.

Introductory Paragraph

Introduction
Thesis sentence
Plan of development:
Points 1, 2, 3

The *introduction* attracts the reader's interest.
The *thesis sentence* states the main idea advanced in the paper.
The *plan of development* is a list of the points that support the thesis. The points are presented in the order in which they will be developed in the paper.

First Supporting Paragraph

Topic sentence (point 1)
Specific evidence

The *topic sentence* advances the first supporting point for the thesis, and the *specific evidence* in the rest of the paragraph develops that first point.

Second Supporting Paragraph

Topic sentence (point 2)
Specific evidence

The *topic sentence* advances the second supporting point for the thesis, and the *specific evidence* in the rest of the paragraph develops that second point.

Third Supporting Paragraph

Topic sentence (point 2)
Specific evidence

The *topic sentence* advances the third supporting point for the thesis, and the *specific evidence* in the rest of the paragraph develops that third point.

Concluding Paragraph

Summary, conclusion, or both

A *summary* is a brief restatement of the thesis and its main points. A *conclusion* is a final thought or two stemming from the subject of the paper.

A MODEL ESSAY

Gene, the writer of the paragraph on working in an apple plant (page 37), later decided to develop his subject more fully. Here is the essay that resulted.

My Job in an Apple Plant

Introductory paragraph

[1]In the course of working my way through school, I have taken many jobs I would rather forget. [2]I have spent nine hours a day lifting heavy automobile and truck batteries off the end of an assembly belt. [3]I have risked the loss of eyes and fingers working a punch press in a textile factory. [4]I have served as a ward aide in a mental hospital, helping care for brain-damaged men who would break into violent fits at unexpected moments. [5]But none of these jobs was as dreadful as my job in an apple plant. [6]The work was physically hard; the pay was poor; and, most of all, the working conditions were dismal.

First supporting paragraph

[7]First of all, the job made enormous demands on my strength and energy. [8]For ten hours a night, I took cartons that rolled down a metal track and stacked them onto wooden skids in a tractor trailer. [9]Each carton contained twelve heavy cans or bottles of apple juice. [10]A carton shot down the track about every fifteen seconds. [11]I once figured out that I was lifting an average of twelve tons of apple juice every night. [12]When a truck was almost filled, I or my partner had to drag fourteen bulky wooden skids into the empty trailer nearby and then set up added sections of the heavy metal track so that we could start routing cartons to the back of the empty van. [13]While one of us did that, the other performed the stacking work of two men.

Second supporting paragraph

[14]I would not have minded the difficulty of the work so much if the pay had not been so poor. [15]I was paid the minimum wage of that time, two dollars an hour, plus the minimum of a quarter extra for working the night shift. [16]Because of the low salary, I felt compelled to get as much overtime pay as possible. [17]Everything over eight hours a night was time-and-a-half, so I typically worked twelve hours a night. [18]On Friday I would sometimes work straight through until Saturday at noon--eighteen hours. [19]I averaged over sixty hours a week but did not take home much more than $100.

Third supporting paragraph

[20]But even more than the low pay, what upset me about my apple plant job was the working conditions. [21]Our humorless supervisor cared only about his production record for each night and tried to keep the assembly line moving at a breakneck pace. [22]During work I was limited to two ten-minute breaks and an unpaid half hour for lunch. [23]Most of my time was spent outside on the truck loading dock in near-zero-degree temperatures. [24]The steel floors of the trucks were like ice; the quickly penetrating cold made my feet feel like stone. [25]I had no shared interests with the man I loaded cartons with, and so I had to work without companionship on the job. [26]And after the production line shut down and most people left, I had to spend two hours alone scrubbing clean the apple vats, which were coated with a sticky residue.

Concluding paragraph

[27]I stayed on the job for five months, all the while hating the difficulty of the work, the poor money, and the conditions under which I worked. [28]By the time I quit, I was determined never to do such degrading work again.

Important Points about the Essay

INTRODUCTORY PARAGRAPH

An introductory paragraph has certain purposes or functions and can be constructed using various methods.

Purposes of the Introduction

An introductory paragraph should do three things:

1. Attract the reader's *interest*. Using one of the suggested methods of introduction described below can help draw the reader into your paper.

2. Present a *thesis sentence* — a clear, direct statement of the central idea that you will develop in your paper. The thesis statement, like a topic sentence, should have a key word or words that reflect your attitude about the subject. For example, in the essay on the apple plant job, the key word is *dreadful.*

3. Indicate a *plan of development*—a preview of the major points that will support your thesis statement, listed in the order in which they will be presented. In some cases, the thesis statement and plan of development may appear in the same sentence. In some cases, also, the plan of development may be omitted.

Activity

1. In "My Job in an Apple Plant," which sentences are used to attract the reader's interest?

    _____ Sentences 1 to 3   _____1 to 4   _____1 to 5

2. The thesis in "My Job in an Apple Plant" is presented in

    _____ Sentence 4   _____ Sentence 5   _____ Sentence 6

3. The thesis is followed by a plan of development.

    _____ Yes   _____ No

4. Which words in the plan of development announce the three major supporting points in the essay? Write them below.

    a. _____

    b. _____

    c. _____

Common Methods of Introduction

Here are some common methods of introduction. Use any one method, or a combination of methods, to introduce your subject in an interesting way.

1 *Broad statement.* Begin with a broad, general statement of your topic and narrow it down to your thesis statement. Broad, general statements ease the reader into your thesis statement by providing a background for it. In ''My Job in an Apple Plant,'' Gene writes generally on the topic of his worst jobs and then narrows down to a specific worst job.

2 *Contrast.* Start with an idea or situation that is the opposite of the one you will develop. This approach works because your readers will be surprised, and then intrigued, by the contrast between the opening idea and the thesis that follows it. Here is an example of a ''contrast'' introduction:

> When I was a girl, I never argued with my parents about differences between their attitudes and mine. My father would deliver his judgment on an issue, and that was usually the end of the matter. Discussion seldom changed his mind, and disagreement was not tolerated. But the situation is different with today's parents and children. My husband and I have to contend with radical differences between what our children think about a given situation and what we think about it. We have had disagreements with all three of our daughters, Stephanie, Diana, and Gisel.

3 *''Relevance.''* Explain the importance of your topic. If you can convince your readers that the subject applies to them in some way, or is something they should know more about, they will want to continue reading. The introductory paragraph of ''Sports-Crazy America'' (page 217) provides an example of a ''relevance'' introduction.

4 *Anecdote.* Use an incident or brief story. Stories are naturally interesting. They appeal to a reader's curiosity. In your introduction, an anecdote will grab the reader's attention right away. The story should be brief and should be related to your central idea. The incident in the story can be something that happened to you, something that you have heard about, or something that you have read about in a newspaper or magazine. Here is an example of a paragraph that begins with a story:

> The husky man pushes open the door of the bedroom and grins as he pulls out a .38 revolver. An elderly man wearing thin pajamas looks at him and whimpers. In a feeble effort at escape, the old man slides out of his bed and moves to the door of the room. The husky man, still grinning, blocks his way. With the face of a small, frightened animal, the old man looks up and whispers, ''Oh God, please don't hurt me.'' The grinning man then fires four times. The television movie cuts now to a soap commercial, but the little boy

who has been watching the set has begun to cry. Such scenes of direct violence on television must surely be harmful to children for a number of psychological reasons.

5   *Questions.* Ask your readers one or more questions. These questions catch the readers' interest and make them want to read on. Here is an example of a paragraph that begins with questions:

> What would happen if we were totally honest with ourselves? Would we be able to stand the pain of our own self-deception? Would the complete truth be too much for us to bear? Such questions will probably never be answered, for in everyday life we protect ourselves from the onslaught of too much reality. All of us cultivate defense mechanisms that prevent us from seeing and hearing and feeling too much. Included among such defense mechanisms are rationalization, reaction formation, and substitution.

Note, however, that the thesis itself must not be a question.

6   *Quotation.* A quotation can be something you have read in a book or an article. It can also be something that you have heard: a popular saying or proverb (''Never give advice to a friend''); a current or recent advertising slogan (''Reach out and touch someone''); a favorite expression used by your friends or family (''My father always says . . .''). Using a quotation in your introductory paragraph lets you add someone else's voice to your own. Here is an example of a paragraph that begins with a quotation:

> ''Evil,'' wrote Martin Buber, ''is lack of direction.'' In my school days as a fatherless boy, with a mother too confused by her own life to really care for me, I strayed down a number of dangerous paths. Before my eighteenth birthday, I had been a car thief, a burglar, and a drug seller.

SUPPORTING PARAGRAPHS

Most essays have three supporting points, developed in three separate paragraphs. (Some essays will have two supporting points; others, four or more.) Each of the supporting paragraphs should begin with a topic sentence that states the point to be detailed in that paragraph. Just as the thesis provides a focus for the entire essay, the topic sentence provides a focus for each supporting paragraph.

Activity

1. What is the topic sentence for the first supporting paragraph of ''My Job in an Apple Plant''? (*Write the sentence number here.*) _____

2. What is the topic sentence for the second supporting paragraph? _____

3. What is the topic sentence for the third supporting paragraph? _____

TRANSITIONAL SENTENCES

In paragraphs, transitions and other connective devices (pages 75–80) are used to help link sentences. Similarly, in an essay *transitional sentences* are used to help tie the supporting paragraphs together. Such transitional sentences usually occur near the end of one paragraph or the beginning of the next.

In ''My Job in an Apple Plant,'' the first transitional sentence is:

> I would not have minded the difficulty of the work so much if the pay had not been so poor.

In this sentence, the key word *difficulty* reminds us of the point of the first supporting paragraph, while *pay* tells us the point to be developed in the second supporting paragraph.

Activity

Here is the other transitional sentence in ''My Job in an Apple Plant'':

> But even more than the low pay, what upset me about my apple plant job were the working conditions.

Complete the following statement: In the sentence above, the key words _____ echo the point of the second supporting paragraph, and the key words _____ announce the topic of the third supporting paragraph.

CONCLUDING PARAGRAPH

The concluding paragraph often summarizes the essay by briefly restating the thesis and, at times, the main supporting points of the essay. Also, the conclusion brings the paper to a natural and graceful end, sometimes leaving the reader with a final thought on the subject.

Activity

1. Which sentence in the concluding paragraph of ''My Job in an Apple Plant'' restates the thesis and supporting points of the essay? _____

2. Which sentence contains the concluding thought of the essay? _____

Essays to Consider

Read the three student essays below and then answer the questions that follow.

Giving Up a Baby

[1]As I awoke, I overheard a nurse say, "It's a lovely baby boy. [2]How could a mother give him up?" [3]"Be quiet," another voice said. [4]"She's going to wake up soon." [5]Then I heard the baby cry, but I never heard him again. [6]Three years ago, I gave up my child to two strangers, people who wanted a baby but could not have one. [7]I was in pain over my decision, and I can still hear the voices of people who said I was selfish or crazy. [8]But the reasons I gave up my child were important ones, at least to me.

[9]I gave up my baby, first of all, because I was very young. [10]I was only seventeen, and I was unmarried. [11]Because I was so young, I did not yet feel the desire to have and raise a baby. [12]I knew that I would be a child raising a child and that, when I had to stay home to care for the baby, I would resent the loss of my freedom. [13]I might also blame the baby for that loss. [14]In addition, I had not had the experiences in life that would make me a responsible, giving parent. [15]What could I teach my child, when I barely knew what life was all about myself?

[16]Besides my age, another factor in my decision was the problems my parents would have. [17]I had dropped out of high school before graduation, and I did not have a job or even the chance of a job, at least for a while. [18]My parents would have to support my child and me, possibly for years. [19]My mom and dad had already struggled to raise their family and were not well off financially. [20]I knew I could not burden them with an unemployed teenager and her baby. [21]Even if I eventually got a job, my parents would have to help raise my child. [22]They would have to be full-time baby-sitters while I tried to make a life of my own. [23]Because my parents are good people, they would have done all this for me. [24]But I felt I could not ask for such a big sacrifice from them.

[25]The most important factor in my decision was, I suppose, a selfish one. [26]I was worried about my own future. [27]I didn't want to marry the baby's father. [28]I realized during the time I was pregnant that we didn't love each other. [29]My future as an unmarried mother with no education or skills would certainly have been limited. [30]I would be struggling to survive, and I would have to give up for years my dreams of getting a job and my own car and apartment. [31]It is hard to admit, but I also considered the fact that, with a baby, I would not have the social life most young people have. [32]I would not be able to stay out late, go to parties, or feel carefree and irresponsible, for I would always have an enormous responsibility waiting for me at home. [33]With a baby, the future looked limited and insecure.

[34]In summary, thinking about my age, my responsibility to my parents, and my own future made me decide to give up my baby. [35]As I look back today at my decision, I know that it was the right one for me at the time.

Sports-Crazy America

[1]Almost all Americans are involved with sports in some way. [2]They may play basketball or volleyball or go swimming or skiing. [3]They may watch football or basketball games on the high school, college, or professional level. [4]Sports may seem like an innocent pleasure, but it is important to look under the surface. [5]In reality, sports have reached a point where they play too large a part in daily life. [6]They take up too much media time, play too large a role in the raising of children, and give too much power and prestige to athletes.

[7]The overemphasis on sports can be seen most obviously in the vast media coverage of athletic events. [8]It seems as if every bowl game play-off, tournament, trial, bout, race, meet, or match is shown on one television channel or another. [9]On Saturday and Sunday, a check of TV Guide will show almost forty sports programs on UHF and VHF alone, and many more on cable stations. [10]In addition, sports makes up about 30 percent of local news at six and eleven, and network news shows often devote several minutes of world news to major American sports events. [11]Radio offers a full roster of games and a wide assortment of sports talk shows. [12]Furthermore, many daily papers such as USA Today are devoting more and more space to sports coverage, often in an attempt to improve circulation. [13]The paper with the biggest sports section is the one people will buy.

[14]The way we raise and educate our children also illustrates our sports mania. [15]As early as six or seven, kids are placed in little leagues, often to play under screaming coaches and pressuring parents. [16]Later, in high school, students who are singled out by the school and by the community are not those who are best academically but those who are best athletically. [17]And college sometimes seems to be more about sports than about learning. [18]The United States may be the only country in the world where people often think of their colleges as teams first and schools second. [19]The names Penn State, Notre Dame, and Southern Cal mean ''sports'' to the public.

[20]Our sports craziness is especially evident in the prestige given to athletes in the United States. [21]For one thing, we reward them with enormous salaries. [22]In 1990, for example, baseball players averaged $350,000 a year; the average annual salary in the United States is $18,000. [23]Besides their huge salaries, athletes receive the awe, admiration, and sometimes the votes of the public. [24]Kids look up to a Michael Jordan or a Roger Clemens as a true hero, while adults wear the jerseys and jackets of their favorite teams. [25]Ex-players become members of Congress. [26]And an athlete like Monica Seles or Jim Kelly needs to make only one commercial for advertisers to see the sales of a product boom.

[27]Americans are truly mad about sports. [28]Perhaps we like to see the competitiveness we experience in our daily lives acted out on playing fields. [29]Perhaps we need heroes who can achieve clear-cut victories in the space of only an hour or two. [30]Whatever the reason, the sports scene in this country is more popular than ever.

An Interpretation of <u>Lord of the Flies</u>

[1]Modern history has shown us the evil that exists in human beings. [2]Assassinations are common, governments use torture to discourage dissent, and six million Jews were exterminated during World War II. [3]In <u>Lord of the Flies</u>, William Golding describes a group of schoolboys shipwrecked on an island with no authority figures to control their behavior. [4]One of the boys soon yields to dark forces within himself, and his corruption symbolizes the evil in all of us. [5]First, Jack Merridew kills a living creature; then, he rebels against the group leader; and finally, he seizes power and sets up his own murderous society.

[6]The first stage in Jack's downfall is his killing of a living creature. [7]In Chapter 1, Jack aims at a pig but is unable to kill. [8]His upraised arm pauses ''because of the enormity of the knife descending and cutting into living flesh, because of the unbearable blood,'' and the pig escapes. [9]Three chapters later, however, Jack leads some boys on a successful hunt. [10]He returns triumphantly with a freshly killed pig and reports excitedly to the others, ''I cut the pig's throat.'' [11]Yet Jack twitches as he says this, and he wipes his bloody hands on his shorts as if eager to remove the stains. [12]There is still some civilization left in him.

[13]After the initial act of killing the pig, Jack's refusal to cooperate with Ralph shows us that this civilized part is rapidly disappearing. [14]With no adults around, Ralph has made some rules. [15]One is that a signal fire must be kept burning. [16]But Jack tempts the boys watching the fire to go hunting, and the fire goes out. [17]Another rule is that at a meeting, only the person holding a special seashell has the right to speak. [18]In Chapter 5, another boy is speaking when Jack rudely tells him to shut up. [19]Ralph accuses Jack of breaking the rules. [20]Jack shouts: ''Bollocks to the rules! We're strong--we hunt! If there's a beast, we'll hunt it down! We'll close in and beat and beat and beat--!'' [21]He gives a ''wild whoop'' and leaps off the platform, throwing the meeting into chaos. [22]Jack is now much more savage than civilized.

[23]The most obvious proof of Jack's corruption comes in Chapter 8, when he establishes his own murderous society. [24]Insisting that Ralph is not a ''proper chief'' because he does not hunt, Jack asks for a new election. [25]After he again loses, Jack announces, ''I'm going off by myself. . . . Anyone who wants to hunt when I do can come too.'' [26]Eventually, nearly all the boys join Jack's ''tribe.'' [27]Following his example, they paint their faces like savages, sacrifice to ''the beast,'' brutally murder two of their schoolmates, and nearly succeed in killing Ralph as well. [28]Jack has now become completely savage--and so have the others.

[29]Through Jack Merridew, then, Golding shows how easily moral laws can be forgotten. [30]Freed from grown-ups and their rules, Jack learns to kill living things, defy authority, and lead a tribe of murdering savages. [31]Jack's example is a frightening reminder of humanity's potential for evil. [32]The ''beast'' the boys try to hunt and kill is actually within every human being.

■ Questions

1. In which essay does the thesis statement appear in the last sentence of the introductory paragraph?

   _____

2. In the essay on *Lord of the Flies,* which sentence of the introductory paragraph contains the plan of development? _____

3. Which method of introduction is used in "Giving Up a Baby"?
   a. General to narrow   c. Incident or story
   b. Stating importance of topic   d. Questions

4. Complete the following brief outline of "Giving Up a Baby":
   I gave up my baby for three reasons:

   a. _____

   b. _____

   c. _____

5. Which *two* essays use a transitional sentence between the first and second supporting paragraphs?

   _____

   _____

6. *Complete the following statement:* Emphatic order is shown in the last supporting paragraph of "Giving Up a Baby" with the words *most important factor;* in the last supporting paragraph of "Sports-Crazy America " with the words

   _____; in the last supporting paragraph of "An Interpretation of *Lord of the Flies*" with the words _____.

7. Which essay uses time order as well as emphatic order to organize its three supporting paragraphs? _____

8. List four major transitions used in the supporting paragraphs of "An Interpretation of *Lord of the Flies*."

   a. _____   c. _____

   b. _____   d. _____

9. Which *two* essays include a sentence in the concluding paragraph that summarizes the three supporting points?

   _____

   _____

10. Which essay includes two final thoughts in its concluding paragraph?

    _____

Planning the Essay

OUTLINING THE ESSAY

When you write an essay, advance planning is crucial for success. You should plan your essay by outlining in two ways:

1 Prepare a scratch outline. This should consist of a short statement of the thesis followed by the main supporting points for the thesis. Here is Gene's scratch outline for his essay on the apple plant:

Working at an apple plant was my worst job.
1. Hard work
2. Poor pay
3. Bad working conditions

Do not underestimate the value of this initial outline—or the work involved in achieving it. Be prepared to do a good deal of plain hard thinking at this first and most important stage of your paper.

2 Prepare a more detailed outline. The outline form that follows will serve as a guide. Your instructor may ask you to submit a copy of this form either before you actually write an essay or along with your finished essay.

FORM FOR PLANNING AN ESSAY

To write an effective essay, use a form like the one that follows.

	Opening remarks
Introduction	***Thesis statement*** _____
	_____
	Plan of development

Body

Topic sentence 1 _____

_____

Specific supporting evidence

Topic sentence 2 _____

_____

Specific supporting evidence

Topic sentence 3 _____

_____

Specific supporting evidence

Conclusion

Summary, closing remarks, or both

Essay Writing Assignments

Hints: Keep the following points in mind when writing an essay on any of the topics below.

1   Your first step must be to plan your essay. Prepare both a scratch outline and a more detailed outline, as explained on the preceding pages.

2   While writing your essay, use the checklist below to make sure your essay touches all four bases of effective writing.

Base 1: Unity

_____ Clearly stated thesis in the introductory paragraph of your paper

_____ All the supporting paragraphs on target in backing up your thesis

Base 2: Support

_____ Three separate supporting points for your thesis

_____ *Specific* evidence for each of the three supporting points

_____ *Plenty* of specific evidence for each supporting point

Base 3: Coherence

_____ Clear method of organization

_____ Transitions and other connecting words

_____ Effective introduction and conclusion

Base 4: Sentence Skills

_____ Clear, error-free sentences (use the checklist on the inside front cover of this book)

■ 1   Your House or Apartment

Write an essay on the advantages *or* disadvantages (not both) of the house or apartment where you live. In your introductory paragraph, describe briefly the place you plan to write about. End the paragraph with your thesis statement and a plan of development. Here are some suggestions for thesis statements:

> The best features of my apartment are its large windows, roomy closets, and great location.

The drawbacks of my house are its unreliable oil burner, tiny kitchen, and old-fashioned bathroom.

An inquisitive landlord, sloppy neighbors, and platoons of cockroaches came along with our rented house.

My apartment has several advantages, including friendly neighbors, lots of storage space, and a good security system.

■ 2   A Big Mistake

Write an essay about the biggest mistake you made within the past year. Describe the mistake and show how its effects have convinced you that it was the wrong thing to do. For instance, if you write about "taking on a full-time job while going to school" as your biggest mistake, show the problems it caused. (You might discuss such matters as low grades, constant exhaustion, and poor performance at work, for example.)

To get started, make a list of all the things you did last year that, with hindsight, now seem to be mistakes. Then choose the action that has had the most serious consequences for you. Make a brief outline to guide you as you write, as in the examples below.

Thesis: Separating from my husband was the worst mistake I made last year.
1. Children have suffered
2. Financial troubles
3. Loneliness

Thesis: Buying a used car to commute to school was the worst mistake I made last year.
1. Unreliable--late for class or missed class
2. Expenses for insurance, repairs
3. Led to an accident

■ 3   A Valued Possession

Write an essay about a valued material possession. Here are some suggestions:

Car	Appliance
Portable radio	Cassette deck
TV set	Photograph album
Piece of furniture	Piece of clothing
Piece of jewelry	Stereo system (car or home)
Camera	Piece of hobby equipment

In your introductory paragraph, describe the possession: tell what it is, when and where you got it, and how long you have owned it. Your thesis statement should center on the idea that there are several reasons this possession is so important to you. In each of your supporting paragraphs, provide details to back up one of the reasons.

For example, here is a brief outline of an essay written about a leather jacket:

Thesis: My favorite garment is my black leather jacket.
1. It is comfortable.
2. It wears well.
3. It makes me look and feel good.

■ 4 Summarizing a Selection

Write an essay in which you summarize three of the study skills described in the selection ''Power Learning'' on pages 483–489. Summarizing involves condensing material by highlighting main points and key supporting details. You can eliminate minor details and most examples given in the original material. You should avoid using the exact language of the original material; put the ideas into your own words.

The introductory paragraph of the essay and suggested topic sentences for the supporting paragraphs are provided below. In addition to developing the supporting paragraphs, you should write a brief conclusion for the essay.

Introductory Paragraph

Using Study Skills

Why do some students in a college class receive A grades, while others get D's and F's? Are some people just naturally smarter? Are other students doomed to failure? Motivation--willingness to do the work--is a factor in good grades. But the main difference between successful and unsuccessful students is that the ones who do well have mastered the specific skills needed to handle college work. Fortunately, these skills can be learned by anyone. Doing well in college depends on knowing how to . . . *[Complete this sentence with the three study skills you decide to write about.]*

Suggested Topic Sentences for the Supporting Paragraphs (Choose Any Three)

Time control is one aid to success as a student. . . .

Another aid is the use of memory techniques. . . .

Knowing how to concentrate is another essential skill. . . .

Studying a textbook effectively is another key to success. . . .

Perhaps the most crucial step of all is effective classroom note-taking. . . .

■ 5   How Study Skills Help

You may already be practicing some of the study skills described in "Power Learning" (pages 483–489). If so, write an essay on how study skills are helping you to succeed in school. Your thesis might be, "Study skills are helping me to succeed in college." You could organize the essay by describing, in separate paragraphs, how three different study skills have improved your work. Your topic sentences might be similar to these:

> First of all, time control has helped me to make the best use of my time.
>
> In addition, taking good notes in class has enabled me to do well in discussions and on tests.
>
> Finally, I can study a textbook effectively now.

Alternatively, begin applying some of the techniques and be prepared to write an essay at a later time on how the study skills helped you become a better student. Or you might want to write about three study techniques of your own that have helped you succeed in your studies.

■ 6   Single Life

Write an essay on the advantages or drawbacks of single life. To get started, make a list of all the advantages and drawbacks you can think of for single life. Advantages might include:

> Fewer expenses
> Fewer responsibilities
> More personal freedom
> More opportunities to move or travel

Drawbacks might include:

> Parental disapproval
> Being alone at social events
> No companion for shopping, movies, and so on
> Sadness at holiday time

After you make up two lists, select the thesis for which you feel you have more supporting material. Then organize your material into a scratch outline. Be sure to include an introduction, a clear topic sentence for each supporting paragraph, and a conclusion.

Alternatively, write an essay on the advantages or drawbacks of married life. Follow the directions given above.

■ 7 Influences on Your Writing

Are you as good a writer as you want to be? Write an essay analyzing the reasons you have become a good writer or explaining why you are not as good as you'd like to be. Begin by considering some factors that may have influenced your level of writing ability.

> *Your family background:* Did you see people writing at home? Did your parents respect and value the ability to write?
>
> *Your school experience:* Did you have good writing teachers? Did you have a history of failure or success with writing? Was writing fun, or was it a chore? Did your school emphasize writing?
>
> *Social influences:* How did your school friends do at writing? What were your friends' attitudes toward writing? What feelings about writing did you pick up from TV or the movies?

You might want to organize your essay by describing the three greatest influences on your writing skill (or lack of writing skill). Show how each of these has contributed to the present state of your writing.

■ 8 A Major Decision

All of us come to various crossroads in our lives — times when we must make an important decision about which course of action to follow. Think about a major decision you have had to make (or one you are planning to make). Then write an essay on the reasons for your decision. In your introduction, describe the decision you reached. Each of the body paragraphs that follow should fully explain one of the reasons for your decision. Here are some examples of major decisions that often confront people:

> Enrolling in or dropping out of college
>
> Accepting or quitting a job
>
> Getting married or divorced
>
> Breaking up with a boyfriend or girlfriend
>
> Having a baby
>
> Moving away from home

Student papers on this topic include the essay on page 216 and the paragraphs on pages 47–48.

■ 9 Reviewing a TV Show or Movie

Write an essay about a television show or movie you have seen very recently. The thesis of your essay will be that the show (or movie) has both good and bad features. (If you are writing about a TV series, be sure that you evaluate only one episode.)

In your first supporting paragraph, briefly summarize the show or movie. Don't get bogged down in small details here; just describe briefly the major characters and give the highlights of the action.

In your second supporting paragraph, explain what you feel are the best features of the show or movie. Listed below are some examples of good features you might write about:

Suspenseful, ingenious, or realistic plot

Good acting

Good scenery or special effects

Surprise ending

Good music

Believable characters

In your third supporting paragraph, explain what you feel are the worst features of the show or movie. Here are some possibilities:

Farfetched, confusing, or dull plot

Poor special effects

Bad acting

Cardboard characters

Unrealistic dialog

Remember to cover only a few features in each paragraph; do not try to include everything.

■ 10 Good Qualities

We are often quick to point out a person's flaws, saying, for example, ''That instructor is conceited,'' ''My boss has no patience,'' or ''My sister is lazy.'' We are usually equally hard on ourselves; we constantly analyze our own faults. We rarely, though, spend as much time thinking about another person's, or our own, good qualities. Write an essay on the good qualities of a particular person. The person might be an instructor, a job supervisor, a friend, a relative, some other person you know well, or even yourself.

In your introductory paragraph, give some brief background information about the person you are describing. And include in your thesis statement a plan of development that names the three qualities you will write about. Here are several suggestions:

Patience, fairness, and kindness are my boss's best qualities.

My boyfriend is hardworking, ambitious, and determined.

Our psychology instructor has a good sense of humor, a strong sense of justice, and a genuine interest in his students.

When planning your paper, you may find it helpful to look at the positive qualities included in the list on page 132.

■ 11   Your High School

Imagine that you are an outside consultant called in as a neutral observer to examine the high school you attended. After your visit, you must send the school board a five-paragraph letter in which you describe the most striking features (good, bad, or a combination of both) of the school and the evidence for each of these features.

In order to write the letter, you may want to think about the following features of your high school:

Attitude of the teachers, student body, or administration

Condition of the buildings, classrooms, recreational areas, and so on

Curriculum

How classes are conducted

Extracurricular activities

Crowded or uncrowded conditions

Be sure to include an introduction, a clear topic sentence for each supporting paragraph, and a conclusion.

PART FOUR
SENTENCE SKILLS

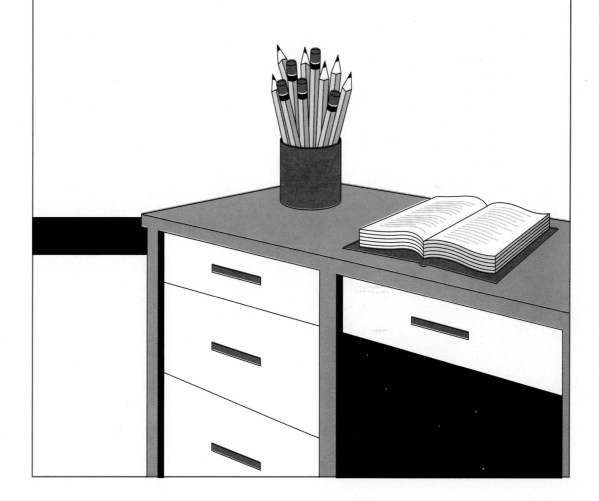

PREVIEW

As explained in Part One, there are four steps, or bases, in effective writing. Part Four is concerned with the *fourth step: the ability to write clear, error-free sentences.* Important sentence skills appear under the general headings "Grammar," "Mechanics," "Punctuation," and "Word Use." "Word Use" includes a chapter on sentence variety which helps develop your sense of the various options and methods available for composing sentences. Finally, there is a "Practice" section which provides editing tests to reinforce many basic writing skills and to give you some experience in proofreading.

SUBJECTS AND VERBS

The basic building blocks of English sentences are subjects and verbs. Understanding them is an important first step toward mastering a number of sentence skills.

Every sentence has a subject and a verb. Who or what the sentence speaks about is called the <u>subject</u>; what the sentence says about the subject is called the <u>verb</u>.

The <u>children</u> <u>laughed</u>.
Several <u>branches</u> <u>fell</u>.
Most <u>students</u> <u>passed</u> the test.
That <u>man</u> <u>is</u> a crook.

A SIMPLE WAY TO FIND A SUBJECT

To find a subject, ask *who* or *what* the sentence is about. As shown below, your answer is the subject.

Who is the first sentence about? <u>Children</u>
What is the second sentence about? Several <u>branches</u>
Who is the third sentence about? Most <u>students</u>
Who is the fourth sentence about? That <u>man</u>

A SIMPLE WAY TO FIND A VERB

To find a verb, ask what the sentence *says about* the subject. As shown below, your answer is the verb.

What does the first sentence *say about* the children? They laughed.

What does the second sentence *say about* the branches? They fell.

What does the third sentence *say about* the students? They passed.

What does the fourth sentence *say about* that man? He is (a crook).

b) A second way to find the verb is to put *I, you, he, she, it,* or *they* in front of the word you think is a verb. If the result makes sense, you have a verb. For example, you could put *they* in front of *laughed* in the first sentence above, with the result, *they laughed,* making sense. Therefore you know that *laughed* is a verb. You could use *they* or *he* to test the other verbs as well.

c) Finally, it helps to remember that most verbs show action. In the sentences already considered, the three action verbs are *laughed, fell,* and *passed.* Certain other verbs, known as *linking verbs,* do not show action. They do, however, give information about the subject. In "That man is a crook," the linking verb *is* tells us that the man is a crook. Other common linking verbs include *am, are, was, were, feel, appear, look, become,* and *seem.*

Activity

In each of the following sentences, draw one line under the subject and two lines under the verb.

1. The heavy purse cut into my shoulder.
2. Small stones pinged onto the windshield.
3. The test directions confused the students.
4. Cotton shirts feel softer than polyester ones.
5. The fog rolled into the cemetery.
6. Sparrows live in the eaves of my porch.
7. A green bottle fly stung her on the ankle.
8. Every other night, garbage trucks rumble down my street on their way to the river.
9. The family played badminton and volleyball, in addition to a game of softball, at the picnic.
10. With their fingers, the children drew pictures on the steamed window.

MORE ABOUT SUBJECTS AND VERBS

1 A pronoun (a word like *he, she, it, we, you,* or *they* used in place of a noun) can serve as the subject of a sentence. For example:

He seems like a lonely person.
They both like to gamble.

Without a surrounding context (so that we know who *He* or *They* refers to), the sentences may not seem clear, but they *are* complete.

2 A sentence may have more than one verb, more than one subject, or several subjects and verbs:

My heart skipped and pounded.
The radio and tape player were stolen from the car.
Dave and Ellen prepared the report together and presented it to the class.

3 The subject of a sentence never appears within a prepositional phrase. A prepositional phrase is simply a group of words that begins with a preposition. Following is a list of common prepositions:

about	before	by	inside	over
above	behind	during	into	through
across	below	except	of	to
among	beneath	for	off	toward
around	beside	from	on	under
at	between	in	onto	with

Cross out prepositional phrases when looking for the subject of a sentence.

Under my pillow I found a quarter left by the Tooth Fairy.
One of the yellow lights at the school crossing began flashing.
The funny pages of the newspaper disappeared.
In spite of my efforts, Bob dropped out of school.
During a rainstorm, I sat in my car reading magazines.

4 Many verbs consist of more than one word. Here, for example, are some of the many forms of the verb *smile*.

smile	smiled	should smile
smiles	were smiling	will be smiling
does smile	have smiled	can smile
is smiling	had smiled	could be smiling
are smiling	had been smiling	must have smiled

Notes

a Words like *not, just, never, only,* and *always* are not part of the verb, although they may appear within the verb.

Larry did not finish the paper before class.
The road was just completed only last week.

b No verb preceded by *to* is ever the verb of a sentence.

My car suddenly began to sputter on the freeway.
I swerved to avoid a squirrel on the road.

c No *-ing* word by itself is ever the verb of a sentence. (It may be part of the verb, but it must have a helping verb in front of it.)

They leaving early for the game. (*not* a sentence, because the verb is not complete)
They are leaving early for the game. (a sentence)

Activity

Draw a single line under the subjects and a double line under the verbs in the following sentences. Be sure to include all parts of the verb.

1. A burning odor from the wood saw filled the room.
2. At first, sticks of gum always feel powdery on your tongue.
3. Vampires and werewolves are repelled by garlic.

4. Three people in the long bank line looked impatiently at their watches.
5. The driving rain had pasted wet leaves all over the car.
6. She has decided to buy a condominium.
7. The trees in the mall were glittering with tiny white lights.
8. The puppies slipped and tumbled on the vinyl kitchen floor.
9. Tony and Lola ate at Pizza Hut and then went to a movie.
10. We have not met our new neighbors in the apartment building.

■ Review Test

Draw a single line under subjects and a double line under verbs. Crossing out prepositional phrases may help you find the subjects.

1. A cloud of fruit flies hovered over the bananas.
2. Candle wax dripped onto the table and hardened into pools.
3. Nick and Fran are both excellent Frisbee players.
4. The leaves of my dying rubber plant resembled limp brown rags.
5. During the first week of vacation, Ken slept until noon every day.
6. They have just decided to go on a diet together.
7. Psychology and word processing are my favorite subjects.
8. The sofa in the living room has not been cleaned for over a year.
9. The water stains on her suede shoes did not disappear with brushing.
10. Fred stayed in bed too long and, as a result, arrived late for work.

SENTENCE FRAGMENTS

Introductory Project

Every sentence must have a subject and a verb and must express a complete thought. A word group that lacks a subject or a verb and that does not express a complete thought is a fragment.

    Listed below are a number of fragments and sentences. See if you can complete the statement that explains each fragment.

1. People. *Fragment*
   People gossip. *Sentence*

   "People" is a fragment because, while it has a subject (*People*), it lacks a ___*verb*___ (*gossip*) and so does not express a complete thought.

2. Wrestles. *Fragment*
   Tony wrestles. *Sentence*

   "Wrestles" is a fragment because, while it has a verb (*Wrestles*), it lacks a ___*subject*___ (*Tony*) and so does not express a complete thought.

3. Drinking more than anyone else at the bar. *Fragment*
   Grandmother was drinking more than anyone else at the bar. *Sentence*

   "Drinking more than anyone else at the bar" is a fragment because it lacks a ___*subject*___ (*Grandmother*) and also part of the ___*verb*___ (*was*) and so does not express a complete thought.

4. When Lola turned eighteen. *Fragment*
   When Lola turned eighteen, she got her own apartment. *Sentence*

   "When Lola turned eighteen" is a fragment because we want to know *what happened when* Lola turned eighteen. The word group does not follow through and ___*does not express a complete thought*___

Answers are on page 573.

WHAT ARE SENTENCE FRAGMENTS?

Every sentence must have a subject and a verb and must express a complete thought. A word group that lacks a subject or a verb and that does not express a complete thought is a *fragment*. The most common types of fragments are:

1 Dependent-word fragments
2 *-ing* and *to* fragments
3 Added-detail fragments
4 Missing-subject fragments

Once you understand the specific kind or kinds of fragments that you might write, you should be able to eliminate them from your writing. The following pages explain all four fragment types.

DEPENDENT-WORD FRAGMENTS

Some word groups that begin with a dependent word are fragments. Here is a list of common dependent words:

Dependent Words		
after	if, even if	when, whenever
although, though	in order that	where, wherever
as	since	whether
because	that, so that	which, whichever
before	unless	while
even though	until	who, whoever
how	what, whatever	whose

Whenever you start a sentence with one of these words, you must be careful that a fragment does not result.

The word group beginning with the dependent word *After* in the example below is a fragment.

After I learned the price of new cars. I decided to keep my old Buick.

A *dependent statement* — one starting with a dependent word like *After* — cannot stand alone. It depends on another statement to complete the thought. "After I learned the price of new cars" is a dependent statement. It leaves us hanging. We expect in the same sentence to find out *what happened after* the writer learned the price of new cars. When a writer does not follow through and complete a thought, a fragment results.

To correct the fragment, simply follow through and complete the thought:

After I learned the price of new cars, I decided to keep my old Buick.

Remember, then, that *dependent statements by themselves are fragments.* They must be attached to a statement that makes sense standing alone.

Here are two other examples of dependent-word fragments:

My daughter refused to stop smoking. Unless I quit also.
Bill asked for a loan. Which he promised to pay back in two weeks.

"Unless I quit also" is a fragment; it does not make sense standing by itself. We want to know in the same statement *what would not happen unless* the writer quit also. The writer must complete the thought. Likewise, "Which he promised to pay back in two weeks" is not in itself a complete thought. We want to know in the same statement what *which* refers to.

Correcting a Dependent-Word Fragment

In most cases you can correct a dependent-word fragment by attaching it to the sentence that comes after it or the sentence that comes before it:

After I learned the price of new cars, I decided to keep my old Buick.
(*The fragment has been attached to the sentence that comes after it.*)
My daughter refused to quit smoking unless I quit also.
(*The fragment has been attached to the sentence that comes before it.*)
Bill asked for a loan which he promised to pay back in two weeks.
(*The fragment has been attached to the sentence that comes before it.*)

Another way of correcting a dependent-word fragment is simply to eliminate the dependent word by rewriting the sentence:

I learned the price of new cars and decided to keep my old Buick.
She wanted me to quit also.
He promised to pay it back in two weeks.

Do not use this second method of correction too frequently, however, for it may cut down on interest and variety in your writing style.

Notes

1   Use a comma if a dependent-word group comes at the beginning of a sentence (see also page 363):

After I learned the price of new cars, I decided to keep my old Buick.

However, do not generally use a comma if the dependent-word group comes at the end of a sentence:

My daughter refused to stop smoking unless I quit also.
Bill asked for a loan which he promised to pay back in two weeks.

2   Sometimes the dependent words *who, that, which,* or *where* appear not at the very start, but near the start, of a word group. A fragment often results:

The town council decided to put more lights on South Street. <u>A place where several people have been mugged.</u>

''A place where several people have been mugged'' is not in itself a complete thought. We want to know in the same statement *where the place was* that several people were mugged. The fragment can be corrected by attaching it to the sentence that comes before it:

The town council decided to put more lights on South Street, a place where several people have been mugged.

Activity 1

Turn each of the following dependent-word groups into a sentence by adding a complete thought. Put a comma after the dependent-word group if a dependent word starts the sentence.

Examples   Although I arrived in class late
Although I arrived in class late, I still did well on the test.

The little boy who plays with our daughter
The little boy who plays with our daughter just came down with

German measles.

1. Because the weather is bad

   Because the weather is bad, the picnic was cancelled.

   _____

2. If I lend you twenty dollars

   If I lend you twenty dollars, don't bother me anymore.

   _____

3. The car that we bought

   The car that we bought did not passed inspection.

   _____

4. Since I was tired

   Since I was tired, my appointments were rescheduled.

   _____

5. Before the instructor entered the room

   Before the instructor entered the room, I spitted the gum.

   _____

Activity 2

<u>Underline</u> the dependent-word fragment or fragments in each of the five items below. Then correct each fragment by attaching it to the sentence that comes before or the sentence that comes after it — whichever sounds more natural. Put a comma after the dependent-word group if it starts the sentence.

1. <u>Whenever our front and back doors are open.</u> The air current causes the back door to slam shut. The noise makes everyone in the house jump.

   Whenever our front and back doors are open, the air current causes
   the back door to slam shut.

2. Bill always turns on the radio in the morning to hear the news. He wants to be sure that World War III has not started. <u>Before he gets on with his day.</u>

   He wants to be sure that World War III has not started before he
   gets on with his day.

   _____

LACK: CARECEN -CARECER DE

3. Since the line at the Motor Vehicle Bureau crawls at a snail's pace. Fred waited two hours there. When there was only one person left in front of him. The office closed for the day.

   Since the line at the Motor Vehicle Bureau crawls at a snail's pace, Fred waited two hours there.

4. My dog ran in joyous circles on the wide beach. Until she found a dead fish. Before I had a chance to drag her away. She began sniffing and nudging the smelly remains.

   My dog ran in joyous circles on the wide beach until she found a dead fish.

5. When the air conditioner broke down. The temperature was over ninety degrees. I then found an old fan. Which turned out to be broken also.

   When the air conditioner broke down, the temperature was over ninety degrees.

-ING AND *TO* FRAGMENTS

When an *-ing* word appears at or near the start of a word group, a fragment may result. Such fragments often lack a subject and part of the verb. Underline the word groups in the examples below that contain *-ing* words. Each is a fragment.

Example 1

I spent almost two hours on the phone yesterday. Trying to find a garage to repair my car. Eventually I had to have it towed to a garage in another town.

Example 2

Maggie was at first very happy with the blue sports car she had bought for only five hundred dollars. Not realizing until a week later that the car averaged seven miles per gallon of gas.

Example 3

He looked forward to the study period at school. It being the only time he could sit unbothered and dream about his future. He imagined himself as a lawyer with lots of money and women to spend it on.

People sometimes write *-ing* fragments because they think the subject in one sentence will work for the next word group as well. Thus, in the first example, the writer thinks that the subject *I* in the opening sentence will also serve as the subject for "Trying to find a garage to repair my car." But the subject must actually be *in* the sentence.

Correcting *-ing* Fragments

1   Attach the *-ing* fragment to the sentence that comes before it or the sentence that comes after it, whichever makes sense. Example 1 could read: "I spent two hours on the phone yesterday, trying to find a garage to repair my car."

2   Add a subject and change the *-ing* verb part to the correct form of the verb. Example 2 could read: "She realized only a week later that the car averaged seven miles per gallon of gas."

3   Change *being* to the correct form of the verb *be* (*am, are, is, was, were*). Example 3 could read: "It was the only time he could sit unbothered and dream about his future."

Correcting *to* Fragments

When *to* appears at or near the start of a word group, a fragment sometimes results:

I plan on working overtime. To get this job finished. Otherwise, my boss may get angry at me.

The second word group here is a fragment and can be corrected by adding it to the preceding sentence:

I plan on working overtime to get this job finished.

Activity 1

Underline the *-ing* fragment in each of the three items that follow. Then make it a sentence by rewriting it, using the method described in parentheses.

Example   A thunderstorm was brewing. A sudden breeze shot through the windows. Driving the stuffiness out of the room.
(Add the fragment to the preceding sentence.)

A sudden breeze shot through the windows, driving the stuffiness

out of the room.

(In the example, a comma is used to set off "driving the stuffiness out of the room," which is extra material placed at the end of the sentence.)

1. <u>Sweating under his heavy load</u>. Brian staggered up the stairs to his apartment. He felt as though his legs were crumbling beneath him.
   (Add the fragment to the sentence that comes after it.)

   Sweating under his heavy load, Brian staggered up the stairs to his apartment.

2. He works ten hours a day. Then <u>going</u> to class for three hours. It is no wonder he writes sentence fragments.
   (Correct the fragment by adding the subject *he* and changing *going* to the proper form of the verb, *goes.*)

   He goes to class for three hours.

3. Charlotte loved the movie *Gone with the Wind,* but Clyde hated it. His chief objection <u>being</u> that it lasted four hours.
   (Correct the fragment by changing *being* to the proper verb form, *was.*)

   His chief objection was that it lasted four hours.

Activity 2

Underline the *-ing* or *to* fragment or fragments in each of the five items that follow. Then rewrite each, correcting the fragments by using one of the three methods of correction described on page 242.

1. A mysterious package arrived on my porch yesterday. <u>Bearing</u> no return address. I half expected to find a bomb inside.

   A mysterious package arrived on my porch yesterday, bearing no return address.

2. Jack bundled up and went outside on the bitterly cold day. <u>To saw wood for his fireplace.</u> He returned half frozen with only two logs.

   Jack bundled up and went outside on the bitterly cold day to saw wood for his fireplace.

3. <u>Looking tired and drawn.</u> The little girl's parents sat in the waiting room. The operation would be over in a few minutes.

   The parents looked tired and drawn.

4. <u>Sighing with resignation.</u> Jill switched on her television set. She knew that the picture would be snowy and crackling with static. <u>Her house being in a weak reception area.</u>

    Sighing with resignation Jill switched on her television set.

    Her house was in a weak reception area

5. <u>Jabbing the ice with a screwdriver.</u> Bill attempted to speed up the defrosting process in his freezer. However, he used too much force. The result <u>being</u> a freezer compartment riddled with holes.

    Bill jabbed the ice with a screwdriver.

    The result was a freezer compartment riddled with holes.

ADDED-DETAIL FRAGMENTS

Added-detail fragments lack a subject and a verb. They often begin with one of the following words:

also	except	including
especially	for example	such as

See if you can locate and underline the one added-detail fragment in each of the examples that follow:

Example 1

I love to cook and eat Italian food. <u>Especially spaghetti and lasagna.</u> I make everything from scratch.

Example 2

The class often starts late. <u>For example, yesterday at quarter after nine instead of at nine sharp.</u> Today the class started at five after nine.

Example 3

He failed a number of courses before he earned his degree. <u>Among</u> them, English I, Economics, and General Biology.

People often write added-detail fragments for much the same reason they write -*ing* fragments. They think the subject and verb in one sentence will serve for the next word group as well. But the subject and verb must be in *each* word group.

Correcting Added-Detail Fragments

1 Attach the fragment to the complete thought that precedes it. Example 1 could read: "I love to cook and eat Italian food, especially spaghetti and lasagna."

2 Add a subject and a verb to the fragment to make it a complete sentence. Example 2 could read: "The class often starts late. For example, yesterday it began at quarter after nine instead of at nine sharp."

3 Change words as necessary to make the fragment part of the preceding sentence. Example 3 could read: "Among the courses he failed before he earned his degree were English I, Economics, and General Biology."

Activity 1

Underline the fragment in each of the three items below. Then make it a sentence by rewriting it, using the method described in parentheses.

Example I am always short of pocket money. <u>Especially for everyday items like magazines and sodas.</u> Luckily my friends often have change.
(Add the fragment to the preceding sentence.)

I am always short of pocket money, especially for everyday items

like magazines and sodas.

1. Nina is trying hard for a promotion. <u>For example, through night classes and a Dale Carnegie course.</u> She is also working overtime for no pay.
(Correct the fragment by adding the subject and verb *she is taking.*)

She is taking night classes and a Dale Carnegie course

2. I could feel Bill's anger building. <u>Like a land mine ready to explode.</u> I was silent because I didn't want to be the one to set it off.
(Add the fragment to the preceding sentence.)

I could feel Bill's anger building like a land mine ready

to explode.

3.   We went on vacation without several essential items. <u>Among other things, our</u>
     <u>sneakers and sweat jackets.</u>
     (Correct the fragment by adding the subject and verb *we forgot.*)

     We forgot our sneakers and sweat jackets.

     _____

Activity 2

Underline the added-detail fragment in each of the five items below. Then rewrite
that part of the item needed to correct the fragment. Use one of the three methods
of correction described above.

1.   It's always hard for me to get up for work. <u>Especially</u> on Mondays after a
     holiday weekend. However, I always wake up early on free days.

     It's always hard for me to get up for work especially on Mondays
     after a holiday weekend.

2.   Tony has enormous endurance. <u>For example</u>, the ability to run five miles in
     the morning and then play basketball all afternoon.

     Tony has the ability to run five miles in the morning
     and then play basketball all afternoon.

3.   A counselor gives you a chance to talk about your problems. <u>Whether</u> with
     your family or the boss at work. You learn how to cope better with life.

     Whether with your family or the boss at work, you learn how
     to cope better with life.

4.   Fred and Martha do most of their shopping through mail-order catalogs.
     Especially the Sears and J. C. Penney catalogs.

     Fred and Martha do most of their shopping through mail-order catalogs.
     Especially they shop through Sears and J. C. Penney catalogs

5.   One of my greatest joys in life is eating desserts. Such as cherry cheesecake
     and vanilla cream puffs. Almond fudge cake makes me want to dance.

     One of my greatest joys in life is eating desserts. I love eating cherry
     cheesecake and vanilla cream puffs.

MISSING-SUBJECT FRAGMENTS

In each example below, underline the word group in which the subject is missing.

Example 1

Patino   ~~the truck~~

The truck skidded on the rain-slick highway. <u>But missed a telephone pole on</u>
<u>the side of the road.</u>

Example 2

                                                           she

Michelle tried each of the appetizers on the table. <u>And then found that, when</u>
<u>the dinner arrived, her appetite had gone.</u>

People write missing-subject fragments because they think the subject in one
sentence will apply to the next word group as well. But the subject, as well as the
verb, must be in each word group to make it a sentence.

Correcting Missing-Subject Fragments

1   Attach the fragment to the preceding sentence. Example 1 could read: "The
truck skidded on the rain-slick highway but missed a telephone pole on the
side of the road."

2   Add a subject (which can often be a pronoun standing for the subject in the
preceding sentence). Example 2 could read: "She then found that, when the
dinner arrived, her appetite had gone."

Activity

Underline the missing-subject fragment in each of the following three items. Then
rewrite that part of the item needed to correct the fragment. Use one of the two
methods of correction described above.

1.   I tried on an old suit hanging in our basement closet. And discovered, to my
surprise, that it was too tight to button.

I tried on an old suit hanging in our basement closet and
discovered, to my surprise, that it was too tight to button

2. When Mary had a sore throat, friends told her to gargle with salt water. Or suck on an ice cube. The worst advice she got was to avoid swallowing.

   When Mary had a sore throat, friends told her to gargle with salt water or suck on an ice cube.

3. One of my grade-school teachers embarrassed us with her sarcasm. Also, seated us in rows from the brightest student to the dumbest. I can imagine the pain the student in the last seat must have felt.

   One of my grade-school teachers embarrassed us with her sarcasm. She, also, seated us in rows from the brightest student to the dumbest.

A Review: How to Check for Sentence Fragments

1 Read your paper aloud from the *last* sentence to the *first*. You will be better able to see and hear whether each word group you read is a complete thought.

2 Ask yourself of any word group you think is a fragment: Does this contain a subject and a verb and express a complete thought?

3 More specifically, be on the lookout for the most common fragments:

- Dependent-word fragments (starting with words like *after, because, since, when,* and *before*)
- *-ing* and *to* fragments (*-ing* or *to* at or near the start of a word group)
- Added-detail fragments (starting with words like *for example, such as, also,* and *especially*)
- Missing-subject fragments (a verb is present but not the subject)

■ Review Test 1

Turn each of the following word groups into a complete sentence. Use the spaces provided.

Example   With sweaty palms
With sweaty palms, I walked in for the job interview.

Even when it rains
The football teams practice even when it rains.

1. When the alarm sounded
   everybody left the building.

2. In order to save some money
   In order to save some money the company laid off 5 people.

3. Was late for the game
   Even though the referee showed up ready he was late for the game.

4. To pass the course
   To pass the course I need a B plus.

5. Peter, who is very impatient
   Peter, who is very impatient, did not wait for the other players.

6. During the holiday season
   Dad and mom are very stingy during the holiday season.

7. The store where I worked
   Mark visited me at the store where I worked.

8. Before the movie started
   Before the movie started, we bought the candy.

9. Down in the basement
   Every one who feared the storm went down in the basement.

10. Feeling very confident
    I just can't help feeling very confident.

■ Review Test 2

Each word group in the student paragraph below is numbered. In the space provided, write C if a word group is a *complete sentence;* write F if it is a *fragment.* You will find seven fragments in the paragraph.

A Disastrous First Date

1. C
2. C
3. F
4. C
5. F
6. C
7. C
8. F
9. C
10. F
11. C
12. C
13. F
14. C
15. C
16. F
17. C
18. F
19. C
20. C

[1]My first date with Donna was a disaster. [2]I decided to take her to a small Italian restaurant. [3]That my friends told me had reasonable prices. [4]I looked over the menu and realized I could not pronounce the names of the dishes. [5]Such as "veal piccante," and "fettucini Alfredo." [6]Then, I noticed a burning smell. [7]The candle on the table was starting to blacken. [8]And scorch the back of my menu. [9]Trying to be casual, I quickly poured half my glass of water on the menu. [10]When the waiter returned to our table. [11]He asked me if I wanted to order some wine. [12]I ordered a bottle of Blue Nun. [13]The only wine that I had heard of and could pronounce. [14]The waiter brought the wine, poured a small amount into my glass, and waited. [15]I said, "You don't have to stand there. We can pour the wine ourselves." [16]After the waiter put down the wine bottle and left. [17]Donna told me I was supposed to taste the wine. [18]Feeling like a complete fool. [19]I managed to get through the dinner. [20]However, for weeks afterward, I felt like jumping out a tenth-story window.

On separate paper, correct the fragments you have found. Attach each fragment to the sentence that comes before or after it, or make whatever other change is needed to turn the fragment into a sentence.

■ Review Test 3

Underline the two fragments in each of the five items below. Then rewrite the item in the space provided, making the changes needed to correct the fragments.

Example   The people at the <u>diner</u> save money. <u>By watering down the coffee.</u> Also, <u>using the cheapest grade of hamburger.</u> Few people go there anymore.

The people at the diner save money by watering down the coffee. Also, they use the cheapest grade of hamburger.

1. <u>Gathering speed with enormous force.</u> The plane was suddenly in the air. Then it began to climb sharply. <u>And several minutes later leveled off.</u>

   Gathering speed with enormous force, the plane was suddenly in the air. The plane began to climb sharply and several minutes later leveled off.

2. <u>Before</u> my neighbors went on vacation. They asked me to watch their house. I agreed to check the premises once a day. <u>Also, to take in their mail.</u>

   Before my neighbors went on vacation, they asked me to watch their house. I agreed to check the premises once a day and to take in their mail.

3. <u>Running untouched into the end zone.</u> The halfback raised his arms in triumph. Then he slammed the football to the ground, <u>And did a little victory dance.</u>

   Running untouched into the end zone, the halfback raised his arms in triumph. He, then, slammed the football to the ground and did a little victory dance.

4. It's hard to keep up with bills. <u>Such as the telephone, gas, and electricity.</u> <u>After you finally mail the checks.</u> New ones seem to arrive a day or two later.

   It is hard to keep up with bills such as the telephone, gas, and electricity. After you finally mail the checks, new ones seem to arrive a day a day or two later.

5. <u>While a woman ordered twenty pounds of cold cuts.</u> Customers at the deli counter waited impatiently. The woman explained that she was in charge of a school picnic. <u>And apologized for taking up so much time.</u>

   While a woman ordered twenty pounds of cold cuts, customers at the deli counter waited impatiently. The woman explained that she was in charge of a school picnic an apologized for taking up so much time.

■ Review Test 4

Write quickly for five minutes about what you like to do in your leisure time. Don't worry about spelling, punctuation, finding exact words, or organizing your thoughts. Just focus on writing as many words as you can without stopping.

After you have finished, go back and make whatever changes are needed to correct any sentence fragments in your writing.

RUN-ONS

Introductory Project

A run-on occurs when two sentences are run together with no adequate sign given to mark the break between them. Shown below are four run-on sentences and four correctly marked sentences. See if you can complete the statement that explains how each run-on is corrected.

1. He is the meanest little kid on his block he eats only the heads of animal crackers. *Run-on*

   He is the meanest little kid on his block. He eats only the heads of animal crackers. *Correct*

   The run-on has been corrected by using a ___COMMA___ and a capital letter to separate the two complete thoughts.

2. Fred Grencher likes to gossip about other people, he doesn't like them to gossip about him. *Run-on*

   Fred Grencher likes to gossip about other people, but he doesn't like them to gossip about him. *Correct*

   The run-on has been corrected by using a joining word, ___But___, to connect the two complete thoughts.

3. The chain on my bike likes to chew up my pants, it leaves grease marks on my ankle as well. *Run-on*

   The chain on my bike likes to chew up my pants; it leaves grease marks on my ankle as well. *Correct*

   The run-on has been corrected by using a ___Semicolon___ to connect the two closely related thoughts.

4. The window shade snapped up like a gunshot, her cat leaped four feet off the floor. *Run-on*

   When the window shade snapped up like a gunshot, her cat leaped four feet off the floor. *Correct*

   The run-on has been corrected by using the subordinating word ___When___ to connect the two closely related thoughts.

Answers are on page 573.

WHAT ARE RUN-ONS?

A *run-on* is two complete thoughts that are run together with no adequate sign given to mark the break between them.* Some run-ons have no punctuation at all to mark the break between the thoughts. Such run-ons are known as *fused sentences:* they are fused or joined together as if they were only one thought.

Fused Sentence

My grades are very good this semester my social life rates only a C.

Fused Sentence

Our father was a madman in his youth he would do anything on a dare.

In other run-ons, known as *comma splices,* a comma is used to connect or ''splice'' together the two complete thoughts. However, a comma alone is *not enough* to connect two complete thoughts. Some stronger connection than a comma alone is needed.

Comma Splice

My grades are very good this semester, my social life rates only a C.

Comma Splice

Our father was a madman in his youth, he would do anything on a dare.

Comma splices are the most common kind of run-on mistake. Students sense that some kind of connection is needed between two thoughts, and so put a comma at the dividing point. But the comma alone is not sufficient, and a stronger, clearer mark between the two thoughts is needed.

* *Note:* Some instructors refer to each complete thought in a run-on as an *independent clause.* A *clause* is simply a group of words having a subject and a verb. A clause may be *independent* (expressing a complete thought and able to stand alone) or *dependent* (not expressing a complete thought and not able to stand alone). A run-on is two independent clauses that are run together with no adequate sign given to mark the break between them.

CORRECTING RUN-ONS

Here are four common methods of correcting a run-on:

1 Use a period and a capital letter to break the two complete thoughts into separate sentences:

My grades are very good this semester. My social life rates only a C.

Our father was a madman in his youth. He would do anything on a dare.

2 Use a comma plus a joining word (*and, but, for, or, nor, so, yet*) to connect the two complete thoughts:

My grades are very good this semester, but my social life rates only a C.

Our father was a madman in his youth, for he would do anything on a dare.

3 Use a semicolon to connect the two complete thoughts:

My grades are very good this semester; my social life rates only a C.

Our father was a madman in his youth; he would do anything on a dare.

4 Use subordination:

Although my grades are very good this semester, my social life rates only a C.

Because my father was a madman in his youth, he would do anything on a dare.

The following pages will give you practice in all four methods of correcting a run-on. The use of subordination will be explained further on page 418, in a section of the book that deals with sentence variety.

Method 1: Period and a Capital Letter

One way of correcting a run-on is to use a period and a capital letter at the break between the two complete thoughts. Use this method especially if the thoughts are not closely related or if another method would make the sentence too long.

Activity 1

Locate the split in each of the following run-ons. <u>Each is a *fused sentence*</u> — that is, each consists of two sentences that are fused or joined together with no punctuation at all between them. Reading each sentence aloud will help you "hear" where a major break or split in the thought occurs. At such a point, your voice will probably drop and pause.

Correct the run-on sentence by putting a period at the end of the first thought and a capital letter at the start of the next thought.

Example Martha Grencher shuffled around the apartment in her slippers. her husband couldn't stand their slapping sound on the floor. [H]

1. The goose down jacket was not well-made little feathers leaked out of the seams. [L]

2. Phil cringed at the sound of the dentist's drill it buzzed like a fifty-pound mosquito. [I]

3. Last summer no one swam in the lake a little boy had dropped his pet piranhas into the water. [A]

4. A horse's teeth never stop growing they will eventually grow outside the horse's mouth. [T]

5. Sue's doctor told her he was an astrology nut she did not feel good about learning that. [S]

6. Ice water is the best remedy for a burn using butter is like adding fat to a flame. [U]

7. In the apartment the air was so dry that her skin felt parched the heat was up to eighty degrees. [T]

8. My parents bought me an ant farm it's going to be hard to find tractors that small. [I]

9. Lobsters are cannibalistic this is one reason they are hard to raise in captivity. [T]

10. Julia placed an egg timer next to the phone she did not want to talk more than three minutes on her long-distance calls. [S]

Activity 2

Locate the split in each of the following run-ons. Some of the run-ons are fused sentences, and some of them are *comma splices* — run-ons spliced or joined together only with a comma. Correct each run-on by putting a period at the end of the first thought and a capital letter at the start of the next thought.

1. A bird got into the house through the chimney, we had to catch it before our cat did.

2. Some so-called health foods are not so healthy, many are made with oils that raise cholesterol levels.

3. We sat only ten feet from the magician, we still couldn't see where all the birds came from.

4. Rich needs only five hours of sleep each night, his wife needs at least seven.

5. Our image of dentistry will soon change, dentists will use lasers instead of drills.

6. Gale entered her apartment and jumped with fright, someone was leaving through her bedroom window.

7. There were several unusual hair styles at the party, one woman had bright green braids.

8. Jon saves all of his magazines, once a month, he takes them to a nursing home.

9. The doctor seemed to be in a rush, I still took time to ask all the questions that were on my mind.

10. When I was little, my brother tried to feed me flies, he told me they were raisins.

A Warning: Words That Can Lead to Run-Ons: People often write run-on sentences when the second complete thought begins with one of the following words. Remember to be on the alert for run-on sentences whenever you use one of these words in writing a paper.

I	we	there	now
you	they	this	then
he, she, it		that	next

Activity

Write a second sentence to go with each of the sentences that follow. Start the second sentence with the word shown at the left. Your sentences can be serious or playful.

Example   *She*   Jackie works for the phone company. *She climbs telephone poles in all kinds of weather.*

It   1. The alarm clock is unreliable. It does not always work.

He   2. My uncle has a peculiar habit. He washes his hands 3 times a day.

Then   3. Lola studied for the math test for two hours. Then she rested for three

It   4. I could not understand why the car would not start. It just came from the garage

There   5. We saw all kinds of litter on the highway. There are no dump sites in the area.

Method 2: Comma and a Joining Word

Another way of correcting a run-on sentence is to use a comma plus a joining word to connect the two complete thoughts. Joining words (also called *conjunctions*) include *and, but, for, or, nor, so,* and *yet.* Here is what the four most common joining words mean:

and   in addition to, along with

His feet hurt from the long hike, and his stomach was growling.

(*And* means ''in addition'': His feet hurt from the long hike; *in addition,* his stomach was growling.)

but   however, except, on the other hand, just the opposite

I remembered to get the cocoa, but I forgot the marshmallows.

(*But* means "however": I remembered to get the cocoa; *however,* I forgot the marshmallows.)

for   because, the reason why, the cause for something

She was afraid of not doing well in the course, for she had always had bad luck with English before.

(*For* means "because" or "the reason why": She was afraid of not doing well in the course; *the reason why* was that she had always had bad luck with English before.)

Note: If you are not comfortable using *for,* you may want to use *because* instead of *for* in the activities that follow. If you do use *because,* omit the comma before it.

so   as a result, therefore

The windshield wiper was broken, so she was in trouble when the rain started.

(*So* means "as a result": The windshield wiper was broken; *as a result,* she was in trouble when the rain started.)

Activity 1

Insert the joining word (*and, but, for, so*) that logically connects the two thoughts in each sentence.

1. The couple wanted desperately to buy the house, __but__ they did not qualify for a mortgage.
2. A lot of men today get their hair styled, __and__ they use perfume and other cosmetics as well.
3. Clyde asked his wife if she had any bandages, __for__ he had just sliced his finger with a paring knife.
4. He failed the vision part of his driver's test, __so__ he did not get his driver's license that day.
5. The restaurant was beautiful, __but__ the food was overpriced.

Activity 2

Add a complete and closely related thought to go with each of the following statements. Use a comma plus the joining word at the left when you write the second thought.

> **Example**   *for*   Lola spent the day walking barefoot, _for the heel of one of_
> _her shoes had come off._

but   1.   She wanted to go to the party, _but she did not have a dress_

and   2.   Tony washed his car in the morning, _and vacuumed the inside._

so   3.   The day was dark and rainy, _so it was good to stay in._

for   4.   I'm not going to eat in the school cafeteria anymore, _for I found a roach._

but   5.   I asked my brother to get off the telephone, _but he did not listen._

Method 3: Semicolon

A third method of correcting a run-on sentence is to use a semicolon to mark the break between two thoughts. A *semicolon* (;) is made up of a period above a comma and is sometimes called a *strong comma*. The semicolon signals more of a pause than a comma alone but not quite the full pause of a period.

Semicolon Alone: Here are some earlier sentences that were connected with a comma plus a joining word. Notice that a semicolon, unlike the comma alone, can be used to connect the two complete thoughts in each sentence:

A lot of men today get their hair styled; they use perfume and other cosmetics as well.

She was afraid of not doing well in the course; she had always had bad luck with English before.

The restaurant was beautiful; the food was overpriced.

Use of the semicolon can add to sentence variety. For some people, however, the semicolon is a confusing mark of punctuation. Keep in mind that if you are not comfortable using it, you can and should use one of the first two methods of correcting a run-on sentence.

Activity

Insert a semicolon where the break occurs between the two complete thoughts in each of the following sentences.

Example I missed the bus by seconds; there would not be another for half an hour.

1. I spend eight hours a day in a windowless office; it's a relief to get out in the open air after work.
2. The audience howled with laughter; the comedian enjoyed a moment of triumph.
3. It rained all week; parts of the highway were flooded.
4. Tony never goes to a certain gas station anymore; he found out that the service manager overcharged him for a valve job.
5. The washer shook and banged with its unbalanced load; then it began to walk across the floor.

Semicolon with a Transitional Word: A semicolon is sometimes used with a transitional word and a comma to join two complete thoughts:

We were short of money; therefore, we decided not to eat out that weekend.

The roots of a geranium have to be crowded into a small pot; otherwise, the plants may not flower.

I had a paper to write; however, my brain had stopped working for the night.

On the following page is a list of common transitional words (also known as *adverbial conjunctions*). Brief meanings are given for most of the words.

Transitional Word	Meaning
however	but
nevertheless	however
on the other hand	however
instead	as a substitute
meanwhile	in the intervening time
otherwise (De lo contrario)	under other conditions
indeed	in fact
in addition	
also	in addition
moreover	in addition
furthermore	in addition
as a result	
thus	as a result
consequently	as a result
therefore	as a result

Activity 1

Choose a logical transitional word from the list in the box and write it in the space provided. Put a semicolon *before* the connector and a comma *after* it.

Example   Exams are over _____ ; however, _____ I still feel tense and nervous.

1. I did not understand her point ; Consequently _____ I asked her to repeat it.
2. With his thumbnail, Tony tried to split open the cellophane covering on the box of crackers ; but, _____ the cellophane refused to tear.
3. Post offices are closed for today's holiday ; Consequently, _____ no mail will be delivered.
4. They decided not to go to the movie ; instead, _____ they went to play miniature golf.
5. I had to skip lunch ; otherwise, _____ I would be late for class.

Activity 2

Punctuate each sentence by using a semicolon and a comma.

Example   My brother's asthma was worsening; as a result, he quit the soccer
team.

1. Bill ate an entire pizza for supper; in addition, he had a big chunk of pound
    cake for dessert.
2. The man leaned against the building in obvious pain; however, no one stopped
    to help him.
3. Our instructor was absent; therefore, the test was postponed.
4. I had no time to type up the paper; instead, I printed it out neatly in black ink.
5. Lola loves the velvety texture of cherry Jell-O; moreover, she loves to squish
    it between her teeth.

Method 4: Subordination

A fourth method of joining related thoughts is to use subordination. *Subordination*
is a way of showing that one thought in a sentence is not as important as another
thought.

Here are three earlier sentences that have been recast so that one idea is
subordinated to (made less important than) the other idea:

> When the window shade snapped up like a gunshot, her cat leaped four feet
> off the floor.
>
> Because it rained all week, parts of the highway were flooded.
>
> Although my grades are very good this year, my social life rates only a C.

Notice that when we subordinate, we use dependent words like *when, because,*
and *although*. Here is a brief list of common dependent words:

Common Dependent Words		
after	before	unless
although	even though	until
as	if	when
because	since	while

Subordination is explained further on page 418.

Activity

Choose a logical dependent word from the box above and write it in the space provided.

Example   _____Because_____ I had so much to do, I never even turned on the TV last night.

1. _____When_____ we emerged from the darkened theater, it took several minutes for our eyes to adjust to the light.

2. _____Although_____ "All Natural" was printed in large letters on the yogurt carton, the fine print listing the ingredients told a different story.

3. I can't study for the test this weekend _____Since_____ my boss wants me to work overtime.

4. _____After_____ the vampire movie was over, my children were afraid to go to bed.

5. _____Even though_____ you have a driver's license and two major credit cards, that store will not accept your check.

A Review: How to Check for Run-On Sentences

1 To see if a sentence is a run-on, read it aloud and listen for a break marking two complete thoughts. Your voice will probably drop and pause at the break.

2 To check an entire paper, read it aloud from the *last* sentence to the *first*. Doing so will help you hear and see each complete thought.

3 Be on the lookout for words that can lead to run-on sentences:

I	he, she, it	they	this	next
you	we	there	that	then

4 Correct run-on sentences by using one of the following methods:

- Period and capital letter
- Comma and joining word (*and, but, for, or, nor, so, yet*)
- Semicolon alone or with a transitional word
- Subordination

■ Review Test 1

Some of the run-ons that follow are fused sentences, having no punctuation between the two complete thoughts; others are comma splices, having only a comma between the two complete thoughts. Correct the run-ons by using one of the following three methods:

■ Period and a capital letter
■ Comma and a joining word
■ Semicolon

Do not use the same method of correction for every sentence.

but

Example   Three people did the job, I could have done it alone.

1. The impatient driver tried to get a jump on the green light, *For* he kept edging his car into the intersection.

2. The course on the history of UFOs sounded interesting, *yet* it turned out to be very dull.

3. That clothing store is a strange place to visit; you keep walking up to dummies that look like real people.

4. Everything on the menu of the Pancake House sounded delicious, *T* they wanted to order the entire menu.

5. Bill pressed a cold washcloth against his eyes; it helped relieve his headache.

6. Craig used to be a fast-food junkie, *but* now he eats only vegetables and sunflower seeds.

7. I knew my term paper was not very good, *so* I placed it in a shiny plastic cover to make it look better.

8. Lola enjoys watching a talk show, Tony prefers watching a late movie.

9. My boss does not know what he is doing half the time, *yet* then he tries to tell me what to do.

10. In the next minute, 100 people will die; over 240 babies will be born.

■ Review Test 2

Correct the run-on in each sentence by using subordination. Choose from among the following dependent words:

after	before	unless
although	even though	until
as	if	when
because	since	while

Example   My eyes have been watering all day, I can tell the pollen count is high.
Because my eyes have been watering all day, I can tell the pollen count is high.

1. There are a number of suits and jackets on sale, they all have very noticeable flaws.
   Although there are a number of suits an jackets on sale, they all have very noticeable flaws.

2. Rust has eaten a hole in the muffler, my car sounds like a motorcycle.
   Because rust has eaten a hole in the muffler, my car sounds like a motorcycle.

3. I finished my household chores, I decided to do some shopping.
   After I finished my household chores, I decided to do some shopping.

4. The power went off for an hour during the night, all the clocks in the house must be reset.
   Since the power went off for an hour during the night, all the clocks in the house must be reset.

5. Electric cars eliminate auto pollution, the limited power of the car's battery is a serious problem.
   Even though electric cars eliminate auto pollution, the limited power of the car's battery is a serious problem.

■ Review Test 3

Write quickly for five minutes about what you did this past weekend. Don't worry about spelling, punctuation, finding exact words, or organizing your thoughts. Just focus on writing as many words as you can without stopping.

After you have finished, go back and make whatever changes are needed to correct any run-ons in your writing.

STANDARD
ENGLISH
VERBS

Introductory Project

Underline what you think is the correct form of the verb in each of the sentences below:

As a boy, he (enjoy, enjoyed) watching nature shows on television.
He still (enjoy, enjoys) watching such shows today as an adult.

When my car was new, it always (start, started) in the morning.
Now it (start, starts) only sometimes.

A couple of years ago, when Alice (cook, cooked) dinner, you needed an antacid tablet.
Now, when she (cook, cooks), neighbors invite themselves over to eat with us.

On the basis of the above examples, see if you can complete the following statements:

1. The first example in each pair refers to a (past, present) action, and the regular verb has an _____ ending.
2. The second example in each pair refers to a (past, present) action, and the regular verb has an _____ ending.

Answers are on page 573.

Many people have grown up in communities where nonstandard verb forms are used in everyday life. Such forms include *I thinks, he talk, it done, we has, you was,* and *she don't.* Community dialects have richness and power but are a drawback in college and the world at large, where standard English verb forms must be used. Standard English helps ensure clear communication among English-speaking people everywhere, and it is especially important in the world of work.

This chapter compares community dialect and standard English forms of one regular verb and three common irregular verbs.

REGULAR VERBS: DIALECT AND STANDARD FORMS

The chart below compares the community dialect (nonstandard) and the standard English forms of the regular verb *smile.*

SMILE

Community Dialect (Do not use in your writing)		Standard English (Use for clear communication)	
Present tense			
~~I smiles~~	~~we smiles~~	I smile	we smile
you smiles	you smiles	you smile	you smile
~~he, she, it smile~~	~~they smiles~~	he, she, it smiles	they smile
Past tense			
~~I smile~~	~~we smile~~	I smiled	we smiled
you smile	you smile	you smiled	you smiled
~~he, she, it smile~~	~~they smile~~	he, she, it smiled	they smiled

One of the most common nonstandard forms results from dropping the endings of regular verbs. For example, people might say "David never *smile* anymore" instead of "David never *smiles* anymore." Or they will say "Before he lost his job, David *smile* a lot" instead of "Before he lost his job, David *smiled* a lot." To avoid such nonstandard usage, memorize the forms shown above for the regular verb *smile.* Then use the activities that follow to help make the inclusion of verb endings a writing habit.

Present Tense Endings

The verb ending *-s* or *-es* is needed with a regular verb in the present tense when the subject is *he, she, it,* or any *one person* or *thing.* Consider the following examples of present tense endings.

He	He yell*s*.
She	She throw*s* things.
It	It really anger*s* me.
One person	Their son storm*s* out of the house.
One person	Their frightened daughter crouch*es* behind the bed.
One thing	At night the house shake*s*.

Activity 1

All but one of the ten sentences that follow need *-s* or *-es* verb endings. Cross out the nonstandard verb forms and write the standard forms in the spaces provided. Mark the one sentence that needs no change with a C for *correct.* One example is given for you.

Example ___*wants*___ Pat always want the teacher's attention.

___Prints___ 1. That newspaper print nothing but bad news.

___Sells___ 2. The gourmet ice cream bar sell for almost two dollars.

___Gossips___ 3. Pat gossip about me all the time.

___Tastes___ 4. Whole-wheat bread taste better to me than rye bread.

___Weakens___ 5. Bob weaken his lungs by smoking so much.

___Screams___ 6. The sick baby scream whenever her mother puts her down.

_____ 7. You make me angry sometimes.

___drives___ 8. Clyde drive twenty-five miles to work each day.

___Lives___ 9. She live in a rough section of town.

___Relaxes___ 10. Martha relax by drinking a glass of wine every night.

To Puzzle over: Tratar de descifrar a resolver, desvanarse los sesos com.

STANDARD ENGLISH VERBS **271**

Activity 2

Rewrite the short selection below, adding present tense -*s* or -*es* verb endings wher-ever needed.

The man lounge on his bed and watch a spider as it crawl across the ceiling. It come closer and closer to a point directly above his head. It reach the point and stop. If it drop now, it will fall right into his mouth. For a while he attempt to ignore the spider. Then he move nervously off the bed.

The man lounges on his bed and watches a spider as it crawls across the ceiling. It comes closer and closer to a point directly above his head. It reaches the point and stops. If it drops now, it will fall right into his mouth. For a while he attempts to ignore the spider. Then he moves nervously off the bed.

Past Tense Endings

The verb ending -*d* or -*ed* is needed with a regular verb in the past tense.

(Pretérita)

A midwife deliver*ed* my baby.

The visitor puzzl*ed* over the campus map.

The children watch*ed* cartoons all morning.

Activity 1

All but one of the ten sentences that follow need -*d* or -*ed* verb endings. Cross out the nonstandard verb forms and write the standard forms in the spaces provided. Mark the one sentence that needs no change with a C.

Example _failed_ This morning I fail a chemistry quiz.

Twisted 1. The customer ~~twist~~ his ankle on the diner's slippery steps.

struggled 2. The Vietnamese student ~~struggle~~ with the new language.

started 3. The sick little boy ~~start~~ to cry again.

_____ 4. The tired mother turned on the TV for him.

missed

5. I ~~miss~~ quite a few days of class early in the semester.

promised

6. The weather forecaster ~~promise~~ blue skies, but rain began early this morning.

attempted

7. Sam ~~attempt~~ to put out the candle flame with his finger.

ended

8. However, he ~~end~~ up burning himself.

threaded

9. Carlo ~~thread~~ the film through the reels of the projector.

ordered

10. As Alice was about to finish work last night, a man came into the diner and ~~order~~ two dozen hamburgers.

Activity 2

Rewrite the short selection below, adding past tense -d or -ed verb endings wherever needed.

     I smoke for two years and during that time suffer no real side effects. Then my body attack me. I start to have trouble falling asleep, and I awaken early every morning. My stomach digest food very slowly, so that at lunchtime I seem to be still full with breakfast. My lips and mouth turn dry and I swallow water constantly. Also, mucus fill my lungs and I cough a lot. I decide to stop smoking when my wife insist I take out more life insurance for our family.

I smoked for two years and during that time suffered no real side effects. Then my body attacked me. I started to have trouble falling asleep, and I awakened early every morning. My stomach digested food very slowly, so that at lunchtime I seemed to be still full with breakfast. My lips and mouth turned dry and I swallowed water constantly. Also, mucus filled my lungs and I coughed a lot. I decided to stop smoking when my wife insisted I take out more life insurance for our family.

THREE COMMON IRREGULAR VERBS:
DIALECT AND STANDARD FORMS

The following charts compare community dialect and standard English forms of the common irregular verbs *be, have,* and *do.* (For more on irregular verbs, see pages 277–284.)

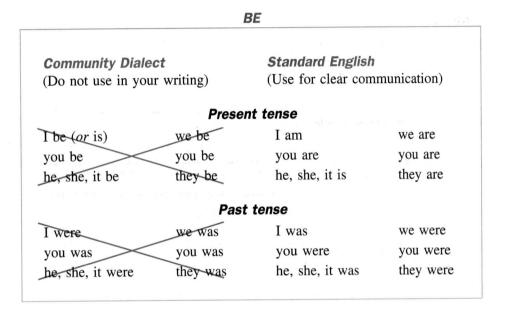

BE

Community Dialect (Do not use in your writing)		Standard English (Use for clear communication)	
Present tense			
I be (*or* is)	we be	I am	we are
you be	you be	you are	you are
he, she, it be	they be	he, she, it is	they are
Past tense			
I were	we was	I was	we were
you was	you was	you were	you were
he, she, it were	they was	he, she, it was	they were

HAVE

Community Dialect (Do not use in your writing)		Standard English (Use for clear communication)	
Present tense			
I has	we has	I have	we have
you has	you has	you have	you have
he, she, it have	they has	he, she, it has	they have
Past tense			
I has	we has	I had	we had
you has	you has	you had	you had
he, she, it have	they has	he, she, it had	they had

DO

Community Dialect		Standard English	
(Do not use in your writing)		(Use for clear communication)	

Present tense

~~I does~~	~~we does~~	I do	we do
you does	you does	you do	you do
~~he, she, it do~~	~~they does~~	he, she, it does	they do

Past tense

~~I done~~	~~we done~~	I did	we did
you done	you done	you did	you did
~~he, she, it done~~	~~they done~~	he, she, it did	they did

Note: Many people have trouble with one negative form of *do*. They will say, for example, "He don't agree" instead of "He doesn't agree," or they will say "The door don't work" instead of "The door doesn't work." Be careful to avoid the common mistake of using *don't* instead of *doesn't.*

Activity 1

Underline the standard form of *be, have,* or *do.*

1. When Walt (have, <u>has</u>) his own house, he will install built-in stereo speakers in every room.
2. The children (is, <u>are</u>) ready to go home.
3. Whenever we (<u>do</u>, does) the laundry, our clothes are spotted with blobs of undissolved detergent.
4. Ed and Arlene (was, <u>were</u>) ready to leave for the movies when the baby began to wail.
5. Our art class (done, <u>did</u>) the mural on the wall of the cafeteria.
6. If Maryanne (have, <u>has</u>) the time, she will help us set up the projector and tape the wires to the floor.
7. Curtis (be, <u>is</u>) the best Ping-Pong player in the college.
8. That mechanic always (do, <u>does</u>) a good job when he fixes my car.
9. The mice in our attic (<u>have</u>, has) chewed several holes in our ceiling.
10. The science instructor said that the state of California (be, <u>is</u>) ready for a major earthquake any day.

Activity 2

Fill in each blank with the standard form of *be, have,* or *do.*

1. My car ___has___ a real personality.
2. It acts as if it ___was___ human.
3. On cold mornings, it ___does___ not want to start.
4. Like me, the car ___has___ a problem dealing with freezing weather.
5. I don't want to get out of bed, and my car ___does___ not like leaving the garage.
6. Also, we ___have___ the same feeling about rainstorms.
7. I hate driving to school in a downpour and so ___does___ the car.
8. When the car ___is___ stopped at a light, it stalls.
9. The habits my car ___has___ may be annoying.
10. But they ___are___ understandable.

■ Review Test 1

Underline the standard verb form.

1. Martha (argue, <u>argues</u>) just to hear herself talk.
2. Those shoppers (<u>do,</u> does) not seem to know their way around the market; they keep retracing their steps.
3. The cheap ballpoint pen (leak, <u>leaked</u>) all over the lining of my pocketbook.
4. Pat (bag, <u>bagged</u>) the dirty laundry and threw it into the car.
5. If you (has, <u>have</u>) any trouble with the assignment, give me a call.
6. Whenever the hairdresser (do, <u>does</u>) my hair, she cuts one side shorter than the other.
7. Lola often (watch, <u>watches</u>) TV after her parents have gone to bed.
8. Two of the players (was, <u>were</u>) suspended from the league for ten games for using drugs.
9. Jeannie (<u>has,</u> have) only one eye; she lost the other years ago after falling on some broken glass.
10. I remember how my wet mittens (use, <u>used</u>) to steam on the hot school radiator.

■ Review Test 2

Cross out the two nonstandard verb forms in each sentence below. Then write the standard English verbs in the spaces provided.

Example   _____is_____   When our teacher be angry, his eyelid begin to twitch.

_____begins_____

WORKS
takes   1. My mother work for the local newspaper; she take classified ads over the phone.

Towed
Picked   2. Last week the city tow away my car; this morning I paid sixty dollars and pick it up from the towing company.

_is_
rushes   3. When my wife be late for work, she rush around the house like a speeded-up cartoon character.

Loves
Removed   4. Henry love to go camping until two thieves in the campground remove his cooler, stove, and sleeping bag from his tent.

Has
take   5. If the baby have a bad cold, I takes her into a steamy bathroom for a while to ease her breathing.

Know
DRESS   6. Although my little girls knows they shouldn't tease the cat, they often dresses up the animal in doll clothes.

watch
KNow   7. When my brothers watches their favorite *Star Trek* reruns, they knows exactly what Captain Kirk is going to say next.

ATTEMPTED
REFUSED   8. Last week my cousin attempt to sell some property in Florida to me, but I refuse to listen to him.

SHOWED
Overcharged.   9. I show the receipt to the manager to prove that the clerk had accidentally overcharge me.

_is_
tastes   10. As far as our son be concerned, oatmeal taste like soggy cardboard.

IRREGULAR VERBS

Introductory Project

You may already have a sense of which common English verbs are regular and which are not. To test yourself, fill in the past tense and past participle of the verbs below. Five are regular verbs and so take *-d* or *-ed* in the past tense and past participle. Five are irregular verbs and will probably not sound right when you try to add *-d* or *-ed*. Write *I* for irregular in front of these verbs. Also, see if you can write in their irregular verb forms. (The item at the top is an example.)

Present	Past	Past Participle
shout	*shouted*	*shouted*
1. crawl		
2. bring		
3. use		
4. do		
5. give		
6. laugh		
7. go		
8. scare		
9. dress		
10. see		

Answers are on page 573.

A BRIEF REVIEW OF REGULAR VERBS

Every verb has four principal parts: present, past, past participle, and present participle. These parts can be used to build all the verb tenses (the times shown by a verb).

The past and past participle of a regular verb are formed by adding *-d* or *-ed* to the present. The *past participle* is the form of the verb used with the helping verbs *have, has,* or *had* (or some form of *be* with passive verbs). The *present participle* is formed by adding *-ing* to the present. Here are the principal forms of some regular verbs:

Present	*Past*	*Past Participle*	*Present Participle*
crash	crashed	crashed	crashing
shiver	shivered	shivered	shivering
kiss	kissed	kissed	kissing
apologize	apologized	apologized	apologizing
tease	teased	teased	teasing

Most verbs in English are regular.

LIST OF IRREGULAR VERBS

Irregular verbs have irregular forms in the past tense and past participle. For example, the past tense of the irregular verb *know* is *knew;* the past participle is *known.*

Almost everyone has some degree of trouble with irregular verbs. When you are unsure about the form of a verb, you can check the list of irregular verbs on the following pages. (The present participle is not shown on this list because it is formed simply by adding *-ing* to the base form of the verb.) Or you can check a dictionary, which gives the principal parts of irregular verbs.

Present	*Past*	*Past Participle*
arise	arose	arisen
awake	awoke *or* awaked	awoken *or* awaked
be (am, are, is)	was (were)	been
become	became	become
begin	began	begun
bend	bent	bent
bite	bit	bitten
blow	blew	blown
break	broke	broken
bring	brought	brought
build	built	built
burst	burst	burst
buy	bought	bought
catch	caught	caught
choose	chose	chosen
come	came	come
cost	cost	cost
cut	cut	cut
do (does)	did	done
draw	drew	drawn
drink	drank	drunk
drive	drove	driven
eat	ate	eaten
fall	fell	fallen
feed	fed	fed
feel	felt	felt
fight	fought	fought
find	found	found
fly	flew	flown
freeze	froze	frozen
get	got	got *or* gotten
give	gave	given
go (goes)	went	gone
grow	grew	grown

Present	Past	Past Participle
have (has)	had	had
hear	heard	heard
hide	hid	hidden
hold	held	held
hurt	hurt	hurt
keep	kept	kept
know	knew	known
lay	laid	laid
lead	led	led
leave	left	left
lend	lent	lent
let	let	let
lie	lay	lain
lose	lost	lost
make	made	made
meet	met	met
pay	paid	paid
ride	rode	ridden
ring	rang	rung
run	ran	run
say	said	said
see	saw	seen
sell	sold	sold
send	sent	sent
shake	shook	shaken
shrink	shrank	shrunk
shut	shut	shut
sing	sang	sung
sit	sat	sat
sleep	slept	slept
speak	spoke	spoken
spend	spent	spent
stand	stood	stood
steal	stole	stolen

Present	Past	Past Participle
stick	stuck	stuck
sting	stung	stung
swear	swore	sworn
swim	swam	swum
take	took	taken
teach	taught	taught
tear	tore	torn
tell	told	told
think	thought	thought
wake	woke *or* waked	woken *or* waked
wear	wore	worn
win	won	won
write	wrote	written

Activity 1

Cross out the incorrect verb form in each of the following sentences. Then write the correct form of the verb in the space provided.

Example *drew* The little boy ~~drawed~~ on the marble table with permanent ink.

grown 1. Tomatoes were once thought to be poisonous, and they were ~~growed~~ only as ornamental shrubs.

ridden 2. Juan has ~~rode~~ the bus to school for two years while saving for a car.

torn 3. My cats have ~~tore~~ little holes in all my good wool sweaters.

frozen 4. The pipes in the bathroom ~~freezed~~ last winter, and they burst when they thawed.

rung 5. Every time my telephone has ~~rang~~ today, there has been bad news on the line.

known 6. Only seven people have ever ~~knowed~~ the formula for Coca-Cola.

blew 7. Amy ~~blowed~~ up animal-shaped balloons for her son's birthday party.

Shook 8. I ~~shaked~~ the bottle angrily until the catsup began to flow.

sat 9. While waiting for the doctor to arrive, I ~~sitted~~ in a plastic chair for over two hours.

eaten 10. The pile of bones on the plate showed how much chicken the family had ~~ate~~.

Activity 2

For each of the italicized verbs, fill in the three missing forms in the following order:

a Present tense, which takes an -*s* ending when the subject is *he, she, it,* or any *one person* or *thing* (see page 270)

b Past tense

c Past participle — the form that goes with the helping verb *have, has,* or *had*

Example My uncle likes to *give* away certain things. He (*a*) _____*gives*_____ old, threadbare clothes to the Salvation Army. Last year he (*b*) _____*gave*_____ me a worthless television set in which the picture tube was burned out. He has (*c*) _*given*_____ away stuff that a junk dealer would reject.

1. I like to *freeze* Hershey bars. A Hershey bar (*a*) _____FREEZES_____ in half an hour. Once I (*b*) _____FROZE_____ a bottle of Pepsi. I put it in the freezer to chill and then forgot about it. Later I opened the freezer and discovered that it had (*c*) _____FROZEN_____ and exploded.

2. I *know* the girl in the lavender bikini. She (*a*) _____KNOWS_____ me, too. I (*b*) _____KNEW_____ her brother before I met her. I have (*c*) _____KNOWN_____ him since boyhood.

3. An acquaintance of mine is a shoplifter, although he knows it's wrong to *steal*. He (*a*) _____STeals_____ candy bars from supermarkets. Last month he (*b*) _____STole_____ a Sony Walkman and was caught by a detective. He has (*c*) _____Stolen_____ pants and shirts by wearing several layers of clothes out of a store.

4. I *go* to parties a lot. Often Camille (*a*) _____goes_____ with me. She (*b*) _____went_____ with me just last week. I have (*c*) _____gone_____ to parties every Friday for the past month.

5. My brother likes to *throw* things. Sometimes he (*a*) _____throws_____ socks into his bureau drawer. In high school he (*b*) _____threw_____ footballs while quarterbacking the team. And he has (*c*) _____thrown_____ Frisbees in our backyard for as long as I can remember.

6. I *see* her every weekend. She (a) _____ sees _____ her other friends during the week. We first (b) _____ saw _____ each other on a cold Saturday night last winter, when we went for supper at an Indian restaurant. Since then we have (c) _____ seen _____ each other every weekend except when my car was broken down.

7. I often *lie* down for a few minutes after a hard day's work. Sometimes my cat (a) _____ lies _____ down near me. Yesterday was Saturday, so I (b) _____ laid _____ in bed all morning. I probably would have (c) _____ lain _____ in bed all afternoon, but I wanted to get some planting done in my vegetable garden.

8. I *do* not understand the assignment. It simply (a) _____ does _____ not make sense to me. I was surprised to learn that Shirley (b) _____ did _____ understand it. In fact, she had already (c) _____ done _____ the assignment.

9. I often find it hard to *begin* writing a paper. The assignment that I must do (a) _____ begins _____ to worry me while I'm watching television, but I seldom turn off the set. Once I waited until the late movie had ended before I (b) _____ began _____ to write. If I had (c) _____ begun _____ earlier, I would have gotten a decent night's sleep.

10. Martha likes to *eat*. She (a) _____ eats _____ as continuously as some people smoke. Once she (b) _____ ate _____ a large pack of cookies in half an hour. Even if she has (c) _____ eaten _____ a heavy meal, she often starts munching snacks right afterward.

■ Review Test 1

Underline the correct verb in the parentheses.

1. I (shaked, <u>shook</u>) the bottle of medicine before I took a teaspoon of it.

2. Chico came into the gym and (<u>began</u>, begun) to practice on the parallel bars.

3. Over half the class has (<u>taken</u>, took) this course on a pass-fail basis.

4. Even though my father (teached, <u>taught</u>) me how to play baseball, I never enjoyed any part of the game.

5. Because I had (lended, <u>lent</u>) him the money, I had a natural concern about what he did with it.

6. The drugstore clerk (gave, gived) him the wrong change.

7. Lola (brang, brought) a sweatshirt with her, for she knew the mountains got cold at night.

8. My sister (was, be) at school when a stranger came asking for her at our home.

9. The mechanic (did, done) an expensive valve job on my engine without getting my permission.

10. The basketball team has (broke, broken) the school record for most losses in one year.

11. Someone (leaved, left) his books in the classroom.

12. That jacket was (tore, torn) during the football game.

13. If I hadn't (threw, thrown) away the receipt, I could have gotten my money back.

14. I would have (become, became) very angry if you had not intervened.

15. As the flowerpot (fell, falled) from the windowsill, the little boy yelled, "Bombs away!"

■ Review Test 2

Write short sentences that use the form requested for the following irregular verbs.

Example   Past of *grow*   *I grew eight inches in one year.*

1. Past of *know*   I knew him.

2. Past of *take*   She took my money

3. Past participle of *give*   I had given her my soul.

4. Past participle of *write*   Lola has written the most beautiful essay.

5. Past of *bring*   the teacher bought in his new car.

6. Past participle of *speak*   It sounded like God had spoken.

7. Present of *begin*   Today begins the semester

8. Past of *go*   my youth is gone like the wind.

9. Past participle of *see*   I have seen the light.

10. Past of *drive*   Mario drove to the lake.

SUBJECT-VERB
AGREEMENT

Introductory Project

As you read each pair of sentences below, place a check mark beside the sentence that you think uses the underlined word correctly.

There <u>was</u> too many people talking at once. _____

There <u>were</u> too many people talking at once. ___✓___

The onions in that spaghetti sauce <u>gives</u> me heartburn. _____

The onions in that spaghetti sauce <u>give</u> me heartburn. ___✓___

The mayor and her husband <u>attends</u> our church. _____

The mayor and her husband <u>attend</u> our church. ___✓___

Everything <u>seem</u> to slow me down when I'm in a hurry. _____

Everything <u>seems</u> to slow me down when I'm in a hurry. ___✓___

Answers are on page 573.

A verb must agree with its subject in number. A *singular subject* (one person or thing) takes a singular verb. A *plural subject* (more than one person or thing) takes a plural verb. Mistakes in subject-verb agreement are sometimes made in the following situations (each situation is explained on the following pages):

1 When words come between the subject and the verb
2 When a verb comes before the subject
3 With compound subjects
4 With indefinite pronouns

WORDS BETWEEN SUBJECT AND VERB

Words that come between the subject and the verb do not change subject-verb agreement. In the sentence

The mean cockroaches (behind my stove) get high on Raid.

Prepositional phrase

the subject (cockroaches) is plural and so the verb (get) is plural. The words *behind my stove* that come between the subject and verb do not affect subject-verb agreement.

To help find the subject of certain sentences, you should cross out prepositional phrases (see page 233):

Nell, ~~with her three dogs close behind~~, runs around the park every day.

The seams ~~in my new coat~~ have split after only two wearings.

Activity

Underline the subject and lightly cross out any words that come between the subject and the verb. Then double-underline the verb choice in parentheses that you believe is correct.

1. The decisions of the judge (seems, seem) questionable.

2. A hamburger with a double order of french fries (is, are) my usual lunch.

3. One of my son's worst habits (is, are) leaving an assortment of dirty plates on the kitchen counter every morning.

4. The rust spots on the back of Emily's car (needs, need) to be cleaned with a special polish.

5. The collection of medicine bottles in my bathroom (overflows, overflow) the cabinet shelves.

VERB BEFORE SUBJECT

A verb agrees with its subject even when the verb comes *before* the subject. Words that may precede the subject include *there, here,* and, in questions, *who, which, what,* and *where.*

> On Bill's doorstep were two police officers.
> There are many pizza places in our town.
> Here is your receipt.
> Where are they going to sleep?

If you are unsure about the subject, ask *who* or *what* of the verb. With the first example above, you might ask, "*Who* were on the doorstep?" The answer, *police officers,* is the subject.

Activity

Write the correct form of the verb in the space provided.

was, were 1. There ____were____ not enough glasses for all the guests at the party.

is, are 2. Here ____are____ the tickets for tonight's ball game.

do, does 3. Where ____do____ you go when you want to be alone?

is, are 4. There ____are____ too many people in the room for me to feel comfortable.

was, were 5. Stuffed into the mailbox ____were____ ten pieces of junk mail and three ripped magazines.

COMPOUND SUBJECTS

Subjects joined by *and* generally take a plural verb.

> Maple syrup and sweet butter taste delicious on pancakes.
> Fear and ignorance have a lot to do with hatred.

When subjects are joined by *either . . . or, neither . . . nor, not only . . . but also,* the verb agrees with the subject closer to the verb.

> Either the Oak Ridge Boys or Randy Travis deserves the award for the best country album of the year.

The nearer subject, *Randy Travis,* is singular, and so the verb is singular.

Activity

Write the correct form of the verb in the space provided.

is, are   1. An egg and a banana _____ are _____ required for the recipe.

was, were   2. Owning a car and having money in my pocket _____ were _____ the chief ambitions of my adolescence.

visits, visit   3. My aunt and uncle from Ireland _____ visit _____ us every other summer.

was, were   4. Before they saw a marriage therapist, Peter and Jenny _____ were _____ planning to get divorced.

acts, act   5. Not only the landlady but also her children _____ act _____ unfriendly to us.

INDEFINITE PRONOUNS

The following words, known as *indefinite pronouns,* always take singular verbs:

(-*one* words)	(-*body* words)	(-*thing* words)	
one	nobody	nothing	each
anyone	anybody	anything	either
everyone	everybody	everything	neither
someone	somebody	something	

Note: *Both* always takes a plural verb.

Activity

Write the correct form of the verb in the space provided.

pitches, pitch   1. If each of us _____ pitches _____ in, we can finish this job in an hour.

was, were   2. Everybody in the theater _____ was _____ getting up and leaving before the movie ended.

provides, provide   3. Neither of the restaurants _____ provides _____ facilities for the handicapped.

likes, like   4. No one <u>in our family</u> _____*likes*_____ housecleaning, but we all take a turn at it.

steals,   5. Someone <u>in our neighborhood</u> _____*steals*_____ vegetables from people's
steal   gardens.

■ **Review Test**

Underline the correct verb in parentheses.

1. The lettuce in most of the stores in our area now (<u>costs,</u> cost) almost one dollar a head.

2. Nobody in the class of fifty students (<u>understands,</u> understand) how to solve the equation on the blackboard.

3. The packages in the shopping bag (was, <u>were)</u> a wonderful mystery to the children.

4. My exercise class of five students (<u>meets,</u> meet) every Thursday afternoon.

5. Anyone who (<u>steals,</u> steal) my purse won't find much inside it.

6. Business contacts and financial backing (is, <u>are)</u> all that I need to establish my career as a dress designer.

7. Each of those breakfast cereals (<u>contains,</u> contain) a high proportion of sugar.

8. The serious look in that young girl's eyes (<u>worries,</u> worry) me.

9. All of the cars on my block (has, <u>have)</u> to be moved one day a month for street cleaning.

10. The job is not for people who (stumbles, stumble) over tough decisions.

CONSISTENT VERB TENSE

Introductory Project

See if you can find and underline the two mistakes in verb tense in the following selection.

Tony's eyes burned and itched all day long. When he looked at them in a mirror, he also discovers there were red blotches on his neck. He spoke to his mother about the symptoms, and she said that maybe he was allergic to something. Then he remembers he had been cuddling the kitten that Lola had just bought the day before. "Good grief. I must be allergic to cats," he said to himself.

Answers are on page 573.

KEEPING TENSES CONSISTENT

Do not shift verb tenses unnecessarily. If you begin writing a paper in the present tense, don't shift suddenly to the past. If you begin in the past, don't shift without reason to the present. Notice the inconsistent verb tenses in the following selection:

> The shoplifter *walked* quickly toward the front of the store. When a clerk *shouts* at him, he *started* to run.

The verbs must be consistently in the present tense:

> The shoplifter *walks* quickly toward the front of the store. When a clerk *shouts* at him, he *starts* to run.

Or the verbs must be consistently in the past tense:

> The shoplifter *walked* quickly toward the front of the store. When a clerk *shouted* at him, he *started* to run.

Activity 1

In each selection one verb must be changed so that it agrees in tense with the other verbs. Cross out the incorrect verb and write the correct form in the space provided.

Example *carried*   Ted wanted to be someplace else when the dentist ~~carries~~ in a long needle.

_____ 1. I played my stereo and watched television before I decide to do some homework.

_____ 2. The hitchhiker stopped me as I walks from the turnpike rest station and said, "Are you on your way to San Jose?"

_____ 3. Some students attend all their classes in school. They listen carefully during lectures but they don't take notes. As a result, they often failed tests.

_____ 4. His parents stayed together for his sake; only after he graduates from college were they divorced.

_____ 5. In the movie, artillery shells exploded on the hide of the reptile monster. It just grinned, tosses off the shells, and kept eating people.

—————   6. Several months a year, monarch butterflies come to live in a spot along the California coast. Thousands and thousands of them hang from the trees and fluttered through the air in large groups.

—————   7. After waking up each morning, Harry stays in bed for a while. First he stretches and yawned loudly, and then he plans his day.

—————   8. The salespeople at Biggs' Department Store are very helpful. When people asked for a product the store doesn't carry or is out of, the salesperson recommends another store.

—————   9. Part-time workers at the company are the first to be laid off. They are also paid less, and they received no union representation.

—————   10. Smashed cars, ambulances, and police cars blocked traffic on one side of the highway. On the other side, traffic slows down as drivers looked to see what happened.

Activity 2

In the following selection, change verbs where needed so that they are consistently in the past tense. Cross out each incorrect verb and write the correct form above it, as shown in the example. You will need to make nine corrections.

Late one rainy night, Sheila woke to the sound of steady dripping. When she got out of bed to investigate, a drop of cold water ~~splashes~~ *splashed* onto her arm. She looks up just in time to see another drop form on the ceiling, hang suspended for a moment, and fall to the carpet. Stumbling to the kitchen, Sheila reaches deep into one of the cabinets and lifts out a large roasting pan. As she did so, pot lids and baking tins clattered out and crash onto the counter. Sheila ignored them, stumbled back to the bedroom, and places the pan on the floor under the drip. But a minute after sliding her icy feet under the covers, Sheila realized she is in trouble. The sound of each drop hitting the metal pan echoed like a gunshot in the quiet room. Sheila feels like crying, but she finally thought of a solution. She got out of bed and returns a minute later with a thick bath towel. She lined the pan with the towel and crawls back into bed.

■ Review Test

In the following selection, change verbs where needed so that they are consistently in the past tense. Cross out each incorrect verb and then write the correct form above it. You will need to make ten corrections in all.

Balancing the green plastic bag full of trash, Craig yanked the front door open. As he stepped onto the front porch, he notices that a light snow was already falling. He remembers that when he called to rent the cabin, he was told that it was not too early to expect snow in this mountain community. He glances up at the sky and then walks briskly to the end of the driveway. There he deposited the overflowing bag into one of the large trash cans. Shivering from the cold, he turned around and starts back toward the house, but then he pauses suddenly. At the southwest corner of the cabin, standing on its hind legs, was an enormous black bear. For a long terrible second, Craig was positive the bear was staring right at him. Looking for a promising direction to run, Craig turns around and saw a small bear cub scampering away from behind another garbage can. Before Craig had time to react, the large bear went down on all fours, sprints past the house, and started after the cub. Craig breathed a sigh of relief, races into the cabin, and locks the door behind him.

1. _____

2. _____

3. _____

4. _____

5. _____

6. _____

7. _____

8. _____

9. _____

10. _____

PRONOUN AGREEMENT, REFERENCE, AND POINT OF VIEW

Introductory Project

Read each pair of sentences below. Then put a check mark beside the sentence that you think uses the underlined word or words correctly.

Someone in my neighborhood lets <u>their</u> dog run loose. _____

Someone in my neighborhood lets <u>his or her</u> dog run loose. _____

After Tony reviewed his notes with Bob, <u>he</u> passed the exam with ease. _____

After reviewing his notes with Bob, <u>Tony</u> passed the exam with ease. _____

I dislike waitressing, for <u>you</u> can never count on a fair tip. _____

I dislike waitressing, for <u>I</u> can never count on a fair tip. _____

Answers are on page 574.

Pronouns are words that take the place of nouns (persons, places, or things). In fact, the word *pronoun* means "for a noun." Pronouns are shortcuts that keep you from unnecessarily repeating words in writing. Here are some examples of pronouns:

> Shirley had not finished *her* paper. (*Her* is a pronoun that takes the place of *Shirley's*.)
>
> Tony swung so heavily on the tree branch that *it* snapped. (*It* replaces *branch.*)
>
> When the three little pigs saw the wolf, *they* pulled out cans of Mace. (*They* is a pronoun that takes the place of *pigs.*)

This section presents rules that will help you avoid three common mistakes people make with pronouns. The rules are as follows:

1   A pronoun must agree in number with the word or words it replaces.
2   A pronoun must refer clearly to the word it replaces.
3   Pronouns should not shift unnecessarily in point of view.

PRONOUN AGREEMENT

A pronoun must agree in number with the word or words it replaces. If the word a pronoun refers to is singular, the pronoun must be singular; if that word is plural, the pronoun must be plural. (Note that the word a pronoun refers to is also known as the *antecedent.*)

> Barbara agreed to lend me (her) Willie Nelson albums.
>
> People walking the trail must watch (their) step because of snakes.

In the first example, the pronoun *her* refers to the singular word *Barbara;* in the second example, the pronoun *their* refers to the plural word *People.*

Activity

Write the appropriate pronoun (*their, they, them, it*) in the blank space in each of the following sentences.

Example   I lifted the pot of hot potatoes carefully, but _____*it*_____ slipped out of my hand.

1.   The value that people receive for _____ dollars these days is rapidly diminishing.

2. Fred never misses his daily workout; he believes _____ keeps him healthy.

3. Sometimes, in marriage, partners expect too much from _____ mates.

4. For some students, college is often their first experience with an undisciplined learning situation, and _____ are not always ready to accept the responsibility.

5. Our new neighbors moved in three months ago, but I have yet to meet _____ .

Indefinite Pronouns

The following words, known as *indefinite pronouns,* are always singular.

(-*one* words)	(-*body* words)	
one	nobody	each
anyone	anybody	either
everyone	everybody	neither
someone	somebody	

If a pronoun in a sentence refers to one of these singular words, the pronoun should be singular.

Each father felt that his child should have won the contest.
One of the women could not find her purse.
Everyone must be in his seat before the instructor takes the roll.

In each example, the circled pronoun is singular because it refers to one of the special singular words.

Note: The last example is correct if everyone in the class is a man. If everyone in the class was a woman, the pronoun would be *her.* If the class had both women and men, the pronoun form would be *his or her:*

Everyone must be in his or her seat before the instructor takes the roll.

Some writers follow the traditional practice of using *his* to refer to both women and men. Many now use *his or her* to avoid an implied sexual bias. To avoid using *his* or the somewhat awkward *his or her,* a sentence can often be rewritten in the plural:

Students must be in their seats before the instructor takes the roll.

Activity

Underline the correct pronoun.

1. Someone has blocked the parking-lot exit with (his or her, their) car.
2. Everyone in the women's group has volunteered some of (her, their) time for the voting drive.
3. Neither of the men arrested as terrorists would reveal information about (his, their) group.
4. Not one of the women coaches will be returning to (her, their) job next year.
5. Each of the President's advisers offered (his or her, their) opinion about the rail strike.

PRONOUN REFERENCE

A sentence may be confusing and unclear if a pronoun appears to refer to more than one word, or if the pronoun does not refer to any specific word. Look at this sentence:

Joe almost dropped out of high school, for he felt *they* emphasized discipline too much.

Who emphasized discipline too much? There is no specific word that *they* refers to. Be clear:

Joe almost dropped out of high school, for he felt *the teachers* emphasized discipline too much.

Following are sentences with other kinds of faulty pronoun references. Read the explanations of why they are faulty and look carefully at how they are corrected.

Faulty	**Clear**
June told Margie that *she* lacked self-confidence.	June told Margie, ''You lack self-confidence.''
(*Who* lacked self-confidence: June or Margie? Be clear.)	(Quotation marks, which can sometimes be used to correct an unclear reference, are explained on pages 353 – 360.)
Nancy's mother is a hairdresser, but Nancy is not interested in *it*.	Nancy's mother is a hairdresser, but Nancy is not interested in becoming one.
(There is no specific word that *it* refers to. It would not make sense to say, ''Nancy is not interested in hairdresser.'')	
Ron blamed the police officer for the ticket, *which* was foolish.	Foolishly, Ron blamed the police officer for the ticket.
(Does *which* mean that the officer's giving the ticket was foolish, or that Ron's blaming the officer was foolish? Be clear.)	

Activity

Rewrite each of the following sentences to make clear the vague pronoun reference. Add, change, or omit words as necessary.

Example   Our cat was friends with our hamster until he bit him.

Until the cat bit the hamster, the two were friends.

1. Maria's mother let her wear her new earrings to school.

2. When I asked why I failed my driver's test, he said I drove too slowly.

3. Dad ordered my brother to paint the garage because he didn't want to do it.

4. Herb dropped his psychology courses because he thought they assigned too much reading.

5. I love Parmesan cheese on veal, but it does not always digest well.

PRONOUN POINT OF VIEW

Pronouns should not shift their point of view unnecessarily. When writing a paper, be consistent in your use of first-, second-, or third-person pronouns.

Type of Pronoun	Singular	Plural
First-person pronouns	I (my, mine, me)	we (our, us)
Second-person pronouns	you (your)	you (your)
Third-person pronouns	he (his, him) she (her) it (its)	they (their, them)

Note: Any person, place, or thing, as well as any indefinite pronoun like *one, anyone, someone,* and so on (page 296), is a third-person word.

For instance, if you start writing in the third person *she,* don't jump suddenly to the second person *you.* Or if you are writing in the first person *I,* don't shift unexpectedly to *one.* Look at the examples.

Inconsistent	*Consistent*
I enjoy movies like *The Return of the Vampire* that frighten *you.* (The most common mistake people make is to let a *you* slip into their writing after they start with another pronoun.)	I enjoy movies like *The Return of the Vampire* that frighten me.
As soon as a person walks into Helen's apartment, *you* can tell that Helen owns a cat. (Again, the *you* is a shift in point of view.)	As soon as a person walks into Helen's apartment, *he or she* can tell that Helen owns a cat. (See also the note about *his or her* references on pages 296–297.)

Activity

Cross out inconsistent pronouns in the following sentences, and write the correct form of the pronoun above each crossed-out word.

Example   My dreams are always the kind that haunt ~~you~~ *me* the next day.

1. Whenever we take our children on a trip, ~~you~~ *we* have to remember to bring snacks, tissues, and toys.

2. In our society, we often need a diploma before ~~you~~ *we* are hired for a job.

3. A worker can take a break only after a relief person comes to take ~~your~~ *its (his or her)* place.

4. If a student organizes time carefully, ~~you~~ *he or she* can accomplish a great deal of work.

5. Although I know you should watch your cholesterol intake, ~~I~~ *you* can never resist an ear of corn dripping with melted butter.

■ Review Test 1

Cross out the pronoun error in each sentence and write the correction in the space provided at the left. Then circle the letter that correctly describes the type of error that was made.

Examples

his (or her)

Each player took ~~their~~ position on the court.
Mistake in: a. pronoun reference   (b.) pronoun agreement

the store

I was angry when ~~they~~ wouldn't give me cash back when I returned the sweater I had bought.
Mistake in: (a.) pronoun reference   b. pronoun point of view

_I_

I love Jello because ~~you~~ can eat about five bowls of it and still not feel full.
Mistake in: a. pronoun agreement   (b.) pronoun point of view

Dan

1. Dan asked Mr. Sanchez if ~~he~~ could stay an extra hour at work today.
Mistake in: (a.) pronoun reference   b. pronoun agreement

their

2. Both the front door and the back door of the abandoned house had fallen off ~~its~~ hinges.
Mistake in: (a.) pronoun agreement   b. pronoun point of view

_I_

3. I hate going to the supermarket because ~~you~~ always have trouble finding a parking space there.
Mistake in: a. pronoun agreement   (b.) pronoun point of view

the state

4. Norm was angry when ~~they~~ raised the state tax on cigarettes again.
Mistake in: (a.) pronoun agreement   b. pronoun reference

his or her   5. Every one of those musicians who played for two hours in the rain truly earned their money last night.
Mistake in: a. pronoun agreement   b. pronoun reference

I   6. As I entered the house, you could hear someone giggling in the hallway.
Mistake in: a. pronoun reference   b. pronoun point of view

her   7. Each of the beauty queens is asked a thought-provoking question and then judged on their answer.
Mistake in: a. pronoun agreement   b. pronoun reference

me   8. Sometimes I take the alternative route, but it costs you five dollars in tolls.
Mistake in: a. pronoun agreement   b. pronoun point of view

the doctor   9. At the dental office, I asked him if it was really necessary to take x-rays of my mouth again.
Mistake in: a. pronoun agreement   b. pronoun reference

me   10. My favorite subject is abnormal psychology because the case studies make you seem so normal by comparison.
Mistake in: a. pronoun agreement   b. pronoun point of view

■ Review Test 2

Underline the correct word in parentheses.

1. As we sat in class waiting for the test results, (you, we) could feel the tension.

2. Hoping to be first in line when (they, the ushers) opened the doors, we arrived two hours early for the concert.

3. If a person really wants to appreciate good coffee, (he or she, you, they) should drink it black.

4. I love science fiction because it lets (you, me) escape to other worlds.

5. Lois often visits the reading center in school, for she finds that (they, the tutors) give her helpful instruction.

6. Nobody seems to know how to add or subtract without (his or her, their) pocket calculator anymore.

7. Cindy is the kind of woman who will always do (their, her) best.

8. Each of my brothers has had (his, their) apartment broken into.

9. If someone is going to write a composition, (he or she, you, they) should prepare at least one rough draft.

10. I've been taking cold medicine, and now (it, the cold) is better.

PRONOUN TYPES

This chapter describes some common types of pronouns: subject and object pronouns, possessive pronouns, and demonstrative pronouns.

SUBJECT AND OBJECT PRONOUNS

Pronouns change their form depending on the purpose they serve in a sentence. In the box that follows is a list of subject and object pronouns.

Subject Pronouns	Object Pronouns
I	me
you	you (no change)
he	him
she	her
it	it (no change)
we	us
they	them

Subject Pronouns

Subject pronouns are subjects of verbs.

> *She* is wearing blue nail polish on her toes. (*She* is the subject of the verb *is wearing*.)
>
> *They* ran up three flights of steps. (*They* is the subject of the verb *ran*.)
>
> *We* children should have some privacy too. (*We* is the subject of the verb *should have*.)

Rules for using subject pronouns, and several kinds of mistakes people sometimes make with subject pronouns, are explained below.

Rule 1: Use a subject pronoun in spots where you have a compound (more than one) subject.

Incorrect	*Correct*
Sally and *me* are exactly the same size.	Sally and *I* are exactly the same size.
Her and *me* share our wardrobes with each other.	*She* and *I* share our wardrobes with each other.

Hint: If you are not sure what pronoun to use, try each pronoun by itself in the sentence. The correct pronoun will be the one that sounds right. For example, "Her shares her wardrobe" does not sound right; "she shares her wardrobe" does.

Rule 2: Use a subject pronoun after forms of the verb *be*. Forms of *be* include *am, are, is, was, were, has been,* and *have been*.

> It was *I* who called you a minute ago and then hung up.
>
> It may be *they* entering the diner.
>
> It was *he* who put the white tablecloth into the washing machine with a red sock.

The sentences above may sound strange and stilted to you because they are seldom used in conversation. When we speak with one another, forms such as "It was me," "It may be them," and "It is her" are widely accepted. In formal writing, however, the grammatically correct forms are still preferred.

Hint: To avoid having to use a subject pronoun form after *be*, you can simply reword a sentence. Here is how the preceding examples could be reworded:

> I was the one who called you a minute ago and then hung up.
>
> They may be the ones entering the diner.
>
> He put the white tablecloth into the washing machine with a red sock.

Rule 3:   Use subject pronouns after *than* or *as*. The subject pronoun is used because a verb is understood after the pronoun.

> Mark can hold his breath longer than *I* (can). (The verb *can* is understood after *I*.)
>
> Her thirteen-year-old daughter is as tall as *she* (is). (The verb *is* is understood after *she*.)
>
> You drive much better than *he* (drives). (The verb *drives* is understood after *he*.)

Hint: Avoid mistakes by mentally adding the ''missing'' verb at the end of the sentence.

Object Pronouns

Object pronouns (*me, him, her, us, them*) are the objects of verbs or prepositions. (*Prepositions* are connecting words like *for, at, about, to, before, by, with,* and *of*. See also page 233.)

> Lee pushed *me*. (*Me* is the object of the verb *pushed*.)
>
> We dragged *them* all the way home. (*Them* is the object of the verb *dragged*.)
>
> She wrote all about *us* in her diary. (*Us* is the object of the preposition *about*.)
>
> Vera passed a note to *him* as she walked to the pencil sharpener. (*Him* is the object of the preposition *to*.)

People are sometimes uncertain about what pronoun to use when two objects follow the verb.

Incorrect	*Correct*
I argued with his sister and *he*.	I argued with his sister and *him*.
The cashier cheated Rick and *I*.	The cashier cheated Rick and *me*.

Hint: If you are not sure what pronoun to use, try each pronoun by itself in the sentence. The correct pronoun will be the one that sounds right. For example, ''I argued with he'' does not sound right; ''I argued with him'' does.

Activity

Underline the correct subject or object pronoun in each of the following sentences. Then show whether your answer is a subject or an object pronoun by circling the S or O in the margin. The first one is done for you as an example.

Ⓢ *O*   1. Kenny and (<u>she</u>, her) kept dancing even after the band stopped playing.

S *O*   2. The letters Mom writes to Estelle and (I, me) are always typewritten in red.

S *O*   3. No one has more nerve than (he, him).

S *O*   4. Their relay team won because they practiced more than (we, us).

S *O*   5. (We, Us) choir members get to perform for the governor.

S *O*   6. The rest of (they, them) came to the wedding by train.

S *O*   7. (She, Her) and Sammy got divorced and then remarried.

S *O*   8. My sister keeps track of all the favors she does for my brother and (I, me).

S *O*   9. Tony and (he, him) look a lot alike, but they're not even related.

S *O* 10. Our neighbors asked Maria and (I, me) to help with their parents' surprise party.

POSSESSIVE PRONOUNS

Possessive pronouns show ownership or possession.

Using a small branch, Stu wrote *his* initials in the wet cement.
The furniture is *mine,* but the car is hers.

Here is a list of possessive pronouns:

my, mine	our, ours
your, yours	your, yours
his	their, theirs
her, hers	
its	

Note: A possessive pronoun *never* uses an apostrophe. (See also page 348.)

Incorrect	**Correct**
That earring is *hers'*.	That earring is *hers*.
The orange cat is *theirs'*.	The orange cat is *theirs*.

Activity

Cross out the incorrect pronoun form in each of the sentences below. Write the correct form in the space at the left.

Example *hers* _____ Those gloves are hers'.

_____ 1. A porcupine has no quills on its' belly.

_____ 2. The stereo set is theirs'.

_____ 3. You can easily tell which team is ours' by when we cheer.

_____ 4. The car with the pink car seats is hers'.

_____ 5. Grandma's silverware and dishes will be yours' when you get married.

DEMONSTRATIVE PRONOUNS

Demonstrative pronouns point to or single out a person or thing. There are four demonstrative pronouns:

this	these
that	those

Generally speaking, *this* and *these* refer to things close at hand; *that* and *those* refer to things farther away. The four pronouns are commonly used in the role of demonstrative adjectives as well.

This milk has gone sour.

My son insists on saving all *these* hot rod magazines.

I almost tripped on *that* roller skate at the bottom of the steps.

Those plants in the corner don't get enough light.

Note: Do not use *them, this here, that there, these here,* or *those there* to point out. Use only *this, that, these,* or *those.*

Activity

Cross out the incorrect form of the demonstrative pronoun and write the correct form in the space provided.

Example ___*Those*___ ~~Those there~~ tires look worn.

_____ 1. This here child has a high fever.

_____ 2. These here pants I'm wearing are so tight I can hardly breathe.

_____ 3. Them kids have been playing in the alley all morning.

_____ 4. That there umpire won't stand for any temper tantrums.

_____ 5. I save them old baby clothes for my daughter's dolls.

■ Review Test

Underline the correct word in the parentheses.

1. If I left dinner up to (he, him), we'd have Cheerios every night.

2. Julia's words may have come from the script, but the smile is all (hers', hers).

3. My boyfriend offered to drive his mother and (I, me) to the mall to shop for his birthday present.

4. (Them, those) little marks on the floor are scratches, not crumbs.

5. I took a picture of my brother and (I, me) looking into the hallway mirror.

6. When Lin and (she, her) drove back from the airport, they talked so much that they missed their exit.

7. (That there, That) orange juice box says ''Fresh,'' but the juice is made from concentrate.

8. Eliot swears that he dreamt about (she, her) and a speeding car the night before Rose was injured in a car accident.

9. The waitress brought our food to the people at the next table, and gave (theirs, theirs') to us.

10. Since it was so hot out, Lana and (he, him) felt they had a good excuse to study at the beach.

ADJECTIVES
AND
ADVERBS

ADJECTIVES

What Are Adjectives?

Adjectives describe nouns (names of persons, places, or things) or pronouns.

Ernie is a *rich* man. (The adjective *rich* describes the noun *man.*)

He is also *generous.* (The adjective *generous* describes the pronoun *he.*)

Our *gray* cat sleeps a lot. (The adjective *gray* describes the noun *cat.*)

She is *old.* (The adjective *old* describes the pronoun *she.*)

Adjectives usually come before the word they describe (as in *rich man* and *gray cat*). But they also come after forms of the verb *be* (*is, are, was, were,* and so on). They also follow verbs such as *look, appear, seem, become, sound, taste,* and *smell.*

That speaker was *boring.* (The adjective *boring* describes the speaker.)

The Petersons are *homeless.* (The adjective *homeless* describes the Petersons.)

The soup looked *good.* (The adjective *good* describes the soup.)

But it tasted *salty.* (The adjective *salty* describes the pronoun *it.*)

Using Adjectives to Compare

For all one-syllable adjectives and some two-syllable adjectives, add *-er* when comparing two things and *-est* when comparing three or more things.

> My sister's handwriting is *neater* than mine, but Mother's is the *neatest*.
>
> Canned juice is sometimes *cheaper* than fresh juice, but frozen juice is often the *cheapest*.

For some two-syllable adjectives and all longer adjectives, add *more* when comparing two things and *most* when comparing three or more things.

> Typing something is *more efficient* than writing it out by hand, but the *most efficient* way to write is on a computer.
>
> Jeans are generally *more comfortable* than slacks, but sweat pants are the *most comfortable* of all.

You can usually tell when to use *more* and *most* by the sound of a word. For example, you can probably tell by its sound that "carefuller" would be too awkward to say and that *more careful* is thus correct. In addition, there are many words for which both *-er* or *-est* and *more* or *most* are equally correct. For instance, either "a more fair rule" or "a fairer rule" is correct.

To form negative comparisons, use *less* and *least*.

> When kids called me "Dum-dum," I tried to look *less* hurt than I felt.
>
> They say men gossip *less* than women do, but I don't believe it.
>
> Suzanne is the most self-centered, *least* thoughtful person I know.

Points to Remember about Comparing

Point 1: Use only one form of comparison at a time. In other words, do not use both an *-er* ending and *more* or both an *-est* ending and *most*:

Incorrect	Correct
My Southern accent is always *more stronger* after I visit my family in Georgia.	My Southern accent is always *stronger* after I visit my family in Georgia.
My *most luckiest* day was the day I met my wife.	My *luckiest* day was the day I met my wife.

Point 2:   Learn the irregular forms of the words shown below.

	Comparative (for Comparing Two Things)	Superlative (for Comparing Three or More Things)
bad	worse	worst
good, well	better	best
little (in amount)	less	least
much, many	more	most

Do not use both *more* and an irregular comparative or *most* and an irregular superlative.

Incorrect

It is *more better* to stay healthy than to have to get healthy.

Yesterday I went on the *most best* date of my life — and all we did was go on a picnic.

Correct

It is *better* to stay healthy than to have to get healthy.

Yesterday I went on the *best* date of my life — and all we did was go on a picnic.

Activity

Add to each sentence the correct form of the word in the margin.

bad   **Examples**   The _____*worst*_____ scare I ever had was when I thought my son was on an airplane that crashed.

wonderful   The day of my divorce was even ___*more wonderful*___ than the day of my wedding.

good   1. The _____ way to diet is gradually.

popular   2. Vanilla ice cream is even _____ than chocolate ice cream.

bad   3. One of the _____ things you can do to people is ignore them.

light   4. A pound of feathers is no _____ than a pound of stones.

little   5. The _____ expensive way to accumulate a wardrobe is by buying used clothing whenever possible.

ADVERBS

What Are Adverbs?

Adverbs describe verbs, adjectives, or other adverbs. They usually end in *-ly*.

The referee *suddenly* stopped the fight.
(The adverb *suddenly* describes the verb *stopped*.)

Her yellow rosebushes are *absolutely* beautiful.
(The adverb *absolutely* describes the adjective *beautiful*.)

The auctioneer spoke so *terribly* fast that I couldn't understand him.
(The adverb *terribly* describes the adverb *fast*.)

A Common Mistake with Adverbs and Adjectives

People often mistakenly use an adjective instead of an adverb after a verb.

Incorrect	*Correct*
I jog *slow*.	I jog *slowly*.
The nervous witness spoke *quiet*.	The nervous witness spoke *quietly*.
The first night I quit smoking, I wanted a cigarette *bad*.	The first night I quit smoking, I wanted a cigarette *badly*.

Activity

Underline the adjective or adverb needed. (Remember that adjectives describe nouns, and adverbs describe verbs or other adverbs.)

1. During a quiet moment in class, my stomach rumbled (loud, loudly).

2. I'm a (slow, slowly) reader, so I have to put aside more time to study than some of my friends.

3. Thinking no one was looking, the young man (quick, quickly) emptied his car's ashtray onto the parking lot.

4. The kitchen cockroaches wait (patient, patiently) in the shadows; at night they'll have the place to themselves.

5. I hang up the phone (immediate, immediately) whenever the speaker is a recorded message.

Well and *Good*

Two words that are often confused are *well* and *good*. *Good* is an adjective; it describes nouns. *Well* is usually an adverb; it describes verbs. *Well* (rather than *good*) is also used when referring to a person's health.

Activity

Write *well* or *good* in each of the sentences that follow.

1. I could tell by the broad grin on Ginny's face that the news was
_____ .

2. They say he sang so _____ that even the wind stopped to listen.

3. The food at the salad bar must not have been too fresh because I didn't feel
_____ after dinner.

4. When I want to do a really _____ job of washing the floor, I do it on my hands and knees.

5. The best way to get along _____ with our boss is to stay out of his way.

■ Review Test

Underline the correct word in the parentheses.

1. In Egypt, silver was once (more valued, most valued) than gold.

2. After seeing Mark get sick, I didn't feel too (good, well) myself.

3. The (littler, less) coffee I drink, the better I feel.

4. Light walls make a room look (more large, larger) than dark walls do.

5. One of the (unfortunatest, most unfortunate) men I know is a millionaire.

6. The moths' (continuous, continuously) thumping against the screen got on my nerves.

7. The Amish manage (good, well) without radios, telephones, or television.

8. A purple crocus had burst (silent, silently) through the snow outside our window.

9. It is (good, better) to teach people to fish than to give them fish.

10. Today a rocket can reach the moon more (quick, quickly) than it took a stagecoach to travel from one end of England to the other.

MISPLACED MODIFIERS

Introductory Project

Because of misplaced words, each of the sentences below has more than one possible meaning. In each case, see if you can explain the intended meaning and the unintended meaning. Also, circle the words that you think create the confusion because they are misplaced.

1. The sign in the restaurant window reads, "Wanted: Young Man— To Open Oysters with References."

   Intended meaning: _____

   Unintended meaning: _____

2. Clyde and Charlotte decided to have two children on their wedding day.

   Intended meaning: _____

   Unintended meaning: _____

3. The students no longer like the math instructor who failed the test.

   Intended meaning: _____

   Unintended meaning: _____

Answers are on page 574.

WHAT MISPLACED MODIFIERS ARE
AND HOW TO CORRECT THEM

Modifiers are descriptive words. *Misplaced modifiers* are words that, because of awkward placement, do not describe the words the writer intended them to describe. Misplaced modifiers often obscure the meaning of a sentence. To avoid them, place words as close as possible to what they describe.

Misplaced Words	*Correctly Placed Words*
Tony bought an old car from a crooked dealer *with a faulty transmission.* (The dealer had a faulty transmission?)	Tony bought an old car with a faulty transmission from a crooked dealer. (The words describing the old car are now placed next to *car.*)
I *nearly* earned a hundred dollars last week. (You just missed earning a hundred dollars, but in fact earned nothing?)	I earned nearly a hundred dollars last week. (The meaning — that you earned a little under a hundred dollars — is now clear.)
Bill yelled at the howling dog *in his underwear.* (The *dog* wore underwear?)	Bill, in his underwear, yelled at the howling dog. (The words describing Bill are placed next to him.)

Activity

Underline the misplaced word or words in each sentence. Then rewrite the sentence, placing related words together and thereby making the meaning clear.

Examples   The suburbs <u>nearly</u> had five inches of rain.

The suburbs had nearly five inches of rain.

We could see the football stadium <u>driving across the bridge.</u>

Driving across the bridge, we could see the football stadium.

1. I saw mountains of uncollected trash walking along the city streets.

_____

2. I almost had a dozen job interviews after I sent out my résumé.

_____

3. Bill swatted the wasp that stung him with a newspaper.

———————————————————————————————————————

4. Joanne decided to live with her grandparents when she attended college to save money.

———————————————————————————————————————

5. Charlotte returned the hamburger to the supermarket that was spoiled.

———————————————————————————————————————

6. Roger visited the old house still weak with the flu.

———————————————————————————————————————

7. The phone almost rang fifteen times last night.

———————————————————————————————————————

8. My uncle saw a kangaroo at the window under the influence of whiskey.

———————————————————————————————————————

9. We decided to send our daughter to college on the day she was born.

———————————————————————————————————————

10. Fred always opens the bills that arrive in the mailbox with a sigh.

———————————————————————————————————————

■ Review Test

Write M for *misplaced* or C for *correct* in front of each sentence.

_____ 1. Rita found it difficult to mount the horse wearing tight jeans.

_____ 2. Rita, wearing tight jeans, found it difficult to mount the horse.

_____ 3. I noticed a crack in the window walking into the delicatessen.

_____ 4. Walking into the delicatessen, I noticed a crack in the window.

_____ 5. A well-worn track shoe was found on the locker bench with holes in it.

_____ 6. A well-worn track shoe with holes in it was found on the locker bench.

_____ 7. I almost caught a hundred lightning bugs.

_____ 8. I caught almost a hundred lightning bugs.

———   9. In a secondhand store, Willie found a television set that had been stolen from me last month.

———   10. Willie found a television set in a secondhand store that had been stolen from me last month.

———   11. Willie found, in a secondhand store, a television set that had been stolen from me last month.

———   12. There were four cars parked outside the café with Minnesota license plates.

———   13. There were four cars with Minnesota license plates parked outside the café.

———   14. The President was quoted on the *NBC Evening News* as saying that the recession was about to end.

———   15. The President was quoted as saying that the recession was about to end on the *NBC Evening News*.

DANGLING
MODIFIERS

Introductory Project

Because of dangling words, each of the sentences below has more than one possible meaning. In each case, see if you can explain the intended meaning and the unintended meaning.

1. While smoking a pipe, my dog sat with me by the crackling fire.

   Intended meaning: ───────────────────────

   Unintended meaning: ─────────────────────

2. Looking at the leather-skirted woman, his sports car went through a red light.

   Intended meaning: ───────────────────────

   Unintended meaning: ─────────────────────

3. After baking for several hours, Grandmother removed the beef pie from the oven.

   Intended meaning: ───────────────────────

   Unintended meaning: ─────────────────────

Answers are on page 574.

WHAT DANGLING MODIFIERS ARE
AND HOW TO CORRECT THEM

A modifier that opens a sentence must be followed immediately by the word it is meant to describe. Otherwise, the modifier is said to be *dangling*, and the sentence takes on an unintended meaning. For example, in the sentence

> While smoking a pipe, my dog sat with me by the crackling fire.

the unintended meaning is that the *dog* was smoking the pipe. What the writer meant, of course, was that *he,* the writer, was smoking the pipe. He should have said,

> While smoking a pipe, *I* sat with my dog by the crackling fire.

The dangling modifier could also be corrected by placing the subject within the opening word group:

> While *I* was smoking my pipe, my dog sat with me by the crackling fire.

Here are other sentences with dangling modifiers. Read the explanations of why they are dangling and look carefully at how they are corrected.

Dangling	*Correct*
Swimming at the lake, a rock cut Sue's foot. (*Who* was swimming at the lake? The answer is not *rock* but *Sue.* The subject *Sue* must be added.)	Swimming at the lake, Sue cut her foot on a rock. *Or:* When Sue was swimming at the lake, she cut her foot on a rock.
While eating my sandwich, five mosquitoes bit me. (*Who* is eating the sandwich? The answer is not *five mosquitoes,* as it unintentionally seems to be, but *I.* The subject *I* must be added.)	While *I* was eating my sandwich, five mosquitoes bit me. *Or:* While eating my sandwich, *I* was bitten by five mosquitoes.
Getting out of bed, the tile floor was so cold that Maria shivered all over. (*Who* got out of bed? The answer is not *tile floor* but *Maria.* The subject *Maria* must be added.)	Getting out of bed, *Maria* found the tile floor so cold that she shivered all over. *Or:* When *Maria* got out of bed, the tile floor was so cold that she shivered all over.

Dangling	Correct
To join the team, a C average or better is necessary. (*Who* is to join the team? The answer is not *C average* but *you.* The subject *you* must be added.)	To join the team, *you* must have a C average or better. *Or:* For *you* to join the team, a C average or better is necessary.

The preceding examples make clear the two ways of correcting a dangling modifier. Decide on a logical subject and do one of the following:

1 Place the subject *within* the opening word group:

When Sue was swimming at the lake, she cut her foot on a rock.

Note: In some cases an appropriate subordinating word such as *When* must be added, and the verb may have to be changed slightly as well.

2 Place the subject right *after* the opening word group:

Swimming at the lake, Sue cut her foot on a rock.

Activity

Ask *Who?* of the opening words in each sentence. The subject that answers the question should be nearby in the sentence. If it is not, provide the logical subject by using either method of correction described above.

Example While sleeping at the campsite, a Frisbee hit Bill on the head.

While Bill was sleeping at the campsite, a Frisbee hit him

on the head.

or *While sleeping at the campsite, Bill was hit on the head by*

a Frisbee.

1. Watching the horror movie, goose bumps covered my spine.

_____

_____

2. After putting on a corduroy shirt, the room didn't seem as cold.

   _____

   _____

3. Flunking out of school, my parents demanded that I get a job.

   _____

   _____

4. Covered with food stains, my mother decided to wash the tablecloth.

   _____

   _____

5. Joining several college clubs, Mike's social life became more active.

   _____

   _____

6. While visiting the Jungle Park Safari, a baboon scrambled onto the hood of their car.

   _____

   _____

7. Under attack by beetles, Charlotte sprayed her roses with insecticide.

   _____

   _____

8. Standing at the ocean's edge, the wind coated my glasses with a salty film.

   _____

   _____

9. Braking the car suddenly, my shopping bags tumbled off the seat.

   _____

   _____

10. Using binoculars, the hawk was clearly seen following its prey.

   _____

   _____

■ Review Test

Write *D* for *dangling* or *C* for *correct* in front of each sentence. Remember that the opening words are a dangling modifier if they have no logical subject to modify.

_____   1. Advertising in the paper, Frank's car was quickly sold.

_____   2. By advertising in the paper, Frank quickly sold his car.

_____   3. After painting the downstairs, the house needed airing to clear out the fumes.

_____   4. After we painted the downstairs, the house needed airing to clear out the fumes.

_____   5. Frustrated by piles of homework, Wanda was tempted to watch television.

_____   6. Frustrated by piles of homework, Wanda's temptation was to watch television.

_____   7. After I waited patiently in the bank line, the teller told me I had filled out the wrong form.

_____   8. After waiting patiently in the bank line, the teller told me I had filled out the wrong form.

_____   9. When dieting, desserts are especially tempting.

_____   10. When dieting, I find desserts especially tempting.

_____   11. Looking through the telescope, I saw a brightly lit object come into view.

_____   12. As I was looking through the telescope, a brightly lit object came into view.

_____   13. Looking through the telescope, a brightly lit object came into my view.

_____   14. Weighing thousands of pounds, no one knows how the enormous stones were brought to Stonehenge.

_____   15. No one knows how the enormous stones, weighing thousands of pounds, were brought to Stonehenge.

FAULTY
PARALLELISM

Introductory Project

Read aloud each pair of sentences below. Put a check mark beside the sentence that reads more smoothly and clearly and sounds more natural.

I made resolutions to study more, to lose weight, and watching less TV. _____

I made resolutions to study more, to lose weight, and to watch less TV. __✓__

A consumer group rates my car as noisy, expensive, and not having much safety. _____

A consumer group rates my car as noisy, expensive, and unsafe. __✓__

Lola likes wearing soft sweaters, eating exotic foods, and to bathe in Calgon bath oil. _____

Lola likes wearing soft sweaters, eating exotic foods, and bathing in Calgon bath oil. __✓__

Single life offers more freedom of choice; more security is offered by marriage. _____

Single life offers more freedom of choice; marriage offers more security. __✓__

Answers are on page 574.

PARALLELISM EXPLAINED

Words in pairs or series should have parallel structure. By balancing the items in a pair or a series so that they have the same kind of structure, you will make a sentence clearer and easier to read. Notice how the parallel sentences that follow read more smoothly than the nonparallel ones.

Nonparallel (Not Balanced)	*Parallel (Balanced)*
I made resolutions to lose weight, to study more, and *watching* less TV.	I made resolutions to lose weight, to study more, and to watch less TV. (A balanced series of *to* verbs: *to lose, to study, to watch*)
A consumer group rates my car as noisy, expensive, and *not having much safety.*	A consumer group rates my car as noisy, expensive, and unsafe. (A balanced series of descriptive words: *noisy, expensive, unsafe*)
Lola likes wearing soft sweaters, eating exotic foods, and *to bathe* in Calgon bath oil.	Lola likes wearing soft sweaters, eating exotic foods, and bathing in Calgon bath oil. (A balanced series of *-ing* words: *wearing, eating, bathing*)
The single life offers more freedom of choice; *more security is offered by marriage.*	The single life offers more freedom of choice; marriage offers more security. (Balanced verbs and word order: *single life offers . . . ; marriage offers . . .*)

You need not worry about balanced sentences when writing first drafts. But when you rewrite, you should try to put matching words and ideas into matching structures. Such parallelism will improve your writing style.

Activity

The unbalanced part of each of the following sentences is *italicized.* Rewrite the unbalanced part so that it matches the rest of the sentence. The first one is done for you as an example.

1. Woody Allen's films are clever, well-acted, and *have a lot of humor.*
   _____humorous_____

2. Filling out an income tax form is worse than wrestling a bear or *to walk* on hot coals. _____*walking*_____

3. The study-skills course taught me how to take more effective notes, to read a textbook chapter, and *preparing* for exams. _____*to prepare*_____

4. Lola plans to become a model, a lawyer, or *to go into nursing.* *to become a nurse.*

5. Martha Grencher likes *to water* her garden, walking her fox terrier, and arguing with her husband. _____*watering*_____

6. Filled with talent and *ambitious,* Charlie plugged away at his sales job. _____*ambition*_____

7. When I saw my roommate with my girlfriend, I felt worried, angry, and *embarrassment* as well. _____*embarrased*_____

8. Cindy's cat likes sleeping in the dryer, lying in the bathtub, and *to chase* squirrels. _____*chasing*_____

9. The bacon was fatty, *grease was on the potatoes,* and the eggs were cold. _____*, the potatoes were greasy and*_____

10. People in the lobby munched popcorn, sipped sodas, and *were shuffling* their feet impatiently. _____*shuffled*_____

■ Review Test 1

On separate paper, write five sentences of your own that use parallel structure.

■ Review Test 2

Draw a line under the unbalanced part of each sentence. Then rewrite the unbalanced part so that it matches the other item or items in the sentence. The first one is done for you as an example.

1. Our professor warned us that he would give surprise tests, the assignment of term papers, and allow no makeup exams.

   assign term papers

2. Pesky mosquitoes, humidity that is high, and sweltering heat make summer an unpleasant time for me.

   _____*high humidity*_____

3. I want a job that pays high wages, provides a complete benefits package, and offering opportunities for promotion.

offers opportunities for promotion.

4. My teenage daughter enjoys shopping for new clothes, to try different cosmetics, and reading beauty magazines.

trying different cosmetics.

5. My car needed the brakes replaced, the front wheels aligned, and recharging of the battery.

and the battery recharged.

6. I had to correct my paper for fragments, misplaced modifiers, and there were apostrophe mistakes.

and mistaken apostrophes.

7. They did not want a black-and-white TV set, but a color set could not be afforded.

TV

8. The neighborhood group asked the town council to repair the potholes and that a traffic light be installed.

install traffic lights

9. Having a headache, my stomach being upset, and a bad case of sunburn did not put me in a good mood for the evening.

an upset stomach,

10. The Gray Panthers is an organization that not only aids older citizens but also providing information for their families.

provides

PAPER FORMAT

When you hand in a paper for any of your courses, probably the first thing you will be judged on is its format. It is important, then, that you do certain things to make your papers look attractive, neat, and easy to read.

Here are guidelines to follow in preparing a paper for an instructor:

1 Use full-sized theme or typewriter paper, 8½ by 11 inches.

2 Leave wide margins (1 to 1½ inches) on all four sides of each page. In particular, do not crowd the right-hand or bottom margin. The white space makes your paper more readable; also, the instructor has room for comments.

3 If you write by hand,

   a Use a blue or black pen (*not* a pencil).

   b Be careful not to overlap letters or to make decorative loops on letters. On narrow-ruled paper, write only on every other line.

   c Make all your letters distinct. Pay special attention to *a, e, i, o,* and *u* — five letters that people sometimes write illegibly.

   d Keep your capital letters clearly distinct from small letters. You may even want to print all the capital letters.

4 Center the title of your paper on the first line of page 1. Do *not* put quotation marks around the title or underline the title or put a period after the title. Capitalize all the major words in a title, including the first word. Small connecting words within a title like *of, for, the, in,* and *to* are not capitalized. Skip a line between the title and the first line of your text.

5 Indent the first line of each paragraph about five spaces (half an inch) from the left-hand margin.

6 Make commas, periods, and other punctuation marks firm and clear. Leave a slight space after each period. When you type, leave a double space after a period.

7 Whenever possible, avoid breaking (hyphenating) words at the end of lines. If you must break a word, break only between syllables (see page 377). Do not break words of one syllable.

8 Write your name, the date, and the course number where your instructor asks for them.

Also keep in mind these important points about the *title* and *first sentence* of your paper:

9 The title should simply be several words that tell what the paper is about. It should usually *not* be a complete sentence. For example, if you are writing a paper about one of the most frustrating jobs you have ever had, the title could be just "A Frustrating Job."

10 Do not rely on the title to help explain the first sentence of your paper. The first sentence must be independent of the title. For instance, if the title of your paper is "A Frustrating Job," the first sentence should *not* be "It was working as a baby-sitter." Rather, the first sentence might be "Working as a baby-sitter was the most frustrating job I ever had."

Activity 1

Identify the mistakes in format in the following lines from a student theme. Explain the mistakes in the spaces provided. One mistake is described for you as an example.

(6) (3) "an unpleasant dining companion" ← (2)
(1) My little brother is often an unpleasant dining companion. Last
night was typical. For one thing, his appearance was disgusting. (5)
His shoes were not tied, and his shirt was unbuttoned and han-(1)
ging out of his pants, which he had forgotten to zip up. Traces
of his afternoon snack of grape juice and chocolate cookies were

1. Hyphenate only between syllables

2. Skip a line between the title and the first line of your text.

3. Capitalize all the major words in a title, including first word.

4. Indent the first line of each paragraph about five spaces.

5. Make commas, periods, and other punctuation marks firm and clear.

6. Do not put quotation marks around the title or underline the title or put a period after the title.

Activity 2

As already stated, a title should tell in several words (but *not* a complete sentence) what a paper is about. Often a title can be based on the topic sentence — the sentence that expresses the main idea of the paper. Following are five topic sentences from student papers. Write a suitable and specific title for each paper, basing the title on the topic sentence. (Note the example.)

Example   *Compromise in a Relationship*

Learning how to compromise is essential to a good relationship.

1. Title: ___Dangerous Houseplants___
   Some houseplants are dangerous to children and pets.

2. Title: ___Childhood Fears.___
   A number of fears haunted me when I was a child.

3. Title: _____
   To insulate a house properly, several important steps should be taken.

4. Title: ___A Compulsive Husband.___
   My husband is compulsively neat.

5. Title: ___Roommate Drawbacks___
   There are a number of drawbacks to having a roommate.

Activity 3

As has already been stated, you must *not* rely on the title to help explain your first sentence. In four of the five sentences that follow, the writer has, inappropriately, used the title to help explain the first sentence.

Rewrite the four sentences so that they stand independent of the title. Write *Correct* under the one sentence that is independent of the title.

Example   Title: My Career Plans
              First sentence: They have changed in the last six months.

              Rewritten: *My career plans have changed in the last six months.*

1. Title: Contending with Dogs
   First sentence: This is the main problem in my work as a mail carrier.
   Rewritten: _As a mail Carrier, my main problem is Contending with Dogs_

   _____

2. Title: Study Skills
   First sentence: They are necessary if a person is to do well in college.
   Rewritten: *To do well in college, It is necessary to have good Study Skills.*

3. Title: Summer Vacation
   First sentence: Contrary to popular belief, a summer vacation can be the most miserable experience of the year.

   Rewritten: _____

   _____

4. Title: My Wife and the Sunday Newspaper
   First sentence: My wife has a peculiar way of reading it.
   Rewritten: *My wife has a peculiar way of reading the Sunday Newspaper.*

5. Title: Traffic Circles
   First sentence: They are one of the chief hazards today's driver must confront.
   Rewritten: *One of the chief hazards of today's driver is confronting traffic circles.*

■ **Review Test**

In the space provided on the next page, rewrite the following sentences from a student paper. Correct the mistakes in format.

	"disciplining our children"
	My husband and I are becoming experts in disciplining our child-
	ren. We have certain rules that we insist upon, and if there are
	any violations, we are swift to act. When our son simply doesn't
	do what he is told to do, he must write that particular action
	twenty times. For example, if he doesn't brush his teeth, he
	writes, "I must brush my teeth." If a child gets home after the

	Disciplining Our Children

CAPITAL
LETTERS

Introductory Project

You probably know a good deal about the uses of capital letters. Answering the questions below will help you check your knowledge.

1. Write the full name of a person you know: _____ *Charles* _____
2. In what city and state were you born? _____ *Lima* _____
3. What is your present street address? _____ *74 Queens Court* _____
4. Name a country where you would like to travel: _____ *China* _____
5. Name a school that you attended: _____ *University of Hartford* _____
6. Give the name of a store where you buy food: _____ *Edwards* _____
7. Name a company where someone you know works: _____ *Aetna* _____
8. What day of the week gives you the best chance to relax? _____ *Friday* _____
9. What holiday is your favorite? _____ *Passover* _____
10. What brand of toothpaste do you use? _____ *Colgate* _____
11. Give the brand name of a candy or gum you like: _____ *Snickers* _____
12. Name a song or a television show you enjoy: _____ *The Nanny* _____
13. Give the title of a magazine you read: _____ *Newsweek* _____

Items 14 – 16: Three capital letters are needed in the lines below. Underline the words that you think should be capitalized. Then write them, capitalized, in the spaces provided.

the masked man reared his silvery-white horse, waved good-bye, and rode out of town. My heart thrilled when i heard someone say, ''that was the Lone Ranger. You don't see his kind much, anymore.''

14. _____ *The* _____   15. _____ *I* _____   16. _____ *That* _____

Answers are on page 574.

MAIN USES OF CAPITAL LETTERS

Capital letters are used with:

1 First word in a sentence or direct quotation
2 Names of persons and the word *I*
3 Names of particular places
4 Names of days of the week, months, and holidays
5 Names of commercial products
6 Names of organizations such as religious and political groups, associations, companies, unions, and clubs
7 Titles of books, magazines, newspapers, articles, stories, poems, films, television shows, songs, papers that you write, and the like

Each use is illustrated on the pages that follow.

First Word in a Sentence or Direct Quotation

The panhandler touched me and asked, "Do you have any change?"

(Capitalize the first word in the sentence.)   (Capitalize the first word in the direct quotation.)

"If you want a ride," said Brenda, "get ready now. Otherwise, I'm going alone."

(*If* and *Otherwise* are capitalized because they are the first words of sentences within a direct quotation. But *get* is not capitalized because it is part of the first sentence within the quotation.)

Names of Persons and the Word *I*

Last night I ran into Tony Curry and Lola Morrison.

Names of Particular Places

Charlotte graduated from Fargone High School in Orlando, Florida. She then moved with her parents to Bakersfield, California, and worked for a time there at Alexander's Gift House. Eventually she married and moved with her husband to the Naval Reserve Center in Atlantic County, New Jersey. She takes courses two nights a week at Stockton State College. On weekends she and her family often visit the nearby Wharton State Park and go canoeing on the Mullica River. She does volunteer work at Atlantic City Hospital in connection with the First Christian Church. In addition, she works during the summer as a hostess at Convention Hall and the Holiday Inn.

But: Use small letters if the specific name of a place is not given.

Charlotte sometimes remembers her unhappy days in high school and at the gift shop where she worked after graduation. She did not imagine then that she would one day be going to college and doing volunteer work for a church and a hospital in the community where she and her husband live.

Names of Days of the Week, Months, and Holidays

I was angry at myself for forgetting that Sunday was Mother's Day.

During July and August, Fred's company works a four-day week, and he has Mondays off.

Bill still has a scar on his ankle from a cherry bomb that exploded near him on a Fourth of July and a scar on his arm where he stabbed himself with a fishhook on a Labor Day weekend.

But: Use small letters for the seasons — summer, fall, winter, spring.

Names of Commercial Products

Clyde uses Scope mouthwash, Certs mints, and Dentyne gum to drive away the taste of the Marlboro cigarettes and White Owl cigars that he always smokes.

My sister likes to play Monopoly and Sorry; I like chess and poker; my brother likes Scrabble, baseball, and table tennis.

But: Use small letters for the *type* of product (mouthwash, mints, gum, cigarettes, and so on).

Names of Organizations Such as Religious and Political Groups, Associations, Companies, Unions, and Clubs

Fred Grencher was a Lutheran for many years but converted to Catholicism when he married. Both he and his wife, Martha, are members of the Democratic Party. Both belong to the American Automobile Association. Martha works part time as a refrigerator salesperson at Sears. Fred is a mail carrier and belongs to the Postal Clerks' Union.

Tony met Lola when he was a Boy Scout and she was a Campfire Girl; she asked him to light her fire.

Titles of Books, Magazines, Newspapers, Articles, Stories, Poems, Films, Television Shows, Songs, Papers That You Write, and the Like

On Sunday Lola read the first chapter of *I Know Why the Caged Bird Sings,* a book required for her writing course. She looked through her parents' copy of *The New York Times.* She then read an article titled "Thinking about a Change in Your Career" and a poem titled "Some Moments Alone" in *Cosmopolitan* magazine. At the same time she played an old Beatles album, *Abbey Road.* In the evening she watched *60 Minutes* on television and a movie, *Sudden Impact,* starring Clint Eastwood. Then from 11 P.M. to midnight she worked on a paper titled "Uses of Leisure Time in Today's Culture" for her sociology class.

Activity

Cross out the words that need capitals in the following sentences. Then write the capitalized forms of the words in the spaces provided. The number of spaces tells you how many corrections to make in each case.

Example   I brush with crest toothpaste but get cavities all the time.   *Crest*

1. A spokesperson for general motors announced that the prices of all chevrolets will rise next year.

    General Motors   Motors   Chevrolets

2. Steve graduated from Maplewood ~~high school~~ in ~~june~~ 1988.

_____High_____   _____School_____   _____June_____

3. The mild-mannered reporter named ~~clark kent~~ said to the Wolfman, "~~you~~'d better think twice before you mess with me, Buddy."

_____Clark_____   _____Kent_____   _____You_____

4. While watching television, Bill drank four ~~pepsis~~, ate an entire package of ~~ritz~~ crackers, and finished up a bag of ~~oreo~~ cookies.

_____Pepsis_____   _____Ritz_____   _____Oreo_____

5. A ~~greyhound~~ bus almost ran over Tony as he was riding his ~~yamaha~~ to a friend's home in ~~florida~~.

_____Greyhound_____   _____Yamaha_____   _____Florida_____

6. Before I lent my ~~polaroid~~ camera to Janet, I warned her, "~~be~~ sure to return it by ~~friday~~."

_____Polaroid_____   _____Be_____   _____Friday_____

7. Before ~~christmas~~ George took his entire paycheck, went to ~~sears~~, and bought a twenty-inch ~~zenith~~ color television.

_____Christmas_____   _____Sears_____   _____Zenith_____

8. On their first trip to New York City, Fred and Martha visited the ~~empire~~ State Building and Times ~~square~~. They also saw the New York ~~mets~~ play at Shea Stadium.

_____Empire_____   _____Square_____   _____Mets_____

9. Clyde was listening to Tina Turner's recording of "Proud ~~mary~~," Charlotte was reading an article in *Reader's ~~digest~~* titled "~~let~~'s Stop Peddling Sex," and their son was watching *~~sesame~~ Street.*

_____Digest_____   "_Let's_   _____Mary_____   _____Sesame_____

10. When a sign for a ~~howard johnson~~'s rest stop appeared on the turnpike, ~~anita~~ said, "~~let~~'s stop here and stretch our legs for a bit."

_____Howard_____   _____Johnson's_____   _____Anita_____   "_Let's_

OTHER USES OF CAPITAL LETTERS

Capital letters are also used with:

1 Names that show family relationships
2 Titles of persons when used with their names
3 Specific school courses
4 Languages
5 Geographic locations
6 Historical periods and events
7 Races, nations, and nationalities
8 Opening and closing of a letter

Each use is illustrated on the pages that follow.

Names That Show Family Relationships

I got Mother to baby-sit for me.

I went with Grandfather to the church service.

Uncle Carl and Aunt Lucy always enclose five dollars with birthday cards.

But: Do not capitalize words like *mother, father, grandmother, aunt,* and so on, when they are preceded by a possessive word (*my, your, his, her, our, their*).

I got my mother to baby-sit for me.

I went with my grandfather to the church service.

My uncle and aunt always enclose five dollars with birthday cards.

Titles of Persons When Used with Their Names

I wrote to Senator Grabbel and Congresswoman Punchie.

Professor Snorrel sent me to Chairperson Ruck, who sent me to Dean Rappers.

He drove to Dr. Helen Thompson's office after the cat bit him.

But: Use small letters when titles appear by themselves, without specific names.

I wrote to my senator and congresswoman.

The professor sent me to the chairperson, who sent me to the dean.

He drove to the doctor's office after the cat bit him.

Specific School Courses

I got an A in both Accounting I and Small Business Management, but I got a C in Human Behavior.

But: Use small letters for general subject areas.

I enjoyed my business courses but not my psychology or language courses.

Languages

She knows German and Spanish, but she speaks mostly American slang.

Geographic Locations

I grew up in the Midwest. I worked in the East for a number of years and then moved to the West Coast.

But: Use small letters in directions.

A new high school is being built at the south end of town.

Because I have a compass in my car, I know that I won't be going east or west when I want to go north.

Historical Periods and Events

Hector did well answering an essay question about the Second World War, but he lost points on a question about the Great Depression.

Races, Nations, Nationalities

The research study centered on African Americans and Hispanics.

They have German knives and Danish glassware in the kitchen, an Indian wood carving in the bedroom, Mexican sculptures in the study, and an Oriental rug in the living room.

Opening and Closing of a Letter

> Dear Sir:
> Dear Madam:
> Sincerely yours,
> Truly yours,

Note: Capitalize only the first word in a closing.

Activity

Cross out the words that need capitals in the following sentences. Then write the capitalized forms of the words in the spaces provided. The number of spaces tells you how many corrections to make in each case.

1. Although my grandfather spoke ~~german~~ and ~~polish~~, my mother never learned either language.

    German   _Polish_

2. The ~~chain~~ letter began, "~~dear~~ friend — You must mail twenty copies of this letter if you want good luck."

    Chain   _Dear_

3. Tomorrow in our history class, ~~dr.~~ ~~connalley~~ will start lecturing on the ~~civil war~~.

    _Dr._   _Connalley_   _Civil_   _War_

4. ~~aunt~~ Sarah and ~~uncle~~ Hal, who are ~~mormons~~, took us to their church services when we visited them in the ~~midwest~~.

    Aunt   _Mormons_   _Uncle_   _Midwest_

5. My sister has signed up for a course titled ~~eastern religions~~; she'll be studying ~~buddhism~~ and ~~hinduism~~.

    Eastern   _Religions_   _Buddhism_   _Hinduism_

UNNECESSARY USE OF CAPITALS

Many errors in capitalization are caused by using capitals where they are not needed.

Activity

Cross out the incorrectly capitalized words in the following sentences. Then write the correct forms of the words in the spaces provided. The number of spaces tells you how many corrections to make in each sentence.

1. Although the ~~Commercials~~ say that ~~Things~~ go better with ~~Coke~~, I prefer Root ~~Beer~~.

    commercials   _things_   _Coke_   _beer_

2. The old man told the ~~Cabdriver~~, ''I want to go out to the ~~Airport~~, and don't try to cheat me.''

    cabdriver   _airport_

3. A front-page ~~Newspaper~~ story about the crash of a commercial ~~Jet~~ has made me nervous about my ~~Overseas~~ trip.

    newspaper   _jet_   _overseas_

4. During a ~~Terrible~~ ~~Blizzard~~ in 1888, ~~People~~ froze to ~~Death~~ on the streets of New York.

    terrible   _blizzard_   _people_   _death_

5. I asked the ~~Bank~~ ~~Officer~~ at Citibank, ''How do I get an identification ~~Card~~ to use the automatic teller machines?''

    bank   _officer_   _card._

■ Review Test 1

Cross out the words that need capitals in the following sentences. Then write the capitalized forms of the words in the spaces provided. The number of spaces tells you how many corrections to make in each sentence.

1. ~~wanda~~ and ~~i~~ agreed to meet on ~~saturday~~ before the football game.

    Wanda   _I_   _Saturday_

2. Between Long ~~island~~ and the ~~atlantic~~ Ocean lies a long, thin sandbar called ~~fire~~ island.

    Island   _Atlantic_   _Fire_   _Island._

3. When I'm in the supermarket checkout line, it seems as if every magazine on display has an article called "~~how~~ You Can Lose Twenty pounds in two weeks."

_____   _____   _____   _____

4. At the bookstore, each student received a free sample pack of ~~bayer~~ aspirin, ~~arrid~~ deodorant, and ~~prell~~ shampoo.

___Bayer___   ___Arrid___   ___Prell___

5. "~~can't~~ you be quiet?" I pleaded. "~~do~~ you always have to talk while I'm watching *general hospital* on television?"

___"Can't___   ___"Do___   ___General___   ___Hospital___

6. On ~~father's day~~, the children drove home and took their parents out to dinner at the ~~ramada inn~~.

___Father's___   ___Day___   ___Ramada___   ___Inn.___

7. I will work at the ~~holly~~ Day School on ~~mondays~~ and ~~fridays~~ for the rest of ~~september~~.

___Holly___   ___Mondays___   ___Fridays___   ___September.___

8. ~~glendale~~ bank, where my ~~sister~~ Kathy works, is paying for her night course titled ~~business accounting~~ I.

___Glendale___   ___Sister___   ___Business___   ___Accounting___

9. I subscribe to one newspaper, the *daily planet;* and two magazines, *people* and *glamour.*

___Daily___   ___Planet___   ___People___   ___Glamour___

10. On ~~thanksgiving~~ my brother said, "~~let's~~ hurry and eat so ~~i~~ can go watch the football game on our new ~~sony~~ TV."

___Thanksgiving___   ___"Let's___   ___I___   ___Sony___

■ **Review Test 2**

On separate paper,

1. Write seven sentences demonstrating the seven main uses of capital letters.
2. Write eight sentences demonstrating the eight additional uses of capital letters.

NUMBERS
AND
ABBREVIATIONS

NUMBERS

1   Spell out numbers that can be expressed in one or two words. Otherwise, use numerals — the numbers themselves.

> During the past five years, over twenty-five barracuda have been caught in the lake.
>
> The parking fine was ten dollars.
>
> In my grandmother's attic are eighty-four pairs of old shoes.

But

> Each year about 250 baby trout are added to the lake.
>
> My costs after contesting a parking fine in court were $135.
>
> Grandmother has 382 back copies of *Reader's Digest* in her attic.

2   Be consistent when you use a series of numbers. If some numbers in a sentence or paragraph require more than two words, then use numerals throughout the selection:

> During his election campaign, State Senator Mel Grabble went to 3 county fairs, 16 parades, 45 cookouts, and 112 club dinners, and delivered the same speech 176 times.

3   Use numerals for dates, times, addresses, percentages, and parts of a book.

> The letter was dated April 3, 1872.
>
> My appointment was at 6:15. (*But:* Spell out numbers before *o'clock*. For example: The doctor didn't see me until seven o'clock.)
>
> He lives at 212 West 19th Street.
>
> About 20 percent of our class has dropped out of school.
>
> Turn to page 179 in Chapter 8 and answer questions 1 – 10.

Activity

Cross out the mistakes in numbers and write the corrections in the spaces provided.

1. Rich was born on February ~~fifteenth~~, ~~nineteen seventy~~.

    _15_

    _1970_

2. When the ~~2~~ children failed to return from school, over ~~50~~ people volunteered to search for them.

    two

    fifty

3. At ~~1~~ o'clock in the afternoon last Thursday, an earthquake destroyed at least ~~20~~ buildings in the town.

    Twenty

    One

ABBREVIATIONS

While abbreviations are a helpful time-saver in note-taking, you should avoid most abbreviations in formal writing. Listed below are some of the few abbreviations that can acceptably be used in compositions. Note that a period is used after most abbreviations.

1 Mr., Mrs., Ms., Jr., Sr., Dr. when used with proper names:

Mr. Tibble   Dr. Stein   Ms. O'Reilly

2 Time references:

A.M. or a.m.   P.M. or p.m.   B.C. or A.D.

3 First or middle name in a signature:

R. Anthony Curry   Otis T. Redding   J. Alfred Prufrock

4 Organizations, technical words, and trade names known primarily by their initials:

FBI   UN   CBS   FM   MTV

Activity

Cross out the words that should not be abbreviated and correct them in the spaces provided.

1. On a Sat. morning I will never forget—Dec. 5, 1992, at ten min. after eight—I came downstairs and discovered that I had been robbed.

    _____   _____   _____

2. For six years I lived at First Ave. and Gordon St., right next to Shore Memorial Hosp., in San Fran., Calif.

    _____   _____   _____   _____   _____

3. Before her biol. and Eng. exams, Linda was so nervous that her doc. gave her a tranq.

    _____   _____   _____   _____

■ Review Test

Cross out the mistakes in numbers and abbreviations and correct them in the spaces provided.

1. At three-fifteen p.m., an angry caller said a bomb was planted in a bus stat. locker.

    _3 : 15_ _____   _Station_ _____

2. Page eighty-two is missing from my chem. book.

    _82_ _____   _Chemistry_ _____

3. Martha has over 200 copies of *People* mag.; she thinks they may be worth money someday.

    magazine _____   _Two Hundred_ _____

4. When I was eight yrs. old, I owned three cats, two dogs, and 4 rabbits.

    years _____   _two, four_ _____

5. Approx. half the striking workers returned to work on Jan. third, nineteen ninety-four.

    _1994_ _____   _Approximately_   _Jan_   _____ _3,_ _____

APOSTROPHE

Introductory Project

1. Larry's motorcycle
   my sister's boyfriend
   Grandmother's shotgun *(handwritten: alone)*
   the men's room
   Dionne Warwick's new album

   What is the purpose of the *'s* in the examples above?
   To Demonstrate Possession

2. They didn't mind when their dog bit people, but now they're leashing him because he's eating all their garden vegetables.

   What is the purpose of the apostrophe in *didn't, they're,* and *he's?*
   To Shortened a word – Contraction

3. I used to believe that vampires lived in the old coal bin of my cellar. *(handwritten: center)*
   The vampire's whole body recoiled when he saw the crucifix.

   Fred ate two baked potatoes.
   One baked potato's center was still hard.

   In each of the sentence pairs above, why is the *'s* used in the second sentence but not in the first? *The first sentences showed simple plurals. The second sentences show possession*

Answers are on page 574.

The two main uses of the apostrophe are:

1   To show the omission of one or more letters in a contraction
2   To show ownership or possession

Each use is explained on the pages that follow.

APOSTROPHE IN CONTRACTIONS

A contraction is formed when two words are combined to make one word. An apostrophe is used to show where letters are omitted in forming the contraction. Here are two contractions:

have + not = haven't (the *o* in *not* has been omitted)

I + will = I'll (the *wi* in *will* has been omitted)

The following are some other common contractions:

I + am = I'm	it + is = it's	
I + have = I've	it + has = it's	
I + had = I'd	is + not = isn't	
who + is = who's	could + not = couldn't	
do + not = don't	I + would = I'd	
did + not = didn't	they + are = they're	

Note: *Will* + *not* has an unusual contraction: *won't.*

Activity 1

Combine the following words into contractions. One is done for you.

1.   we + are = _we're_
2.   are + not = _aren't_
3.   you + are = _You're_
4.   they + have = _they're_
5. would + not = _woldn't_

6.   you + have = _you've_
7.   has + not = _hasn't_
8.   who + is = _who's_
9.   does + not = _doesn't_
10.   there + is = _there's_

Activity 2

Write the contractions for the words in parentheses. One is done for you.

1. (Are not) _____Aren't_____ you coming with us to the concert?

2. (I am) __I'm____ going to take the car if (it is) ____its____ all right with you.

3. (There is) ____There's____ an extra bed upstairs if (you would) ____You'd____ like to stay here for the night.

4. (I will) ____I'll____ give you the name of the personnel director, but there (is not) ____isn't____ much chance that (he will) ____he'll____ speak to you.

5. Linda (should not) ____shouldn't____ complain about the cost of food if (she is) ____she's____ not willing to grow her own by planting a backyard garden.

Note: Even though contractions are common in everyday speech and in written dialog, usually it is best to avoid them in formal writing.

APOSTROPHE TO SHOW OWNERSHIP OR POSSESSION

To show ownership or possession, we can use such words as *belongs to, possessed by, owned by,* or (most commonly) *of.*

> the jacket that *belongs to* Tony
> the grades *possessed by* James
> the gas station *owned by* our cousin
> the footprints *of* the animal

But the apostrophe plus *s* (if the word is not a plural ending in -*s*) is often the quickest and easiest way to show possession. Thus we can say:

> Tony's jacket
> James's grades
> our cousin's gas station
> the animal's footprints

Points to Remember

1   The *'s* goes with the owner or possessor (in the examples given, *Tony, cousin, the animal*). What follows is the person or thing possessed (in the examples given, *the jacket, gas station, footprints*).

2   When *'s* is handwritten, there should always be a break between the word and the *'s*.

Tony's   not   Tony's

Yes   No

3   A singular word ending in *-s* (such as *James* on the preceding page) also shows possession by adding an apostrophe plus *s* (*James's*).

Activity 1

Rewrite the italicized part of each of the sentences below, using the *'s* to show possession. Remember that the *'s* goes with the owner or possessor.

Examples   *The toys belonging to the children* filled an entire room.

The children's toys

1. *The roller skates owned by Pat* have been stolen.

Pat's roller skates

2. *The visit of my cousin* lasted longer than I wanted it to.

My cousin's visit

3. *The fenders belonging to the car* are badly rusted.

the car's fenders

4. *The prescription of a doctor* is needed for the pills.

the doctor's prescription

5. *The jeep owned by Doris* was recalled because of an engine defect.

Doris's Jeep

6. Is this *the hat of somebody*?

Somebody's hat

7. The broken saddle produced a sore on *the back of the horse*.

the horse's back

8. *The two dogs belonging to my neighbor* ripped open the trash bags.

My neighbor's two dogs

9. *The energy level possessed by the little boy* is much higher than hers.

The little boy's energy level

10. *The foundation of the house* is crumbling.

The house's foundation is crumbling

Activity 2

Add *'s* to each of the following words to make them the possessors or owners of something. Then write sentences using the words. Your sentences can be serious or playful. One is done for you.

1. dog ___dog's___   That dog's bite is worse than his bark.

2. instructor ___instructor's___   My team was penalized according to the instructor's rules.

3. Lola ___Lola's___   Lola's migraine headache was due to stress.

4. store ___store's___   The walmart store's success story is due to perseverance.

5. mother ___mother's___   I did not know that was my mother's purse.

Apostrophe versus Possessive Pronouns

Do not use an apostrophe with possessive pronouns. They already show ownership. Possessive pronouns include *his, hers, its, yours, ours,* and *theirs.*

Incorrect	*Correct*
The bookstore lost its' lease.	The bookstore lost its lease.
The racing bikes were theirs'.	The racing bikes were theirs.
The change is yours'.	The change is yours.
His' problems are ours', too.	His problems are ours, too.
His' skin is more sunburned than hers.'	His skin is more sunburned than hers.

Apostrophe versus Simple Plurals

When you want to make a word plural, just add an *-s* at the end of the word. Do *not* add an apostrophe. For example, the plural of the word *movie* is *movies,* not *movie's* or *movies'*. Look at this sentence:

Lola adores Tony's broad shoulders, rippling muscles, and warm eyes.

The words *shoulders, muscles,* and *eyes* are simple plurals, meaning *more than one shoulder, more than one muscle, more than one eye*. The plural is shown by adding *-s* only. On the other hand, the *'s* after *Tony* shows possession — that Tony owns the shoulders, muscles, and eyes.

Activity

In the space provided under each sentence, add the one apostrophe needed and explain why the other word or words ending in *s* are simple plurals.

Example   Karens tomato plants are almost six feet tall.

Karens: *Karen's, meaning "the plants belonging to Karen"*

plants: *simple plural meaning "more than one plant"*

1. My fathers influence on his brothers has been enormous.

fathers: _____

brothers: _____

2. Phils job — slaughtering pigs — was enough to make him a vegetarian.

Phils: _____

pigs: _____

3. As Tinas skill at studying increased, her grades improved.

Tinas: _____

grades: _____

4. When I walked into my doctors office, there were six people waiting who also had appointments.

doctors: _____

appointments: _____

5. I asked the record store clerk for several blank cassette tapes and Whitney Houston's new album.

   tapes: _____

   Houstons: _____

6. After six weeks without rain, the nearby streams started drying up, and the lakes' water level fell sharply.

   weeks: _____

   streams: _____

   lakes: _____

7. Everyone wanted to enroll in Dr. Lerner's class, but all the sections were closed.

   Lerners: _____

   sections: _____

8. When the brakes failed on Phil's truck, he narrowly avoided hitting several parked cars and two trees.

   Phils: _____

   cars: _____

   trees: _____

9. My family's favorite breakfast is bacon, eggs, and home-fried potatoes.

   familys: _____

   eggs: _____

   potatoes: _____

10. We like Florida's winters, but we prefer to spend the summers in other states.

    Floridas: _____

    winters: _____

    summers: _____

    states: _____

Apostrophe with Plural Words Ending in *-s*

Plurals that end in *-s* show possession simply by adding the apostrophe, rather than an apostrophe plus *s*.

My *parents'* station wagon is ten years old.

The many *students'* complaints were ignored by the high school principal.

All the *Boy Scouts'* tents were damaged by the hail storm.

Activity

In each sentence, cross out the one plural word that needs an apostrophe. Then write the word correctly, with the apostrophe, in the space provided.

Example _____*soldiers'*_____ All the soldiers rifles were cleaned for inspection.

1. My ~~parents~~ car was stolen last night.

     ____*parents'*____

2. The transit ~~workers~~ strike has just ended.

     ____*workers'*____

3. Two of our ~~neighbors~~ homes are up for sale.

     ____*neighbors'*____

4. The door to the ~~ladies~~ room is locked.

     ____*ladies'*____

5. When students gripes about the cafeteria were ignored, many started to bring their own lunches.

     ____*students'*____

■ **Review Test 1**

In each sentence, cross out the two words that need apostrophes. Then write the words correctly in the spaces provided.

1. The ~~contestants~~ face fell when she learned she had won a years supply of Ajax cleanser.

     ____*contestants'*____   ____*year's*____

2. ~~Weve~~ been trying for weeks to see that movie, but ~~theres~~ always a long line.

     ____*we're*____   ____*there's*____

3. ~~Freds~~ car ~~wouldnt~~ start until the baby-faced mechanic replaced its spark plugs and points.

   _____Fred's_____   _____wouldn't_____

4. The ~~citys~~ budget director has trouble balancing his own ~~familys~~ books.

   _____city's_____   _____family's_____

5. Taking ~~Dianes~~ elderly parents to church every week is one example of ~~Toms~~ generous behavior.

   _____Diane's_____   _____Tom's_____

6. ~~Heres~~ a checklist of points to follow when ~~youre~~ writing your class reports.

   _____Here's_____   _____You're_____

7. Lola shops in the mens store for jeans and the ~~childrens~~ department for belts.

   _____men's_____   _____children's_____

8. The ~~cats~~ babies are under my chair again; I ~~cant~~ find a way to keep her from bringing them near me.

   _____cat's_____   _____can't_____

9. Because of a family feud, Julie ~~wasnt~~ invited to a barbecue at her ~~cousins~~ house.

   _____wasn't_____   _____cousin's_____

10. ~~Phyllis~~ grade was the highest in the class, and ~~Lewis~~ grade was the lowest.

    _____Phylli's_____   _____Lewi's_____

■ Review Test 2

Make the following words possessive and then—on separate paper—use at least five of them in a not-so-serious paragraph that tells a story. In addition, use at least three contractions in the paragraph.

mugger	restaurant	Tony	student
New York	sister	children	vampire
duck	Jay Leno	boss	Eddie Murphy
customer	bartender	police car	yesterday
instructor	someone	mob	Chicago

QUOTATION
MARKS

SET OFF:

STROLL:

Introductory Project

Read the following scene and underline all the words enclosed within quotation marks. Your instructor may also have you dramatize the scene, with one person reading the narration and two persons acting the two speaking parts of the young man and the old woman. The two speakers should imagine the scene as part of a stage play and try to make their words seem as real and true-to-life as possible.

An old woman in a Rolls-Royce was preparing to back into a parking space. Suddenly a small sports car appeared and pulled into the space. "That's what you can do when you're young and fast," the young man in the car yelled to the old woman. As he strolled away, laughing, he heard a terrible crunching sound. "What's that noise?" he said. Turning around, he saw the old woman backing repeatedly into and crushing his small car. "You can't do that, old lady!" he yelled.

"What do you mean, I can't?" she chuckled, as metal grated against metal. "This is what you can do when you're old and rich."

1. On the basis of the above selection, what is the purpose of quotation marks?

   To SET OFF the exact words of the Speaker.

2. Do commas and periods that come after a quotation go inside or outside the quotation marks?

   inside

Answers are on page 574.

GRATE:

The two main uses of quotation marks are:

1 To set off the exact words of a speaker or a writer
2 To set off the titles of short works

Each use is explained on the pages that follow.

QUOTATION MARKS TO SET OFF
EXACT WORDS OF A SPEAKER OR A WRITER

Use quotation marks when you want to show the exact words of a speaker or a writer.

"Say something tender to me," whispered Lola to Tony.
(Quotation marks set off the exact words that Lola spoke to Tony.)

Mark Twain once wrote, "The more I know about human beings, the more I like my dog."
(Quotation marks set off the exact words that Mark Twain wrote.)

"The only dumb question," the instructor said, "is the one you don't ask."
(Two pairs of quotation marks are used to enclose the instructor's exact words.)

Sharon complained, "I worked so hard on this paper. I spent two days getting information in the library and two days writing it. Guess what grade I got on it."
(Note that the end quotation marks do not come until the end of Sharon's speech. Place quotation marks before the first quoted word of a speech and after the last quoted word. As long as no interruption occurs in the speech, do not use quotation marks for each new sentence.)

Punctuation Hint: In the four examples above, notice that a comma sets off the quoted part from the rest of the sentence. Also observe that commas and periods at the end of a quotation always go *inside* quotation marks.

Complete the following statements that explain how capital letters, commas, and periods are used in quotations. Refer to the four examples as guides.

1. Every quotation begins with a ____Capital____ letter.
2. When a quotation is split (as in the sentence above about dumb questions), the second part does not begin with a capital letter unless it is a ____new____ sentence.

3. _____Commas_____ are used to separate the quoted part of a sentence from the rest of the sentence.

4. Commas and periods that come at the end of a quotation should go _____inside_____ the quotation marks.

The answers are *capital, new, Commas,* and *inside.*

Activity 1

Place quotation marks around the exact words of a speaker or writer in the sentences that follow.

1. "Take some vitamin C for your cold," Lola told Tony.
2. "How are you doing in school?" my uncle always asks me.
3. An epitaph on a tombstone in Georgia reads, "I told you I was sick!"
4. Dave said, "Let's walk faster. I think the game has already started."
5. Lincoln wrote, "To sin by silence when they should protest makes cowards of men."
6. Thelma said, "My brother is so lazy that, if opportunity knocked, he'd resent the noise."
7. "It's extremely dangerous to mix alcohol and pills," Dr. Wilson reminded us. "The combination could kill you."
8. "Ice-cold drinks!" shouted the vendor selling lukewarm drinks. (TIBIOS)
9. "Be careful not to touch the fence," the guard warned. "It's electrified."
10. "Just because I'm deaf," Lynn said, "many people treat me as if I were stupid."

Activity 2

1. Write a sentence in which you quote a favorite expression of someone you know. Identify the relationship of the person to you.

   Example   _One of my father's favorite expressions is, "Don't sweat_
   the small stuff."

   "What a dummy'," my mom used to tell us when were kids.

2. Write a quotation that contains the words *Tony asked Lola.* Write a second quotation that includes the words *Lola replied.*

"Do you read the Bible often?" Tony asked Lola

"Of course, I do it religiously," Lola replied.

3. Copy a sentence or two that interests you from a book or magazine. Identify the title and author of the work.

Example   *In Night Shift, Stephen King writes, "I don't like to sleep with one leg sticking out. ... If a cool hand ever reached out from under the bed and grasped my ankle, I might scream."*

In The Bible, you can read the word of God that promises, "a New Heaven and a New Earth where righteousness is to dwell."

Indirect Quotations

An indirect quotation is a rewording of someone else's comments, rather than a word-for-word direct quotation. The word *that* often signals an indirect quotation. Quotation marks are *not* used with indirect quotations.

Direct Quotation

Fred said, "The distributor cap on my car is cracked."
(Fred's exact spoken words are given, so quotation marks are used.)

Sally's note to Jay read, "I'll be working late. Don't wait up for me."
(The exact words that Sally wrote in the note are given, so quotation marks are used.)

Indirect Quotation

Fred said that the distributor cap on his car was cracked.
(We learn Fred's words *in*directly, so no quotation marks are used.)

Sally left a note for Jay saying she would be working late and he should not wait up for her.
(We learn Sally's words indirectly, so no quotation marks are used.)

Activity

Rewrite the following sentences, changing words as necessary to convert the indirect quotations into direct quotations. The first one is done for you as an example.

1. Fred asked Martha if he could turn on the football game.
   Fred asked Martha, "May I turn on the football game?"

2. Martha said that he could listen to the game on the radio.
   Martha said, "You can listen to the game on the radio."

3. Fred replied he was tired of being told what to do.
   "I am tired of being told what to do," Fred replied.

4. Martha said that as long as she was bigger and stronger, she would make the rules.
   Martha said, "as long as I am bigger and stronger, I will make the rules"

5. Fred said that the day would come when the tables would be turned.
   "The day will come when the tables would be turned," Fred said.

QUOTATION MARKS TO SET OFF TITLES OF SHORT WORKS

Titles of short works are usually set off by quotation marks, while titles of long works are underlined. Use quotation marks to set off the titles of such short works as articles in books, newspapers, or magazines; chapters in a book; short stories; poems; and songs.

On the other hand, you should underline the titles of books, newspapers, magazines, plays, movies, record albums, and television shows.

Quotation Marks	Underlines
the article ''The Mystique of Lawyers''	in the book Verdicts on Lawyers
the article ''Getting a Fix on Repairs''	in the newspaper The New York Times
the article ''Animal Facts and Fallacies''	in the magazine Reader's Digest
the chapter ''Why Do Men Marry?''	in the book Passages
the story ''The Night the Bed Fell''	in the book A Thurber Carnival

Quotation Marks

the poem ''A Prayer for My Daughter''

the song ''Beat It''

Underlines

in the book <u>Poems of W. B. Yeats</u>

in the album <u>Thriller</u>

the television show <u>Cheers</u>

the movie <u>Gone with the Wind</u>

Note: In printed works, titles of books, newspapers, and so on are set off by italics — slanted type that looks *like this* — instead of being underlined.

Activity

Use quotation marks or underlines as needed.

1. ''I Was a Playboy Bunny'' is the first chapter of Gloria Steinem's book <u>Outrageous Acts and Everyday Rebellions</u>.

2. No advertising is permitted in <u>Consumer Reports</u>, a nonprofit consumer magazine.

3. I cut out an article from <u>Newsweek</u> called ''The Bad News about Our High Schools'' to use in my sociology report.

4. Tony's favorite television show is <u>Star Trek</u>, and his favorite movie is <u>The Night of the Living Dead</u>.

5. Our instructor gave us a week to buy the textbook titled <u>Personal Finance</u> and to read the first chapter, ''Work and Income.''

6. Every holiday season, our family watches the movie <u>A Christmas Carol</u> on television.

7. Fred bought the <u>Ladies' Home Journal</u> because he wanted to read the cover article titled ''Secrets Men Never Tell You.''

8. Edgar Allan Poe's short story ''The Murders in the Rue Morgue'' and his poem ''The Raven'' are in a paperback titled <u>Great Tales and Poems of Edgar Allan Poe</u>.

9. When Elaine got her <u>TV Guide</u>, she read an article titled ''The New Comedians'' and then thumbed through the listings to see who would be the guests that week on the <u>Tonight Show</u>.

10. The night before his exam, he discovered with horror that the chapter ''Becoming Mature'' was missing from <u>Childhood and Adolescence</u>, the psychology text that he had bought secondhand.

OTHER USES OF QUOTATION MARKS

1 Quotation marks are used to set off special words or phrases from the rest of a sentence:

Many people spell the words ''a lot'' as *one* word, ''alot,'' instead of correctly spelling them as two words.

I have trouble telling the difference between ''their'' and ''there.''

Note: In printed works, *italics* are often used to set off special words or phrases. That is usually done in this book, for example.

2 Quotation marks are also used to mark off a quotation within a quotation:

The instructor said, ''Know the chapter titled 'Status Symbols' in *Adolescent Development* if you expect to pass the test.''

Lola said, ''One of my favorite Mae West lines is 'I used to be Snow White, but I drifted.' ''

Note: A quotation within a quotation is indicated by *single* quotation marks.

■ Review Test 1

Insert quotation marks where needed in the sentences that follow.

1. "Don't you ever wash your car?" Lola asked Tony.
2. When the washer tilted and began to buzz, Martha shouted, "Let's get rid of that blasted machine!"
3. "Take all you want," read the sign above the cafeteria salad bar, "but please eat all you take."
4. After scrawling formulas all over the board with lightning speed, my math instructor was fond of asking, "Any questions now?"
5. "Move that heap!" the truck driver yelled. "I'm trying to make a living here."
6. I did a summary of an article titled "Aspirin and Heart Attacks" in the latest issue of Time.

7. "Writer's block is something that happens to everyone at times," the instructor explained. "You simply have to keep writing to break out of it."

8. A passenger in the car ahead of Clyde threw food wrappers and empty cups out the window. "That man," said Clyde to his son, "is a human pig."

9. "If you are working during the day," said the counselor, "the best way to start college is with a night course or two."

10. I told the dentist that I wanted Novocain. "Don't be a sissy," he said. "A little pain won't hurt you." I told him that a little pain wouldn't bother him, but it would bother me.

■ Review Test 2

Go through the comics section of a newspaper to find a comic strip that amuses you. Be sure to choose a strip where two or more characters are speaking to each other. Write a full description that will enable people who have not read the comic strip to visualize it clearly and appreciate its humor. Describe the setting and action in each panel, and enclose the words of the speakers in quotation marks.

COMMA

Introductory Project

Commas often (though not always) signal <u>a minor break</u>, or <u>pause</u>, in a sentence. Each of the six pairs of sentences below illustrates one of the six main uses of the comma. Read each pair of sentences aloud and place a comma wherever you feel a slight pause occurs.

1. a. Frank's interests are Maria, television, and sports.
   b. My mother put her feet up, sipped some iced tea, and opened the newspaper.

2. a. Although the Lone Ranger used lots of silver bullets, he never ran out of ammunition.
   b. To open the cap of the aspirin bottle, you must first press down on it.

3. a. Kitty Litter and Dredge Rivers, Hollywood's leading romantic stars, have made several movies together.
   b. Sarah, who is my next-door neighbor, just entered the hospital with an intestinal infection.

4. a. The wedding was scheduled for four o'clock, but the bride changed her mind at two.
   b. Verna took three coffee breaks before lunch, and then she went on a two-hour lunch break.

5. a. Lola's mother asked her, "What time do you expect to get home?"
   b. "Don't bend over to pat the dog," I warned, "or he'll bite you."

6. a. Roy ate seventeen hamburgers on July 29, 1992, and lived to tell about it.
   b. Roy lives at 817 Cresson Street, Detroit, Michigan.

Answers are on page 575.

SIX MAIN USES OF THE COMMA

Commas are used mainly as follows:

1   To separate items in a series
2   To set off introductory material
3   Before and after words that interrupt the flow of thought in a sentence
4   Between two complete thoughts connected by *and, but, for, or, nor, so, yet*
5   To set off a direct quotation from the rest of a sentence
6   For certain everyday material

Each use is explained on the pages that follow.

You may find it helpful to remember that the comma often marks a slight pause, or break, in a sentence. Read aloud the sentence examples given for each rule, and listen for the minor pauses, or breaks, that are signaled by commas.

Comma between Items in a Series

Use commas to separate items in a series.

> Do you drink tea with milk, lemon, or honey?
> Today the dishwasher stopped working, the garbage bag split, and the refrigerator turned into an icebox.
> The television talk shows enraged him so much he did not know whether to laugh, cry, or throw up.
> Jan awoke from a restless, nightmare-filled sleep.

Note: A comma is used between two descriptive words in a series only if *and* inserted between the words sounds natural. You could say:

> Jan awoke from a restless *and* nightmare-filled sleep.

But notice in the following sentence that the descriptive words do not sound natural when *and* is inserted between them. In such cases, no comma is used.

> Wanda drove a bright blue Corvette. (A bright *and* blue Corvette doesn't sound right, so no comma is used.)

Activity

Place commas between items in a series.

1. Superman believes in truth, justice, and the American way.
2. My father taught me to swim by talking to me calmly, holding my hand firmly, and throwing me into the pool.
3. Paul added white wine mushrooms, salt, pepper, and oregano, to his spaghetti sauce.
4. Baggy threadbare jeans, feel more comfortable than pajamas to me.
5. Mark grabbed a tiny towel <u>bolted out</u> of the bathroom, and ran toward the ringing phone.

Comma after Introductory Material

Use a comma to set off introductory material.

> After punching the alarm clock with his fist, Bill turned over and went back to sleep.
>
> Looking up to the sky, I saw a man who was flying faster than a speeding bullet.
>
> Holding a baited trap, Clyde cautiously approached the gigantic mousehole.
>
> In addition, he held a broom in his hand.
>
> Also, he wore a football helmet in case a creature should leap out at his head.

Notes:

a If the introductory material is brief, the comma is sometimes omitted. In the activities here, you should use the comma.

b A comma is also used to set off extra material at the end of a sentence. Here are two earlier sentences where this comma rule applies:

> A sudden breeze shot through the windows, driving the stuffiness out of the room.
>
> I love to cook and eat Italian food, especially spaghetti and lasagna.

Activity

Place commas after introductory material.

1. When the president entered, the room became hushed.
2. Feeling brave and silly at the same time, Tony volunteered to go on stage and help the magician.
3. While I was eating my tuna sandwich, the cats circled my chair like hungry sharks.
4. Because my parents died when I was young, I have learned to look after myself. Even though I am now independent, I still carry a special loneliness within me.
5. At first, putting extra hot pepper flakes on the pizza seemed like a good idea. However, I felt otherwise when flames seemed about to shoot out of my mouth.

Comma around Words Interrupting the Flow of Thought

Use commas before and after words or phrases that interrupt the flow of thought in a sentence.

> My brother, a sports nut, owns over five thousand baseball cards.
> That game show, at long last, has been canceled.
> The children used the old Buick, rusted from disuse, as a backyard clubhouse.

Usually you can "hear" words that interrupt the flow of thought in a sentence. However, if you are not sure that certain words are interrupters, remove them from the sentence for a moment. If it still makes sense without the words, you know that the words are interrupters and the information they give is nonessential. Such nonessential information is set off with commas. In the sentence

> Dody Thompson, who lives next door, won the javelin-throwing competition.

the words *who lives next door* are extra information, not needed to identify the subject of the sentence, *Dody Thompson*. Put commas around such nonessential information. On the other hand, in the sentence

> The woman who lives next door won the javelin-throwing competition.

the words *who lives next door* supply essential information — information needed for us to identify the woman being spoken of. If the words were removed from the sentence, we would no longer know who won the competition. Commas are *not* used around such essential information.

Here is another example:

Wilson Hall, which the tornado destroyed, was ninety years old.

Here the words *which the tornado destroyed* are extra information, not needed to identify the subject of the sentence, *Wilson Hall.* Commas go around such non-essential information. On the other hand, in the sentence

The building which the tornado destroyed was ninety years old.

the words *which the tornado destroyed* are needed to identify the building. Commas are *not* used around such essential information.

As noted above, however, most of the time you will be able to ''hear'' words that interrupt the flow of thought in a sentence and will not have to think about whether the words are essential or nonessential.

Activity

Use commas to set off interrupting words.

1. On Friday, my day off, I went to get a haircut.
2. Dracula, who had a way with women, is Tony's favorite movie hero. He feels that the Wolfman, on the other hand, showed no class in handling women.
3. Many people forget that Franklin Roosevelt, one of our most effective presidents, was also handicapped.
4. Mowing the grass, especially when it is six inches high, is my least favorite job.
5. A jar of chicken noodle soup, which was all there was in the refrigerator, did not make for a very satisfying meal.

Comma between Complete Thoughts

Use a comma between two complete thoughts connected by *and, but, for, or, nor, so, yet.*

The wedding was scheduled for four o'clock, but the bride changed her mind at two.

We could always tell when our instructor felt disorganized, for his shirt would not be tucked in.

Rich has to work on Monday nights, so he tapes the TV football game on his video recorder.

Note: Be careful not to use a comma in sentences having *one* subject and a *double* verb. The comma is used only in sentences made up of two complete thoughts (two subjects and two verbs). In the following sentence, there is only one subject (*Bill*) with a double verb (*will go* and *forget*). Therefore, no comma is needed:

Bill will go partying tonight and forget all about tomorrow's exam.

Likewise, the following sentence has only one subject (*Rita*) and a double verb (*was* and *will work*); therefore, no comma is needed:

Rita was a waitress at the Holiday Inn last summer and probably will work there this summer.

Activity

Place a comma before a joining word that connects two complete thoughts (two subjects and two verbs). Remember, do *not* place a comma within sentences that have only one subject and a double verb.

1. The oranges in the refrigerator were covered with blue mold, and the potatoes in the cupboard felt like sponges.
2. All the slacks in the shop were on sale, but not a single pair was my size.
3. Martha often window-shops in the malls for hours and comes home without buying anything.
4. Tony left the dentist's office with his mouth still numb from Novocain, and he talked with a lisp for two hours.
5. I covered the walls with three coats of white paint, but the purple color underneath still showed through.
6. The car squealed down the entrance ramp and sped recklessly out onto the freeway.
7. The dancers in the go-go bar moved like wound-up Barbie dolls, and the men in the audience sat as motionless as stones.
8. The aliens in the science fiction film visited our planet in peace, but we greeted them with violence.
9. I felt like shouting at the gang of boys, but didn't dare open my mouth.
10. Lenny claims he wants to succeed in college, but he has missed classes all semester.

Comma with Direct Quotations

Use a comma to set off a direct quotation from the rest of a sentence.

His father shouted, "Why don't you go out and get a job?"

"Our modern world has lost a sense of the sacredness of life," the speaker said.

"No," said Celia to Jerry. "I won't go to the roller derby with you."

"Can anyone remember," wrote Emerson, "when the times were not hard and money not scarce?"

Note: Commas and periods at the end of a quotation go inside quotation marks. See also page 354.

Activity

Use commas to set off quotations from the rest of the sentence.

1. The man yelled, "Call an ambulance, somebody!"
2. My partner on the dance floor said, "Don't be so stiff. You look as if you'd swallowed an umbrella."
3. The question on the anatomy test read, "What human organ grows faster than any other, never stops growing, and always remains the same size?"
4. The student behind me whispered, "The skin."
5. "My stomach hurts," Bruce said, "and I don't know whether it was the hamburger or the math test."

Comma with Everyday Material

Use a comma with certain everyday material.

Persons Spoken To

Tina, go to bed if you're not feeling well.

Cindy, where did you put my shoes?

Are you coming with us, Bob?

Dates

March 4, 1992, is when Martha buried her third husband.

Addresses

Tony's grandparents live at 183 Roxborough Avenue, Cleveland, Ohio 44112.

Note: No comma is used to mark off the zip code.

Openings and Closings of Letters

Dear Santa,
Dear Larry,
Sincerely yours,
Truly yours,

Note: In formal letters, a colon is used after the opening: Dear Sir: *or* Dear Madam:

Numbers

The dishonest dealer turned the used car's odometer from 98,170 miles to 39,170 miles.

Activity

Place commas where needed.

1. I expected you to set a better example for the others, Mike.
2. Janet, with your help I passed the test.
3. The movie stars Kitty Litter, and Dredge Rivers were married on September 12, 1991, and lived at 3865 Sunset Boulevard, Los Angeles, California for one month.
4. They received 75000 congratulatory fan letters and were given picture contracts worth $3000000 in the first week of their marriage.
5. Kitty left Dredge on October 12, 1991, and ran off with their marriage counselor.

■ Review Test 1

Insert commas where needed. In the space provided below each sentence, summarize briefly the rule that explains the use of the comma or commas.

1. The best features of my new apartment are its large kitchen, its bay windows, and its low rent.

   To separate items in series

2. Because we got in line at dawn, we were among the first to get tickets for the concert.

   To set off introductory material

3. "When will someone invent a telephone," Lola asked, "that will let you know who's calling before you answer it?"

   To set off a direct quotation from the rest of a sentence

4. Without opening his eyes, Simon stumbled out of bed and opened the door for the whining dog.

   to set off introductory material

5. I think, David, that you had better ask someone else for your $2500 loan.

   Before and after words that

6. Hot dogs are the most common cause of choking deaths in children for a bite-size piece can easily plug up a toddler's throat.

7. Tax forms though shortened and revised every year never seem to get any simpler.

8. Sandra may decide to go to college full-time or she may enroll in a couple of evening courses.

9. I remember how with the terrible cruelty of children we used to make fun of the retarded girl who lived on our street.

10. Although that old man on the corner looks like a Skid Row bum he is said to have a Swiss bank account.

■ Review Test 2

Insert commas where needed.

1. My dog who is afraid of the dark sleeps with a night-light.
2. ''I wish there were some pill'' said Chuck ''that would give you the equivalent of eight hours' sleep in four hours.''
3. The hot dogs at the ball park tasted delicious but they reacted later like delayed time bombs.
4. Janice attended class for four hours worked at the hospital for three hours and studied at home for two hours.
5. The old man as he gasped for air tried to assure the hospital clerk that he had an insurance card somewhere.
6. George and Ida sat down to watch the football game with crackers sharp cheese salty pretzels and two frosty bottles of beer.
7. Although I knew exactly what was happening the solar eclipse gave me a strong feeling of anxiety.
8. The company agreed to raise a senior bus driver's salary to $28000 by January 1 1995.
9. Even though King Kong was holding her at the very top of the Empire State Building Fay Wray kept yelling at him ''Let me go!''
10. Navel oranges which Margery as a little girl called belly-button oranges are her favorite fruit.

■ Review Test 3

On separate paper, write six sentences, with each sentence demonstrating one of the six main comma rules.

OTHER PUNCTUATION MARKS

Introductory Project

Each of the sentences below needs one of the following punctuation marks:

; — - ( ) :

See if you can insert the correct mark in each sentence. Each mark is used once.

1. The following holiday plants are poisonous and should be kept away from children and pets holly, mistletoe, and poinsettias.
2. The freeze-dried remains of Annie's canary were in a clear bottle on her bookcase.
3. William Shakespeare (1564 – 1616) married a woman eight years his senior when he was eighteen.
4. Grooming in space is more difficult than on Earth no matter how much astronauts comb their hair, for instance, it still tends to float loosely around their heads.
5. I opened the front door, and our cat walked in proudly with a live bunny hanging from his mouth.

Answers are on page 575.

COLON (:)

Use the colon at the end of a complete statement to introduce a list, a long quotation, or an explanation.

List

The following were my worst jobs: truck loader in an apple plant, assembler in a battery factory, and attendant in a state mental hospital.

Long Quotation

Thoreau explains in *Walden:* "I went to the woods because I wished to live deliberately, to front only the essential facts of life, and see if I could not learn what it had to teach, and not, when I came to die, discover that I had not lived."

Explanation

There are two softball leagues in our town: the fast-pitch league and the lob-pitch league.

Activity

Place colons where needed.

1. Foods that are high in cholesterol include the following: eggs, butter, milk, cheese, shrimp, and well-marbled meats.
2. All the signs of the flu were present: hot and cold spells, heavy drainage from the sinuses, a bad cough, and an ache through the entire body.
3. In his book *Illiterate America*, Jonathan Kozol has written: "Twenty-five million American adults cannot read the poison warnings on a can of pesticide, a letter from their child's teacher, or the front page of a daily paper. An additional 35 million read only at a level which is less than equal to the full survival needs of our society. Together, these 60 million people represent more than one-third of the entire adult population."

SEMICOLON (;)

The main use of the semicolon is to mark a break between two complete thoughts, as explained on page 260. Another use of the semicolon is to mark off items in a series when the items themselves contain commas. Here are some examples:

> Winning prizes at the national flower show were Roberta Collins, Alabama, azaleas; Sally Hunt, Kentucky, roses; and James Weber, California, Shasta daisies.

> The following books must be read for the course: *The Color Purple,* by Alice Walker; *In Our Time,* by Ernest Hemingway; and *Man's Search for Meaning,* by Viktor Frankl.

Activity

Place semicolons where needed.

1. The specials at the restaurant today are eggplant Parmesan, for $3.95; black beans and rice, for $2.95; and chicken potpie, for $4.95.
2. The top of the hill offered an awesome view of the military cemetery; thousands of headstones were ranged in perfect rows.
3. Lola's favorite old movies are *To Catch a Thief,* starring Cary Grant and Grace Kelly; *Animal Crackers,* a Marx Brothers comedy; and *The Wizard of Oz,* with Judy Garland.

DASH (—)

A dash signals a degree of pause longer than a comma but not as complete as a period. Use a dash to set off words for dramatic effect:

> I didn't go out with him a second time — once was more than enough.
> Some of you — I won't mention you by name — cheated on the test.
> It was so windy that the VW passed him on the highway — overhead.

Notes

a   The dash is formed on a typewriter by striking the hyphen twice (- -). In handwriting, the dash is as long as two letters would be.

b   Be careful not to overuse dashes.

Activity

Place dashes where needed.

1. Riding my bike, I get plenty of exercise—especially when dogs chase me.
2. I'm advising you—in fact, I'm telling you—not to bother me again.
3. The package finally arrived—badly damaged.

HYPHEN (-)

1 Use a hyphen <u>with two or more words that act as a single unit</u> <u>describing a noun.</u>

The fast-talking salesman was so good that he went into politics. (*Fast* and *talking* combine to describe the salesman.)

I both admire and envy her well-rounded personality.

When the dude removed his blue-tinted shades, Lonnell saw the spaced-out look in his eyes.

2 Use a hyphen to divide a word at the end of a line of writing or typing. When you need to divide a word at the end of a line, divide it between syllables. Use your dictionary to be sure of correct syllable divisions (see also page 377).

When Tom lifted up the hood of his Toyota, he realized that one of the radiator hoses had broken.

Notes

a Do not divide words of one syllable.
b Do not divide a word if you can avoid doing so.

Activity

Place hyphens where needed.

1. High-flying jets and gear-grinding trucks are constant sources of noise pollution in our neighborhood, and consequently we are going to move.
2. When Linda turned on the porch light, ten-legged creatures scurried every where over the crumb-filled floor.
3. Fred had ninety-two dollars in his pocket when he left for the supermarket, and he had twenty-two dollars when he got back.

PARENTHESES ( )

Parentheses are <u>used to set off extra</u> or <u>incidental information</u> from the rest of a sentence:

The section of that book on the medical dangers of abortion (pages 35 to 72) is outdated.

Yesterday at Hamburger House (my favorite place to eat), the guy who makes french fries asked me to go out with him.

Note: Do not use parentheses too often in your writing.

Activity

Add parentheses where needed.

1.   Certain sections of the novel (especially Chapter 5) made my heart race with suspense.
2.   Did you hear that George (Linda's first husband) just got remarried?
3.   Sigmund Freud (1856 – 1939) was the founder of psychoanalysis.

■ Review Test

At the appropriate spot, place the punctuation mark shown in the margin.

;   1.   Mary's savings have dwindled to nothing; she's been borrowing from me to pay her rent.

—   2.   There's the idiot I'd know him anywhere who dumped trash on our front lawn.

-   3.   Today's two-career couples spend more money on eating out than their parents did.

:   4.   Ben Franklin said: "If a man empties his purse into his head, no man can take it away from him. An investment in knowledge always pays the best interest."

( )   5.   One-fifth of our textbook (pages 401 – 498) consists of footnotes and a bibliography.

USING
THE
DICTIONARY

The dictionary is a valuable tool. To take advantage of it, you need to understand the main kinds of information that a dictionary gives about a word. Look at the information provided for the word *murder* in the following entry from the *American Heritage Dictionary of the English Language:**

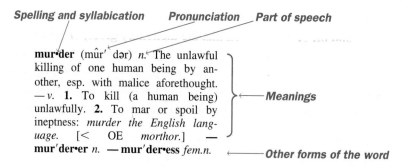

Spelling and syllabication   Pronunciation   Part of speech

mur•der (mûr′ dər) *n.* The unlawful killing of one human being by another, esp. with malice aforethought. —*v.* **1.** To kill (a human being) unlawfully. **2.** To mar or spoil by ineptness: *murder the English language.* [< OE *morthor.*] — **mur′der•er** *n.* — **mur′der•ess** *fem.n.*

Meanings

Other forms of the word

* © 1969, 1970, 1976, 1980, Houghton Mifflin Company. Reprinted by permission from the *American Heritage Dictionary of the English Language,* paperback edition.

SPELLING

The first bit of information, in the boldface (heavy type) entry itself, is the spelling of *murder*. You probably already know the spelling of *murder,* but if you didn't, you could find it by pronouncing the syllables in the word carefully and then looking it up in the dictionary.

Use your dictionary to correct the spelling of the following words:

compatable	_Compatible_	insite	_inside / insight_
althogh	_Although_	troble	_Trouble_
aksident	_Accident_	untill	_Until_
embelish	_Embellish_	easyer	_easier_
systimatise	_Systematize_	prepostrous	_Preposterous_
shedule	_Schedule_	comotion	_Commotion_
attenshun	_Attention_	Vasaline	_Vaseline_
wierd	_Weird_	fatel	_Fatal_
hurryed	_Hurried_	busines	_business_
alright	_All Right_	jenocide	_Genocide_
fony	_Phony_	poluted	_Polluted_
kriterion	_Criterion_	perpose	_Purpose_
hetirosexual	_Heterosexual_	chalange	_Challenge_

SYLLABICATION

The second bit of information that the dictionary gives, also in the boldface entry, is the syllabication of *murder*. Note that a dot separates the syllables.

Use your dictionary to mark the syllable divisions in the following words. Also indicate how many syllables are in each word.

j i t t e r	(_2_ syllables)
m o/t i/v a t e	(_3_ syllables)
o r a n g/u t a n	(_2_ syllables)
in/c o n/t r o/v e r/t i b l e	(_5_ syllables)

Noting syllable divisions will enable you to *hyphenate* a word: divide it at the end of one line of writing and complete it at the beginning of the next line. You can correctly hyphenate a word only at a syllable division, and you may have to check your dictionary to make sure of a word's syllable divisions.

PRONUNCIATION

The third bit of information in the dictionary entry is the pronunciation of *murder:* (mûr′dər). You already know how to pronounce *murder,* but if you didn't, the information within the parentheses would serve as your guide. Use your dictionary to complete the following exercises that relate to pronunciation.

Vowel Sounds

You will probably use the pronunciation key in your dictionary mainly as a guide to pronouncing different vowel sounds. (Vowels are the letters *a, e, i, o,* and *u.*) Here is part of the pronunciation key in the *American Heritage Dictionary:*

ă bat / ā way / ĕ ebb / ē equal / ĭ if

The key tells you, for example, that the sound of the short *a* is pronounced like the *a* in *bat,* the sound of the long *a* is like the *a* in *way,* and the sound of the short *e* is like the *e* in *ebb.*

Now look at the pronunciation key in your dictionary. The key is probably located in the front of the dictionary or at the bottom of every page. What common word in the key tells you how to pronounce each of the following sounds?

ī _____   ŭ _____

ŏ _____   o͞o _____

ō _____   o͞o _____

(Note that the long vowel always has the sound of its own name.)

The Schwa (ə)

The symbol ə looks like an upside-down *e.* It is called a *schwa,* and it stands for the unaccented sound in such words as *ago, item, easily, gallop,* and *circus.* More approximately, it stands for the sound *uh* — like the *uh* that speakers sometimes make when they hesitate. Perhaps it would help to remember that *uh,* as well as ə, could be used to represent the schwa sound.

Here are some of the many words in which the sound appears: *imitation* (im-uh-tā′shuhn or im-ə-tā′shən); *elevate* (el′uh-vāt or el′ə-vāt); *horizon* (huh-rī′zuhn or hə-rī′zən). Open your dictionary to any page, and you will almost surely be able to find words that make use of the schwa in the pronunciation in parentheses after the main entry.

In the spaces below, write three words that make use of the schwa, and their pronunciations.

1. _DISTANCE_ (_dis-tən(t)s_)
2. _Disputation_ (_dis-pyə-ta-shən_)
3. _Carbon_ (_kär-bən_)

Accent Marks

Some words contain both a primary accent, shown by a heavy stroke ('), and a secondary accent, shown by a lighter stroke ('). For example, in the word *controversy* (kon'trə vûr'se), the stress, or accent, goes chiefly on the first syllable (*kon'*), and to a lesser extent, on the third syllable (*vûr'*).

Use your dictionary to add accent marks to the following words:

preclude (pri klōōd)
atrophy (at rə fē)
inveigle (in vā gəl)
ubiquitous (yōō bik wi təs)
prognosticate (prog nos ti kāt)

Full Pronunciation

Now use your dictionary to write the full pronunciation (the information given in parentheses) for each of the following words.

1. inveigh _____
2. diatribe _____
3. raconteur _____
4. panacea _____
5. esophagus _____
6. Cesarean _____
7. clandestine _____
8. vicarious _____
9. quiescent _____
10. parsimony _____

11. penchant _____

12. antipathy _____

13. capricious _____

14. schizophrenia _____

15. euphemism _____

16. internecine _____

17. amalgamate _____

18. quixotic _____

19. laissez-faire _____

20. antidisestablishmentarianism (This word is probably not in a paperback dictionary, but if you can say *establish* and if you break the rest of the word into individual syllables, you should be able to pronounce it.)

_____

Now practice pronouncing each word. Use the pronunciation key in your dictionary as an aid to sounding out each syllable. Do *not* try to pronounce a word all at once; instead, work on mastering *one syllable at a time*. When you can pronounce each of the syllables in a word successfully, then say them in sequence, add the accent, and pronounce the entire word.

PARTS OF SPEECH

The next bit of information that the dictionary gives about *murder* is *n*. This abbreviation means that the meanings of *murder* as a noun will follow.

Use your dictionary if necessary to fill in the meanings of the following abbreviations:

v. = _____   sing. = _____

adj. = _____   pl. = _____

PRINCIPAL PARTS OF IRREGULAR VERBS

Murder is a regular verb and forms its principal parts by adding -*ed*, -*ed*, and -*ing* to the stem of the verb. When a verb is irregular, the dictionary lists its principal parts. For example, with *give* the present tense comes first (the entry itself, *give*). Next comes the past tense (*gave*), and then the past participle (*given*) — the form of the verb used with such helping words as *have*, *had*, and *was*. Then comes the present participle (*giving*) — the -*ing* form of the verb.

Look up the parts of the following irregular verbs and write them in the spaces provided. The first one is done for you.

Present	Past	Past Participle	Present Participle
tear	*tore*	*torn*	*tearing*
go	WenT	Gone	Going
know	KNOWN	KNOWN	KNOWING
steal	Stole	Stolen	Stealing

PLURAL FORMS OF IRREGULAR NOUNS

The dictionary supplies the plural forms of all irregular nouns. (Regular nouns like *murder* form the plural by adding *-s* or *-es*.) Give the plurals of the following nouns. If two forms are shown, write down both.

analysis   Analyses

dictionary   dictionaries

criterion   Criterions

activity   activities

thesis   Theses

MEANINGS

When a word has more than one meaning, the meanings are numbered in the dictionary, as with the verb *murder*. In many dictionaries, the most common meanings of a word are presented first. The introductory pages of your dictionary will explain the order in which meanings are presented.

Use the sentence context to try to explain the meaning of the underlined word in each of the following sentences. Write your definition in the space provided. Then look up and record the dictionary meaning of the word. Be sure you pick out the meaning that fits the word as it is used in the sentence.

1. I spend an <u>inordinate</u> amount of time watching television.

     Your definition: _____

     Dictionary definition: _____

2. I appreciated her <u>candid</u> remark that my pants were so baggy they made me look like a clown.

Your definition: _____

Dictionary definition: _____

3. The FBI <u>squelched</u> the terrorists' plan to plant a bomb in the White House.

Your definition: _____

Dictionary definition: _____

4. One of the <u>cardinal</u> rules in our house was, "Respect other people's privacy."

Your definition: _____

Dictionary definition: *of basic Importance; main, chief, Primary*

5. A special <u>governor</u> prevents the school bus from traveling more than fifty-five miles an hour.

Your definition: _____

Dictionary definition: *An attachment to a machine (as a gasoline Engine) for automatic Control or limitation of speed*

ETYMOLOGY

Etymology refers to the origin and historical development of a word. Such information is usually enclosed in brackets and is more likely to be present in a hardbound desk dictionary than in a paperback one. Good desk dictionaries include the following:

American Heritage Dictionary of the English Language
The Random House College Dictionary
Webster's New Collegiate Dictionary
Webster's New World Dictionary

A good desk dictionary will tell you, for example, that the word *berserk* derives from the name of a tribe of Scandinavian warriors who would work themselves into a frenzy during battle. The word is now a general term to describe someone whose actions are frenzied or crazed.

See if your dictionary says anything about the origins of the following words:

bikini _____

sandwich _____

tantalize _____

breakfast _____

USAGE LABELS

As a general rule, use only standard English words in your writing. If a word is not standard English, your dictionary will probably give it a usage label like one of the following: *informal, nonstandard, slang, vulgar, obsolete, archaic, rare.*

Look up the following words and record how your dictionary labels them. Remember that a recent hardbound desk dictionary will always be the best source of information about usage.

flunk _____

tough (meaning "unfortunate, too bad") _____

creep (meaning "an annoying person") _____

ain't _____

scam _____

SYNONYMS

A *synonym* is a word that is close in meaning to another word. Using synonyms helps you avoid unnecessary repetition of the same word in a paper. A paperback dictionary is not likely to give you synonyms for words, but a good desk dictionary will. (You might also want to own a *thesaurus,* a book that lists synonyms and antonyms. An *antonym* is a word approximately opposite in meaning to another word.)

Consult a desk dictionary that gives synonyms for the following words, and write the synonyms in the spaces provided.

heavy _____

escape _____

necessary _____

IMPROVING SPELLING

Poor spelling often results from bad habits developed in early school years. With work, such habits can be corrected. If you can write your name without misspelling it, there is no reason why you can't do the same with almost any word in the English language. Following are six steps you can take to improve your spelling.

STEP 1: USE THE DICTIONARY

Get into the habit of using the dictionary. When you write a paper, allow yourself time to look up the spelling of all those words you are unsure about. Do not overlook the value of this step just because it is such a simple one. By using the dictionary, you can probably make yourself a 95 percent better speller.

STEP 2: KEEP A PERSONAL SPELLING LIST

Keep a list of words you misspell and study the words regularly. Use the chart on page 578 as a starter. When you accumulate additional words, put them on the back page of a frequently used notebook or on a separate sheet of paper titled "Personal Spelling List."

To master the words on your list, do the following:

1 Write down any hint that will help you remember the spelling of a word. For example, you might want to note that *occasion* is spelled with two *c*'s, or that *all right* is two words, not one word.

2 Study a word by looking at it, saying it, and spelling it. You may also want to write out the word one or more times, or ''air-write'' it with your finger in large, exaggerated motions.

3 When you have trouble spelling a long word, try to break the word down into syllables and see whether you can spell the syllables. For example, *inadvertent* can be spelled easily if you can hear and spell in turn its four syllables: *in ad ver tent.* The word *consternation* can be spelled easily if you hear and spell in turn its four syllables: *con ster na tion.* Remember, then: try to see, hear, and spell long words in terms of their syllables.

4 Keep in mind that review and repeated self-testing are keys to effective learning. When you are learning a series of words, go back after studying each new word and review all the preceding ones.

STEP 3: MASTER COMMONLY CONFUSED WORDS

Master the meanings and spellings of the commonly confused words on pages 397–406. Your instructor may assign twenty words for you to study at a time and give you a series of quizzes until you have mastered the words.

STEP 4: UNDERSTAND BASIC SPELLING RULES

Explained briefly here are three rules that may improve your spelling. While exceptions sometimes occur, the rules hold true most of the time.

1 *Changing* y *to* i. When a word ends in a consonant plus *y*, change *y* to *i* when you add an ending.

try	+ ed	= tried	easy	+ er	= easier
defy	+ es	= defies	carry	+ ed	= carried
ready	+ ness	= readiness	penny	+ less	= penniless

2 **Final silent e.** Drop a final *e* before an ending that starts with a vowel (the vowels are *a, e, i, o,* and *u*).

create + ive = creative   believe + able = believable
nerve + ous = nervous   share + ing = sharing

Keep the final *e* before an ending that starts with a consonant.

extreme + ly = extremely   life   + less = lifeless
hope   + ful = hopeful   excite + ment = excitement

3 **Doubling a final consonant.** Double the final consonant of a word when all three of the following are true:

a The word is one syllable or is accented on the last syllable.
b The word ends in a single consonant preceded by a single vowel.
c The ending you are adding starts with a vowel.

shop + er = shopper   thin   + est = thinnest
equip + ed = equipped   submit + ed = submitted
swim + ing = swimming   drag   + ed = dragged

Activity

Combine the following words and endings by applying the three rules above.

1. worry + ed   = _worried_
2. write + ing = _writing_
3. marry + es   = _marries_
4. run   + ing = _running_
5. terrify + ed   = _terrified_
6. dry   + es   = _dries_
7. forget + ing = _forgetting_
8. care   + ful = _careful_
9. control + ed   = _controlled_
10. debate + able = _debatable_

STEP 5: STUDY A BASIC WORD LIST

Study the spellings of the words in the following list. They are five hundred of the words most often used in English. Your instructor may assign twenty-five or fifty words for you to study at a time and give you a series of quizzes until you have mastered the list.

Five Hundred Basic Words

ability	another	begin	chair
absent	answer	being	change
accept	anxious	believe	charity
accident	appetite	between	cheap
ache	apply	bicycle	cheat
across	approach	black	cheek
address	approve	blue	chicken
advertise	argue	board	chief
advice	around	borrow	children
after	arrange	bottle	choose
again	attempt	bottom	church
against	attention	brake	cigarette
agree	August	breast	citizen
all right	automobile	breathe	city
almost	autumn	brilliant	close
a lot	avenue	brother	clothing
already	awful	building	coffee
also	awkward	bulletin	collect
although	back	bureau	college
always	balance	business	color
amateur	bargain	came	come
American	beautiful	can't	comfortable **100**
among	because	careful **75**	company
amount	become **50**	careless	condition
angry **25**	been	cereal	conversation
animal	before	certain	copy

daily	eight	general	into
danger	either	get	iron
daughter	empty	good	itself
daybreak	English	grammar	January
dear	enough	great **175**	July
death	entrance	grocery	June
December	evening	grow	just
decide	everything	guess	kindergarten
deed	examine	half	kitchen
dentist	except	hammer	knock
deposit	exercise	hand	knowledge
describe	exit	handkerchief	labor
did	expect **150**	happy	laid
died	fact	having	language
different	factory	head	last
dinner	family	heard	laugh
direction	far	heavy	learn
discover	February	high	led
disease	few	himself	left
distance	fifteen	hoarse	leisure
doctor **125**	fight	holiday	length
does	flower	home	lesson **225**
dollar	forehead	hospital	letter
don't	foreign	house	life
doubt	forty	however	light
down	forward	hundred	listen
dozen	found	hungry	little
during	fourteen	husband	loaf
each	Friday	instead	loneliness
early	friend	intelligence **200**	long
earth	from	interest	lose
easy	gallon	interfere	made
education	garden	interrupt	making

many	not	pillow	repeat
March	nothing	place	resource
marry	November **275**	plain	restaurant
match	now	please	ribbon
matter	number	pocket	ridiculous
may	ocean	policeman	right **350**
measure	o'clock	possible	said
medicine	October	post office	same
men	offer	potato	sandwich
middle	often	power	Saturday
might	old	prescription	say
million	omit	president	school
minute	once	pretty	scissors
mistake **250**	one	probably	season
Monday	only	promise	see
money	operate	psychology	sentence
month	opinion	public **325**	September
more	opportunity	pursue	service
morning	optimist	put	seventeen
mother	original	quart	several
mountain	ought	quarter	shoes
mouth	ounce	quick	should
much	overcoat	quiet	sight
must	pain	quit	since
nail	paper	quite	sister
near	part	quiz	sixteenth
needle	peace	raise	sleep
neither	pear **300**	read	smoke
never	pencil	ready	soap
newspaper	penny	really	soldier
nickel	people	reason	something **375**
niece	perfect	receive	sometimes
night	period	recognize	soul
ninety	person	refer	soup
noise	picture	religion	south
none	piece	remember	stamp

state	they	upon	well
still	thing	used	went
stockings	thirteen	usual	were
straight	this	valley	what
street	though	value	whether **475**
strong	thousand	variety	which
student	thread	vegetable	while
studying	three	very	white
such	through	view	whole
suffer	Thursday	villain **450**	whose
sugar	ticket	visitor	wife
suit	time	voice	window
summer	tired	vote	winter
Sunday	today	wage	without
supper	together **425**	wagon	woman
sure	tomorrow	waist	wonder
sweet	tongue	wait	won't
take	tonight	wake	work
teach	touch	walk	world
tear **400**	toward	warm	worth
telegram	travel	warning	would
telephone	trouble	Washington	writing
tenant	trousers	watch	written
tenth	truly	water	wrong
than	twelve	wear	year
Thanksgiving	uncle	weather	yesterday
that	under	Wednesday	yet
theater	understand	week	young
them	United States	weigh	your
there	until	welcome	you're **500**

Note: Two spelling mistakes that students often make are to write _a lot_ as one word (_alot_) and to write _all right_ as one word (_alright_). Do not write either _a lot_ or _all right_ as one word.

√STEP 6: USE ELECTRONIC AIDS

There are three electronic aids that may help your spelling. First, many _electronic typewriters_ on the market today will beep automatically when you misspell a word. They include built-in dictionaries that will then give you the correct spelling. Smith-Corona, for example, has a series of portable typewriters with an "Auto-Spell" feature that start at around $150 at discount stores.

Second, a _computer with a spell-checker_ will identify incorrect words and suggest correct spellings. If you know how to write on the computer, you will have no trouble learning how to use the spell-check feature.

Third, _electronic spell-checkers_ are pocket-size devices that look much like the pocket calculators you may carry to your math class. They are the latest example of how technology can help the learning process. Electronic spellers can be found in the typewriter or computer section of any discount store, at prices in the $100 range. The checker includes a tiny keyboard. You type out the word the way you think it is spelled, and the checker quickly provides you with the correct spelling of related words. Some of these checkers even _pronounce_ the word aloud for you.

VOCABULARY DEVELOPMENT

A good vocabulary is a vital part of effective communication. A command of many words will make you a better writer, speaker, listener, and reader. Studies have shown that students with a strong vocabulary, and students who work to improve a limited vocabulary, are more successful in school. And one research study found that *a good vocabulary, more than any other factor, was common to people enjoying successful careers.* This section will describe three ways of developing your word power: (1) regular reading, (2) vocabulary wordsheets, and (3) vocabulary study books. You should keep in mind from the start, however, that none of the approaches will help unless you truly decide that vocabulary development is an important goal. Only when you have this attitude can you begin doing the sustained work needed to improve your word power.

REGULAR READING

Through reading a good deal, you will learn words by encountering them a number of times in a variety of sentences. Repeated exposure to a word in context will eventually make it a part of your working language.

You should develop the habit of reading a daily newspaper and one or more weekly magazines like *Time, Newsweek,* or even *People,* as well as monthly magazines suited to your interests. In addition, you should try to read some books for pleasure. This may be especially difficult at times when you also have textbook reading to do. Try, however, to redirect a regular half hour to one hour of your recreational time to reading books, rather than watching television, listening to music, or the like. Doing so, you may eventually reap the rewards of an improved vocabulary *and* the discovery that reading can be truly enjoyable. If you would like some recommendations, ask your instructor for a copy of the "List of Interesting Books" in the Instructor's Manual of *English Skills with Readings.*

VOCABULARY WORDSHEETS

Vocabulary wordsheets are another means of vocabulary development. First, as you read, you should mark off words that you want to learn. Then, after you have accumulated a number of words, sit down with a dictionary and look up basic information about each of them. Put this information on a wordsheet like the one shown below. Be sure also to write down a sentence in which each word appears. A word is always best learned not in a vacuum but in the context of surrounding words.

Study each word as follows. First, make sure you can correctly pronounce the word and its derivations. (Pages 378–380 explain the dictionary pronunciation key that will help you pronounce each word properly.) Second, study the main meanings of the word until you can say them without looking at them. Finally, spend a moment looking at the example of the word in context. Follow the same process with the second word. Then, after testing yourself on the first and the second words, go on to the third word. Remember to continue to test yourself on all the words you have studied after you learn each new word. Repeated self-testing is a key to effective learning.

Activity

Locate four words in your reading that you would like to master. Enter them in the spaces on the vocabulary wordsheet below and fill in all the needed information. Your instructor may then check your wordsheet and perhaps give you a quick oral quiz on selected words.

You may receive a standing assignment to add five words a week to a wordsheet and to study the words. Note that you can create your own wordsheets using loose-leaf paper, or your instructor may give you copies of the wordsheet that appears below.

Vocabulary Wordsheet

1. Word: _____*formidable*_____ Pronunciation: _(fôr' mi də bəl)_

    Meanings: ___1. *feared or dreaded*___

    _____2. *extremely difficult*_____

    _____

    Other forms of the word: *formidably   formidability*

    Use of the word in context: *Several formidable obstacles stand between*

    Matt and his goal.

2. Word: _____ Pronunciation: _____

   Meanings: _____

   _____

   _____

   Other forms of the word: _____

   Use of the word in context: _____

   _____

3. Word: _____ Pronunciation: _____

   Meanings: _____

   _____

   _____

   Other forms of the word: _____

   Use of the word in context: _____

   _____

4. Word: _____ Pronunciation: _____

   Meanings: _____

   _____

   _____

   Other forms of the word: _____

   Use of the word in context: _____

   _____

5. Word: _____ Pronunciation: _____

   Meanings: _____

   _____

   _____

   Other forms of the word: _____

   Use of the word in context: _____

   _____

VOCABULARY STUDY BOOKS

A third way to increase your word power is to use vocabulary study books. One well-known series of books that may be available in the learning-skills center at your school is the EDL *Word Clues.* These books help you learn a word by asking you to look at the context — or the words around the unfamiliar word — to unlock its meaning. This method is called *using context clues,* or *word clues.*

Many vocabulary books and programs are available. The best are those that present words in one or more contexts and then provide several reinforcement activities for each word. These books will help you increase your vocabulary if you have the determination required to work with them on a regular basis.

COMMONLY
CONFUSED
WORDS

Introductory Project

Circle the five words that are misspelled in the following passage. Then see if you can write the correct spellings in the spaces provided.

You're mind and body are not as separate as you might think. Their is a lot of evidence, for instance, that says if you believe that a placebo (a substance with no medicine) will help you, than it will. One man is said too have rapidly recovered from an advanced case of cancer after only one dose of a drug that he believed was highly effective. Its not clear just how placebos work, but they do show how closely the mind and body are related.

1. You are
2. There is
3. then it will.
4. is said to have
5. It is not clear.

Answers are on page 575.

HOMONYMS

The commonly confused words on the following pages have the <u>same sounds</u> but different meanings and spellings; such words are known as *homonyms*. Complete the activity for each set of words, and check off and study the words that give you trouble.

all ready   completely prepared
already   previously; before

> We were *all ready* to start the play, but the audience was still being seated.
>
> I have *already* called the police.

Fill in the blanks: I am ___All ready___ for the economics examination because I have ___already___ studied the chapter three times.

brake   stop; the stopping device in a vehicle
break   come apart

> His car bumper has a sticker reading, ''I *brake* for animals.''
>
> ''I am going to *break* up with Bill if he keeps seeing other women,'' said Rita.

Fill in the blanks: When my car's emergency ___brake___ slipped, the car rolled back and demolished my neighbor's rose garden, causing a ___break___ in our good relations with each other.

coarse   rough
course   part of a meal; school subject; direction; certainly (as in *of course*)

> By the time the waitress served the customers the second *course* of the meal, she was aware of their *coarse* eating habits.

Fill in the blanks: Ted felt that the health instructor's humor was too ___coarse___ for his taste and was glad when he finished the ___course___ .

hear   perceive with the ear
here   in this place

"The salespeople act as though they don't see or *hear* me, even though I've been standing *here* for fifteen minutes," the woman complained.

Fill in the blanks: "Did you ___*hear*___ about the distinguished visitor who just came into town and is staying ___*here*___ at this very hotel?"

hole   empty spot
whole   entire

"I can't believe I ate the *whole* pizza," moaned Ralph. "I think it's going to make a *hole* in my stomach lining."

Fill in the blanks: The ___*whole*___ time I was at the party I tried to conceal the ___*hole*___ I had in my trousers.

its   belonging to it
it's   shortened form for *it is* or *it has*

The car blew *its* transmission (the transmission belonging to it, the car).
It's (it has) been raining all week and *it's* (it is) raining now.

Fill in the blanks: ___*It is*___ hot and unsanitary in the restaurant kitchen I work in, and I don't think the restaurant deserves ___*its*___ good reputation.

knew   past form of *know*
new   not old

"I had *new* wallpaper put up," said Sarah.
"I *knew* there was some reason the place looked better," said Bill.

Fill in the blanks: Lola ___*knew*___ that getting her hair cut would give her face a ___*new*___ look.

know   to understand
no   a negative

"I don't *know* why my dog Fang likes to attack certain people," said Martha. "There's *no* one thing the people have in common."

Fill in the blanks: I ___*know*___ of ___*no*___ way of telling whether that politician is honest or not.

pair   set of two
pear   fruit

"What a great *pair* of legs Tony has," said Lola to Vonnie. Tony didn't hear her, for he was feeling very sick after munching on a green *pear.*

Fill in the blanks: In his lunch box was a ___*pair*___ of ___*pear*___ s .

passed   went by; succeeded in; handed to
past   time before the present; beyond, as in "We worked past closing time."

Someone *passed* him a wine bottle; it was the way he chose to forget his unhappy *past.*

Fill in the blanks: I walked ___*past*___ the instructor's office but was afraid to ask her whether or not I had ___*passed*___ the test.

peace   calm
piece   a part

Nations often risk world *peace* by fighting over a *piece* of land.

Fill in the blanks: Martha did not have any ___*peace*___ until she gave her pet dog a ___*piece*___ of her meat loaf.

plain   simple; flat area
plane   aircraft

The *plain,* unassuming young man on the *plane* suddenly jumped up with a grenade in his hand and announced, "We're all going to Tibet."

Fill in the blanks: The game-show contestant opened the small box wrapped in

_____*plain*_____ brown paper and found inside the keys to his own jet

_____*plane*_____.

principal   main; person in charge of a school
principle   law, standard, or rule
              Ley   Norma   Regla

Note: It might help to remember that the *e* in *principle* is also in *rule* — the meaning of *principle.*

Pete's high school *principal* had one *principal* problem: Pete. This was because there were only two *principles* in Pete's life: rest and relaxation.

Fill in the blanks: The _____*Principal*_____ reason she dropped out of school

was that she believed in the _____*principle*_____ of complete freedom of choice.

right   correct; opposite of *left*
write   what you do in English

If you have the *right* course card, I'll *write* your name on the class roster.

Fill in the blanks: Eddie thinks I'm weird since I _____*write*_____ with both

my _____*right*_____ and my left hands.

than (thăn)   word used in comparisons
then (thĕn)   at that time

Note: It might help to remember that the*n* is also a time signal.

> When we were kids, my friend Elaine had prettier clothes *than* I did. I really envied her *then.*

Fill in the blanks: Marge thought she was better ____than____ the rest of us, but ____then____ she got the lowest grade on the history test.

their   belonging to them
there   at that place; neutral word used with verbs like *is, are, was, were, have,* and *had*
they're   short form of *they are*

> Two people own that van over *there* (at that place). *They're* (they are) going to move out of *their* apartment (the apartment belonging to them) and into the van, in order to save money.

Fill in the blanks: ____They are____ not going to invite us to ____their____ table because ____there____ is no room for us to sit down.

threw   past form of *throw*
through   from one side to the other; finished

> The fans *threw* so much litter on the field that the teams could not go *through* with the game.

Fill in the blanks: When Mr. Jefferson was ____through____ screaming about the violence on television, he ____threw____ the newspaper at his dog.

to   verb part, as in *to smile;* toward, as in ''I'm going *to* heaven''

too   overly, as in ''The pizza was *too* hot''; <u>also,</u> as in ''The coffee was hot, *too.*''

two   the number 2

hacia

Tony drove *to* the park *to* be alone with Lola. (The first <u>*to* means ''toward'';</u> the second *to* is a verb part that goes with *be.*)

Tony's shirt is *too* tight; his pants are tight, *too.* (The first *too* means ''overly''; the second *too* means ''also.'')

Cosa enorme.

You need *two* hands (2 hands) to handle a Whopper.

Fill in the blanks: _____two_____ times tonight, you have been _____too_____ ready _____to_____ make assumptions without asking questions first.

wear   to have on

where   in what place

Fred wanted to *wear* his light pants on the hot day, but he didn't know *where* he had put them.

Fill in the blanks: _____where_____ exactly on my leg should I _____wear_____ this elastic bandage?

weather   atmospheric conditions

whether   <u>if it happens that;</u> <u>in case;</u> <u>if</u>

Some people go on vacations *whether* or not the *weather* is good.

Fill in the blanks: I always ask Bill _____whether_____ or not we're going to have a storm, for he can feel rainy _____weather_____ approaching in his bad knee.

whose   belonging to whom

who's   short form for *who is* and *who has*

Who's the teacher *whose* students are complaining?

Fill in the blanks: _____who's_____ the guy _____whose_____ car I saw you in?

your   belonging to you
you're   short form of *you are*

> *You're* (meaning "you are") not going to the fair unless *your* brother (the brother belonging to you) goes with you.

Fill in the blanks: _____*You are*_____ going to have to put aside individual differences and play together for the sake of _____*your*_____ team.

OTHER WORDS FREQUENTLY CONFUSED

Following is a list of other words that people frequently confuse. Complete the activities for each set of words, and check off and study the words that give you trouble.

a, an   Both *a* and *an* are used before other words to mean, approximately, "one."

Generally you should use *an* before words starting with a vowel (*a, e, i, o, u*):

   an ache   an experiment   an elephant   an idiot   an ox

Generally you should use *a* before words starting with a consonant (all other letters):

   a Coke   a brain   a cheat   a television   a gambler

Fill in the blanks: The girls had _____*an*_____ argument over _____*a*_____ former boyfriend.

accept (ăk sĕpt′)   receive; agree to
except (ĕk sĕpt′)   exclude; but

> "I would *accept* your loan," said Bill to the bartender, "*except* that I'm not ready to pay 25 percent interest."

Fill in the blanks: _____*Except*_____ that she can't _____*accept*_____ any criticism, Lori is a good friend.

advice (ăd vīs′)   noun meaning "an opinion"
advise (ăd vīz′)   verb meaning "to counsel, to give advice"

I *advise* you to take the *advice* of your friends and stop working so hard.

Fill in the blanks: I ____*advise*____ you to listen carefully to any ____*advice*____ you get from your boss.

affect (uh fĕkt′)   verb meaning "to influence"
effect (ĭ fĕkt′)   verb meaning "to bring about something"; noun meaning "result"

The full *effects* of marijuana and alcohol on the body are only partly known; however, both drugs clearly *affect* the brain in various ways.

Fill in the blanks: The new tax laws go into ____*effect*____ next month, and they are going to ____*affect*____ your income tax deductions.

among   implies three or more
between   implies only two

We had to choose from *among* 125 shades of paint but *between* only 2 fabrics.

Fill in the blanks: The layoff notices distributed ____*among*____ the unhappy workers gave them a choice ____*between*____ working for another month at full pay and leaving immediately with two weeks' pay.

beside   along the side of
besides   in addition to

I was lucky I wasn't standing *beside* the car when it was hit.
Besides being unattractive, these uniforms are impractical.

Fill in the blanks: ____*Besides*____ the alarm system hooked up to the door, our neighbors keep a gun ____*beside*____ their beds.

desert (děz'ərt)   stretch of dry land; (di zûrt') to abandon one's post or duty
dessert (dǐ zûrt')   last part of a meal

Sweltering in the *desert*, I was tormented by the thought of an icy *dessert.* *Postre ·*

Fill in the blanks: After their meal, they carried their _____*dessert*_____ into the living room so that they would not miss the start of the old *desert* _____ movie about Lawrence of Arabia.

fewer   word used with things that can be counted
less   refers to amount, value, or degree

There were *fewer* than seven people in all my classes today.
I seem to feel *less* tired when I exercise regularly.

Fill in the blanks: With _____*fewer*_____ people driving large cars, we are *g can be counted* importing _____*less*_____ oil than we used to.

loose (loos)   not fastened; not tight-fitting
lose (looz)   misplaced; fail to win

Phil's belt is so *loose* that he always looks ready to *lose* his pants.

Fill in the blanks: At least once a week our neighbors _____*lose*_____ their dog; it's because they let him run _____*loose*_____.

quiet (kwī'ĭt)   peaceful
quite (kwīt)   entirely; really; rather *Bastante*

After a busy day, the children are now *quiet,* and their parents are *quite* tired.

Fill in the blanks: The _____*quiet*_____ halls of the church become _____*quite*_____ lively during square-dance evenings.

though (thō)   despite the fact that
thought (thôt)   past form of *think*

Even *though* she worked, she *thought* she would have time to go to school.

Fill in the blanks: Susan _____thought_____ she would like the job, but even _____though_____ the pay was good, she hated the traveling involved.

■ Review Test 1

Underline the correct word in the parentheses. If necessary, look back at the explanations of the words instead of trying to guess.

1. Please take my (advice, advise) and (where, wear) something warm and practical, rather (than, then) something fashionable and flimsy.

2. Glen felt that if he could (loose, lose) twenty pounds, the (affect, effect) on his social life might be dramatic.

3. (Their, There, They're) going to show seven horror films at (their, there, they're) Halloween night festival; I hope you'll be (their, there, they're).

4. (Your, You're) going to have to do (a, an) better job on (your, you're) final exam if you expect to pass the (coarse, course).

5. Those (to, too, two) issues are (to, too, two) hot for any politician (to, too, two) handle.

6. Even (though, thought) the (brakes, breaks) on my car were worn, I did not have (quiet, quite) enough money to get them replaced (right, write) away.

7. (Accept, Except) for the fact that my neighbor receives most of his mail in (plain, plane) brown wrappers, he is (know, no) stranger (than, then) anyone else in this rooming house.

8. Because the Randalls are so neat and fussy, (its, it's) hard (to, too, two) feel comfortable when (your, you're) in (their, there, they're) house.

9. (Whose, Who's) the culprit who left the paint can on the table? The paint has ruined a (knew, new) tablecloth, and (its, it's) soaked (threw, through) the linen and (affected, effected) the varnish stain on the table.

10. I would have been angry at the car that (passed, past) me at ninety miles an hour on the highway, (accept, except) that I (knew, new) it would not get (passed, past) the speed trap (to, too, two) miles down the road.

■ Review Test 2

On separate paper, write short sentences using the ten words shown below.

their	principal
its	except
you're	past
too	through
then	who's

EFFECTIVE
WORD
CHOICE

Introductory Project

Put a check beside the sentence in each pair that you feel makes more effective use of words.

1. I flipped out when Faye broke our date. _____
   I got very angry when Faye broke our date. __✓__

2. Doctors as dedicated as Dr. Curtin are few and far between. _____
   Doctors as dedicated as Dr. Curtin are rare. __✓__

3. Yesterday I ascertained that Elena and Judd broke up. _____
   Yesterday I found out that Elena and Judd broke up. __✓__

4. Judging by the looks of things, it seems to me that it will probably rain very soon. _____
   It looks as though it will rain soon. __✓__

Now see if you can circle the correct number in each case:

    Pair (①, 2, 3, 4) contains a sentence with slang.
    Pair (1, ②, 3, 4) contains a sentence with a cliché.
    Pair (1, 2, ③, 4) contains a sentence with a pretentious word.
    Pair (1, 2, 3, ④) contains a wordy sentence.

Answers are on page 575.

Choose your words carefully when you write. Always take the time to think about your word choices rather than simply using the first word that comes to mind. You want to develop the habit of selecting words that are appropriate and exact for your purposes. One way you can show sensitivity to language is by avoiding slang, clichés, pretentious words, and wordiness.

Palabrería

SLANG

We often use slang expressions when we talk because they are so vivid and colorful. However, slang is usually out of place in formal writing. Here are some examples of slang expressions:

My girlfriend *got straight* with me by saying she wanted to see other men.

Rick spent all Saturday *messing around* with his stereo.

My boss keeps *riding* me about coming to work on time.

The tires on the Corvette make the car look like *something else.*

The crowd was *psyched up* when the game began.

Slang expressions have a number of drawbacks: they go out of date quickly, they become tiresome if used excessively in writing, and they may communicate clearly to some readers but not to others. Also, the use of slang can be a way of evading the specific details that are often needed to make one's meaning clear in writing. For example, in ''The tires on the Corvette make the car look like something else,'' the writer has not provided the specific details about the tires necessary for us to understand the statement clearly. In general, then, you should avoid slang in your writing. If you are in doubt about whether an expression is slang, it may help to check a recently published hardbound dictionary.

Activity

Rewrite the following sentences, replacing the italicized slang words with more formal ones.

Example   The movie was a *real bomb,* so we *cut out* early.

The movie was terrible, so we left early.

1. My boss *came down on me* for *goofing off* on the job.

    My boss reprimanded me for procrastinating on the Job

2. The car was a *steal* for the money until the owner *jacked up* the price.

   The car was a bargain for the money until the owner
   raised the price.

3. If the instructor stops *hassling* me, I am going to *get my act together* in the course.

   If the instructor stops picking on me, I am going to do better in
   the course,

CLICHÉS

A cliché is an expression that has been worn out through constant use. Some typical clichés are listed below:

Clichés

all work and no play	saw the light
at a loss for words	short but sweet
better late than never	sigh of relief
drop in the bucket	singing the blues
easier said than done	taking a big chance
had a hard time of it	time and time again
in the nick of time	too close for comfort
in this day and age	too little, too late
it dawned on me	took a turn for the worse
it goes without saying	under the weather
last but not least	where he (she) is
make ends meet	coming from
on top of the world	word to the wise
sad but true	work like a dog

Clichés are common in speech but make your writing seem tired and stale. Also, clichés—like slang—are often a way of evading the specific details that you must work to provide in your writing. You should, then, avoid clichés and try to express your meaning in fresh, original ways.

Activity

Underline the cliché in each of the following sentences. Then substitute specific, fresh words for the (trite) expression.
ESTEREOTIPADO

Example   I passed the test by the skin of my teeth.

I barely passed the test

1. Anyone turning in a paper late is throwing caution to the winds.

   Anyone turning in a paper late is a fool.

2. Judy doesn't make any bones about her ambition.

   Judy doesn't get picky about her ambition

3. I met with my instructor to try to iron out the problems in my paper.

   I met with my instructor to try to solve the problems in my paper.

PRETENTIOUS WORDS

Some people feel they can improve their writing by using fancy and elevated words rather than simple and natural words. They use artificial and (stilted) language
ALTISONANTE
that more often obscures their meaning than communicates it clearly.

Here are some unnatural-sounding sentences:

I comprehended her statement.
UNDERSTOOD
While partaking of our morning meal, we engaged in an animated conversation.
SHARING
I am a stranger to excessive financial sums.
Law enforcement officers directed traffic when the lights malfunctioned.
BROKE DOWN

The same thoughts can be expressed more clearly and effectively by using plain, natural language, as below:

I understood what she said.
While eating breakfast, we had a lively talk.
I have never had much money.
Police officers directed traffic when the lights stopped working.

UPON: EN EL MOMENTO DE — INMEDIATAMENTE DESPUES DE

Apprehensive: Aprehensivo- intoligento, Capaz -Temeroso, receloso

ENCOMPASS; CERCAR, RODEAR — abarcar, Comprender — llevar a cabo

Activity

Cross out the artificial words in each sentence. Then substitute clear, simple language for the artificial words.

Example The manager ~~reproached~~ me for my ~~tardiness~~.

The manager criticized me for being late.

1. One of Tina's <u>objectives</u> in life is <u>to accomplish</u> a large family.

   One of Tina's Goals in life is To have a large family

2. <u>Upon</u> entering our <u>residence</u>, we detected smoke in <u>the atmosphere</u>.

   After entering our house, we detected smoke in the air

3. I am not <u>apprehensive</u> about the test, which <u>encompasses</u> five chapters of the book.
   Temeroso   *abarca*

   I am not scare about The test, which include five chapters of the book.

WORDINESS

Wordiness — using more words than necessary to express a meaning — is often a sign of lazy or careless writing. Your readers may resent the extra time and energy they must spend when you have not done the work needed to make your writing direct and concise. — Conciso — Breve

Here are examples of wordy sentences:

Anne is of the opinion that the death penalty should be allowed.

I would like to say that my subject in this paper will be the kind of generous person that my father was.

Omitting needless words improves the sentences:

Anne supports the death penalty.

My father was a generous person.

In the box on the opposite page is a list of some wordy expressions that could be reduced to single words.

Wordy Form	Short Form
a large number of	many
a period of a week	a week
arrive at an agreement	agree
at an earlier point in time	before
at the present time	now
big in size	big
owing to the fact that	because
during the time that	while
five in number	five
for the reason that	because
good benefit	benefit
in every instance	always
in my own opinion	I think
in the event that	if
in the near future	soon
in this day and age	today
is able to	can
large in size	large
plan ahead for the future	plan
postponed until later	postponed
red in color	red
return back	return

Activity

Rewrite the following sentences, omitting needless words.

1. After a lot of careful thinking, I have arrived at the conclusion that drunken drivers should receive jail terms.

    Drunken Drivers should be put in jail

    _____

2. The movie that I went to last night, which was fairly interesting, I must say, was enjoyed by me and my girlfriend.

    My girlfriend and I enjoyed the movie last night.

    _____

3. Owing to inclement weather conditions of wind and rain, we have decided not to proceed with the athletic competition about to take place on the baseball diamond.

Competition on the baseball diamond was cancelled.

4. Without any question, there should be a law making it a requirement for parents of young children to buckle the children into car seats for safety.

Parents should buckle their children's car seats for safety

5. Beyond a doubt, the only two things you can rely or depend on would be the sure facts that death comes to everyone and that the government will tax your yearly income.

You can only depend on death to come and for the government to tax your income.

■ Review Test 1

Certain words are italicized in the following sentences. In the space provided, identify the words as *slang (S)*, *clichés (C)*, or *pretentious words (PW)*. Then rewrite the sentences, replacing the words with more effective diction.

S 1. We're *psyched* for tonight's concert, which is going to be *totally awesome*.

We're ready for tonight's concert, which is going to be great.

C 2. Getting good grades in college courses is sometimes *easier said than done*.

Getting good grades in college courses is sometimes difficult.

PW 3. I *availed myself* of the chance to *participate* in the computer course.

I take advantage of the chance to enroll in the computer course

C 4. The victims of the car accident were shaken but *none the worse for wear.*

The victims of the car accident were shaken but not injured

S 5. My roommate *pulled an all-nighter* and almost *conked out* during the exam.

My roommate studied all night and almost fell asleep during the exam

■ Review Test 2

Rewrite the following sentences, omitting needless words.

1. Workers who are on a part-time basis are attractive to a business because they do not have to be paid as much as full-time workers for a business.

   Part-time workers are preferable to a business than full-time workers.

2. During the time that I was sick and out of school, I missed a total of three math tests.

   I missed three tests because I was sick.

3. The game, which was scheduled for later today, has been canceled by the officials because of the rainy weather.

   Rain made the game to be canceled.

4. At this point in time, I am quite undecided and unsure about just which classes I will take during this coming semester.

   I do not know which classes to take this semester.

5. An inconsiderate person located in the apartment next to mine keeps her radio on too loud a good deal of the time, with the result being that it is disturbing to everyone in the neighboring apartments.

   The neighbor likes to play the music to loud.

SENTENCE VARIETY

One aspect of effective writing is to vary the kinds of sentences you write. If every sentence follows the same pattern, writing may become monotonous to read. This chapter explains four ways you can create variety and interest in your writing style. The first two ways involve coordination and subordination—important techniques for achieving different kinds of emphasis in writing.

The following are four methods you can use to make your sentences more varied and more sophisticated:

1 Add a second complete thought (coordination)
2 Add a dependent thought (subordination)
3 Begin with a special opening word or phrase
4 Place adjectives or verbs in a series

Each method will be discussed in turn.

ADD A SECOND COMPLETE THOUGHT

When you add a second complete thought to a simple sentence, the result is a compound (or double) sentence. The two complete statements in a compound sentence are usually connected by a comma plus a joining, or coordinating, word (*and, but, for, or, nor, so, yet*).

A compound sentence is used when you want to give equal weight to two closely related ideas. The technique of showing that ideas have equal importance is called *coordination*.

Following are some compound sentences. Each contains two ideas that the writer regards as equal in importance.

Bill has stopped smoking cigarettes, but he is now addicted to chewing gum.

I repeatedly failed the math quizzes, so I decided to drop the course.

Stan turned all the lights off, and then he locked the office door.

Activity

Combine the following pairs of simple sentences into compound sentences. Use a comma and a logical joining word (*and, but, for, so*) to connect each pair.

Note: If you are not sure what *and, but, for,* and *so* mean, review pages 258–259.

Example ■ The record kept skipping.

■ There was dust on the needle.

The record kept skipping, for there was dust on the needle.

1. ■ The line at the deli counter was long.

 ■ Jake took a numbered ticket anyway.

 _____

2. ■ Vandals smashed the car's headlights.

 ■ They slashed the tires as well.

 _____

3. ■ I married at age seventeen.

 ■ I never got a chance to live on my own.

 _____

4. ■ Mold grew on my leather boots.

 ■ The closet was warm and humid.

 _____

5. ■ My father has a high cholesterol count.

 ■ He continues to eat red meat almost every day.

 _____

 _____

ADD A DEPENDENT THOUGHT

When you add a dependent thought to a simple sentence, the result is a complex sentence.* A dependent thought begins with a word or phrase like one of the following:

Dependent Words		
after	if, even if	when, whenever
although, though	in order that	where, wherever
as	since	whether
because	that, so that	which, whichever
before	unless	while
even though	until	who, whoever
how	what, whatever	whose

A complex sentence is used when you want to emphasize one idea over another within the sentence. Look at the following complex sentence:

Although I lowered the thermostat, my heating bill remained high.

The idea that the writer wants to emphasize here — *my heating bill remained high* — is expressed as a complete thought. The less important idea — *Although I lowered my thermostat* — is subordinated to this complete thought. The technique of giving one idea less emphasis than another is called *subordination.*

Following are other examples of complex sentences. In each case, the part starting with the dependent word is the less emphasized part of the sentence.

Even though I was tired, I stayed up to watch the horror movie.

Before I take a bath, I check for spiders in the tub.

When Ivy feels nervous, she pulls on her earlobe.

---

* The two parts of a complex sentence are sometimes called an *independent clause* and a *dependent clause.* A *clause* is simply a word group that contains a subject and a verb. An independent clause expresses a complete thought and can stand alone. A dependent clause does not express a complete thought in itself and ''depends on'' the independent clause to complete its meaning. Dependent clauses always begin with a dependent, or subordinating, word.

Activity

Use logical subordinating words to combine the following pairs of simple sentences into sentences that contain a dependent thought. Place a comma after a dependent statement when it starts the sentence.

Example   ■ Our team lost.

          ■ We were not invited to the tournament.

        Because our team lost, we were not invited to the tournament.

1. ■ I receive my degree in June.
   ■ I will begin applying for jobs.

    _____

    _____

2. ■ Lola doesn't enjoy cooking.
   ■ She often eats at fast-food restaurants.

    _____

    _____

3. ■ I sent several letters of complaint.
   ■ The electric company never corrected my bill.

    _____

    _____

4. ■ Neil's car went into a skid.
   ■ He took his foot off the gas pedal.

    _____

    _____

5. ■ The final exam covered sixteen chapters.
   ■ The students complained.

    _____

    _____

BEGIN WITH A SPECIAL OPENING WORD OR PHRASE

Among the special openers that can be used to start sentences are *-ed* words, *-ing* words, *-ly* word, *to* word groups, and prepositional phrases. Here are examples of all five kinds of openers:

-ed *word*	Tired from a long day of work, Sharon fell asleep on the sofa.
-ing *word*	Using a thick towel, Mel dried his hair quickly.
-ly *word*	Reluctantly, I agreed to rewrite the paper.
to *word group*	To get to the church on time, you must leave now.
Prepositional phrase	With Fred's help, Martha planted the evergreen shrubs.

Activity

Combine the simple sentences into one sentence by using the opener shown in the margin and omitting repeated words. Use a comma to set off the opener from the rest of the sentence.

Example   -ing *word*   ■ The toaster refused to pop up.

■ It buzzed like an angry hornet.

Buzzing like an angry hornet, the toaster refused

to pop up.

-ed *word*   1. ■ Bill was annoyed by the poor TV reception.

■ He decided to get a new antenna.

_____

_____

-ing *word*   2. ■ The star player glided down the court.

■ He dribbled the basketball like a pro.

_____

_____

-ly *word*   3. ■ Food will run short on our crowded planet.

■ It is inevitable.

_____

_____

to *word*
group

4. ■ Bill rented a limousine for the night.
   ■ He wanted to make a good impression.

_____

_____

prepositional
phrase

5. ■ Lisa answered the telephone.
   ■ She did this at 4 A.M.

_____

_____

-ed *word*

6. ■ Nate dreaded the coming holidays.
   ■ He was depressed by his recent divorce.

_____

_____

-ing *word*

7. ■ The people pressed against the doors of the theater.
   ■ They pushed and shoved each other.

_____

_____

-ly *word*

8. ■ I waited in the packed emergency room.
   ■ I was impatient.

_____

_____

to *word*
group

9. ■ The little boy likes to annoy his parents.
   ■ He pretends he can't hear them.

_____

_____

Prepositional
phrase

10. ■ People must wear white-soled shoes.
    ■ They must do this in the gym.

_____

_____

PLACE ADJECTIVES OR VERBS IN A SERIES

Various parts of a sentence may be placed in a series. Among these parts are adjectives (descriptive words) and verbs. Here are examples of both in a series.

Adjectives The *black, smeary* newsprint rubbed off on my *new butcher-block* table.

Verbs The quarterback *fumbled* the ball, *recovered* it, and *sighed* with relief.

Activity

Combine the simple sentences into one sentence by using adjectives or verbs in series and by omitting repeated words. In most cases, use a comma between the adjectives or verbs in a series.

Example   ■ Before Christmas, I made fruitcakes.

■ I decorated the house.

■ I wrapped dozens of toys.

Before Christmas, I made fruitcakes, decorated the house, and wrapped dozens of toys.

1. ■ My lumpy mattress was giving me a cramp in my neck.

   ■ It was causing pains in my back.

   ■ It was making me lose sleep.

   _____

   _____

2. ■ Lights appeared in the fog.

   ■ The lights were flashing.

   ■ The lights were red.

   ■ The fog was gray.

   ■ The fog was soupy.

   _____

   _____

3. ■ Before going to bed, I locked all the doors.
    ■ I activated the burglar alarm.
    ■ I slipped a kitchen knife under my mattress.

    _____

    _____

4. ■ Lola picked sweater hairs off her coat.
    ■ The hairs were fuzzy.
    ■ The hairs were white.
    ■ The coat was brown.
    ■ The coat was suede.

    _____

    _____

5. ■ The contact lens fell onto the floor.
    ■ The contact lens was thin.
    ■ The contact lens was slippery.
    ■ The floor was dirty.
    ■ The floor was tiled.

    _____

    _____

■ Review Test 1

On separate paper, use coordination or subordination to combine the following groups of simple sentences into one or more longer sentences. Omit repeated words. Since various combinations are possible, you might want to jot down several combinations in each case. Then read them aloud to find the combination that sounds best.

Keep in mind that very often, the relationship among ideas in a sentence will be clearer when subordinating rather than coordinating words are used.

Example ■ I don't like to ask for favors.
       ■ I must borrow money from my brother-in-law.
       ■ I know he won't turn me down.
       ■ I still feel guilty about it.

   I don't like to ask for favors, but I must borrow money from my

   brother-in-law. Although I know he won't turn me down, I still

   feel guilty about it.

Comma Hints

a   Use a comma at the end of a word group that starts with a subordinating word (as in ''Although I know he won't turn me down, . . .'').

b   Use a comma between independent word groups connected by *and, but, for, or, nor, so, yet* (as in ''I don't like to ask for favors, but . . .'').

1. ▪ My grandmother is eighty-six.
   ▪ She drives to Florida alone every year.
   ▪ She believes in being self-reliant.

2. ▪ His name was called.
   ▪ Luis walked into the examining room.
   ▪ He was nervous.
   ▪ He was determined to ask the doctor for a straight answer.

3. ▪ They left twenty minutes early for class.
   ▪ They were late anyway.
   ▪ The car overheated.

4. ▪ John failed the midterm exam.
   ▪ He studied harder for the final.
   ▪ He passed it.

5. ▪ A volcano erupts.
   ▪ It sends tons of ash into the air.
   ▪ This creates flaming orange sunsets.

6. ▪ Tony got home from the shopping mall.
   ▪ He discovered his rented tuxedo did not fit.
   ▪ The jacket sleeves covered his hands.
   ▪ The pants cuffs hung over his shoes.

7. ▪ The boys waited for the bus.
   ▪ The wind shook the flimsy shelter.
   ▪ They shivered with cold.
   ▪ They were wearing thin jackets.

8. ■ The engine almost caught.

   ■ Then it died.

   ■ I realized no help would come.

   ■ I was on a lonely road.

   ■ It was very late.

9. ■ Miriam wanted white wall-to-wall carpeting.

   ■ She knew it was a bad buy.

   ■ It would look beautiful.

   ■ It would be very hard to clean.

10. ■ Gary was leaving the store.

    ■ The shoplifting alarm went off.

    ■ He had not stolen anything.

    ■ The clerk had forgotten to remove the magnetic tag.

    ■ The tag was on a shirt Gary had bought.

■ **Review Test 2**

On separate paper, write two sentences of your own that begin with (1) -*ed* words, (2) -*ing* words, (3) -*ly* words, (4) *to* word groups, and (5) prepositional phrases. Also write two sentences of your own that contain (6) a series of adjectives and (7) a series of verbs.

EDITING
TESTS

EDITING AND PROOFREADING
FOR SENTENCE-SKILLS MISTAKES

The five tests in this section will give you practice in editing and proofreading for sentence-skills mistakes. People often find it hard to edit and proofread a paper carefully. They have put so much work into their writing, or so little, that it's almost painful for them to look at the paper one more time. You may simply have to *force* yourself to edit and proofread. Remember that eliminating sentence-skills mistakes will improve an average paper and help ensure a strong grade on a good paper. Further, as you get into the habit of checking your papers, you will also get into the habit of using sentence skills consistently. They are a basic part of clear and effective writing.

■ Editing Test 1

Identify the five mistakes in paper format in the student paper that follows. From the box below, choose the letters that describe the five mistakes and write those letters in the spaces provided.

a. The title should not be underlined.
b. The title should not be set off in quotation marks.
c. There should not be a period at the end of the title.
d. All the major words in the title should be capitalized.
e. The title should be just several words and not a complete sentence.
f. The first line of the paper should stand independent of the title.
g. A line should be skipped between the title and the first line of the paper.
h. The first line of the paper should be indented.
i. The right-hand margin should not be crowded.
j. Hyphenation should occur only between syllables.

"my candy apple adventure"

	It was the best event of my day. I loved the sweetness that
	filled my mouth as I bit into the sugary coating. With my second
	bite, I munched contentedly on the apple underneath. Its
	crunchy tartness was the perfect balance to the smooth sweet-
	ness of the outside. Then the apple had a magical effect on me.
	Suddenly I remembered when I was seven years old, walking
	through the county fair grounds, holding my father's hand. We
	stopped at a refreshment stand, and he bought us each a
	candy apple. I had never had one before, and I asked him what it
	was. "This is a very special fruit," he said. "If you ever feel sad,
	all you have to do is eat a candy apple, and it will bring you
	sweetness." Now, years later, his words came back to me, and
	as I ate my candy apple, I felt the world turn sweet once more.

1. _____   2. _____   3. _____   4. _____   5. _____

■ Editing Test 2

Identify the sentence-skills mistakes at the underlined spots in the selection that follows. From the box below, choose the letter that describes each mistake and write it in the space provided. The same mistake may appear more than once.

---

a.   sentence fragment

b.   run-on

c.   mistake in subject-verb
      agreement

d.   apostrophe mistake

e.   faulty parallelism

Looking Out for Yourself

It's sad but true that "If you don't look out for yourself, no one else will." For example, some people have a false idea about the power of a college <u>degree, they</u> think ₁ that once they <u>possesses</u> the degree, the world will be waiting on their doorstep. In fact, ₂ nobody is likely to be on their doorstep unless, through advance planning, they <u>has</u> ₃ prepared themselves for a career. <u>The kind in which good job opportunities exist.</u> Even ₄ after a person has landed a job, however, a healthy amount of self-interest is needed. People who hide in corners or <u>with hesitation</u> to let others know about their skills <u>doesn't</u> ₅   ₆ get promotions or raises. <u>Its</u> important to take credit for a job well done, whether it ₇ involves writing a report, <u>organized the office filing system</u>, or calming down an angry ₈ customer. Also, people should feel free to ask the boss for a raise. <u>If they work hard</u> ₉ <u>and really deserve it</u>. Those who look out for themselves get the <u>rewards, people</u> who ₁₀ depend on others to help them along get left behind.

1. _____   3. _____   5. _____   7. _____   9. _____

2. _____   4. _____   6. _____   8. _____   10. _____

■ Editing Test 3

Identify the sentence-skills mistakes at the underlined spots in the selection that follows. From the box below, choose the letter that describes each mistake and write it in the space provided. The same mistake may appear more than once.

a. sentence fragment	e. missing commas around an interrupter
b. run-on	
c. mistake in verb tense	f. mistake with quotation marks
d. irregular verb mistake	g. apostrophe mistake

Deceptive Appearances

Appearances can be deceptive. While looking through a library window yesterday, I saw a neatly groomed woman walk by. Her clothes were skillfully <u>tailored her makeup</u> [1] was perfect. Then <u>thinking no one was looking she</u> crumpled a piece of paper in her hand. [2] <u>And tossed it into a nearby hedge.</u> Suddenly she no longer <u>looks</u> attractive to me. On [3] [4] another occasion, I started talking to a person in my psychology class named Eric. Eric seemed to be a great person. He always got the class laughing with his <u>jokes, on the days</u> [5] when Eric was absent, I think even the professor missed his lively personality. Eric asked me <u>"if I wanted to get a Coke in the cafeteria,"</u> and I felt happy he had <u>chose</u> me to be a [6] [7] friend. <u>While we were sitting in the cafeteria.</u> Eric took out an envelope with several kinds [8] of pills inside. "Want one?" he asked. "They're uppers." I didn't want <u>one, I felt dis-</u> [9] appointed. <u>Erics</u> terrific personality was the product of the pills he took. [10]

1. _____   3. _____   5. _____   7. _____   9. _____

2. _____   4. _____   6. _____   8. _____   10. _____

■ Editing Test 4

Identify the sentence-skills mistakes at the underlined spots in the selection that follows. From the box below, choose the letter that describes each mistake and write it in the space provided. The same mistake may appear more than once.

a. sentence fragment	e. apostrophe mistake
b. run-on	f. dangling modifier
c. irregular verb mistake	g. missing quotation marks
d. missing comma after introductory words	

A Horrifying Moment

The most horrifying moment in my life occurred in the dark hallway. <u>Which led to</u>
<u>my apartment house.</u> Though the hallway light was <u>out I</u> managed to find my apartment
door. However, I could not find the keyhole with my door key. I then pulled a book of
matches from my pocket. <u>Trying to strike a match,</u> the entire book of matches <u>bursted</u>
into flames. I flicked the matches away but not before my coat sleeve <u>catched</u> fire.
Within seconds, my arm was like a torch. <u>Struggling to unsnap the buttons of my coat,</u>
flames began to sear my skin. I was quickly going into shock. <u>And began screaming in</u>
<u>pain.</u> A <u>neighbors</u> door opened and a voice cried out, <u>My God!</u> I was pulled through an
apartment and put under a bathroom shower, which extinguished the flames. I suffered
third degree burns on my <u>arm, I</u> felt lucky to escape with my life.

1. _____   3. _____   5. _____   7. _____   9. _____

2. _____   4. _____   6. _____   8. _____   10. _____

■ Editing Test 5

Identify the sentence-skills mistakes at the underlined spots in the selection that follows. From the box below, choose the letter that describes each mistake and write it in the space provided. The same mistake may appear more than once.

a. sentence fragment	e. faulty parallelism
b. run-on	f. apostrophe mistake
c. missing capital letter	g. missing quotation mark
d. mistake in subject-verb agreement	h. missing comma after introductory words

Why I Didn't Go to Church

I almost never attended church in my boyhood years. There was an unwritten code that the guys on the corner <u>was</u> not to be seen in <u>churches'</u>. Although there <u>was</u> many
1   2   3
days when I wanted to attend a church, I felt I had no choice but to stay away. If the guys had heard I had gone to church, they would have said things like, <u>"hey,</u> angel,
4
when are you going to <u>fly?</u> With my group of friends, <u>its</u> amazing that I developed any
5   6
religious feeling at all. Another reason for not going to church was my father. When he was around the <u>house he</u> told my mother, "Mike's not going to church. No boy of mine
7
is a sissy." My mother and sister went to <u>church, I</u> sat with my father and read the
8
Sunday paper or <u>watching television.</u> I did not start going to church until years later.
9
<u>When I no longer hung around with the guys on the corner or let my father have power
10
over me.</u>

1. _____	3. _____	5. _____	7. _____	9. _____
2. _____	4. _____	6. _____	8. _____	10. _____

PART FIVE

FIFTEEN
READING
SELECTIONS

PREVIEW

This book assumes that writing and reading are closely connected skills—so that practicing one helps the other, and neglecting one hurts the other. Part Five will enable you to work on becoming a better reader as well as a stronger writer. Following an introductory section that offers a series of tips on effective reading, there are fifteen reading selections. Each selection begins with a preview that supplies background information about the piece. After the selection are ten questions to give you practice in key reading comprehension skills. A set of discussion questions is also provided, both to deepen your understanding of the selection and to point out basic writing techniques used in the essay. Then come several writing assignments, along with guidelines to help you think about the assignments and get started working on them.

INTRODUCTION
TO THE
READINGS

The reading selections in Part Five will help you find topics for writing. Some of the selections provide helpful practical information. For example, you'll learn how to study more efficiently and how to go about deciding on a career and finding a job. Other selections deal with thought-provoking aspects of contemporary life. One article, for instance, argues that friendship may be the most important ingredient for health in a stressful world; another dramatizes in a vivid and painful way the tragedy that can result when teenagers drink and drive. Still other selections are devoted to an exploration of human goals and values; one essay, for example, celebrates a person who, despite a disability, dares to pursue his dream. The varied subjects should inspire lively class discussions as well as serious individual thought. The selections should also provide a continuing source of high-interest material for a wide range of writing assignments.

The selections serve another purpose as well. They will help develop reading skills with direct benefits to you as a writer. First, through close reading, you will learn how to recognize the main idea or point of a selection and how to identify and evaluate the supporting material that develops the main idea. In your writing, you will aim to achieve the same essential structure: an overall point followed by detailed and valid support for that point. Second, close reading will help you explore a selection and its possibilities thoroughly. The more you understand about what is said in a piece, the more ideas and feelings you may have about writing on an assigned topic or a related topic of your own. A third benefit of close reading is becoming more aware of authors' stylistic devices—for example, their introductions and conclusions, their ways of presenting and developing a point, their use of transitions, their choice of language to achieve a particular tone. Recognizing these devices in other people's writing will help you enlarge your own range of writing techniques.

THE FORMAT OF EACH SELECTION

Each selection begins with a short overview that gives helpful background information. The selection is then followed by two sets of questions.

- First, there are ten reading comprehension questions to help you measure your understanding of the material. These questions involve several important reading skills: recognizing a subject or topic, determining the thesis or main idea, identifying key supporting points, making inferences, and understanding vocabulary in context. Answering the questions will enable you and your instructor to check quickly your basic understanding of a selection. More significantly, as you move from one selection to the next, you will sharpen your reading skills as well as strengthen your thinking skills—two key factors in making you a better writer.

- Following the comprehension questions are several discussion questions. In addition to dealing with issues of content, these questions focus on matters of structure, style, and tone as well.

Finally, several writing assignments accompany each selection. Many of the assignments provide guidelines on how to proceed, including suggestions for prewriting and appropriate methods of development. When writing your responses to the readings, you will have opportunities to apply all the methods of development presented in Part Two of this book.

HOW TO READ WELL: FOUR GENERAL STEPS

Skillful reading is an important part of becoming a skillful writer. Following are four steps that will make you a better reader—both of the selections here and in your reading at large.

1   Concentrate as You Read

To improve your concentration, follow these tips. First, read in a place where you can be quiet and alone. Don't choose a spot where a TV or stereo is on or where friends or family are talking nearby. Next, sit in an upright position when you read. If your body is in a completely relaxed position, sprawled across a bed or nestled in an easy chair, your mind is also going to be completely relaxed. The light muscular tension that comes from sitting in an upright chair promotes concentration and keeps your mind ready to work. Finally, consider using your index finger (or a pen) as a pacer while you read. Lightly underline each line of print with your index finger as you read down a page. Hold your hand slightly above the page and move your finger at a speed that is a little too fast for comfort. This pacing with your index finger, like sitting upright on a chair, creates a slight physical tension that will keep your body and mind focused and alert.

2   Skim Material before You Read It

In skimming, you spend about two minutes rapidly surveying a selection, looking for important points and skipping secondary material. Follow this sequence when skimming:

- Begin by reading the overview that precedes the selection.

- Then study the title of the selection for a few moments. A good title is the shortest possible summary of a selection; it often tells you in several words what a selection is about. For example, the title "The Tryout" suggests that you're going to read about a time when someone took a chance and tried out for some event.

- Next, form a basic question (or questions) out of the title. For instance, for the selection titled "The Tryout," you might ask, "What exactly was the tryout?" "What was someone's reason for trying out?" "What was the result of the tryout?" Forming questions out of the title is often a key to locating a writer's main idea—your next concern in skimming.

- Read the first two or three paragraphs and the last two or three paragraphs in the selection. Very often a writer's main idea, *if* it is directly stated, will appear in one of these paragraphs and will relate to the title. For instance, in "What It Means to Be Young Today," the author states in the third paragraph that "life in the Western world provides a scarcity of delights for youngsters and many blighting and bruising experiences."

- Finally, look quickly at the rest of the selection for other clues to important points. Are there any subheads you can relate in some way to the title? Are there any words the author has decided to emphasize by setting them off in *italic* or **boldface** type? Are there any major lists of items signaled by words such as *first, second, also, another,* and so on?

3   Read the Selection Straight Through with a Pen Nearby

Don't slow down or turn back; just aim to understand as much as you can the first time through. Place a check or star beside answers to basic questions you formed from the title, and beside other ideas that seem important. Number as 1, 2, 3 . . . lists of important points. Circle words you don't understand. Put question marks in the margin next to passages that are unclear and that you will want to reread.

4   Work with the Material

Go back and reread passages that were not clear the first time through. Look up words that block your understanding of ideas and write their meanings in the margin. Also, reread carefully the areas you identified as most important; doing so will enlarge your understanding of the material. Now that you have a sense of the whole, prepare a short outline of the selection by answering the following questions on a sheet of paper:

- What is the main idea?
- What key points support the main idea?
- What seem to be other important points in the selection?

By working with the material in this way, you will significantly increase your understanding of a selection. Effective reading, just like effective writing, does not happen all at once. Rather, it is a process. Often you begin with a general impression of what something means, and then, by working at it, you move to a deeper level of understanding of the material.

HOW TO ANSWER THE COMPREHENSION QUESTIONS: SPECIFIC HINTS

Several important reading skills are involved in the ten reading comprehension questions that follow each selection. The skills are:

- Summarizing the selection by providing a title for it
- Determining the main idea
- Recognizing key supporting details
- Making inferences
- Understanding vocabulary in context

The following hints will help you apply each of these reading skills:

- *Subject or title.* Remember that the title should accurately describe the *entire* selection. It should be neither too broad nor too narrow for the material in the selection. It should answer the question "What is this about?" as specifically as possible. Note that you may at times find it easier to do the "title" question *after* the "main idea" question.

- *Main idea.* Choose the statement that you think best expresses the main idea or thesis of the entire selection. Remember that the title will often help you focus on the main idea. Then ask yourself the question, "Does most of the material in the selection support this statement?" If you can answer *Yes* to this question, you have found the thesis.

■ *Key details.* If you were asked to give a two-minute summary of a selection, the major details are the ones you would include in that summary. To determine the key details, ask yourself the question, "What are the major supporting points for the thesis?"

■ *Inferences.* Answer these questions by drawing on the evidence presented in the selection and on your own common sense. Ask yourself, "What reasonable judgments can I make on the basis of the information in the selection?"

■ *Vocabulary in context.* To decide on the meaning of an unfamiliar word, consider its context. Ask yourself, "Are there any clues in the sentence that suggest what this word means?"

On pages 580–581 is a chart on which you can keep track of your performance as you answer the ten questions for each selection. The chart will help you identify reading skills you may need to strengthen.

GOALS
AND
VALUES

The Tryout

Bob Greene

 In a monthly column in *Esquire* magazine called "American Beat," Bob Greene reported on interesting events or people in American life. The following piece is about Greg Talerico, a young man confined to a wheelchair who decided to try out as a sports commentator for a basketball league. The feature received the biggest response that Greene has ever had for any "American Beat" column; as a result, he decided to write a sequel to the story. Reading about Greg Talerico, who had the courage to take charge of his life, we recognize a choice we all must make at times. That choice is between playing it safe and trying to make something happen, even if we may fail in the attempt.

At first I didn't notice him. There were about a dozen people in the hotel's third-floor hallway, and most of them were standing up. He was in his wheelchair. His head was down; he was studying the Continental Basketball Association's official guidebook.   1

■

The idea of the story was supposed to be sort of a joke. In last month's American   2
Beat, I wrote about what it was like to be guest host—for one night—of a nationally televised talk show. I had done that, and I had written the column about the Walter Mitty-like experience of it all.

Then I heard about this stunt that the Continental Basketball Association was staging. The CBA is a minor league; it is composed of teams with names such as the Albany Patroons, the Wyoming Wildcatters, and the Tampa Bay Thrillers. The goal for basketball players in the CBA is someday to make it to the National Basketball Association. 3

One CBA game each week of the season is telecast on a cable network. The league's executives had thought up a clever promotional idea: the play-by-play man on the cablecasts would be a broadcast professional—but for a color commentator, the CBA would conduct a "nationwide search" for a regular fan who could do the job. One fan would be chosen to be the CBA's color man for the entire season. The only requirement was that the fan must have had no prior broadcast experience. 4

I thought it might make a funny counterpoint to my column about guest-hosting the talk show. Apparently this was a common fantasy; the CBA color commentator tryouts were being held in cities all over the United States and were drawing big crowds of entrants. Today the tryouts were in Chicago, at the Westin Hotel; I thought I would drop by and watch. 5

■

It was just after 10:00 A.M.; 122 contestants had been scheduled for tryouts, at five-minute intervals throughout the day. The ones who were waiting for their chance were talking with one another in the corridor. 6

"I read about this in *USA Today,* and I thought I'd come down and give it a try," said Jim Lutz, twenty-four, a mechanical engineer. "I'm just doing this on a whim. I'd like to be a color man on TV. A lot of people kind of idolize color men." 7

Lutz's fiancée, Karen Schulz, twenty-two, said, "I hope he gets it, but if he wins I hope there aren't a lot of women around him." 8

David Schneider, twenty-one, a college student, said, "Everyone looks up to a good color man. Billy Packer is the best basketball color man on the networks, and everyone knows who he is. A color man can walk into any restaurant and have people say, 'Hey, there's Billy Packer.' 'Hey, there's Al McGuire.' I'd like that." 9

I noticed that the man in the wheelchair was still studying the CBA guidebook. But I didn't go up to him yet. 10

■

I went into the room where the tryouts were being held. Chris Tomasson, the basketball league's media information director, was seated next to a television monitor that was hooked up to a videotape recorder. Tomasson would do the play-by-play for the tryouts; there was an empty chair next to him, where the aspiring color commentators would sit. Two judges sat at another table across the room. 11

Tomasson explained the procedure to me. A videotape of a game from last season would be shown. The game was between the Sarasota Stingers and the Toronto Tornados; the first 4½ minutes of the fourth quarter would be shown on the TV monitor. The audio track was crowd noise: a mixture of applause and cheers. Over that, Tomasson would provide a description of the action, and each contestant would provide the color. 12

A labor-union official named George Poppers, fifty-four, entered the room. 13
Tomasson outlined the setup to him. Then Tomasson pressed the PLAY button on
the VCR. The game came onto the screen.

"This is the CBA Game of the Week," Tomasson said. "I'm Chris Tomasson, 14
along with George Poppers, and we're back at Varsity Arena in Toronto, Canada.
Sarasota leads Toronto 99-98 at the beginning of the fourth quarter. George, what
can we look for in this quarter?"

"Well," George Poppers said, "Sarasota hasn't done too well on the road this 15
season. We hope that will change tonight."

The two men watched the game on the screen, talking back and forth; when 16
the 4½ minutes were up, Tomasson thanked Poppers and asked him to wait in the
hallway. After every ten contestants, one would be selected as a finalist for the
day. At the end of the day the finalists would compete, and one would be chosen
to go to the national finals in New York.

I sat and watched as the contestants had their 4½ minutes each. Some were 17
glib; some were nervous. All seemed to be doing this as a lark. "Sarasota isn't
using the ball as much as it should," said Felix Rojas, thirty-seven, a probation
officer. Jeff Carlson, twenty-eight, a desk clerk, said, "That was a beautiful pass
from perennial all-star Robert Smith." The same 4½ minutes of the same game
kept flashing by; each new contestant gave his own commentary.

I kept half-expecting the man in the wheelchair to be the next person through 18
the door. After about forty-five minutes, when he hadn't come in, I went back into
the hallway.

■

He was still studying the guidebook. When I got closer to the wheelchair, I saw that 19
he had a Chicago Cubs bumper sticker applied to one side of it. I noticed that his
limbs were underdeveloped; he was bent over in the wheelchair.

I introduced myself and said that he seemed to have been waiting a long time. 20

"I'm not scheduled to go in until 1:00," he said. "They told me that they'd had 21
some cancellations, and that I can go earlier if I want. But I'd rather study the
statistics right up until my time comes."

He said that his name was Greg Talerico and that he was twenty-three years 22
old. When I asked him why he was trying out, his answer was simple.

"If I could win, it would mean my entire life," he said. 23

He said that he had been born with hydrocephalus—commonly referred to as 24
water on the brain. As he grew older, he developed other ailments. When he learned
how to walk, it was with the aid of crutches.

"I read about this in *The Sporting News*," he said. "I love sports, but I never 25
could play. When I was a little boy, I used to watch all the games on TV. I've never
done anything like this before—tried out for anything.

"But if I could win—it would mean for the first time in my life that I was doing 26
something productive. I honestly don't think I'm doing anything constructive with
my life. But if I could win . . ."

He said that he lived in a center for handicapped adults. "It's clean," he said.   27
"It's a comfortable place to sleep."

A young woman named Cindy Copp, who had been hired for the day to be   28
secretary for the tryouts, came over and said, "We have some openings, if you'd
like to go in before your scheduled time."

"No, thank you," Talerico said. "I'm just going to use all the time until 1:00   29
to study."

■

I had noticed a dignified-looking, gray-haired man standing in the vicinity of Talerico's   30
wheelchair. I went over to say hello to him, and he said that he was Greg's father.
His name was Patrick Talerico, he was forty-three, and he was a truck driver.

"I think it's good that he's attempting this," the father said. "He's been inter-   31
ested in sports since he was seven or eight. It was tough on him, never being able
to play. Greg has had ten operations on his brain, starting when he was three years
old, and it hasn't been easy."

He said that his son had traveled 150 miles from the center where he lived for   32
today's tryouts. "If nothing else, at least he can say he tried," his father said.

■

I went back into the room where the tryouts were being held. Everyone was in high   33
spirits. As the Sarasota-Toronto game flickered on the screen, sports clichés filled
the air: "There's no love lost between these teams." "They're being very physical
on the boards." "You can tell he's not happy about that call."

I found myself thinking about Greg Talerico, so I went back into the hallway to   34
talk with him some more.

■

"I was on the crutches until I was fourteen," he said. "Then I began to fall down   35
too many times, and I was told that I'd be in a wheelchair permanently.

"As I grow older, I slow down more and more. They really don't know how long   36
I'm going to live. I'm told that I've already lived longer than anyone thought I would."

He said he had made a point of arriving three hours early so that he would be   37
sure to be prepared when his turn arrived.

"I've got butterflies," he said. "I'm trying to think positive, but that's hard to   38
do sometimes."

■

Just before 1:00 I went into the room, so I would be seated when Greg came in.   39
His father wheeled him through the door, and to the spot next to Chris Tomasson
and the TV monitor. In a soft voice his father said, "Is there enough room under
the table for your feet?"

Tomasson explained the procedure to him. He started the video recorder.   40

"This is the CBA Game of the Week," Tomasson said. "I'm Chris Tomasson,   41
along with Greg Talerico, and we're back at the Varsity Arena in Toronto, Canada. . . ." I could see Talerico's face light up at the sound of his words.

Tomasson turned to him and said, "Well, Greg, what can we expect in this fourth quarter?" 42

"Chris, we just saw some good play there from both sides," Talerico began. I realized that he was the only contestant I had seen so far who had bothered to remember Tomasson's name. 43

The 4½ minutes went quickly. During one play Talerico watched all of the superbly conditioned athletes race down the court; one of the players tried and failed to stop the basketball from going out of bounds. "He looks a little frustrated," Talerico said. "He feels he should have gotten the ball." 44

When the tape ended, Tomasson asked Talerico to wait in the hallway until a finalist from his group of ten contestants was chosen. 45

∎

I walked back out into the hallway and asked Talerico what he had thought. 46

"It started up so fast," he said. "I was worried about saying a dumb thing. 47

"But I had fun. I don't know how I did, but I had a great time. It was great. It was everything that I hoped." 48

∎

Because Talerico had been one of the first of his group of ten to try out, he had to wait almost an hour for the others to have their turns. Then there was a brief delay while the judges made their decision. 49

Finally Cindy Copp, the secretary, walked up to people in the corridor who were milling around. 50

"First of all, I'd like to thank all of you for coming today, and for your great enthusiasm," she said. "You were all very good. We have picked one finalist. He is . . ." 51

I was looking at Greg Talerico's face. 52

". . . Al Pote." 53

Pote, a twenty-six-year-old civil engineer, broke into a wide grin and accepted everyone's applause and congratulations. Greg Talerico, still holding his Continental Basketball Association guidebook, joined the rest in wishing him well. 54

Talerico's father waited for the hallway to clear, then started to push the wheelchair toward the bank of elevators. 55

"I'm going to take this guidebook home with me tonight," Greg said to his dad. "It's really interesting, and I didn't get to finish it all." 56

"That's fine, Greg," his father said. We all have our dreams in this life. Some manage to attain glory. For others, at least there is a clean, comfortable place to sleep. 57

Sequel

In the six years that American Beat has been appearing in this space, we have never done a follow-up—never done a column updating what has happened to a person or place written about in a previous column. 58

This month we make an exception. There are few enough stories in this world 59
that have happy endings; we thought we would share this one with you.

■

In the March American Beat there appeared the story of Greg Talerico. Greg was a 60
twenty-three-year-old man who had come to the Westin Hotel in Chicago to try out
as a color commentator for something called the Continental Basketball Association.
The CBA is a minor league that, as a gimmick, was holding tryouts around the
country for the position of color commentator on its game-of-the-week cablecasts.

Many of the people who showed up to try out were doing it as a lark. Not Greg 61
Talerico. He was confined to a wheelchair; he had been born with hydrocephalus,
commonly referred to as *water on the brain,* and as he had grown older, he had
developed other ailments. He had endured ten operations on his brain, beginning
at the age of three. His limbs had lost so much strength that he could get around
only in the wheelchair.

For the tryouts, he had traveled 150 miles from the center for physically handi- 62
capped adults where he lived. When I asked him why he was trying out, his answer
was: "If I could win, it would mean my entire life. . . . I love sports, but I never could
play. When I was a little boy, I used to watch all the games on TV. I've never done
anything like this before—tried out for anything.

"But if I could win—it would mean for the first time in my life that I was doing 63
something productive. I honestly don't think I'm doing anything constructive with
my life. But if I could win . . ."

■

Greg didn't win. He didn't even make it to the finals of the tryouts. 64

But after the column about him appeared here, something remarkable hap- 65
pened. From all over the country, people called and wrote to my office with messages
of support for Greg, saying that his courage had inspired them. It was the biggest
reaction that any American Beat column has ever had.

The first letter, sent to Greg by a woman in Georgia, set the tone: 66

I just wanted to let you know how much the story about you meant to me. For some
time now, I've had a secret dream to try to be a free-lance writer. I've just never had
the nerve or the follow-through to go for it.

When I read your story, I made a promise to myself that I would at least give it a
try. I just couldn't shake off the image of you sitting in that hallway, going over that
guidebook until the last possible moment, putting in all the preparation you could. I
thought, That's the kind of guts and persistence I need if I'm ever going to get anywhere.

I don't know whether or not I'll be successful, but at least now I know that I'll give
it my best shot.

I hope this letter doesn't sound too corny. I really got a new sense of determination
from reading [the column], and I just wanted to let you know that.

There was a letter from a banker in Denver: 67

Although I have made many presentations in my life, I cannot imagine doing anything as terrifying as being a sports commentator, and I really admire you for being a contestant.

Mr. Talerico, you were quoted as saying you had never done anything constructive in your life. [But] you had a very constructive effect on me and have made me reevaluate my current situation. You exhibited persistence and stamina by studying so hard and traveling so far for the audition, grace under pressure by performing so well during the audition, and good sportsmanship by congratulating the winner. I wish that more of the people I worked with exhibited these qualities, and I wish that I exhibited them more often myself.

And then there was the letter from Olympic champion gymnast Bart Conner: 68

It seems every so often, perhaps not often enough, we are reminded of how fortunate we really are. Today I read [the column] about Greg Talerico's dream to be a TV color commentator. Thanks for helping me to remember that I am a very lucky man.

I happened to win a couple of gold medals in the Los Angeles Olympics. Because of that success plenty of opportunities have come my way—one of them being a spot as a CBS-TV commentator. And yet I won the gold by only .025 in parallel bars—it was very close! Just because I won by .025 points, does it mean that my opinions carry any more weight than Greg Talerico's?

Life is strange and very unfair. The tears that welled in my eyes for Greg Talerico reminded me that I'm a very lucky man.

■

The most important response to the column, though, came from Salt Lake City.   69

Dave Blackwell, the sports director of KLUB radio, got in touch to say that he   70
was the host of an evening talk show called *Sports Club Open Line.* He wondered if Greg Talerico might want to become a part of the show.

"Broadcasting is such a tough business for anyone to get into," Blackwell   71
explained. "When I read the article, I realized that here was a guy who had more going against him than most. I have the forum to put Greg on the air. I went to the station manager, and if Greg would like the opportunity, we'd like to give it to him."

I put Blackwell in touch with Greg Talerico at Winning Wheels, the Prophetstown,   72
Illinois, center where he lives. Blackwell talked to Talerico, and explained that he would like to make him a guest commentator on the program. Greg could simply prepare for the show during the day, and then talk on the telephone to Blackwell with his comments.

The results have been phenomenal. "The first couple of times he was a little   73
nervous," Blackwell said. "But now he's fine. He's on the show at least once a week, and he's very good and very knowledgeable. At first I explained to the listeners about the *Esquire* column, and about Greg's handicap. But now I just say, 'Here's our friend Greg Talerico from Prophetstown, Illinois,' and there we go.

"I think he's developing a following on the station. What I'll do is call Winning 74
Wheels at the beginning of the week and tell the nurse supervisor what nights the
show is on that week. And then Greg will pick out a topic, and that night he'll call
collect—he and my engineer are buddies by now, and the engineer knows to accept
the call. Greg and I are very comfortable on the air together, and everything goes
as smoothly as can be."

■

Greg Talerico himself feels overwhelmed by what has happened. 75
"It's great," he said. "For the first time in my life, I feel I'm doing something. 76
I feel I'm important, at least a little bit. A lot of people around here say that I've
changed 100 percent."

At first, he said, it was the letters that got to him. "Those people who told me 77
that I had inspired them—I never thought that I could inspire anybody.

"Even my own little sister is proud of me. Her name is Amanda, and she's eight 78
years old. She's crazy about me and I'm crazy about her. But you know how other
kids can be to a little girl when they find out her brother is in a wheelchair.

"When *Esquire* came out, though, she took the magazine with my picture in it 79
to school—and no one could believe that her big brother was actually in a national
magazine! That was probably as important to me as anything that has happened—
the fact that it helped make my little sister proud of me."

As for the show on KLUB, Greg said, "Dave Blackwell and I get along well on 80
the air. He takes the time to listen to me and lead me through the conversations.
On the day of the show, I start getting nervous. I look forward to it all week, and
then on the day when I'm supposed to go on, I think about it all day. Being on the
show really makes my week—it keeps me going from one week to the next. And
now I'm taking classes at Sauk Valley College, in Dixon, Illinois. I'm studying
composition and English."

■

People who are close to Greg have noticed the difference. 81
"You can hear it in his voice," said his father, Patrick Talerico. "It's more 82
enthusiastic and full of life. You can tell from his voice that he's looking forward to
some kind of a future now. He never was before. He didn't feel he had a future.

"When he first told me he wanted to go to Chicago for the color-commentator 83
tryouts, I was a little apprehensive for him. I knew he wouldn't have much of a
chance, but I thought he was brave for being willing to give it a try. Who could have
known that all this would result from it?

"He always used to seem down all the time. Now, you can tell that he wants 84
to live, where before he seemed willing to give up everything. I never dreamed that
there would be a change like this."

Greg's mother, Mrs. Patricia Timke, said, "I guess this proves that the world 85
is not all bad. Greg got sort of a rotten deal from life, but this whole thing has
turned things around. It's clear to me that now Greg has something to live for. He
feels that life is worth something.

"I remember the first time that I took him to a Chicago Cubs baseball game at   86
Wrigley Field; he absolutely fell in love with the game. I felt so bad for him, knowing
that he could never go out onto a field and play it. But he never wavered in his
interest in sports. And now, finally, he is being rewarded."

At Winning Wheels, Paul Yackley, an administrator, said, "From the time Greg   87
came here, he always felt he was inferior. He always felt he was a step below
everyone else.

"This is the first time in his life that anything has happened to make him feel   88
special. He gets tired awfully easily—as a person with his condition gets older,
there is more and more loss of physical strength—but in spite of that, he is always
excited and happy now. I don't think he ever dared dream of anything like this. Now
he knows that, even if he never accomplishes anything else in his life, he has
done this."

Joyce Gladhill, a nurse at Winning Wheels, said, "When the letters started   89
coming in, they just put him on top of the world. The thought that his example could
encourage someone made him feel, for the first time, that he was worth something.

"And now the radio show—Greg has a wonderful knowledge of sports. You can   90
ask him anything about sports, and he knows it. On the nights that he's on the air,
he uses the director of nursing's office, so that he has privacy. We never listen in,
but we can tell when he comes out of the office that he's feeling terrific. There's
real pride there.

"He feels that they must really like him at the radio station, because they keep   91
putting him back on. He tells me that he has to believe that he's doing something
right, or they wouldn't have him back. And I can tell that he feels a sense of
responsibility to keep coming up with fresh topics. I really like this change in him."

■

At KLUB, Dave Blackwell says that Greg is welcome to be a part of the radio show   92
for as long as he wishes. "As far as I'm concerned, he has done a great job,"
Blackwell said. "It's really up to Greg, but from our end, he's a permanent member
of the show."

And Greg himself sometimes ponders what that means. "I think about all the   93
people who live in Salt Lake City," he said. "What do they think of me when they
hear me on the air, and what do they say to each other? I never thought about
having listeners before."

Dave Blackwell has sent me some audio tapes of Greg's appearances on the   94
radio program. Sometimes, on those long, cold nights when you wonder why you
do what you do, I'll get out of bed and go into the living room and put one of the
cassettes on the tape player.

I'll sit back in the dark. There will be Dave Blackwell introducing Greg Talerico.   95
And then there will be Greg's voice—strong and confident and full of enthusiasm,
talking about sports with authority and insight. I'll listen for a while, and then I'll
head back to bed. But the voice stays with me; the voice stays with me.

■ Reading Comprehension Questions

1. Which of the following would be the best alternative title for this selection?
   a. How to Become a Sportscaster
   b. A Dream Come True
   c. The Helpful Columnist
   d. The Contestant

2. Which sentence best expresses the main idea of the selection?
   a. People in wheelchairs can find jobs in broadcasting.
   b. It takes guts and persistence to become a sportscaster.
   c. Americans want to help handicapped people.
   d. Being courageous changed Greg Talerico's life.

3. Most of the contestants wanted to be color commentators because
   a. the pay was good.
   b. they had played basketball.
   c. they had broadcasting experience.
   d. they thought it would be fun.

4. *True or false?* _____ When Greg lost the tryout, he was angry and frustrated.

5. Greg is an example of a handicapped person whose life changed because he
   a. was given an opportunity to do something.
   b. received good health care.
   c. was a personal friend of Bob Greene.
   d. finally got a college education.

6. The author implies that Greg's broadcasting job has
   a. made his mother proud of him.
   b. made Greg nervous all the time.
   c. encouraged him to try new experiences.
   d. required him to move to Salt Lake City.

7. *True or false?* _____ "Sequel" implies that Greg has inspired the author himself as well as inspiring others.

8. The author implies that Greg's father
   a. never worries about his son.
   b. lives with his son.
   c. has been a caring parent.
   d. doesn't want Greg to work.

9. The word *glib* in "Some were glib; some were nervous" (paragraph 17) means
   a. surprised.
   b. angry.
   c. smooth-talking.
   d. uninterested.

10. The word *apprehensive* in "I was a little apprehensive for him. I knew he wouldn't have much of a chance" (paragraph 83) means
    a. confident.
    b. excited.
    c. expectant.
    d. afraid.

■ **Discussion Questions**

About Content

1. Why did Greg Talerico decide to try out? How were his reasons different from those of the other contestants?
2. What is the attitude of Greg's father toward his son's tryout and later success as a broadcaster?
3. According to the "Sequel," how have Greg's life and his attitude toward life changed since the story about his tryout?
4. In the "Sequel," Greene tells us that his story about Greg inspired the biggest response of any of his magazine columns. Why do you think people reacted so strongly to "The Tryout"? What was your reaction?

About Structure

5. How does Greene focus our interest on Greg Talerico even though the first half of his piece is mostly about the contest itself or the other contestants?
6. Greene quotes three letters out of all those that were sent in response to his first column about Greg. Why do you think he chose these particular three? Why did he put Bart Conner's letter last?
7. The "Sequel" is organized with topic sentences that are followed by several supporting paragraphs. One such sentence is, "From all over the country, people called and wrote to my office with messages of support for Greg, saying that his courage had inspired them" (paragraph 65), which is followed by support in the next three paragraphs. Identify two other such topic sentences and write them below:

_____

_____

About Style and Tone

8. What is Greene's attitude toward Talerico? How is it conveyed at the end of the piece?

■ Writing Assignments

Assignment 1: Writing a Paragraph

A writing assignment based on this selection is on page 151.

Assignment 2: Writing a Paragraph

Greg Talerico, who was willing to try his best, also brought out the best in other people. Write a paragraph supporting the idea that Greg brought out the best in those around him. Your topic sentence might be, "The example of Greg Talerico helped bring out the best in some of the adults around him."

To get started, reread the article; and as you do, make up a list of the people around Greg who acted in a decent or loving manner on his behalf. Under the name of each person, jot down particulars of words and actions. Then use the evidence you have accumulated to decide on the three or four people you will focus on in your paragraph. In addition, decide on the person who has been most supportive of Greg and his needs, and be sure to end with an account of that person's behavior.

Assignment 3: Writing an Essay

Greg Talerico showed courage and persistence in competing to be the color commentator for the Continental Basketball Association's broadcasts. But it was not just his own determination that was a factor in his success: the assistance of other people was important as well. Probably all of us have benefited at times from the help of family, acquaintances, or even strangers. Write an essay describing three ways that you have been aided by the decency and goodwill of others.

To get started, make up a list of specific benefits that you have received from others. Here, for example, are just a few suggestions of ways you may have been helped:

Money	Job
Information	Place to stay
Encouragement	Service
Needed item	Time spent listening
Help with moving	Friendly advice

In your introductory paragraph, be sure to include a thesis statement and to mention the three kinds of help that you plan to discuss. Then go on to write about each kind of help in a separate paragraph. Describe the exact situation in each case and just how you benefited. Finally, end your essay with one or two summarizing sentences and a final thought.

While working on your paper, you may also want to look at the guidelines for writing essays on pages 207–228.

They Call Him a Miracle Worker

Michael Ryan

Do you think that bad luck has held you down? Do you feel that your life is limited by circumstances beyond your control? If so, consider Benjamin Carson's life. By giving in to a violent temper and peer pressure, Carson started down a path of danger and failure. But a belief in the power of the individual turned his life around. Carson's story appears to be a miracle, but its real message may be that we can all make our lives "miraculous."

The TV cameras had gone, and Benjamin Carson, M.D., was off the world's front pages, at least temporarily. The media long ago decided that this understated, hospitable young man was a miracle worker. First, he performed a rare operation that saved the life of a hydrocephalic baby still in the womb. Then, last year, he was part of a team that separated Siamese twins, born joined at the skull and sharing major blood systems in the brain, and left each one alive and intact. But, as I talk with this thirty-six-year-old neurosurgeon, I realize why people say that he would be a great man even if he had never picked up a scalpel.   1

Dr. Benjamin Carson is director of pediatric neurosurgery at the Johns Hopkins Children's Center. A Yale graduate who has won two of the most prestigious awards in surgery, he is already almost a legend in his field. But just twenty-one years ago, he was a poor black teenager in inner-city Detroit who nearly threw his life away.   2

"I had a pathological temper," he recalls. "It was out of control. When I perceived that people had infringed upon my rights, I took pains to be sure that they suffered as a result. Whatever was available—rock, hammer, bottle, knife—I would go after them with. One day I tried to stab another teenager with a camping knife. He had a large metal belt buckle, and it broke the knife. It struck me then that if he hadn't had that belt buckle on, I would be on my way to jail or reform school, and he would be on his way to a hospital, or dead. I went and sat in the bathroom, on the edge of the bathtub, for several hours, and I thought about my temper. I prayed to the Lord to take my temper away."   3

Ben Carson was the second son of divorced parents. His mother worked at two and sometimes three jobs to keep the family together. Even more important, she worked hard to convince her boys that they could make something of their lives— even if their environment was telling them they couldn't. "We got lots of negative messages in society," Carson says. "But my mother just put an end to those kinds of thoughts quickly—you might say she brainwashed us into believing we could do anything."   4

By the eighth grade—which he spent in a largely white junior high school— Carson did so well that he won a prize as the best student in the class. That infuriated his white teacher. "That teacher blasted the rest of the class for letting me be number one. Obviously, they weren't working hard enough if a black kid was number one. I'll never forget that," he says, in a quiet, earnest voice.   5

High school took Benjamin Carson back to an inner-city environment—and almost, again, to a dead end. "I started listening to my peers," he says. "They were into all kinds of alcohol and drugs. It was ridiculous, but I started listening to them. I wanted to be part of the crowd." His grades dropped, and what looked like a bright future began to dim. Carson says that his mother worked on him constantly, trying to convince him that he was headed nowhere fast. And, after a year, he agreed and started studying again. He graduated and won a scholarship to Yale. There, he discovered that the science courses were tougher than anything his high school had prepared him for. He almost flunked. "I realized I had to do a substantial rearrangement in the way I studied and become an in-depth learner," he says. "But I did, and rectified the problem. I just have never, under any circumstances, thought of giving up on anything I do."

This was the attitude that propelled Ben Carson through medical school, through an internship, and into a series of prestigious posts. He took up his current job two years ago. "The big difference between people who succeed and people who don't is not that the ones who are successful don't have barriers and obstacles," he says. "Everybody has barriers and obstacles. If you look at them as fences that don't allow you to advance, then you're going to be a failure. If you look at them as hurdles that strengthen you each time you go over one, then you're going to be a success."

Carson got over his hurdles with a combination of decency, compassion, courage, and brains. He is himself something of a medical marvel: he may be the only great surgeon without an ego to match. He makes no secret of his belief that God has given him his talent—even though he knows his religious faith makes him an anomaly in a hospital setting. "It's not fashionable by any stretch of the imagination," Carson admits. "But it's what I believe, and I don't have any qualms about telling people."

The simplicity of Carson's life contrasts with the intricacy of his skills. He does not drink, smoke, or eat meat. He married his college sweetheart and is the father of three children. He has always resisted the chance to earn many times his income in private practice. Instead, he stays in academic medicine and looks for new challenges to keep his facile mind engaged. Last year, just out of curiosity, he read an account of twenty-one sets of Siamese twins joined at the head whom surgeons had tried to separate. In the majority of cases, one child survived but the other either died or was mentally destroyed. The problem, he saw, was the mammoth loss of blood the operation entailed. If he ever was involved in such a case, he decided, he would stop the babies' circulation beforehand, lower their body temperature, and then operate. But the chance of his ever seeing such a case, Carson knew, was minute.

Three weeks later, a West German doctor arrived at Johns Hopkins with the records of a pair of Siamese newborns in his native country. Their mother was unwilling to sacrifice either child to save the other, but no surgeon in Europe knew any other way to separate them. Benjamin Carson was called in to consult. "I went up and looked at the films and said, 'Yeah, I can do this,' " he recalls.

The operation took twenty-two hours, and for fourteen of them Carson worked   11
as a leading member of a seventy-person team—some of whom were doctors senior
to him. "I guess I would have been afraid if I didn't have so much faith in God," he
says. "I never have the feeling He's going to let me get into something He can't
get me out of."

Today, Benjamin and Patrick Binder, who will be two in February, are back in   12
West Germany. They probably won't remember that they were born Siamese twins,
and they will have to be told how Benjamin Carson changed their lives. But hundreds
of other young people may remember the day this young surgeon came into their
worlds. Almost every week, on his own time, this dedicated doctor visits schoolchildren around the country. "I tell them that there are opportunities, and they have
to be willing to take advantage of them," he says. "I tell them to take responsibility
for their lives. I tell them that education gives them independence and an ability to
control their own lives. That message has got to get across to our young people."

If the teenagers of America need a role model—and all teenagers do—they   13
could hardly do better than Dr. Benjamin Carson.

■ Reading Comprehension Questions

1. Which of the following would be the best alternative title for this selection?
   a. Overcoming a Dangerous Temper
   b. Separating Siamese Twins
   c. Difficulties of Life in the Inner City
   d. The Inspiring Story of Dr. Benjamin Carson

2. Which sentence best expresses the main idea of the selection?
   a. Dr. Carson overcame obstacles to become a great success and an inspiring role model.
   b. Dr. Carson believes that young people can take responsibility for their own destiny.
   c. Benjamin and Patrick Binder, Siamese twins, are both alive because of Dr. Carson's skill.
   d. While Dr. Carson's medical skills are complex, his life-style is simple.

3. A significant point in Carson's life was when he realized he had almost
   a. lost his mother's love and support because of his friends.
   b. lost his scholarship to Yale.
   c. overdosed on drugs.
   d. stabbed someone.

4. When Benjamin Carson won a prize in eighth grade,
   a. his mother was surprised that he could do so well.
   b. his teacher was proud.
   c. his teacher was angry.
   d. he was angry.

5. *True or false?* _____ Dr. Carson performed the "miracle" operation on the Siamese twins by himself.

6. According to Dr. Carson, we should consider obstacles as
   a. hurdles.
   b. useless.
   c. fences.
   d. bad luck.

7. Dr. Carson's great sense of social responsibility is evidenced by his
   a. poverty as a youth.
   b. scholarship to Yale.
   c. visits to schoolchildren.
   d. medical skills.

8. The author clearly implies that Dr. Carson's success
   a. was gained through luck.
   b. is both professional and personal.
   c. was mainly motivated by financial goals.
   d. is the result of encouragement from friends.

9. The word *rectified* in "I realized I had to do a substantial rearrangement in the way I studied. . . . But I did, and rectified the problem" (paragraph 6) means
   a. increased.
   b. misunderstood.
   c. corrected.
   d. destroyed.

10. The word *intricacy* in "The simplicity of Carson's life contrasts with the intricacy of his skills" (paragraph 9) means
    a. suitability.
    b. sensitivity.
    c. effectiveness.
    d. complexity.

■ Discussion Questions

About Content

1. Why do you think people say that Dr. Carson would have been "a great man even if he had never picked up a scalpel"?

2. How did Dr. Carson's mother influence his life?

3. What does the reaction of Dr. Carson's eighth-grade teacher reveal about the kind of world in which he grew up?

4. What does Dr. Carson consider the important difference between "people who succeed and people who don't"? How has that difference affected his life?

About Structure

5. What method of introduction does Ryan use for his article?
    a. Broad-to-narrow
    b. Anecdote
    c. Explaining the importance of the topic
    d. Situation that is the opposite of the one developed

6. The first two paragraphs introduce Dr. Carson to the reader, and then the article jumps to Carson's teenage years. Find the sentence which Ryan uses as a transition between the introduction and Carson's teenage years. Write the first few words of that sentence here:

    _____

7. To enliven his article and bring the reader closer to his subject, Ryan frequently quotes Dr. Carson. To see how often the author wove Dr. Carson's own words into the article, find the paragraphs with *no* quotation at all, and write their numbers here:

    _____   _____   _____   _____

About Style and Tone

8. Find two places in the article where Ryan's attitude toward Carson is revealed, and write the sentences or phrases below. Also, identify each sentence or phrase with the number of its paragraph.

    _____

    _____

    _____

■ **Writing Assignments**

Assignment 1: Writing a Paragraph

"Everyone has barriers and obstacles," Dr. Carson tells us. In order to be successful, however, you need to "look at them as hurdles that strengthen you each time you go over one." Think of a person you know well who has overcome several obstacles on his or her way to success. What "hurdles" has he or she had to jump? Write a paragraph describing a few of the obstacles this person has had to overcome in order to succeed. You might begin your paragraph with a topic sentence similar to these:

> My friend George had to learn how to deal with several problems before he was able to return to school.

My boss, now the owner of a successful diner, had to overcome three major obstacles to reach success.

Get started by listing several of the obstacles overcome by the person you decide to write about. Next, choose two or three of the most interesting or significant items on your list to write about. Also, decide how it would be best to present those items—in time order or emphatic order.

Assignment 2: Writing a Paragraph

Ryan considers Dr. Carson a good role model for teenagers, but Carson could be considered a role model for everyone. For example, despite his skill and fame as a surgeon, he lives a simple life. In addition, he has chosen the challenges of academic life over "the chance to earn many times his income in private practice." Write a paragraph about someone you know who has lived in such an admirable way that he or she is a good role model. Begin your paragraph with a topic sentence similar to this one: "_____ is a good role model for people of all ages." Then go on to describe the admirable aspects of your subject's life.

Assignment 3: Writing an Essay

Peer pressure was once a negative influence on Dr. Carson. What role has peer pressure played in your life? Write about three ways or events in which peer pressure influenced you during your junior high or high school days.

Begin with a brief paragraph of introduction, perhaps using the broad-to-narrow approach or explaining the importance of your topic. Then go on to write a paragraph on each of the three ways or events in which peer pressure influenced you. In deciding on the topic for each of your supporting paragraphs, you might consider these areas in which peer pressure often plays a role:

Time spent on study

Clothing

Hairstyles

Drugs

Attitudes toward parents

The opposite sex

The law

What Good Families Are Doing Right

Delores Curran

It isn't easy to be a successful parent these days. Pressured by the conflicting demands of home and workplace, confused by changing moral standards, and drowned out by their offspring's rock music and television, today's parents seem to be facing impossible odds in their struggle to raise healthy families. Yet some parents manage to "do it all"—and even remain on speaking terms with their children. How do they do it? Delores Curran's survey offers some significant suggestions; her article could serve as a recipe for a successful family.

I have worked with families for fifteen years, conducting hundreds of seminars, workshops, and classes on parenting, and I meet good families all the time. They're fairly easy to recognize. Good families have a kind of visible strength. They expect problems and work together to find solutions, applying common sense and trying new methods to meet new needs. And they share a common shortcoming—they can tell me in a minute what's wrong with them, but they aren't sure what's right with them. Many healthy families with whom I work, in fact, protest at being called *healthy.* They don't think they are. The professionals who work with them do. 1

To prepare the book on which this article is based, I asked respected workers in the fields of education, religion, health, family counseling, and voluntary organizations to identify a list of possible traits of a healthy family. Together we isolated fifty-six such traits, and I sent this list to five hundred professionals who regularly work with families—teachers, doctors, principals, members of the clergy, scout directors, YMCA leaders, family counselors, social workers—asking them to pick the fifteen qualities they most commonly found in healthy families. 2

While all of these traits are important, the one most often cited as central to close family life is communication: The healthy family knows how to talk—and how to listen. 3

"Without communication you don't know one another," wrote one family counselor. "If you don't know one another, you don't care about one another, and that's what the family is all about." 4

"The most familiar complaint I hear from wives I counsel is 'He won't talk to me' and 'He doesn't listen to me,' " said a pastoral marriage counselor. "And when I share this complaint with their husbands, they don't hear *me,* either." 5

"We have kids in classes whose families are so robotized by television that they don't know one another," said a fifth-grade teacher. 6

Professional counselors are not the only ones to recognize the need. The phenomenal growth of communication groups such as Parent Effectiveness Training, Parent Awareness, Marriage Encounter, Couple Communication, and literally hundreds of others tells us that the need for effective communication—the sharing of deepest feelings—is felt by many. 7

Healthy families have also recognized this need, and they have, either instinctively or consciously, developed methods of meeting it. They know that conflicts are to be expected, that we all become angry and frustrated and discouraged. And they know how to reveal those feelings—good and bad—to each other. Honest communication isn't always easy. But when it's working well, there are certain recognizable signs or symptoms, what I call the hallmarks of the successfully communicating family. 8

The Family Exhibits a Strong Relationship between the Parents

According to Dr. Jerry M. Lewis—author of a significant work on families, *No Single Thread*—healthy spouses complement, rather than dominate, each other. Either husband or wife could be the leader, depending on the circumstances. In the unhealthy families he studied, the dominant spouse had to hide feelings of weakness while the submissive spouse feared being put down if he or she exposed a weakness. 9

Children in the healthy family have no question about which parent is boss. Both parents are. If children are asked who is boss, they're likely to respond, "Sometimes Mom, sometimes Dad." And, in a wonderful statement, Dr. Lewis adds, "If you ask if they're comfortable with this, they look at you as if you're crazy—as if there's no other way it ought to be." 10

My survey respondents echo Dr. Lewis. One wrote, "The healthiest families I know are ones in which the mother and father have a strong, loving relationship. This seems to flow over to the children and even beyond the home. It seems to breed security in the children and, in turn, fosters the ability to take risks, to reach out to others, to search for their own answers, become independent and develop a good self-image." 11

The Family Has Control over Television

Television has been maligned, praised, damned, cherished, and even thrown out. It has more influence on children's values than anything else except their parents. Over and over, when I'm invited to help families mend their communication ruptures, I hear "But we have no time for this." These families have literally turned their "family-together" time over to television. Even those who control the quality of programs watched and set "homework-first" regulations feel reluctant to intrude upon the individual's right to spend his or her spare time in front of the set. Many families avoid clashes over program selection by furnishing a set for each family member. One of the women who was most desperate to establish a better sense of communication in her family confided to me that they owned nine sets. Nine sets for seven people! 12

Whether the breakdown in family communication leads to excessive viewing or whether too much television breaks into family lives, we don't know. But we do know that we can become out of one another's reach when we're in front of a TV set. The term *television widow* is not humorous to thousands whose spouses are absent even when they're there. One woman remarked, "I can't get worried about whether there's life after death. I'd be satisfied with life after dinner." 13

In family-communication workshops, I ask families to make a list of phrases they most commonly hear in their home. One parent was ⸤aghast⸥ to discover that his family's most familiar comments were "What's on?" and "Move." In families like this one, communication isn't hostile—it's just missing. 14

But television doesn't have to be a villain. A 1980 Gallup Poll found that the public sees great potential for television as a positive force. It can be a tremendous device for initiating discussion on subjects that may not come up elsewhere, subjects such as sexuality, corporate ethics, sportsmanship, and marital fidelity. 15

Even very bad programs offer material for values clarification if family members view them together. My sixteen-year-old son and his father recently watched a program in which hazardous driving was part of the hero's characterization. At one point, my son turned to his dad and asked, "Is that possible to do with that kind of truck?" 16

"I don't know," replied my husband, "but it sure is dumb. If that load shifted . . ." With that, they launched into a discussion on the responsibility of drivers that didn't have to originate as a parental lecture. Furthermore, as the discussion became more ⸤engrossing⸥ to them, they turned the sound down so that they could continue their conversation. 17

Parents frequently report similar experiences; in fact, this use of television was recommended in the widely publicized 1972 Surgeon General's report as the most effective form of television gatekeeping by parents. Instead of turning off the set, parents should view programs with their children and make moral judgments and initiate discussion. Talking about the problems and attitudes of a TV family can be a ⸤lively⸥, nonthreatening way to risk sharing real fears, hopes, and dreams. 18

The Family Listens and Responds

"My parents say they want me to come to them with problems, but when I do, either they're busy or they only half-listen and keep on doing what they were doing—like shaving or making a grocery list. If a friend of theirs came over to talk, they'd stop, be polite, and listen," said one of the children quoted in a *Christian Science Monitor* interview by Ann McCarroll. This child put his finger on the most difficult problem of communicating in families: the inability to listen. 19

It is usually easier to react than to respond. When we react, we reflect our own experiences and feelings; when we respond, we get into the other person's feelings. For example: 20

Tom, age seventeen: "I don't know if I want to go to college. I don't think I'd do very well there."
Father: "Nonsense. Of course you'll do well."

That's reacting. This father is cutting off communication. He's refusing either 21
to hear the boy's fears or to consider his feelings, possibly because he can't accept
the idea that his son might not attend college. Here's another way of handling the
same situation:

> *Tom:* "I don't know if I want to go to college. I don't think I'd do very well there."
> *Father:* "Why not?"
> *Tom:* "Because I'm not that smart."
> *Father:* "Yeah, that's scary. I worried about that, too."
> *Tom:* "Did you ever come close to flunking out?"
> *Father:* "No, but I worried a lot before I went because I thought college would be full of
> brains. Once I got there, I found out that most of the kids were just like me."

This father has responded rather than reacted to his son's fears. First, he 22
searched for the reason behind his son's lack of confidence and found it was fear
of academic ability (it could have been fear of leaving home, of a new environment,
of peer pressure, or of any of a number of things); second, he accepted the fear
as legitimate; third, he empathized by admitting to having the same fear when he
was Tom's age; and, finally, he explained why his, not Tom's, fears turned out to
be groundless. He did all this without denigrating or lecturing.

And that's tough for parents to do. Often we don't want to hear our children's 23
fears, because those fears frighten us; or we don't want to pay attention to their
dreams because their dreams aren't what we have in mind for them. Parents who
deny such feelings will allow only surface conversation. It's fine as long as a child
says, "School was okay today," but when she says, "I'm scared of boys," the
parents are uncomfortable. They don't want her to be afraid of boys, but since they
don't quite know what to say, they react with a pleasant "Oh, you'll outgrow it."
She probably will, but what she needs at the moment is someone to hear and
understand her pain.

In Ann McCarroll's interviews, she talked to one fifteen-year-old boy who said 24
he had "*some* mother. Each morning she sits with me while I eat breakfast. We
talk about anything and everything. She isn't refined or elegant or educated. She's
a terrible housekeeper. But she's interested in everything I do, and she always
listens to me—even if she's busy or tired."

That's the kind of listening found in families that experience real communication. 25
Answers to the routine question, "How was your day?" are heard with the eyes and
heart as well as the ears. Nuances are picked up and questions are asked, although
problems are not necessarily solved. Members of a family who really listen to one
another instinctively know that if people listen to you, they are interested in you.
And that's enough for most of us.

The Family Recognizes Unspoken Messages

Much of our communication—especially our communication of feelings—is non- 26
verbal. Dr. Lewis defines *empathy* as "someone responding to you in such a way
that you feel deeply understood." He says, "There is probably no more important

dimension in all of human relationships than the capacity for empathy. And healthy families teach empathy." Its members are allowed to be mad, glad, and sad. There's no crime in being in a bad mood, nor is there betrayal in being happy while someone else is feeling moody. The family recognizes that bad days and good days attack everyone at different times.

Nonverbal expressions of love, too, are the best way to show children that   27 parents love each other. A spouse reaching for the other's hand, a wink, a squeeze on the shoulder, a "How's-your-back-this-morning?" a meaningful glance across the room—all these tell children how their parents feel about each other.

The most destructive nonverbal communication in marriage is silence. Silence   28 can mean lack of interest, hostility, denigration, boredom, or outright war. On the part of a teen or preteen, silence usually indicates pain, sometimes very deep pain. The sad irony discovered by so many family therapists is that parents who seek professional help when a teenager becomes silent have often denied the child any other way of communicating. And although they won't permit their children to become angry or to reveal doubts or to share depression, they do worry about the withdrawal that results. Rarely do they see any connection between the two.

Healthy families use signs, symbols, body language, smiles, and other gestures   29 to express caring and love. They deal with silence and withdrawal in a positive, open way. Communication doesn't mean just talking or listening; it includes all the clues to a person's feelings—his bearing, her expression, their resignation. Family members don't have to say, "I'm hurting," or, "I'm in need." A quick glance tells that. And they have developed ways of responding that indicate caring and love, whether or not there's an immediate solution to the pain.

The Family Encourages Individual Feelings and Independent Thinking

Close families encourage the emergence of individual personalities through open   30 sharing of thoughts and feelings. Unhealthy families tend to be less open, less accepting of differences among members. The family must be Republican, or Bronco supporters, or gun-control advocates, and woe to the individual who says, "Yes, but . . . ."

Instead of finding differing opinions threatening, the healthy family finds them   31 exhilarating. It is exciting to witness such a family discussing politics, sports, or the world. Members freely say, "I don't agree with you," without risking ridicule or rebuke. They say, "I think it's wrong . . ." immediately after Dad says, "I think it's right . . ."; and Dad listens and responds.

Give-and-take gives children practice in articulating their thoughts at home so   32 that eventually they'll feel confident outside the home. What may seem to be verbal rambling by preteens during a family conversation is a prelude to sorting out their thinking and putting words to their thoughts.

Rigid families don't understand the dynamics of give-and-take. Some label it   33 disrespectful and argumentative; others find it confusing. Dr. John Meeks, medical director of the Psychiatric Institute of Montgomery County, Maryland, claims that argument is a way of life with normally developing adolescents. "In early adolescence they'll argue with parents about anything at all; as they grow older, the quantity of argument decreases but the quality increases." According to Dr. Meeks, arguing is something adolescents need to do. If the argument doesn't become too bitter, they have a good chance to test their own beliefs and feelings. "Incidentally," says Meeks, "parents can expect to 'lose' most of these arguments, because adolescents are not fettered by logic or even reality." Nor are they likely to be polite. Learning how to disagree respectfully is a difficult task, but good families work at it.

Encouraging individual feelings and thoughts, of course, in no way presumes 34 that parents permit their children to do whatever they want. There's a great difference between permitting a son to express an opinion on marijuana and allowing him to use it. That his opinion conflicts with his parents' opinion is OK as long as his parents make sure he knows their thinking on the subject. Whether he admits it or not, he's likely at least to consider their ideas if he respects them.

Permitting teenagers to sort out their feelings and thoughts in open discussions 35 at home gives them valuable experience in dealing with a bewildering array of situations they may encounter when they leave home. Cutting off discussion of behavior unacceptable to us, on the other hand, makes our young people feel guilty for even thinking about values contrary to ours and ends up making those values more attractive to them.

The Family Recognizes Turn-Off Words and Put-Down Phrases

Some families deliberately use hurtful language in their daily communication. "What 36 did you do all day around here?" can be a red flag to a woman who has spent her day on household tasks that don't show unless they're not done. "If only we had enough money" can be a rebuke to a husband who is working as hard as he can to provide for the family. "Flunk any tests today, John?" only discourages a child who may be having trouble in school.

Close families seem to recognize that a comment made in jest can be insulting. 37 A father in one of my groups confided that he could tease his wife about everything but her skiing. "I don't know why she's so sensitive about that, but I back off on it. I can say anything I want to about her cooking, her appearance, her mothering— whatever. But not her skiing."

One of my favorite exercises with families is to ask them to reflect upon phrases 38 they most like to hear and those they least like to hear. Recently, I invited seventy-five fourth- and fifth-graders to submit the words they most like to hear from their mothers. Here are the five big winners:

> *"I love you."*
> *"Yes."*
> *"Time to eat."*
> *"You can go."*
> *"You can stay up late."*

And on the children's list of what they least like to hear from one another are   39
the following:

"I'm telling."
"Mom says!"
"I know something you don't know."
"You think you're so big."
"Just see if I ever let you use my bike again."

It can be worthwhile for a family to list the phrases members like most and   40
least to hear, and post them. Often parents aren't even aware of the reaction of
their children to certain routine comments. Or keep a record of the comments heard
most often over a period of a week or two. It can provide good clues to the level
of family sensitivity. If the list has a lot of "shut ups" and "stop its," that family
needs to pay more attention to its relationships, especially the role that communication plays in them.

The Family Interrupts, but Equally

When Dr. Jerry M. Lewis began to study the healthy family, he and his staff videotaped   41
families in the process of problem solving. The family was given a question, such
as, "What's the main thing wrong with your family?" Answers varied, but what was
most significant was what the family actually did: who took control, how individuals
responded or reacted, what were the put-downs, and whether some members were
entitled to speak more than others.

The researchers found that healthy families expected everyone to speak openly   42
about feelings. Nobody was urged to hold back. In addition, these family members
interrupted one another repeatedly, but no one person was interrupted more than
anyone else.

Manners, particularly polite conversational techniques, are not hallmarks of the   43
communicating family. This should make many parents feel better about their family's dinner conversation. One father reported to me that at their table people had
to take a number to finish a sentence. Finishing sentences, however, doesn't seem
all that important in the communicating family. Members aren't sensitive to being
interrupted, either. The intensity and spontaneity of the exchange are more important
than propriety in conversation.

The Family Develops a Pattern of Reconciliation

"We know how to break up," one man said, "but who ever teaches us to make up?"   44
Survey respondents indicated that there is indeed a pattern of reconciliation in
healthy families that is missing in others. "It usually isn't a kiss-and-make-up situation," explained one family therapist, "but there are certain rituals developed over
a long period of time that indicate it's time to get well again. Between husband and
wife, it might be a concessionary phrase to which the other is expected to respond
in kind. Within a family, it might be that the person who stomps off to his or her
room voluntarily reenters the family circle, where something is said to make him or
her welcome."

When I asked several families how they knew a fight had ended, I got remarkably 45
similar answers from individuals questioned separately. "We all come out of our
rooms," responded every member of one family. Three members of another family
said, "Mom says, 'Anybody want a Pepsi?' " One five-year-old scratched his head
and furrowed his forehead after I asked him how he knew the family fight was over.
Finally, he said, "Well, Daddy gives a great big yawn and says, 'Well . . . ' " This
scene is easy to visualize, as one parent decides that the unpleasantness needs
to end and it's time to end the fighting and to pull together again as a family.

Why have we neglected the important art of reconciling? "Because we have 46
pretended that good families don't fight," says one therapist. "They do. It's essential
to fight for good health in the family. It gets things out into the open. But we need
to learn to put ourselves back together—and many families never learn this."

Close families know how to time divisive and emotional issues that may cause 47
friction. They don't bring up potentially explosive subjects right before they go out,
for example, or before bedtime. They tend to schedule discussions rather than
allow a matter to explode, and thus they keep a large measure of control over the
atmosphere in which they will fight and reconcile. Good families know that they
need enough time to discuss issues heatedly, rationally, and completely—and
enough time to reconcile. "You've got to solve it right there," said one father. "Don't
let it go on and on. It just causes more problems. Then when it's solved, let it be.
No nagging, no remembering."

The Family Fosters Table Time and Conversation

Traditionally, the dinner table has been a symbol of socialization. It's probably the 48
one time each day that parents and children are assured of uninterrupted time with
one another.

Therapists frequently call upon a patient's memory of the family table during 49
childhood in order to determine the degree of communication and interaction there
was in the patient's early life. Some patients recall nothing. Mealtime was either
so unpleasant or so unimpressive that they have blocked it out of their memories.
Therapists say that there is a relationship between the love in a home and life
around the family table. It is to the table that love or discord eventually comes.

But we are spending less table time together. Fast-food dining, even within the 50
home, is becoming a way of life for too many of us. Work schedules, individual
organized activities, and television all limit the quantity and quality of mealtime
interaction. In an informal study conducted by a church group, 68 percent of the
families interviewed in three congregations saw nothing wrong with watching television while eating.

Families who do a good job of communicating tend to make the dinner meal 51
an important part of their day. A number of respondents indicated that adults in
the healthiest families refuse dinner business meetings as a matter of principle
and discourage their children from sports activities that cut into mealtime hours.
"We know which of our swimmers will or won't practice at dinnertime," said a coach,
with mixed admiration. "Some parents never allow their children to miss dinners.

Some don't care at all." These families pay close attention to the number of times they'll be able to be together in a week, and they rearrange schedules to be sure of spending this time together.

The family that wants to improve communication should look closely at its   52
attitudes toward the family table. Are family table time and conversation important? Is table time open and friendly or warlike and sullen? Is it conducive to sharing more than food—does it encourage the sharing of ideas, feelings, and family intimacies?

We all need to talk to one another. We need to know we're loved and appreciated   53
and respected. We want to share our intimacies, not just physical intimacies but all the intimacies in our lives. Communication is the most important element of family life because it is basic to loving relationships. It is the energy that fuels the caring, giving, sharing, and affirming. Without genuine sharing of ourselves, we cannot know one another's needs and fears. Good communication is what makes all the rest of it work.

■ Reading Comprehension Questions

1. Which of the following would be the best alternative title for this selection?
    a. Successful Communication
    b. How to Solve Family Conflicts
    c. Characteristics of Families
    d. Hallmarks of the Communicating Family

2. Which sentence best expresses the article's main point?
    a. Television can and often does destroy family life.
    b. More American families are unhappy than ever before.
    c. A number of qualities mark the healthy and communicating family.
    d. Strong families encourage independent thinking.

3. *True or false?* _False_ According to the article, healthy families have no use for television.

4. Healthy families
    a. never find it hard to communicate.
    b. have no conflicts with each other.
    c. know how to reveal their feelings.
    d. permit one of the parents to make all final decisions.

5. The author has found that good families frequently make a point of being together
    a. in the mornings.
    b. after school.
    c. during dinner.
    d. before bedtime.

6. *True or false?* _True_ The article implies that the most troublesome non-verbal signal is silence.

7. The article implies that
   a. verbal messages are always more accurate than nonverbal ones.
   b. in strong families, parents practice tolerance of thoughts and feelings.
   c. parents must avoid arguing with their adolescent children.
   d. parents should prevent their children from watching television.

8. From the article, we can conclude that
   a. a weak marital relationship often results in a weak family.
   b. children should not witness a disagreement between parents.
   c. children who grow up in healthy families learn not to interrupt other family members.
   d. parents always find it easier to respond to their children than to react to them.

9. The word *aghast* in "One parent was aghast to discover that his family's most familiar comments were 'What's on?' and 'Move' " (paragraph 14) means
   a. horrified.
   b. satisfied.
   c. curious.
   d. amused.

10. The word *engrossing* in "as the discussion became more engrossing to them, they turned the sound down so that they could continue their conversation" (paragraph 17) means
    a. disgusting.
    b. intellectual.
    c. foolish.
    d. interesting.

■ **Discussion Questions**

About Content

1. What are the nine hallmarks of a successfully communicating family? Which of the nine do you feel are most important?

2. How do good parents control television watching? How do they make television a positive force instead of a negative one?

3. In paragraph 20, the author says, "It is usually easier to react than to respond." What is the difference between the two terms *react* and *respond*?

4. Why, according to Curran, is a "pattern of reconciliation" (paragraph 44) crucial to good family life? Besides those patterns mentioned in the essay, can you describe a reconciliation pattern you have developed with friends or family?

About Structure

5. What is the thesis of the selection? Write here the number of the paragraph in which it is stated: _____

6. What purpose is achieved by Curran's introduction (paragraphs 1–2)? Why is a reader likely to feel her article will be reliable and worthwhile?

7. Curran frequently uses dialog or quotations from unnamed parents or children as the basis for her examples. The conversation related in paragraphs 16–17 is one instance. Find three other dialogs used to illustrate points in the essay and write the numbers below:

    Paragraphs _____ to _____

    Paragraphs _____ to _____

    Paragraphs _____ to _____

About Style and Tone

8. Curran enlivens the essay by using some interesting and humorous remarks from parents, children, and counselors. One is the witty comment in paragraph 5 from a marriage counselor: "And when I share this complaint with their husbands, they don't hear *me,* either." Find two other places where the author keeps your interest by using humorous or enjoyable quotations, and write the numbers of the paragraphs here:

    _____ _____

■ Writing Assignments

Assignment 1: Writing a Paragraph

A writing assignment based on this selection is on page 171.

Assignment 2: Writing a Paragraph

Curran tells us five phrases that some children say they most like to hear from their parents (paragraph 38). When you were younger, what statement or action of one of your parents (or another adult) would make you especially happy—or sad? Write a paragraph that begins with a topic sentence like one of the following:

A passing comment my grandfather once made really devastated me.

When I was growing up, there were several typical ways my mother treated me that always made me sad.

A critical remark by my fifth-grade teacher was the low point of my life.

My mother has always had several lines that make her children feel very pleased.

You may want to write a narrative that describes in detail the particular time and place in which a statement or action occurred. Or you may want to provide three or so examples of statements or actions and their effect upon you.

To get started, make up two long lists of childhood memories involving adults—happy memories and sad memories. Then decide which memory or memories you could most vividly describe in a paragraph. Remember that your goal is to help your readers see for themselves why a particular time was sad or happy for you.

Assignment 3: Writing an Essay

In light of Curran's description of what healthy families do right, examine your own family. Which of Curran's traits of communicative families fit your family? Write an essay pointing out three things that your family is doing right in creating a communicative climate for its members. Or, if you feel your family could work harder at communicating, write the essay about three specific ways your family could improve. In either case, choose three of Curran's nine "hallmarks of the successfully communicating family" and show how they do or do not apply to your family.

In your introductory paragraph, include a thesis statement as well as a plan of development that lists the three traits you will talk about. Then present these traits in turn in three supporting paragraphs. Develop each paragraph by giving specific examples of conversations, arguments, behavior patterns, and so on, that illustrate how your family communicates. Finally, conclude your essay with a summarizing sentence or two and a final thought about your subject.

Adolescent Confusion

Maya Angelou

In this selection from her highly praised autobiographical work, *I Know Why the Caged Bird Sings,* Maya Angelou writes with honesty, humor, and sensitivity about her sexual encounter with a neighborhood boy. Angelou captures some of the confused feelings about sex we all experience when we are growing up; she is frightened but curious, outwardly aggressive yet inwardly shy; calculating and innocent at the same time. Angelou's outrageous plan for finding out what it is like to be a "real woman" may seem shocking. But her candor makes us respond to her account with understanding and delight.

A classmate of mine, whose mother had rooms for herself and her daughter in a ladies' residence, had stayed out beyond closing time. She telephoned me to ask if she could sleep at my house. Mother gave her permission, providing my friend telephoned her mother from our house. 1

When she arrived, I got out of bed and we went to the upstairs kitchen to make hot chocolate. In my room we shared mean gossip about our friends, giggled over boys, and whined about school and the tedium of life. The unusualness of having someone sleep in my bed (I'd never slept with anyone except my grandmothers) and the frivolous laughter in the middle of the night made me forget simple courtesies. My friend had to remind me that she had nothing to sleep in. I gave her one of my gowns, and without curiosity or interest I watched her pull off her clothes. At none of the early stages of undressing was I in the least conscious of her body. And then suddenly, for the briefest eye span, I saw her breasts. I was stunned. 2

They were shaped like light-brown falsies in the five-and-ten-cent store, but they were real. They made all the nude paintings I had seen in museums come to life. In a word, they were beautiful. A universe divided what she had from what I had. She was a woman. 3

My gown was too snug for her and much too long, and when she wanted to laugh at her ridiculous image I found that humor had left me without a promise to return. 4

Had I been older I might have thought that I was moved by both an esthetic sense of beauty and the pure emotion of envy. But those possibilities did not occur to me when I needed them. All I knew was that I had been moved by looking at a woman's breasts. So all the calm and casual words of Mother's explanation a few weeks earlier and the clinical terms of Noah Webster did not alter the fact that in a fundamental way there was something queer about me. 5

I somersaulted deeper into my snuggery of misery. After a thorough self-examination, in the light of all I had read and heard about dykes and bulldaggers, I reasoned that I had none of the obvious traits—I didn't wear trousers, or have big shoulders or go in for sports, or walk like a man or even want to touch a woman. I wanted to be a woman, but that seemed to me to be a world to which I was to be eternally refused entrance. 6

What I needed was a boyfriend. A boyfriend would clarify my position to the world and, even more important, to myself. A boyfriend's acceptance of me would guide me into that strange and exotic land of frills and femininity. 7

Among my associates, there were no takers. Understandably the boys of my age and social group were captivated by the yellow- or light-brown-skinned girls, with hairy legs and smooth little lips, whose hair "hung down like horses' manes." And even those sought-after girls were asked to "give it up or tell where it is." They were reminded in a popular song of the times, "If you can't smile and say yes, please don't cry and say no." If the pretties were expected to make the supreme sacrifice in order to "belong," what could the unattractive female do? She who had been skimming along on life's turning but never-changing periphery had to be ready to be a "buddy" by day and maybe by night. She was called upon to be generous only if the pretty girls were unavailable. 8

I believe most plain girls are virtuous because of the scarcity of opportunity to be otherwise. They shield themselves with an aura of unavailableness (for which after a time they begin to take credit) largely as a defense tactic. 9

In my particular case, I could not hide behind the curtain of voluntary goodness. I was being crushed by two unrelenting forces: the uneasy suspicion that I might not be a normal female and my newly awakening sexual appetite. 10

I decided to take matters into my own hands. (An unfortunate but apt phrase.) 11

Up the hill from our house, and on the same side of the street, lived two handsome brothers. They were easily the most eligible young men in the neighborhood. If I was going to venture into sex, I saw no reason why I shouldn't make my experiment with the best of the lot. I didn't really expect to capture either brother on a permanent basis, but I thought if I could hook one temporarily I might be able to work the relationship into something more lasting. 12

I planned a chart for seduction with surprise as my opening ploy. One evening as I walked up the hill suffering from youth's vague malaise (there was simply nothing to do), the brother I had chosen came walking directly into my trap. 13

"Hello, Marguerite." He nearly passed me. 14

I put the plan into action. "Hey." I plunged, "Would you like to have a sexual intercourse with me?" Things were going according to the chart. His mouth hung open like a garden gate. I had the advantage and so I pressed it. 15

"Take me somewhere." 16

His response lacked dignity, but in fairness to him I admit that I had left him little chance to be suave. 17

He asked, "You mean, you're going to give me some trim?" 18

I assured him that that was exactly what I was about to give him. Even as the scene was being enacted, I realized the imbalance in his values. He thought I was giving him something, and the fact of the matter was that it was my intention to take something from him. His good looks and popularity had made him so inordinately conceited that they blinded him to that possibility.   19

We went to a furnished room occupied by one of his friends, who understood the situation immediately and got his coat and left us alone. The seductee quickly turned off the lights. I would have preferred them left on, but didn't want to appear more aggressive than I had been already—if that was possible.   20

I was excited rather than nervous, and hopeful instead of frightened. I had not considered how physical an act of seduction would be. I had anticipated long soulful tongued kisses and gentle caresses. But there was no romance in the knee which forced my legs, nor in the rub of hairy skin on my chest.   21

Unredeemed by shared tenderness, the time was spent in laborious gropings, pullings, yankings, and jerkings.   22

Not one word was spoken.   23

My partner showed that our experience had reached its climax by getting up abruptly, and my main concern was how to get home quickly. He may have sensed that he had been used, or his lack of interest may have been an indication that I was less than gratifying. Neither possibility bothered me.   24

Outside on the street we left each other with little more than "OK, see you around."   25

Thanks to Mr. Freeman nine years before, I had had no pain of entry to endure, and because of the absence of romantic involvement neither of us felt much had happened.   26

At home I reviewed the failure and tried to evaluate my new position. I had had a man. I had been had. Not only didn't I enjoy it, but my normality was still a question.   27

What happened to the moonlight-on-the-prairie feeling? Was there something so wrong with me that I couldn't share a sensation that made poets gush out rhyme after rhyme, that made Richard Arlen brave the Arctic wastes and Veronica Lake betray the entire free world?   28

There seemed to be no explanation for my private infirmity, but being a product (is "victim" a better word?) of the Southern Negro upbringing, I decided that I "would understand it all better by and by." I went to sleep.   29

Three weeks later, having thought very little of the strange and strangely empty night, I found myself pregnant.   30

■ Reading Comprehension Questions

1. Which of the following would be the best alternative title for this selection?
   a. A Wasted Life
   b. The Story of a Teenage Pregnancy
   c. The Pain and Confusion of Growing Up
   d. A Handsome Young Man

2. Which sentence best expresses the main idea of the selection?
   a. Teenage girls feel more insecure about sex than teenage boys do.
   b. A sexual experience is the first step toward adulthood.
   c. Maya Angelou's innocence led her to a joyless experience with sex and an unplanned pregnancy.
   d. Women who are sexually aggressive often become pregnant.

3. In the days following her sexual experience, the author
   a. talked to her mother about her feelings.
   b. wrote about the incident.
   c. asked her classmates for advice.
   d. virtually ignored what had happened.

4. The author chose the boy she did to experiment with because
   a. he had shown some interest in her.
   b. she wanted to start with one of the two most eligible boys in the neighborhood.
   c. she knew he would be kind to her.
   d. she had a crush on him.

5. The author expected that
   a. having a boyfriend would help her become a woman.
   b. she would feel guilty about her actions.
   c. she would no longer be plain.
   d. she would probably get pregnant.

6. The author implies that
   a. she would become a homosexual.
   b. she had little sense of right and wrong.
   c. she had little idea of what love, sex, or femininity really mean.
   d. none of the girls she knew had had a sexual experience.

7. *True or false?* _____ The author implies that she had discussed the facts of womanhood with her mother.

8. The author implies that
   a. she wanted the boy to marry her.
   b. she was raped as a child.
   c. the boy's lack of tenderness was expected.
   d. the movies had taught her the facts of life.

9. The word *inordinately* in "His good looks and popularity had made him so inordinately conceited" (paragraph 19) means
   a. timidly.
   b. excessively.
   c. unexpectedly.
   d. unknowingly.

10. The word *malaise* in "I walked up the hill suffering from youth's vague malaise" (paragraph 13) means
     a. patience.
     b. pleasure.
     c. ambition.
     d. uneasiness.

■ **Discussion Questions**

About Content

1. For what reasons did Angelou decide she needed a boyfriend?
2. In what ways did Angelou's actual experience differ from what she expected it to be? Find passages in the selection that describe (a) Angelou's expectations and (b) the reality of the experience.
3. What was the young man's reaction to Angelou's seduction? What does his reaction reveal about him?

About Structure

4. A narrative selection most often focuses on a single event. But this selection is developed through two narratives. What are the two narratives? Why does Angelou include both?
5. Within her narratives, Angelou uses contrast to develop her paragraphs. For example, she contrasts her body and her classmate's body, and the "pretties" and "unattractive females." Find two other areas of contrast and write them below:

     _____

     _____

6. Paragraph 23 consists of just one sentence: "Not one word was spoken." What effect does Angelou achieve by making this paragraph so short?

About Style and Tone

7. Angelou enlivens her narrative with humor. Find two places where she touches on the humorous side of her experience and write the paragraph numbers here:

     _____   _____

8. Find two other places where the tone is quite serious.

     _____   _____

■ Writing Assignments

Assignment 1: Writing a Paragraph

A writing assignment based on this selection is on page 197.

Assignment 2: Writing a Paragraph

Because of her confusion and insecurity, Angelou acted without consulting anyone else about her problem. Pretend that the young Maya has come to you with her doubts and her plan to seduce a boy. What advice would you give her? In a paragraph written in the form of a letter to Maya, explain what you would say to her.

EDUCATION AND SELF-IMPROVEMENT

Let's Really Reform Our Schools

Anita Garland

A few years back, a National Commission on Excellence in Education published *A Nation at Risk*, in which the commission reported on a "rising tide of mediocrity" in our schools. Other studies have pointed to students' poor achievement in science, math, communication, and critical thinking. What can our schools do to improve students' performance? Anita Garland has several radical ideas, which she explains in this selection. As you read it, think about whether or not you agree with her points.

American high schools are in trouble. No, that's not strong enough. American high schools are disasters. "Good" schools today are only a rite of passage for American kids, where the pressure to look fashionable and act cool outweighs any concern for learning. And "bad" schools—heaven help us—are havens for the vicious and corrupt. There, metal detectors and security guards wage a losing battle against the criminals that prowl the halls.

Desperate illnesses require desperate remedies. And our public schools are desperately ill. What is needed is no meek, faint-hearted attempt at "curriculum revision" or "student-centered learning." We need to completely restructure our thinking about what schools are and what we expect of the students who attend them.

The first change needed to save our schools is the most fundamental one. Not only must we stop *forcing* everyone to attend school; we must stop *allowing* the attendance of so-called students who are not interested in studying. Mandatory school attendance is based upon the idea that every American has a right to basic education. But as the old saying goes, your rights stop where the next guy's begin.

A student who sincerely wants an education, regardless of his or her mental or physical ability, should be welcome in any school in this country. But "students" who deliberately interfere with other students' ability to learn, teachers' ability to teach, and administrators' ability to maintain order should be denied a place in the classroom. They do not want an education. And they should not be allowed to mark time within school walls, waiting to be handed their meaningless diplomas while they make it harder for everyone around them to either provide or receive a quality education.

4   By requiring troublemakers to attend school, we have made it impossible to deal with them in any effective way. They have little to fear in terms of punishment. Suspension from school for a few days doesn't improve their behavior. After all, they don't want to be in school anyway. For that matter, mandatory attendance is, in many cases, nothing but a bad joke. Many chronic troublemakers are absent so often that it is virtually impossible for them to learn anything. And when they *are* in school, they are busy shaking down other students for their lunch money or jewelry. If we permanently banned such punks from school, educators could turn their attention away from the troublemakers and toward those students who realize that school is a serious place for serious learning.

5   You may ask, "What will become of these young people who aren't in school?" But consider this: What is becoming of them now? They are not being educated. They are merely names on the school records. They are passed from grade to grade, learning nothing, making teachers and fellow students miserable. Finally they are bumped off the conveyor belt at the end of twelfth grade, oftentimes barely literate, and passed into society as "high school graduates." Yes, there would be a need for alternative solutions for these young people. Let the best thinkers of our country come up with some ideas. But in the meanwhile, don't allow our schools to serve as a holding tank for people who don't want to be there.

6   Once our schools have been returned to the control of teachers and genuine students, we could concentrate on smaller but equally meaningful reforms. A good place to start would be requiring students to wear school uniforms. There would be cries of horror from the fashion slaves, but the change would benefit everyone. If students wore uniforms, think of the mental energy that could be redirected into more productive channels. No longer would young girls feel the need to spend their evenings laying out coordinated clothing, anxiously trying to create just the right look. The daily fashion show that currently absorbs so much of students' attentions would come to a halt. Kids from modest backgrounds could stand out because of their personalities and intelligence, rather than being tagged as losers because they can't wear the season's hottest sneakers or jeans. Affluent kids might learn they have something to offer the world other than a fashion statement. Parents would be relieved of the pressure to deal with their offsprings' constant demands for wardrobe additions.

7   Next, let's move to the cafeteria. What's for lunch today? How about a Milky Way bar, a bag of Fritos, a Coke, and just to round out the meal with a vegetable, maybe some french fries. And then back to the classroom for a few hours of intense mental activity, fueled on fat, salt, and sugar. What a joke! School is an institution of education, and that education should be continued as students sit down to eat.

Here's a perfect opportunity to teach a whole generation of Americans about nutrition, and we are blowing it. School cafeterias, of all places, should demonstrate how a healthful, low-fat, well-balanced diet produces healthy, energetic, mentally alert people. Instead, we allow school cafeterias to dispense the same junk food that kids could buy in any mall. Overhaul the cafeterias! Out with the candy, soda, chips, and fries! In with the salads, whole grains, fruits, and vegetables!

Turning our attention away from what goes on during school hours, let's consider what happens after the final bell rings. Some school-sponsored activites are all to the good. Bands and choirs, foreign-language field trips, chess or skiing or drama clubs are sensible parts of an extracurricular plan. They bring together kids with similar interests to develop their talents and leadership ability. But other common school activities are not the business of education. The prime example of inappropriate school activity is in competitive sports between schools.   8

Intramural sports are great. Students need an outlet for their energies, and friendly competition against one's classmates on the basketball court or baseball diamond is fun and physically beneficial. But the wholesome fun of sports is quickly ruined by the competitive team system. School athletes quickly become the campus idols, encouraged to look down upon classmates with less physical ability. Schools concentrate enormous amounts of time, money, and attention upon their teams, driving home the point that competitive sports are the *really* important part of school. Students are herded into gymnasiums for "pep rallies" that whip up adoration of the chosen few and encourage hatred of rival schools. Boys' teams are supplied with squads of cheerleading girls. . . . Let's not even get into what the subliminal message is *there.* If communities feel they must have competitive sports, let local businesses or even professional teams organize and fund the programs. But school budgets and time should be spent on programs that benefit more than an elite few.   9

Another school-related activity that should get the ax is the fluff-headed, money-eating, misery-inducing event known as the prom. How in the world did the schools of America get involved in this showcase of excess? Proms have to be the epitome of everything that is wrong, tasteless, misdirected, inappropriate, and just plain sad about the way we bring up our young people. Instead of simply letting the kids put on a dance, we've turned the prom into a bloated nightmare that ruins young people's budgets, self-image, and even their lives. The pressure to show up at the prom with the best-looking date, in the most expensive clothes, wearing the most exotic flowers, riding in the most extravagant form of transportation, dominates the thinking of many students for months before the prom itself. Students cling to doomed, even abusive romantic relationships rather than risk being dateless for this night of nights. They lose any concept of meaningful values as they implore their parents for more, more, more money to throw into the jaws of the prom god. The adult trappings of the prom—the slinky dresses, emphasis on romance, slow dancing, nightclub atmosphere—all encourage kids to engage in behavior that can have tragic consequences. Who knows how many unplanned pregnancies and alcohol-related accidents can be directly attributed to the pressures of prom night? And yet, not going to the prom seems a fate worse than death to many young people—because of all the hype about the "wonder" and "romance" of it all. Schools are not in the business of providing wonder and romance, and it's high time we remembered that.   10

We have lost track of the purpose of our schools. They are not intended to   11
be centers for fun, entertainment, and social climbing. They are supposed to be
institutions for learning and hard work. Let's institute the changes suggested here—
plus dozens more—without apology, and get American schools back to business.

■ Reading Comprehension Questions

1. Which of the following would be the best alternative title for this selection?
    a. America's Youth
    b. Education of the Future
    c. Social Problems of Today's Students
    d. Changes Needed in the American School System

2. Which sentence best expresses the main idea of the selection?
    a. Excesses such as the prom and competitive sports should be eliminated from school budgets.
    b. Major changes are needed to make American schools real centers of learning.
    c. Attendance must be voluntary in our schools.
    d. The best thinkers of our country must come up with ideas on how to improve our schools.

3. Garland believes that mandatory attendance at school
    a. gives all students an equal chance at getting an education.
    b. allows troublemakers to disrupt learning.
    c. is cruel to those who don't really want to be there.
    d. helps teachers maintain control of their classes.

4. Garland is against school-sponsored competitive sports because she believes that
    a. exercise and teamwork should not have a role in school.
    b. they overemphasize the importance of sports and athletes.
    c. school property should not be used in any way after school hours.
    d. they take away from professional sports.

5. We can infer that Garland believes
    a. teens should not have dances.
    b. proms promote unwholesome values.
    c. teens should avoid romantic relationships.
    d. proms are even worse than mandatory education.

6. The author clearly implies that troublemakers
    a. are not intelligent.
    b. really do want to be in school.
    c. should be placed in separate classes.
    d. don't mind being suspended from school.

7. *True or false?* _____ We can conclude that the author feels that teachers and genuine students have lost control of our schools.

8. The essay suggests that the author would also oppose
   a. school plays.
   b. serving milk products in school cafeterias.
   c. the selection of homecoming queens.
   d. stylish school uniforms.

9. The word *affluent* in "Kids from modest backgrounds could stand out because of their personalities and intelligence. . . . Affluent kids might learn they have something to offer the world other than a fashion statement" (paragraph 6) means
   a. intelligent.
   b. troubled.
   c. wealthy.
   d. poor.

10. The word *implore* in "They lose any concept of meaningful values as they implore their parents for more, more, more money to throw into the jaws of the prom god" (paragraph 10) means
    a. ignore.
    b. beg.
    c. pay.
    d. obey.

■ Discusssion Questions

About Content

1. What reforms does Garland suggest in her essay? Think back to your high school days. Which of the reforms that Garland suggests do you think might have been most useful at your high school?

2. Garland's idea of voluntary school attendance directly contradicts the "stay in school" campaigns. Do you agree with her idea? What do you think might become of students who choose not to attend school?

3. At the end of her essay, Garland writes, "Let's institute the changes suggested here—plus dozens more." What other changes do you think Garland may have in mind? What are some reforms you think might improve schools?

About Structure

4. The thesis of this essay can be found in the introduction, which is made up of the first two paragraphs. Find the thesis statement, and write it here:

    _____

    _____

5. The first point on Garland's list of reforms is the elimination of mandatory (that is, required) education. Then she goes on to discuss other reforms. Find the transition sentence which signals that she is leaving the discussion about mandatory education and going on to other needed changes. Write that sentence here:

    _____

    _____

6. What are two transitional words that Garland uses to introduce two of the other reforms?

    _____   _____

Style and Tone

7. Garland uses some colofrul images to communicate her ideas. For instance, in paragraph 5 she writes, "Finally they [the troublemakers] are bumped off the conveyor belt at the end of twelfth grade, oftentimes barely literate, and passed into society as 'high school graduates.' " What does the image of a conveyor belt imply about schools and about the troublemakers? What do the quotation marks around *high school graduates* imply?

8. Below are three other colorful images from the essay. What do the italicized words imply about today's schools and students?

    . . . don't allow our schools to serve as a *holding tank* for people who don't want to be there. (paragraph 5)

    A good place to start would be requiring students to wear school uniforms. There would be cries of horror from the *fashion slaves* . . . (paragraph 6)

    Students are *herded* into gymnasiums for "pep rallies" that whip up adoration of the chosen few . . . (paragraph 9)

9. To convey her points, does the author use a formal and straightforward tone or an informal and impassioned tone? Give examples from the essay to support your answer.

■ Writing Assignments

Assignment 1: Writing a Paragraph

A writing assignment based on this selection is on page 206.

Assignment 2: Writing a Paragraph

If troublemakers were excluded from schools, what would become of them? Write a paragraph in which you suggest two or three types of programs that troublemakers could be assigned to. Explain why each program would be beneficial to the troublemakers themselves and society in general. You might want to include in your paragraph one or more of the following:

Apprentice programs

Special neighborhood schools for troublemakers

Reform schools

Work-placement programs

Community service programs

Assignment 3: Writing an Essay

Garland suggests ways to make schools "institutions for learning and hard work." She wants to get rid of anything that greatly distracts students from their education, such as having to deal with troublemakers, overemphasis on fashion, and interschool athletics. When you were in high school, what tended most to divert your attention from learning? Write an essay explaining in full detail the three things that interfered most with your high school education. You may include any of Garland's points, but present details that apply specifically to you. Organize your essay by using emphatic order—in other words, save whatever interfered most with your education for the last supporting paragraph.

It is helpful to write a sentence outline for this kind of essay. Here, for example, is one writer's outline for an essay titled "Obstacles to My High School Education."

Thesis: There were three main things that interfered with my high school education.

Topic sentence 1: Concern about my appearance took up too much of my time and energy.
a. Since I was concerned about my looking good, I spent too much time shopping for clothes.
b. In order to afford the clothes, I worked twenty hours a week, which cut drastically into my study time.
c. Spending even more time on clothes, I fussed every evening over what I would wear to school the next day.

Topic sentence 2: Cheerleading was another major obstacle to my academic progress in high school.
a. I spent many hours practicing in order to make the cheerleading squad.
b. Once I made the squad, I had to spend even more time practicing and then attending games.
c. Once when I didn't make the squad, I was so depressed for a while that I couldn't study, which had serious consequences.

Topic sentence 3: The main thing that inferfered with my high school education was my family situation.
a. Even when I had time to study, I often found it impossible to do so at home since my parents were often fighting, which was noisy and upsetting.
b. My parents showed little interest in my school work, which gave me little reason to work hard for my classes.
c. When I was in eleventh grade, my parents divorced, which was a major distraction for me for a long time.

To round off your essay with a conclusion, you may simply want to restate your thesis and main supporting points.

As an alternative to the above assignment, you can write about current obstacles to your college education.

Power Learning

Sheila Akers

 For many students, cramming for tests, staying up late to do assignments, and having an incomplete grasp of information are a natural part of college life. After all, there is so much to do, and almost none of it is easy. If you are one of those students who never seem able to catch up, you may find the following selection a revelation. It might convince you that even though you study hard in school, you may need to learn more about how to study better.

Jill had not been as successful in high school as she would have liked. Since college   1
involved even more work, it was no surprise that she was not doing any better there.

The reason for her so-so performance was not a lack of effort. She attended 2 most of her classes and read her textbooks. And she never missed handing in any assignment, even though it often meant staying up late the night before homework was due. Still, she just got by in her classes. Before long, she came to the conclusion that she just couldn't do any better.

Then one day, one of her instructors said something to make her think otherwise. 3 "You can probably build some sort of house by banging a few boards together," he said. "But if you want a sturdy home, you'll have to use the right techniques and tools. Building carefully takes work, but it gets better results. The same can be said of your education. There are no shortcuts, but there are some proven study skills that can really help. If you don't use them, you may end up with a pretty flimsy education."

Prompted by this advice, Jill signed up for a course in study skills at her school. 4 She then found out a crucial fact—that learning how to learn is the key to success in school. There are certain dependable skills that have made the difference between disappointment and success for generations of students. These techniques won't free you from work, but they will make your work far more productive. They include three important areas: time control, classroom note-taking, and textbook study.

Time Control

Success in college depends on time control. Time control means that you deliberately 5 organize and plan your time, instead of letting it drift by. Planning means that you should never be faced with a night-before-the-test "cram" session or an overdue term paper.

There are three steps involved in time control. The *first step* is to prepare a 6 large monthly calendar. Buy a calendar with a large white block around each date, or make one yourself. At the beginning of the college semester, circle important dates on this calendar. Circle the days on which tests are scheduled; circle the days when papers are due. This calendar can also be used to schedule study plans. You can jot down your plans for each day at the beginning of the week. An alternative method would be to make plans for each day the night before. On Tuesday night, for example, you might write down "Read Chapter 5 in psychology" in the Wednesday block. Be sure to hang this calendar in a place where you will see it every day— your kitchen, your bedroom, even your bathroom!

The *second step* in time control is to have a weekly study schedule for the 7 semester. To prepare this schedule, make up a chart that covers all the days of the week and all the waking hours in each day. Part of one student's schedule is shown opposite. On your schedule, mark in all the fixed hours in each day—hours for meals, classes, job (if any), and travel time. Next, mark in time blocks that you can *realistically* use for study each day. Depending on the number of courses you are taking and the demands of the courses, you may want to block off five, ten, or even twenty or more hours of study time a week. Keep in mind that you should not block off time for study that you do not truly intend to use for study. Otherwise, your schedule will be a meaningless gimmick. Also, remember that you should allow time for rest and relaxation in your schedule. You will be happiest, and able to accomplish the most, when you have time for both work and play.

	Monday	Tuesday	Wednesday	Thursday	Friday	Saturday	Sunday
6:00 A.M.							
7:00	B	B	B	B	B		
8:00	Math	STUDY	Math	STUDY	Math		
9:00	STUDY	Biology	STUDY	Biology	STUDY	Job	
10:00	Psychology	↓	Psychology	↓	Psychology		
11:00	STUDY	English		English			
12:00 NOON	L		L	↓	L	↓	

The *third step* in time control is to make a daily or weekly "to do" list. This may be the most valuable time-control method you ever use. On this list, you write down the things you need to do for the following day or the following week. If you choose to write a weekly list, do it on Sunday night. If you choose to write a daily list, do it the night before. You may use a three- by five-inch notepad or a small spiral-bound notebook for this list. Carry the list around with you during the day. Always concentrate on doing first the most important items on your list. Mark high-priority items with an asterisk and give them precedence over low-priority items in order to make the best use of your time. For instance, you may find yourself wondering what to do after dinner on Thursday evening. Among the items on your list are "Clean inside of car" and "Review chapter for math quiz." It is obviously more important for you to review your notes at this point; you can clean the car some other time. As you complete items on your "to do" list, cross them out. Do not worry about unfinished items. They can be rescheduled. You will still be accomplishing a great deal and making more effective use of your time. Part of one student's daily list is shown below.

8

To Do   **Tuesday**

 *1   Review biology notes before class
 *2   Proofread English paper due today
  3   See Dick about game on Friday
 *4   Gas for car
  5   Read next chapter of psychology text

Classroom Note-Taking

One of the most important single things you can do to perform well in a college   9
course is to take effective class notes. The following hints should help you become
a better note-taker.

First, attend class faithfully. Your alternatives—reading the text or someone   10
else's notes, or both—cannot substitute for the experience of hearing ideas in
person as someone presents them to you. Also, in class lectures and discussions,
your instructor typically presents and develops the main ideas and facts of the
course—the ones you will be expected to know on exams.

Another valuable hint is to make use of abbreviations while taking notes. Using   11
abbreviations saves time when you are trying to get down a great deal of information.
Abbreviate terms that recur frequently in a lecture and put a key to your abbreviations
at the top of your notes. For example, in a sociology class, *eth* could stand for
ethnocentrism; in a psychology class, *STM* could stand for *short-term memory.*
(When a lecture is over, you may want to go back and write out the terms you have
abbreviated.) In addition, abbreviate words that often recur in any lecture. For
instance, use *ex* for *example, def* for *definition, info* for *information,* + for *and,* and
so on. If you use the same abbreviations all the time, you will soon develop a kind
of personal shorthand that makes taking notes much easier.

A third hint when taking notes is to be on the lookout for signals of importance.   12
Write down whatever your instructor puts on the board. If he or she takes the time
to put material on the board, it is probably important, and the chances are good
that it will come up later on exams. Always write down definitions and enumerations.
Enumerations are lists of items. They are signaled in such ways as: "The four steps
in the process are . . ."; "There were three reasons for . . ."; "The two effects
were . . ."; "Five characteristics of . . ."; and so on. Always number such enumerations in your notes (1, 2, 3, etc.). They will help you understand relationships among
ideas and organize the material of the lecture. Watch for emphasis words—words
your instructor may use to indicate that something is important. Examples of
such words are "This is an important reason . . ."; "A point that will keep coming
up later . . ."; "The chief cause was . . ."; "The basic idea here is . . ."; and so on.
Always write down the important statements announced by these and other emphasis words. Finally, if your instructor repeats a point, you can assume it is important.
You might put an R for *repeated* in the margin, so that later you will know that your
instructor has stressed it.

Next, be sure to write down the instructor's examples and mark them with an   13
X. The examples help you understand abstract points. If you do not write them
down, you are likely to forget them later when they are needed to help make sense
of an idea.

Also, be sure to write down the connections between ideas. Too many students   14
merely copy the terms the instructor puts on the board. They forget that, as time
passes, the details that serve as connecting bridges between ideas quickly fade.
You should, then, write down the relationships and connections in class. That way
you'll have them to help tie your notes together later on.

Review your notes as soon as possible after class. You must make them as 15
clear as possible while they are fresh in your mind. A day later may be too late,
because forgetting sets in very quickly. Make sure that punctuation is clear, that
all words are readable and correctly spelled, and that unfinished sentences are
completed (or at least marked off so that you can check your notes with another
student's). Add clarifying or connecting comments whenever necessary. Make sure
important ideas are clearly marked. Improve the organization if necessary, so that
you can see at a glance main points and relationships among them.

Finally, try in general to get down a written record of each class. You must do 16
this because forgetting begins almost immediately. Studies have shown that within
two weeks you are likely to have forgotten 80 percent or more of what you have
heard. And in four weeks you are lucky if 5 percent remains! This is so crucial that
it bears repeating: to guard against the relentlessness of forgetting, it is absolutely
essential to write down what you hear in class. Later on you can concentrate on
working to understand fully and to remember the ideas that have been presented
in class. And the more complete your notes are at the time of study, the more you
are likely to learn.

Textbook Study

In many college courses, success means being able to read and study a textbook 17
skillfully. For many students, unfortunately, textbooks are heavy going. After an hour
or two of study, the textbook material is as formless and as hard to understand as
ever. But there is a way to attack even the most difficult textbook and make sense
of it. Use a sequence in which you preview a chapter, mark it, take notes on it, and
then study the notes.

Previewing. Previewing a selection is an important first step to understanding. 18
Taking the time to preview a section or chapter can give you a bird's-eye view of
the way the material is organized. You will have a sense of where you are beginning,
what you will cover, and where you will end.

There are several steps in previewing a selection. First, study the title. The title 19
is the shortest possible summary of a selection and will often tell you the limits of
the material you will cover. For example, the title "FDR and the Supreme Court"
tells you to expect a discussion of President Roosevelt's dealings with the Court.
You know that you will probably not encounter any material dealing with FDR's
foreign policies or personal life. Next, read over quickly the first and last paragraphs
of the selection; these may contain important introductions to, and summaries of,
the main ideas. Then examine briefly the headings and subheadings in the selection.
Together, the headings and subheadings are a brief outline of what you are reading.
Headings are often main ideas or important concepts in capsule form; subheadings
are breakdowns of ideas within main areas. Finally, read the first sentence of some
paragraphs, look for words set off in **boldface** or *italics,* and look at pictures or
diagrams. After you have previewed a selection in this way, you should have a good
general sense of the material to be read.

Marking. You should mark a textbook selection at the same time that you read   20
it through carefully. Use a felt-tip highlighter to shade material that seems important,
or use a regular ballpoint pen and put symbols in the margin next to the material:
stars, checks, or NBs (for *nota bene,* a Latin phrase meaning "note well"). What
to mark is not as mysterious as some students believe. You should try to find main
ideas by looking for the following clues: definitions and examples, enumerations,
and emphasis words.

1   *Definitions and examples:* Definitions are often among the most important ideas   21
in a selection. They are particularly significant in introductory courses in almost
any subject area, where much of your learning involves mastering the specialized
vocabulary of that subject. In a sense, you are learning the "language" of
psychology or business or whatever the subject might be.

Most definitions are abstract, and so they usually are followed by one or   22
more examples to help clarify their meaning. Always mark off definitions and
at least one example that makes a definition clear to you. In a psychology text,
for example, we are told that "rationalization is an attempt to reduce anxiety
by deciding that you have not really been frustrated." Several examples follow,
among them: "A young man, frustrated because he was rejected when he asked
for a date, convinces himself that the woman is not very attractive and is much
less interesting than he had supposed."

2   *Enumerations:* Enumerations are lists of items (causes, reasons, types, and   23
so on) that are numbered 1, 2, 3, . . . or that could easily be numbered in an
outline. They are often signaled by addition words. Many of the paragraphs in
a textbook use words like *first of all, another, in addition,* and *finally* to signal
items in a series. This is a very common and effective organizational method.

3   *Emphasis words:* Emphasis words tell you that an idea is important. Common   24
emphasis words include phrases such as *a major event, a key feature, the
chief factor, important to note, above all,* and *most of all.* Here is an example:
"The most significant contemporary use of marketing is its application to non-
business areas, such as political parties."

Note-Taking. Next, you should take notes. Go through the chapter a second   25
time, rereading the most important parts. Try to write down the main ideas in a
simple outline form. For example, in taking notes on a psychology selection, you
might write down the heading "Kinds of Defense Mechanisms." Below the heading
you would number and describe each kind and give an example of each.

Defense Mechanisms
a. *Definition: Unconscious attempts to reduce anxiety*
b. *Kinds:*
    *(1) Rationalization: Attempt to reduce anxiety by deciding that you have not really
    been frustrated*
    *Example: Man turned down for a date decides that the woman was not worth
    going out with anyway*
    (2) Projection: Attributing to other people motives or thoughts of one's own
    Example: Wife who wants to have an affair accuses her husband of having one

Studying Notes. To study your notes, use the method of repeated self-testing. 26
For example, look at the heading "Kinds of Defense Mechanisms" and say to
yourself, "What are the kinds of defense mechanisms?" When you can recite them,
then say to yourself, "What is rationalization?" "What is an example of rationalization?" Then ask yourself, "What is projection?" "What is an example of projection?"
After you learn each section, review it, and then go on to the next section.

Do not simply read your notes; keep looking away and seeing if you can recite 27
them to yourself. This self-testing is the key to effective learning.

In summary, remember this sequence in order to deal with a textbook: previewing, 28
marking, taking notes, studying the notes. Approaching a textbook in this methodical
way will give you very positive results. You will no longer feel bogged down in a
swamp of words, unable to figure out what you are supposed to know. Instead, you
will understand exactly what you have to do and how to go about doing it.

■

Take a minute now to evaluate your own study habits. Do you practice many of the 29
above skills in order to control your time, take effective classroom notes, and learn
from your textbooks? If not, perhaps you should. The skills are not magic, but they
are too valuable to ignore. Use them carefully and consistently, and they will make
academic success possible for you. Try them, and you won't need convincing.

■ Reading Comprehension Questions

1. Which of the following would be the best alternative title for this selection?
    a. The Importance of Note-Taking
    b. Good Study Skills: The Key to Success
    c. Easy Ways to Learn More
    d. How to Evaluate Your Study Habits

2. Which sentence best expresses the main idea of the selection?
    a. Good study skills can increase academic success.
    b. Note-taking is the best way to study difficult subjects.
    c. More and more schools are offering courses on study skills.
    d. Certain study techniques make college work easy for everyone.

3. Which of these is *not* a good way to organize your time?
    a. Make a monthly calendar.
    b. Keep a weekly study schedule.
    c. Prepare a "to do" list.
    d. Always use extra time for studying.

4. Which is the correct sequence of steps in studying from a textbook?
    a. Preview, self-test, take notes.
    b. Take notes, preview, mark, self-test.
    c. Take notes, mark, preview, self-test.
    d. Preview, mark, take notes, self-test.

5.   When marking the textbook for main ideas, do *not*
     a.   mark it while you are previewing.
     b.   highlight definitions and examples.
     c.   include lists of items.
     d.   look for "emphasis" words.

6.   *True or false?* _____ The author implies that it is better to write too much rather than too little when taking classroom notes.

7.   The author implies that one value of class attendance is that you
     a.   need to get the next assignment.
     b.   will please the instructor, which can lead to better grades.
     c.   can begin to improve your short-term memory.
     d.   increase your understanding by hearing ideas in person.

8.   *True or false?* _____ The author implies that studying does not require any memorization.

9.   The word *abstract* in "The examples help you understand abstract points" (paragraph 13) means
     a.   simple.
     b.   difficult.
     c.   ordinary.
     d.   correct.

10. The word *capsule* in "Headings are often main ideas or important concepts in capsule form" (paragraph 19) means
     a.   adjustable.
     b.   larger.
     c.   complicated.
     d.   abbreviated.

■ Discussion Questions

About Content

1.   Evaluate Jill's college course work. What was she doing right? What was she probably doing wrong?

2.   When taking notes in class, how can we tell what information is important enough to write down?

3.   What are the three steps in time control? Which do you think would be most helpful to you?

4.   What are some of the ways you can spot main ideas when marking a textbook chapter?

About Structure

5. Does Akers use time order or emphatic order in presenting the three study skills?

6. Write down seven different transitional words and phrases used in "Classroom Note-Taking":

   _____   _____

   _____   _____

   _____   _____

   _____

7. Akers tells us that emphasis words (paragraphs 12 and 24) are keys to important ideas. What are three emphasis words or phrases that she herself uses at different places in the article?

   _____   (paragraph _____)

   _____   (paragraph _____)

   _____   (paragraph _____)

About Style and Tone

8. Why has Akers chosen to present most of her essay in the second person— "you"? Why didn't she continue to use Jill, or another student, as an example?

■ Writing Assignments

Assignment 1: Writing a Paragraph

A writing assignment based on this selection is on page 142.

Assignment 2: Writing a Paragraph

Akers says, "A third hint on taking notes is to be on the lookout for signals of importance." Pay close attention to these signals in your classes over the next few days. Watch for use of the board, for definitions, for enumerations, and for other ways your instructors might stress information. On a special sheet of paper, keep track of these signals as they occur. Then use your notes to write a paragraph on ways that your instructors signal that certain ideas are important. Be sure to provide specific examples of what your instructors say and do. Possible topic sentences for this paragraph might be: "My psychology instructor has several ways of signalling important points in her lectures" or "My instructors use several signals in common to let students know that ideas are important."

Assignment 3: Writing an Essay

For many students, the challenge of college is not just to learn good study skills. It is also to overcome the various temptations that interfere with study time. What pulls you away from success at school? Time with friends or family? Card games? Extracurricular activities? Cable TV? Time spent daydreaming or listening to music? An unneeded part-time job?

Make a list of all the temptations that distract you from study time. Then decide on the three that interfere most with your studying time. Use these three as the basis for an essay, "Temptations in College Life."

Here is one student's outline for an essay:

Thesis statement: The local coffee shop, television, and my girlfriend often tempt me away from what I should be doing in school.

Topic sentence 1: The time I spend at the coffee shop interferes with school in three ways.
a. Skipping classes
b. Going right after class, instead of checking notes
c. Long lunches with friends, instead of studying

Topic sentence 2: I also find that the time I spend watching television interferes with school.
a. Time away from study because of sports and other shows
b. Getting to sleep too late because of late-night TV

Topic sentence 3: Finally, I am often with my girlfriend, who is not a student and does not need to study.
a. Time spent together on nonschool activities
b. Studying poorly when she is around

In your final paragraph, include one or two sentences of summary and, perhaps, a comment on any changes you plan to make to improve your study time.

As an alternative, you may want to write generally (rather than personally) about "Temptations Faced by College Students." In such a paper, you will use a third-person point of view rather than the first person ("I"), and you will provide examples based on your observations of others.

Old Before Her Time

Katherine Barrett

Most of us wait for our own advanced years to learn what it is like to be old. Patty Moore decided not to wait. At the age of twenty-six, she disguised herself as an eighty-five-year-old woman. What she learned suggests that to be old in our society is both better and worse than is often thought. This selection may give you a different perspective on the older people in your life—on what they are really like inside and on what life is really like for them.

This is the story of an extraordinary voyage in time, and of a young woman who devoted three years to a singular experiment. In 1979, Patty Moore—then aged twenty-six—transformed herself for the first of many times into an eighty-five-year-old woman. Her object was to discover firsthand the problems, joys, and frustrations of the elderly. She wanted to know for herself what it's like to live in a culture of youth and beauty when your hair is gray, your skin is wrinkled, and no men turn their heads as you pass. 1

Her time machine was a makeup kit. Barbara Kelly, a friend and professional makeup artist, helped Patty pick out a wardrobe and showed her how to use latex to create wrinkles and wrap Ace bandages to give the impression of stiff joints. "It was peculiar," Patty recalls, as she relaxes in her New York City apartment. "Even the first few times I went out, I realized that I wouldn't have to act that much. The more I was perceived as elderly by others, the more 'elderly' I actually became. . . . I imagine that's just what happens to people who really are old." 2

What motivated Patty to make her strange journey? It was partly her career—as an industrial designer, Patty often focuses on the needs of the elderly. But the roots of her interest are also deeply personal. Extremely close to her own grandparents—particularly her maternal grandfather, now ninety—and raised in a part of Buffalo, New York, where there was a large elderly population, Patty always drew comfort and support from the older people around her. When her own marriage ended in 1979 and her life seemed to be falling apart, she dove into her "project" with all her soul. In all, she donned her costume more than two hundred times in fourteen different states. Here is the remarkable story of what she found. 3

Columbus, Ohio, May 1979. Leaning heavily on her cane, Pat Moore stood alone in the middle of a crowd of young professionals. They were all attending a gerontology conference, and the room was filled with animated chatter. But no one was talking to Pat. In a throng of men and women who devoted their working lives to the elderly, she began to feel like a total nonentity. "I'll get us all some coffee," a young man told a group of women next to her. "What about me?" thought Pat. 4

"If I were young, they would be offering me coffee, too." It was a bitter thought at the end of a disappointing day—a day that marked Patty's first appearance as "the old woman." She had planned to attend the gerontology conference anyway, and almost as a lark decided to see how professionals would react to an old person in their midst.

Now, she was angry. All day she had been ignored . . . counted out in a way   5
she had never experienced before. She didn't understand. Why didn't people help her when they saw her struggling to open a heavy door? Why didn't they include her in conversations? Why did the other participants seem almost embarrassed by her presence at the conference—as if it were somehow inappropriate that an old person should be professionally active?

And so, eighty-five-year-old Pat Moore learned her first lesson: The old are often   6
ignored. "I discovered that people really do judge a book by its cover," Patty says today. "Just because I looked different, people either condescended or totally dismissed me. Later, in stores, I'd get the same reaction. A clerk would turn to someone younger and wait on her first. It was as if he assumed that I—the older woman—could wait because I didn't have anything better to do."

New York City, October 1979. Bent over her cane, Pat walked slowly toward   7
the edge of the park. She had spent the day sitting on a bench with friends, but now dusk was falling and her friends had all gone home. She looked around nervously at the deserted area and tried to move faster, but her joints were stiff. It was then that she heard the barely audible sound of sneakered feet approaching and the kids' voices. "Grab her, man." "Get her purse." Suddenly an arm was around her throat and she was dragged back, knocked off her feet.

She saw only a blur of sneakers and blue jeans, heard the sounds of mocking   8
laughter, felt fists pummeling her—on her back, her legs, her breasts, her stomach. "Oh, God," she thought, using her arms to protect her head and curling herself into a ball. "They're going to kill me. I'm going to die. . . ."

Then, as suddenly as the boys attacked, they were gone. And Patty was left   9
alone, struggling to rise. The boy's punches had broken the latex makeup on her face, the fall had disarranged her wig, and her whole body ached. (Later she would learn that she had fractured her left wrist, an injury that took two years to heal completely.) Sobbing, she left the park and hailed a cab to return home. Again the thought struck her: What if I really lived in the gray ghetto? . . . What if I couldn't escape to my nice safe home . . . ?

Lesson number two: the fear of crime is paralyzing. "I really understand now   10
why the elderly become homebound," the young woman says as she recalls her ordeal today. "When something like this happens, the fear just doesn't go away. I guess it wasn't so bad for me. I could distance myself from what happened . . . and I was strong enough to get up and walk away. But what about someone who is really too weak to run or fight back or protect herself in any way? And the elderly often can't afford to move if the area in which they live deteriorates, becomes unsafe. I met people like this and they were imprisoned by their fear. That's when the bolts go on the door. That's when people starve themselves because they're afraid to go to the grocery store."

New York City, February, 1980. It was a slushy, gray day, and Pat had laboriously   11
descended four flights of stairs from her apartment to go shopping. Once outside,
she struggled to hold her threadbare coat closed with one hand and manipulate
her cane with the other. Splotches of snow made the street difficult for anyone to
navigate, but for someone hunched over, as she was, it was almost impossible.
The curb was another obstacle. The slush looked ankle-deep—and what was she
to do? Jump over it? Slowly, she worked her way around to a drier spot, but the
crowds were impatient to move. A woman with packages jostled her as she rushed
past, causing Pat to nearly lose her balance. If I really were old, I would have fallen,
she thought. Maybe broken something. On another day, a woman had practically
knocked her over by letting go of a heavy door as Pat tried to enter a coffee shop.
Then there were the revolving doors. How could you push them without strength?
And how could you get up and down stairs, on and off a bus, without risking a
terrible fall?

Lesson number three: If small, thoughtless deficiencies in design were cor-   12
rected, life would be so much easier for older people. It was no surprise to Patty
that the "built" environment is often inflexible. But even she didn't realize the extent
of the problems, she admits. "It was a terrible feeling. I never realized how difficult
it is to get off a curb if your knees don't bend easily. Or the helpless feeling you
get if your upper arms aren't strong enough to open a door. You know, I just felt
so vulnerable—as if I was at the mercy of every barrier or rude person I encountered."

Fort Lauderdale, Florida, May 1980. Pat met a new friend while shopping, and   13
they decided to continue their conversation over a sundae at a nearby coffee shop.
The woman was in her late seventies, "younger" than Pat, but she was obviously
reaching out for help. Slowly, her story unfolded. "My husband moved out of our
bedroom," the woman said softly, fiddling with her coffee cup and fighting back
tears. "He won't touch me anymore. And when he gets angry at me for being stupid,
he'll even sometimes . . . " The woman looked down, too embarrassed to go on.
Pat took her hand. "He hits me; . . . he gets so mean." "Can't you tell anyone?"
Pat asked. "Can't you tell your son?" "Oh, no!" the woman almost gasped. "I would
never tell the children; they absolutely adore him."

Lesson number four: Even a fifty-year-old marriage isn't necessarily a good one.   14
While Pat met many loving and devoted elderly couples, she was stunned to find
others who had stayed together unhappily—because divorce was still an anathema
in their middle years. "I met women who secretly wished their husbands dead,
because after so many years they just ended up full of hatred. One woman in
Chicago even admitted that she deliberately angered her husband because she
knew it would make his blood pressure rise. Of course, that was pretty extreme. . . . "

Patty pauses thoughtfully and continues. "I guess what really made an impres-   15
sion on me, the real eye-opener, was that so many of these older women had the
same problems as women twenty, thirty, or forty—problems with men . . . problems
with the different roles that are expected of them. As a 'young woman' I, too, had
just been through a relationship where I spent a lot of time protecting someone by
covering up his problems from family and friends. Then I heard this woman in Florida
saying that she wouldn't tell her children their father beat her because she didn't
want to disillusion them. These issues aren't age-related. They affect everyone."

Clearwater, Florida, January 1981. She heard the children laughing, but she   16
didn't realize at first that they were laughing at her. On this day, as on several
others, Pat had shed the clothes of a middle-income woman for the rags of a bag
lady. She wanted to see the extremes of the human condition, what it was like to
be old and poor, and outside traditional society as well. Now, tottering down the
sidewalk, she was most concerned with the cold, since her layers of ragged clothing
did little to ease the chill. She had spent the afternoon rummaging through garbage
cans, loading her shopping bags with bits of debris, and she was stiff and tired.
Suddenly, she saw that four little boys, five or six years old, were moving up on
her. And then she felt the sting of the pebbles they were throwing. She quickened
her pace to escape, but another handful of gravel hit her and the laughter continued.
They're using me as a target, she thought, horror-stricken. They don't even think
of me as a person.

Lesson number five: Social class affects every aspect of an older person's   17
existence. "I found out that class is a very important factor when you're old," says
Patty. "It was interesting. That same day, I went back to my hotel and got dressed
as a wealthy woman, another role that I occasionally took. Outside the hotel, a little
boy of about seven asked if I would go shelling with him. We walked along the
beach, and he reached out to hold my hand. I knew he must have a grandmother
who walked with a cane, because he was so concerned about me and my footing.
'Don't put your cane there, the sand's wet,' he'd say. He really took responsibility
for my welfare. The contrast between him and those children was really incredible.
The little ones who were throwing pebbles at me because they didn't see me as
human. And then the seven-year-old taking care of me. I think he would have
responded to me the same way even if I had been dressed as the middle-income
woman. There's no question that money does make life easier for older people,
not only because it gives them a more comfortable lifestyle, but because it makes
others treat them with greater respect."

New York City, May 1981. Pat always enjoyed the time she spent sitting on the   18
benches in Central Park. She'd let the whole day pass by, watching young children
play, feeding the pigeons and chatting. One spring day she found herself sitting
with three women, all widows, and the conversation turned to the few available men
around. "It's been a long time since anyone hugged me," one woman complained.
Another agreed. "Isn't that the truth. I need a hug, too." It was a favorite topic, Pat
found—the lack of touching left in these women's lives, the lack of hugging, the
lack of men.

In the last two years, she found out herself how it felt to walk down Fifth Avenue   19
and know that no men were turning to look after her. Or how it felt to look at models
in magazines or store mannequins and know that those gorgeous clothes were just
not made for her. She hadn't realized before just how much casual attention was
paid to her because she was young and pretty. She hadn't realized it until it stopped.

Lesson number six: You never grow old emotionally. You always need to feel   20
loved. "It's not surprising that everyone needs love and touching and holding," says
Patty. "But I think some people feel that you reach a point in your life when you
accept that those intimate feelings are in the past. That's wrong. These women
were still interested in sex. But more than that, they—like everyone—needed to

be hugged and touched. I'd watch two women greeting each other on the street and just holding onto each other's hands, neither wanting to let go. Yet, I also saw that there are people who are afraid to touch an old person; . . . they were afraid to touch me. It's as if they think old age is a disease and it's catching. They think that something might rub off on them."

New York City, September 1981. He was a thin man, rather nattily dressed, with a hat that he graciously tipped at Pat as he approached the bench where she sat. "Might I join you?" he asked jauntily. Pat told him he would be welcome and he offered her one of the dietetic hard candies that he carried in a crumpled paper bag. As the afternoon passed, they got to talking . . . about the beautiful buds on the trees and the world around them and the past. "Life's for the living, my wife used to tell me," he said. "When she took sick, she made me promise her that I wouldn't waste a moment. But the first year after she died, I just sat in the apartment. I didn't want to see anyone, talk to anyone or go anywhere. I missed her so much." He took a handkerchief from his pocket and wiped his eyes, and they sat in silence. Then he slapped his leg to break the mood and change the subject. He asked Pat about herself, and described his life alone. He belonged to a "senior center" now, and went on trips and had lots of friends. Life did go on. They arranged to meet again the following week on the same park bench. He brought lunch—chicken salad sandwiches and decaffeinated peppermint tea in a thermos—and wore a carnation in his lapel. It was the first date Patty had had since her marriage ended.

Lesson number seven: Life does go on . . . as long as you're flexible and open to change. "That man really meant a lot to me, even though I never saw him again," says Patty, her eyes wandering toward the gray wig that now sits on a wig-stand on the top shelf of her bookcase. "He was a real old-fashioned gentleman, yet not afraid to show his feelings—as so many men my age are. It's funny, but at that point I had been through months of self-imposed seclusion. Even though I was in a different role, that encounter kind of broke the ice for getting my life together as a single woman."

In fact, while Patty was living her life as the old woman, some of her young friends had been worried about her. After several years, it seemed as if the lines of identity had begun to blur. Even when she wasn't in makeup, she was wearing unusually conservative clothing, she spent most of her time with older people and she seemed almost to revel in her role—sometimes finding it easier to be in costume than to be a single New Yorker.

But as Patty continued her experiment, she was also learning a great deal from the older people she observed. Yes, society often did treat the elderly abysmally; . . . they were sometimes ignored, sometimes victimized, sometimes poor and frightened, but so many of them were survivors. They had lived through two world wars, through the Depression, and into the computer age. "If there was one lesson to learn, one lesson that I'll take with me into my old age, it's that you've got to be flexible," Patty says. "I saw my friend in the park, managing after the loss of his wife, and I met countless other people who picked themselves up after something bad—or even something catastrophic—happened. I'm not worried about them. I'm worried about the others who shut themselves away. It's funny, but seeing these two extremes helped me recover from the trauma in my own life, to pull my life together."

Today, Patty is back to living the life of a single thirty-year-old, and she rarely   25
dons her costumes anymore. "I must admit, though, I do still think a lot about
aging," she says. "I look in the mirror and I begin to see wrinkles, and then I realize
that I won't be able to wash those wrinkles off." Is she afraid of growing older?
"No. In a way, I'm kind of looking forward to it," she smiles. "I know it will be
different from my experiment. I know I'll probably even look different. When they
aged Orson Welles in *Citizen Kane* he didn't resemble at all the Orson Welles
of today."

But Patty also knows that in one way she really did manage to capture the   26
feeling of being old. With her bandages and her stooped posture, she turned her
body into a kind of prison. Yet, inside she didn't change at all. "It's funny, but that's
exactly how older people always say they feel," says Patty. "Their bodies age, but
inside they are really no different from when they were young."

■ Reading Comprehension Questions

1. Which of the following would be the best alternative title for this selection?
   a. How Poverty Affects the Elderly
   b. Similarities Between Youth and Old Age
   c. One Woman's Discoveries about the Elderly
   d. Violence against the Elderly

2. Which sentence best expresses the main idea of the selection?
   a. The elderly often have the same problems as young people.
   b. Pat Moore dressed up like an elderly woman over two hundred times.
   c. By making herself appear old, Pat Moore learned what life is like for the elderly in the United States.
   d. Elderly people often feel ignored in a society that glamorizes youth.

3. *True of false?* _____ As they age, people need others less.

4. Pat Moore learned that the elderly often become homebound because of the
   a. high cost of living.
   b. fear of crime.
   c. availability of in-home nursing care.
   d. lack of interesting places for them to visit.

5. One personal lesson Pat Moore learned from her experiment was that
   a. she needs to start saving money for her retirement.
   b. by being flexible she can overcome hardships.
   c. she has few friends her own age.
   d. her marriage could have been saved.

6. From paragraph 2, we can infer that
    a. behaving like an old person was difficult for Moore.
    b. many older people wear Ace bandages.
    c. people sometimes view themselves as others see them.
    d. Barbara Kelly works full-time making people look older than they really are.

7. The article suggests that fifty years ago
    a. young couples tended to communicate better than today's young couples.
    b. divorce was less acceptable than it is today.
    c. verbal and physical abuse was probably extremely rare.
    d. the elderly were treated with great respect.

8. We can conclude that Pat Moore may have disguised herself as an elderly woman over two hundred times in fourteen states because
    a. she and her friend Barbara Kelly continuously worked at perfecting Moore's costumes.
    b. her company made her travel often.
    c. she was having trouble finding locations with large numbers of elderly people.
    d. she wanted to see how the elderly were seen and treated all over the country, rather than in just one area.

9. The author implies that Moore's experiences dressed as an old woman
    a. were helpful to Moore personally and professionally.
    b. were not typical of real elderly people.
    c. were paid for by her employer.
    d. did Moore permanent harm.

10. The word *abysmally* in "society often did treat the elderly abysmally; . . . they were sometimes ignored, sometimes victimized, sometimes poor and frightened" (paragraph 24) means
    a. politely.
    b. absentmindedly.
    c. very badly.
    d. angrily.

■ Discussion Questions

About Content

1. Why did Pat Moore decide to conduct her experiment? Which of her discoveries surprised you?

2. Using the information Moore learned from her experiment, list some of the things that could be done to help the elderly. What are some things you personally could do?

3. How do the elderly people Moore met during her experiment compare with the elderly people you know?

4. Lesson number seven in the article is "Life does go on . . . as long as you're flexible and open to change" (paragraph 22). What do you think that really means? How might that lesson apply to situations and people you're familiar with—in which people either were or were not flexible and open to change?

About Structure

5. Most of the selection is made up of a series of Pat Moore's experiences and the seven lessons they taught. Find the sentence used by the author to introduce those experiences and lessons, and write that sentence here:

_____

6. The details of paragraph 21 are organized in time order, and the author has used a few time transition words to signal time relationships. Find two of those time words, and write them here:

_____   _____

About Style and Tone

7. What device does the author use to signal that she is beginning a new set of experiences and the lesson they taught? How does she ensure that the reader will recognize what each of the seven lessons are?

8. Do you think Barrett is objective in her treatment of Patty Moore? Or does the author allow whatever her feelings might be for Moore to show in her writing? Find details in the article to support your answer.

■ **Writing Assignment**

Assignment 1: Writing a Paragraph

In her experiment, Moore discovered various problems faced by the elderly. Choose one of these areas of difficulty, and write a paragraph in which you discuss what could be done in your city to help solve the problem. Following are a few possible topic sentences for this assignment:

Fear of crime among the elderly could be eased by a program providing young people to accompany them on their errands.

The courthouse and train station in our town need to be redesigned to allow easier access for the elderly.

Schools should start adopt-a-grandparent programs, which would enrich the emotional lives of both the young and the old participants.

Assignment 2: Writing a Paragraph

What did you learn from the selection, or what do you already know, about being older in our society that might influence your own future? Write a paragraph in which you list three or four ways in which you plan to minimize or avoid some of the problems often faced by elderly people. For instance, you may decide to do whatever you can to remain as healthy and strong as possible throughout your life. That might involve quitting smoking and incorporating exercise into your schedule. Your topic sentence might simply be: "There are three important ways in which I hope to avoid some of the problems often faced by the elderly."

Assignment 3: Writing an Essay

Lesson number seven in Barrett's article is "Life does go on . . . as long as you're flexible and open to change" (paragraph 22). Think about one person of any age whom you know well (including yourself). Write an essay in which you show how being (or not being) flexible and open to change was important in that person's life. Develop your essay with three main examples.

In preparation for writing, think of several key times in your subject's life. Select three times in which being flexible or inflexible had a significant impact on that person. Then narrate and explain each of those times in a paragraph of its own. Here are two possible thesis statements for this essay:

> My grandmother generally made the most of her circumstances by being flexible and open to change.

> When I was a teenager, I could have made life easier for myself by being more flexible and open to change.

Your conclusion for this essay might summarize the value of being flexible or the problems of being inflexible, or both, for the person you are writing about.

Finding a Career and a Job: A No-Nonsense Guide

Ann McClintock

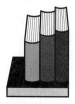

If you knew you were going to spend about two thousand hours a year at one activity, you'd be very careful about what that activity would be. You would want it to be enjoyable and to make good use of your talents. And you'd take enough time to make sure you chose the *right* activity. For most of us, that activity is work. Do you think about your career in this way? Many people don't. They risk ending up with a job that is only a place to pass time until the end of the workday, until the end of the week, and, finally, until retirement. In the following selection, you'll see that there is a great deal you can do to determine how you will spend the eighty thousand or more work hours of your life.

1   Of all his high school subjects, Larry liked history best. So when it came time to pick his college major, that's what he chose.

2   Larry enjoyed his classes and got good grades. But when he finally received his bachelor's degree and began looking for work, he discovered that there weren't many jobs waiting for graduates with a degree in history.

3   After floundering for a while, he began to look for a job in other fields. He started this search by answering a few want ads and signing up with two employment agencies.

4   When several months passed and he still hadn't received an offer, Larry realized that getting a job required more effort and strategy than he was putting into it. So he began to study the job market more carefully and to take more time with his application letters. He finally took the first offer he got—a job as a clothing salesman in a department store.

5   Now he's saving up his money to get training in a field that appeals to him more. In his investigation of the job market, Larry discovered that there's a growing need for hotel managers and travel agents, two types of work that interest him. He plans to talk to a few hotel managers and travel agents and decide which area appeals to him more. Next, he'll find a good school where he can get some training, and then he'll really begin his career.

6   It turned out that Larry's college education gave him a fine background in liberal arts and history, but it was of no practical value in his work life.

7   When Larry's younger sister started college, he gave her this advice: Remember that you're going to college for just several years, but you'll be working most of your life. Now is the time to think about what kind of work you want to do. Then during college you can get a good start in your career. You should take some classes just for the sake of learning, but that's not enough. You've got to get a degree that's marketable. And once you've got it, you should be ready for an all-out job search.

■

Larry's advice, in spirit, is applicable to everyone aiming for a job. You'll find it useful whether you're a student, unemployed, or switching careers. 8

In all cases, you'll do yourself a favor by taking time to select an appealing and marketable career path, get the necessary training, and then make a full-time job of finding an employer. 9

How does one choose a career? The answer is "carefully." You have two important questions to ask yourself: 10

1   What kind of work do you want to spend your life doing?
2   Are there good career opportunities in that line of work?

Begin by analyzing yourself. Are you outgoing? Then perhaps working in front of a computer all day may not satisfy you or bring out your best. Are you shy? Then you should probably not think of being a salesperson. 11

If you aren't sure what you'd like to do, get help from your college job counseling office. Such an office will have tests that can help you find out what kind of careers you might enjoy and do well at. These are called *interest inventory tests* and *vocational preference tests.* After you take such tests, a counselor can sit down with you and help you decide what your major should be. Taking courses in your prospective major as soon as possible can help confirm that choice. Talking to people employed in the field you're interested in can also be very useful. 12

Of course, it's essential to check on the marketability of your career choice. Again, your job placement counselor may be able to give you information on what the job market is like for various fields, especially locally. 13

Another source to check is the *Occupational Outlook Handbook,* published by the Bureau of Labor Statistics. This is an extremely valuable source of information about the current and future job market. Copies are usually available in libraries and your college placement office. But if you want to buy this book for easy reference, write to the New Orders, Superintendent of Documents, P.O. Box 371954, Pittsburgh, PA 15250-7950, and ask for the latest paperback edition of the *Occupational Outlook Handbook;* or call 1-312-533-1886. The book will cost you about $23. 14

According to the *Handbook* and the 1994 career guide in *U.S. News & World Report,* here are some of the jobs expected to be widely available in the mid-1990s. 15

Flight attendants

Travel agents

Car rental and hotel sales and reservations agents

Switchboard operators and telecommunications personnel

Cashiers

Restaurant cooks

Food service and lodging personnel

Bartenders

Insurance claims adjusters

Corrections officers

Security guards

Banking sales and marketing personnel

Cable ad sales reps and customer service representatives

Retail sales workers

Secretaries and office clerks

Cosmetologists

Dental hygienists

Clinical laboratory and X-ray technicians

Registered and licensed practical nurses

Nursing aides and attendants

Home care aides

Child-care workers

Social workers

Veterinary-care technicians

Computer programmers and operators

Computer repair technicians

Teacher aides

Teachers, especially elementary, bilingual, and special education

■

16 Eventually, you will have decided on your career goals and completed a two- or four-year degree in your intended field. You're then ready to do at least entry-level work, and the time has come to begin the demanding pursuit of a job. Getting hired involves four basic steps:

1 Finding potential employers
2 Preparing written materials
3 Going out on interviews
4 Following up on the interviews

17 When most people think of looking for a job, they think of the want ads. Want ads are a good place to begin, and you should check those in your chosen field in various newspapers, as well as in trade publications. Want ads can be divided into three types: agency ads, blind ads, and company ads. Agency ads, of course, are placed by employment agencies. Blind ads are those that give no company name—only a post office box number. With a blind ad, you're unable to follow up on your application, so be especially sure your letter demonstrates your qualifications thoroughly. Company ads—ads that give the name of the employer—are the best to deal with. They allow you to follow up your written application with another letter or a phone call, perhaps even to contact the person who's doing the hiring.

Research has shown that another route to finding employment, and one too often ignored by job seekers, is direct contact with people in your intended field. This contact, in the form of information-gathering interviews, helps you learn more about the specific nature of the work you would be doing. It has the added value of acquainting you with a given company and acquainting that company with you. Such interviews are best conducted *before* you actually want a job. In a nutshell, what you do is call the switchboard of a company you might like to work for, get the name of a person in your field of interest, and then call that person and ask if you can have a half hour of time to learn about his or her job. Most people respond favorably to such a request; they are flattered and happy to talk about their work. Information-gathering interviews are described in a separate chapter of a classic book on careers, *What Color Is Your Parachute?* by Richard Bolles. This highly recommended text is updated frequently and is available in the reference section of almost any bookstore. 18

Finally, in your search for employment, don't forget to use your network of personal acquaintances to get out the message that you're available. Tell class-mates, professors, high school teachers, church members—everyone you can think of. Don't hide your need for a job; you may get a name, a lead, or even an invitation to an interview—possibilities you can't afford to ignore. 19

Once you're ready to begin the application process, you'll need a *résumé* and *cover letters*. Because these materials may be all a potential employer sees of you when deciding whether or not to call you in for an interview, they must be written as if they'll be on exhibit. You must be *absolutely sure* to type them with a fresh ribbon on good-quality paper and to make them error-free. It's an excellent idea to have someone proofread your work for spelling, grammar, and punctuation. 20

If the cover letter and résumé are not perfect, save yourself the cost of a stamp and throw them into a wastebasket. Employers often get hundreds of applications for one job, so they have no incentive to spend any time on candidates who send in messy or poorly written work. "This candidate will be a careless worker" will run through employers' minds as they throw out applications that look unprofessional. 21

Keep in mind that résumé preparation services are advertised at most schools. Such ads are often posted on bulletin boards in the campus bookstore or near the job placement and counseling offices. The people who run such services may be very helpful to you as you put together your résumé. If you are not a strong typist, or if you are not strong on writing and proofreading skills, it's worth spending money to use such a service. 22

Your résumé should be a brief one- or two-page summary of personal and work-related information. A model is shown on the following page. 23

Note that after beginning with your name, address, and phone number, you should indicate your career objective and then detail your educational and work histories. If you're a recent graduate with limited work experience, put your educa-tional background first. Otherwise, begin with your employment history. In either case, be concise. Begin each section with the most recent information and work backwards in time. As a general rule, you should not include information about high school unless it's particularly useful. For example, if you were an art student at a high school for the arts and are applying for a graphic-arts position, then that information is relevant. 24

Sample Résumé

Carol Phillips
67 Russell Street
Chicago Heights, Illinois 60003
(312) 223-4547

Objective

Career in the paralegal field

Education

1993–present　Midwestern Paralegal Institute, Homewood, Illinois
Expect to graduate with a paralegal certificate in August of 1990.

1991–1993　Truman College of Chicago
Graduated with an Associate of Science degree in business.
Grade point average: 3.2 of possible 4.0.

1987–1991　Chicago Heights High School
Concentrated in business courses.

Job experience

1992–present　Secretary at James & Hall, Attorneys at Law, Park Forest, Illinois
General secretarial duties, including word processing.

1990–1992　Assistant evening manager at Fairmont Hall Gifts
Sales, employee scheduling, inventory control.

1988–1990　Part-time salesperson at Marshall Fields, Orland Park, Illinois

Summer 1987　Part-time salesperson at Kane Family Shoes, Chicago Heights

Personal data

Single. 21 years old. Excellent health.

References

Furnished on request.

End the résumé by saying that references are available on request. Such refer- 25
ences should be one-page statements from former or present teachers or employers. The statements testify to your character and abilities, and to your work and study habits. You should hold the originals of such recommendations and then make copies as needed to give to prospective employers. It's important to keep in mind as you're going through school and working at jobs that you want your teachers and bosses to see you at your best; that way, they'll be in a position to prepare solid letters of recommendation on your behalf.

Every résumé should be accompanied by an individually typed cover letter, no 26
more than one page long and addressed to a specific person at the company (unless it's in response to a blind help-wanted ad, where only a box number is given). A sample cover letter is shown below.

Sample Cover Letter

67 Russell Street
Chicago Heights, Illinois 60003
June 23, 1994

Mr. George McNeal
McNeal & Schneider
10 Michigan Avenue
Chicago, Illinois 60111

Dear Mr. McNeal:

I am responding to your ad for a paralegal in yesterday's Courier-Gazette. I feel I am a strong candidate for the job.

The enclosed résumé will tell you about my educational and employment background. I will receive my paralegal certification in August, and I expect to rank in the top quarter of my class. In addition, my present position as a legal secretary for a general-practice law firm has given me a solid overview of law practice. Both kinds of experiences prepare me to take on the challenge of the job you have described.

I am aware that your firm specializes in personal injury, a field that especially interests me. With the hope that we can arrange an interview, I will call you next Wednesday, July 1, to discuss my qualifications.

Sincerely yours,

Carol Phillips

Carol Phillips

Begin the letter by stating what position you're applying for and, if applicable, how you heard about the opening. Then, in the body of the letter, be sure to point out how your talents, experience, and education, as more fully described in your résumé, will help you succeed in the job. In a low-key way, do your best to sell yourself effectively. Finally, in the last paragraph, express your wish for an interview and say that you will call on a particular day—about a week after your letter will probably arrive—to discuss your qualifications.   27

It is often necessary to send out many résumés and letters for each interview you'll actually be granted. For twenty applications, you might get one response. Once you land an interview, you must prepare to deal successfully with it, for the interview is the next important hurdle on your road to a job. The best candidate for a position does not always get a job; sometimes, the best interviewee is chosen.   28

Prepare yourself for the interview, first of all, by keeping in mind that all companies are interested in candidates who will work hard, be reliable, and get along well with others. More specifically, develop well-thought-out answers for these four typical interview questions: 29

1   Why are you interested in this job?

2   What are your greatest strengths and weaknesses?

3   What were your accomplishments in your past jobs?

4   Why should we hire you?

Write out your answers to these questions, polish them, and go over them repeatedly. There is no need to memorize answers, but do go over them so thoroughly that they become part of you.

During interviews, you'll have opportunities to ask your own questions. They can help you understand the position better and, equally important, demonstrate that you'll be an alert and motivated worker. Here are four questions to ask: 30

1   What are the most important qualifications for the job?

2   Does the job involve a training period?

3   What might a typical first assignment be?

4   If a person does well in this job, what would the next step be in the company?

Save questions about salary, vacations, benefits, and any problems (such as child-care needs) until after you've received a job offer.

On the day of the interview, pay attention to "interview etiquette." Show up slightly early, and don't overdress or underdress. Dirty, rumpled, or tight clothing is taboo, as are chewing gum, smoking, and slouching. Dress neatly in a business suit. Bring along a copy of your résumé, just in case it is needed, and a list of references with addresses and phone numbers.   31

Sample Follow-Up Letter

67 Russell Street
Chicago Heights, Illinois 60003
July 15, 1994

Mr. George McNeal
McNeal & Schneider
10 Michigan Avenue
Chicago, Illinois 60111

Dear Mr. McNeal:

Thank you for an enjoyable and informative interview. Now that I know more about your practice, I am eager to join your staff. The position of paralegal with your firm sounds demanding, but I know that my paralegal education and my experience as a legal secretary have well prepared me for the responsibilities involved.

Again, thank you for your time. I hope to hear from you soon.

Sincerely yours,

Carol Phillips

Carol Phillips

32   When you meet your interviewer, smile and shake hands firmly. During the interview, try to appear confident but not conceited. Interviewers are impressed by applicants who are at ease, know their goals, are articulate, and listen well. When you finish the interview, thank the interviewer for his or her time and shake hands again.

33   Finally, follow the interview up with a brief follow-up letter. Send it out within a day of the interview. A sample is shown above.

34   Such a note will give you the chance to reaffirm to the interviewer your enthusiasm for the position and to review your qualifications. If there are any important points you didn't make in the interview, the follow-up letter is a good place for them, too.

35   Your final weapon in seeking a job is to be thick-skinned. It may take some time before interviews start coming your way. And when they do, you may feel that some didn't go very well. Don't despair. The more interviews you have, the better you'll get at being interviewed. Some people even go so far as to seek interviews for jobs they don't want, just for practice.

36   There are a lot of jobs out there, but there's also lots of competition. Rejection is a natural part of the process—but so is finally getting a job.

37   Remember that even successful people have encountered their share of disappointment and failure along the way. They then went on to succeed because they kept trying.

■ Reading Comprehension Questions

1. Which of these would be the best alternative title for this selection?
   a. College and Careers
   b. How to Choose a Career and Get a Job
   c. Preparing for the Future
   d. Getting Employed

2. Which sentence best expresses the main idea of the selection?
   a. Getting hired involves four basic steps.
   b. The time to select a career is during college.
   c. Larry did not have any career skills when he finished college.
   d. Both selecting the right career and choosing a job require careful planning.

3. When you are choosing a career, two important considerations are
   a. high school grades and college courses.
   b. pay scale and personal acquaintances.
   c. appeal and marketability.
   d. a good résumé and a good interview.

4. To find a job, the author recommends all of the following except
   a. want ads.
   b. personal acquaintances.
   c. taking a year off from college.
   d. direct contacts.

5. A good cover letter will
   a. always result in an interview.
   b. be very detailed and lengthy.
   c. help the candidate sell himself or herself.
   d. be prepared ahead of time by a professional service.

6. *True or false?* _____ The author implies that being the best-prepared candidate can be more important than being the best-qualified.

7. The author implies that you are more likely to get a job if you
   a. get a liberal arts degree.
   b. are outgoing, not shy.
   c. take a business program in college.
   d. choose a growth occupation.

8. The author implies that good work and study habits
   a. are rarely noticed by teachers and employers.
   b. should be mentioned in the résumé.
   c. will help lead to good letters of recommendation.
   d. are seldom considered during job interviews.

9. The word *prospective* in "Taking courses in your prospective major" (paragraph 12) and "prospective employers" (paragraph 25) means
    a. unusual.
    b. potential.
    c. challenging.
    d. hardest.
10. The word *network* in "use your network of personal acquaintances" (paragraph 19) means
    a. view.
    b. handful.
    c. choice.
    d. interrelated group.

■ **Discussion Questions**

About Content

1. Why does the author emphasize that one should choose a career *carefully?*
2. The author mentions several ways that a college job counseling office can be helpful in the search for a career. What are they?
3. What is the reason for writing error-free résumés, cover letters, and follow-up letters?
4. In what ways does the author suggest that job candidates improve their interview skills?

About Structure

5. The thesis of the article can be found in a paragraph that follows the introduction. Write the number of that paragraph here: _____
6. In the spaces provided, write the numbers of the paragraphs that correspond to the three basic parts of the article:
    a. Introduction   (paragraphs _____ to _____)
    b. Finding a Career   (paragraphs _____ to _____)
    c. Finding a Job   (paragraphs _____ to _____)

About Style and Tone

7. Find the paragraph in which the author tells us what audience this article is written for. Write the paragraph number here: _____
8. The final three paragraphs of the article (paragraphs 35, 36, and 37) have two purposes. One is to provide information. What is the second purpose? Which words and phrases express this purpose?

■ Writing Assignments

Assignment 1: Writing a Paragraph

What jobs would you most like doing? Which would you absolutely despise? For the sake of this assignment, do not consider such factors as job market, pay, and location. Just free your imagination and think of a few of the best and worst possible positions you could work at. Then write a paragraph on one or two of the most appealing and one or two of the least appealing jobs. Explain the qualities of each job that make it so attractive or so unattractive to you. A possible topic sentence might be, "There are a few jobs I would love to do and a few I would absolutely hate."

Assignment 2: Writing a Paragraph

To reach a long-term goal, you must plan and achieve a continuing series of short-term goals. What will you do over the next several years in pursuing your chosen career? Will you take certain required or recommended courses? Will you prepare for special certification? Will you seek internships or part-time jobs in your field?

Write a paragraph describing the steps you intend to take to advance your career goals. Explain the nature and purpose of each step in detail, and comment on which will be most challenging. Here is a sample topic sentence for such a paragraph: "In my pursuit of a nursing career, I plan to achieve the following goals over the next several years."

If you do not yet know your career goal, write a paragraph describing the steps you might take to discover what work you would like to do. A topic sentence for this paragraph might be: "In my search for a career, I plan to take the following steps."

Following is a list of several steps it is helpful to consider in planning a career search:

Taking vocational and interest inventory tests

Taking courses in potential job fields

Reading through the *Occupational Outlook Handbook*

Speaking to college job counselors and placement officers

Speaking to people working in fields you may be interested in

Working at part-time jobs and internships in fields of interest

Assignment 3: Writing an Essay

What jobs appeal to you? Do some thinking and make a list of what seem the best careers for you. Then speak to someone who works at one of these jobs. He or she may be someone you already know or a person at a company or store that interests you. In the latter case, contact someone in the position you have chosen (you can get his or her name and number by calling the switchboard of the company) and explain that you would like to interview him or her briefly for a school assignment. Most people will be pleased to help you.

At the interview, ask about the education, job experience, and abilities and talents needed for the position. Find out in detail why these requirements are useful. Take notes during your interview and then use them to write an essay on the recommended background for the job in question.

Your three supporting paragraphs will cover, in turn, recommended education, useful experience, and desirable abilities. Your introductory paragraph should refer to these three areas and should explain when, where, and with whom the interview took place. As you develop your body paragraphs, remember to use details and examples from your interview to back up each of your three topic sentences.

Here are several sample thesis statements:

A candidate for a position as a corporate salesperson is well advised to have a business education, selling experience, and an outgoing personality.

According to a local accountant, prospective accountants should take as many business courses as possible, get at least a two-year accounting degree, and have the ability to do detail work.

A nursing candidate should have an R.N. certificate, a willingness to work with others, and a good deal of patience.

Assignment 4: Writing a Résumé and Cover Letter

Clip a job listing from a newspaper or copy a job description posted in your school placement office. The job should be one that you feel you are presently qualified for or that you might be qualified for in the future.

Prepare and type a résumé and a cover letter for the job. Use the models in the article as guides. Unless your instructor tells you otherwise, feel free to invent some of the specific supporting material needed to make you appear a strong candidate for the job.

Concentrate on preparing a résumé and cover letter that are neat and error-free. Use the checklist of sentence skills on the inside front cover of this book as a guide in your writing. Assume that your instructor will not accept or give you credit for these materials unless they are absolutely *perfect*.

How to Think Clearly

Earl Ubell

You are probably familiar with the phrases *jumping to conclusions* and *making a mountain out of a molehill.* They refer to a common mistake: making distorted judgments. We all like to believe we think clearly, but all too often our logic is muddied by our fears, expectations, and desires. We fear that people will not like us, for example, and so we interpret their friendly greetings as hypocrisy or mere courtesy. We experience rejection and conclude that we are failures. It is not easy to make sense of ourselves and our relationships with others, but that becomes even more difficult if our thinking is distorted. The following selection lists some common patterns of twisted logic and suggests how to avoid them. Perhaps you will recognize some of your own ways of "jumping to conclusions" and will see how they make your life more frustrating than necessary.

Sally: *"Judy is five minutes late."*
Jean: *"Yeah, Judy is always late."*

Bill: *"That's a pretty nice tie, Harry."*
Harry thinks: *"Bill has no taste. This tie must be terrible. I'll throw it away."*

1   Jean and Harry are thinking illogically. Just because Judy may have been late once or twice, Jean jumps to the conclusion that Judy is *always* late. And Harry does not know how to accept a compliment—he sees only the negative side.

2   Jean's and Harry's twisted logic provides only two examples of a dozen kinds of distorted thoughts that hold us in their grip, producing depression, anxiety, and frustration, ruining our relationships with others, and making it difficult for us to think, to work, to love.

3   I call them the "dirty dozen of distorted thinking." Psychologists call them *cognitive distortions.* The word *cognitive* comes from the Latin *cognoscere,* which means "to know." *Cognitive* refers to what you know and believe rather than how you feel, your emotions.

4   Psychologists say that almost no one escapes cognitive distortions. If twisted logic is giving you trouble with your spouse, your children, your friends, or your boss, or if you are ever anxious, depressed, or puzzled over emotional problems, you too may be a victim of one or more of these "dirty dozen."

The "Every" Distortion

Although psychologists call the first distortion *overgeneralization,* I call it the *"every"*   5
distortion. After only one or two instances of an event, you leap to the conclusion
that it happens *every* time or to *every*body or *every*where. A prime example of the
"every" distortion is Jean's twisted thinking at the beginning of this article. Jean
thinks her friend is *always* late even though Judy may have been late only once
before. And Harry, when one dog growls at him, leaps to the conclusion, "Dogs hate
me." But what if the next dog he meets wags its tail at Harry and licks his hand?

Poisoning the Positive

Like Harry at the beginning of this article, you find reasons to distrust and dismiss   6
compliments or friendly moves. Such poisoned thinking discourages friendships
and undermines intimacy. A man says to Jean, "I like you." Jean says to herself,
"Ha! Sure he 'likes me.' I bet. Ha! He can't really mean that. Ha!" Will Jean ever
be able to accept signs of his regard as genuine?

The Shoulds

You set up impossible standards of behavior for yourself or for others, telling yourself   7
and others what *should* or *must* be done. It's easy to fail this way. Reasonable people
make suggestions more tentatively. "Such and such *might* be better," they say.

All or Nothing

Some of us see everything in terms of one extreme or the other; there is no   8
in-between. For example, we either love or hate something; or we think everybody is either good or bad. We view everything in stringent black-and-white terms
when, figuratively speaking, real life is shades of gray.

No! No! No!

If there is something even remotely negative in another person's actions or words,   9
you will find it and harp on it.

Mind Reading

You really believe that you know what another person is thinking. ("I *know* my boss   10
likes long memos—even though he *says* he doesn't.") Then when you act on your
beliefs, you get into trouble. The success rate of all mind reading is low, no matter
what you've seen in the movies or on televison. Harry thinks, "Maybe Mabel will
think my necktie is terrible; I'd better take it off." What if, before he has a chance
to take it off, Mabel comes along and says, "Nice tie"?

Catastrophizing

If you suffer from this distortion, you view everything as a catastrophe. One gray   11
hair on your head means that you are old. One lost sale signals the end of your
job. Catastrophizing paralyzes action; if you fear the worst, you won't make a move.

I! I! I!

You think that everything happens because of you or to you. If your best friend gets   12
the flu, you think it's because you served her iced tea on the rainy afternoon that
she visited—and then you fret that you're sure to catch an even worse case.
Most such occurrences have more than one cause, the least of which is probably
your contribution.

Mislabeling

With mislabeling, you tend to paint a picture of reality that you want or fear rather   13
than what exists. You may say, "I'm a failure," and think that you really are, when
all you actually did was make a mistake.

Thoughts as Things

You take something that exists only in your head and you make it real. This, in turn,   14
leads to a form of mislabeling. You *think* you're being given all the bad jobs in the
office when in fact you are not.

Emotional Reasoning

Essentially, you think, "I feel it, therefore it must be true." For example, you feel   15
anxious, so you conclude that something terrible will happen to you.

Magnify-Minimize

You either exaggerate or downplay a situation, depending on your needs rather than   16
the reality. If you have a pimple, you may say it's skin cancer. Or you insult someone
and minimize the effect by saying, "I was only joking."

■

As you read about the twelve types of warped thought, did you recognize some of   17
your own? If so, you may be a victim of cognitive distortions. And as a result you
may be anxious, depressed, or puzzled over your emotional problems.

Dr. Aaron T. Beck, professor of psychiatry at the University of Pennsylvania,   18
identified many of these cognitive distortions. He says that unless cognitive distortions are caught early, they can mushroom.

"They are particularly deadly in marriage," Dr. Beck says. "You get a couple   19
who have a controversy about a minor point. Instead of seeking a common ground,
they begin to look at each other as adversaries and look at their differences.
The husband thinks the wife is just being 'hysterical'; the wife sees the husband
as 'tyrannical.' "

Then one or more of the dirty dozen will take over. First, the "every" distortion. 20
The wife—after one or two battles—thinks the husband is *always* tyrannical; the husband sees the wife as *always* hysterical. From then on, the relationship spirals downward.

Enter the second distortion: "poisoning the positive." When the wife cozies up 21
to the husband in an attempt to make up, the husband thinks: "She's manipulating me." And when he rejects her overture, she thinks: "He's trying to control me." And they are trapped.

People troubled by illogical thinking often need the help of a psychologist or 22
psychiatrist who is trained in recognizing cognitive distortions. The expert can point out illogical thinking and actually train a couple to think clearly.

You also can train yourself. The primary rule for clear thinking is to confront 23
your belief with *reality,* that is, with real evidence. For example, what are the real chances that something you do will end in catastrophe? How many catastrophes have you actually had? Are you really ugly? Or do you have nice features, such as eyes or hair?

Therapists often ask their clients to make lists of good or bad things about 24
themselves. This exercise shows patients that reality is different from their negative ideas. (Likewise, if you believe that nobody likes you, try writing down the names of people with whom you are friendly.)

Dr. Beck has shown that many depressed individuals owe their condition to 25
cognitive distortions. By removing the distortions, Dr. Beck and his colleagues say, they have been able to clear up depressive symptoms as effectively as drugs do.

In depressed patients, cognitive distortions foster a sense of worthlessness. 26
For example, the patient thinks, "If *everybody* hates me," or "if I am ugly" or "if *everything* I do is a catastrophe"—"then I must be worthless." A feeling of worthlessness often attacks nondepressed people who think this way too.

Dr. Albert Ellis of the Institute for Rational Emotive Therapy in New York City 27
thinks the tendency to distort is built into the human brain.

"When the human race was running through the jungle, thinking that a lion was 28
around the corner was not unreasonable," Dr. Ellis says lightheartedly. "Even if your perception was distorted—that is, there was no lion—you could live to run another day. Today, perceiving danger where there is none can be crippling."

Much illogical thinking, he says, also comes from copying the thinking style of 29
one's parents, teachers, and peers, many of whom may have been trapped by their own distortions.

Dr. Beck reports that, once your thinking is crooked, you will distort what you see 30
and hear and not know you've done so. As evidence, he videotaped confrontations between spouses. Later, he asked them to list the good things said. Couples in trouble could not list any. Yet when the videotape revealed otherwise, neither the husbands nor the wives could remember having heard anything positive. Such distorted perceptions reinforce our mental distortions.

Dr. Ellis says many of the distortions come from unrealistic needs to be totally 31
loved by everyone. Other unrealistic needs include: "I must be 100 percent right all the time." "I must have adoring, well-behaved children." "I must be fashionably dressed all the time." "Nobody matters but me."

The bottom line is that the outside world cannot *make* you feel bad. Unbelievable   32
as it sounds, it isn't the actual loss of money, fame, or loved ones that affects
your feelings. It is what you believe that counts.

Dr. Ellis cites the Roman philosopher Epictetus, who said: "What disturbs men's   33
minds is not events but their judgments on events."

■ Reading Comprehension Questions

1. Which of the following would be the best alternative title for this selection?
    a. Distorted Thinking
    b. Causes of Depression
    c. Reason versus Emotion
    d. How to Take a Compliment

2. Which sentence best expresses the article's main point?
    a. Marriages fail because spouses think in distorted ways.
    b. Most people cannot solve their emotional problems.
    c. Depressed people feel that they are complete failures.
    d. Illogical thinking is extremely common and causes problems in our
        relationships and moods.

3. Disbelieving a compliment that someone pays you is an example of
    which distortion?
    a. Mind reading
    b. Mislabeling
    c. Poisoning the positive
    d. No, no, no

4. One way to think realistically is to
    a. make lists of your good and bad points.
    b. imitate the thought processes of parents and peers.
    c. say,"I feel it, therefore it must be true."
    d. believe that you must be loved by everyone.

5. Thinking that a pimple means you have skin cancer is an example of
    which distortion?
    a. Catastrophizing
    b. Shoulds
    c. All or nothing
    d. Magnify-minimize

6. From the article, we can conclude that illogical thinkers
    a. are more creative than other people.
    b. are less intelligent than other people.
    c. are often less secure than other people.
    d. understand people's hidden motivations.

7. The author implies that many people who think illogically have
   a. few friends.
   b. poor images of themselves.
   c. unsatisfying jobs.
   d. poor health.

8. *True or false?* _____ The author implies that illogical thinkers tend to be female rather than male.

9. The word *undermines* in "poisoned thinking . . . undermines intimacy" (paragraph 6) means
   a. promotes.
   b. weakens.
   c. popularizes.
   d. quickens.

10. The word *foster* in "distortions foster a sense of worthlessness" (paragraph 26) means
   a. communicate.
   b. promote.
   c. resist.
   d. prevent.

■ Discussion Questions

About Content

1. Explain four common types of distorted thinking. Give examples of each, drawing on your own experience or your observation of others.

2. Who are the two authorities that Ubell cites in the article? According to these authorities, what are the reasons why people develop illogical thoughts?

3. How can a person help himself or herself overcome distorted thinking?

About Structure

4. What method of introduction does Ubell use in the essay?
   a. broad to narrow
   b. anecdote
   c. beginning with an opposite
   d. question

5. What two methods of development does Ubell use in the essay?
   a. comparing and contrasting
   b. dividing and classifying
   c. providing examples
   d. describing a person or event

6. Ubell finishes explaining the distortions in paragraph 16. What does he do in the remainder of the essay?
    a. narrates cases of distorted thinking
    b. discusses the effects and causes of distorted thinking
    c. warns the reader to change illogical thoughts
    d. summarizes the kinds of distorted thinking

About Style and Tone

7. In paragraph 3, Ubell tells us that the term *cognitive distortions* means the same as his term, the *dirty dozen of distorted thinking*. Find two other terms which he uses as synonyms for cognitive distortion. Write in the spaces below the terms and the paragraphs in which they appear:

    _____ (paragraph _____)

    _____ (paragraph _____)

8. Is this article directed toward a specialized audience of psychologists or toward a general audience? In which of the following publications do you think the article appeared?
    a. *Psychology Today*   c. *Parade Magazine*
    b. *Newsweek*   d. *Wall Street Journal*

■ Writing Assignments

Assignment 1: Writing a Paragraph

A writing assignment based on this selection is on page 179.

Assignment 2: Writing a Paragraph

Write a one-paragraph explanation of cognitive distortion, addressing your remarks to a friend at another college. Tell your friend that you've learned something new and important about how people's minds work, and that you want to share it. Then explain what cognitive distortion is in terms that your friend will understand. Include three examples of distorted thinking that you or other college students are prone to use. Be sure to describe them in a way that will be meaningful to your friend.

Assignment 3: Writing an Essay

Your friend Larry is going through an emotionally troublesome time. His parents are divorcing, and he worries that they would have stayed together if he had been a more obedient teenager who caused fewer arguments at home. He also worries that because he has failed his most recent math test, he is on the road to additional failures in other subjects and eventual suspension from college, despite his fairly decent study habits and his otherwise average grades. Finally, he thinks other students look down on him and that his girlfriend is staying with him only because she feels sorry for him.

Write an essay in which you describe how Larry can get over his emotional slump. In each of three supporting paragraphs, use the ideas presented by Ubell to explain the illogical thinking in one of Larry's three worries.

To begin, you will have to describe which three of the twelve cognitive distortions apply in Larry's situation. Then, in an introductory paragraph, mention Larry's worries and conclude with a thesis statement such as the following: "To feel better about his life, Larry might become aware of the three kinds of distorted thinking in his life: _____, _____, and _____."

HUMAN GROUPS AND SOCIETY

Television Changed My Family Forever

Linda Ellerbee

 We have all heard people complain that television is too violent, that too many programs are mediocre, and so on. But it can be argued that one of television's greatest disadvantages is simply that it takes "center stage" in our living rooms. One way to evaluate that argument is to consider what life was like before TV sets took their place in American homes. Television producer and writer Linda Ellerbee remembers well what life was like then—and what it was like after her family bought a television set. In this selection from her book *Move On*, she details some of the differences.

Santa Claus brought us a television for Christmas. See, said my parents, television doesn't eat people. Maybe not. But television changed people. Television changed my family forever. We stopped eating dinner at the dining-room table after my mother found out about TV trays. We kept the TV trays behind the kitchen door and served ourselves from pots on the stove. Setting and clearing the dining-room table used to be my job; now, setting and clearing meant unfolding and wiping out TV trays, then, when we'd finished, wiping and folding our TV trays. Dinner was served in time for one program and finished in time for another. During dinner we used to talk to one another. Now television talked to us. If you had something you absolutely had to say, you waited until the commercial, which is, I suspect, where I learned to speak in thirty-second bursts. As a future writer, it was good practice in editing my thoughts. As a little girl, it was lonely as hell. Once in a while, I'd pass our dining-room table and stop, thinking I heard our ghosts sitting around talking to one another, saying stuff.

1

Before television, I would lie in bed at night listening to my parents come   2
upstairs, enter their bedroom and say things to one another that I couldn't hear,
but it didn't matter, their voices rocked me to sleep. My first memory, the first one
ever, was of my parents and their friends talking me to sleep when we were living
in Bryan and my bedroom was right next to the kitchen. I was still in my crib then.
From the kitchen I could hear them, hear the rolling cadence of their speech, the
rising and falling of their voices and the sound of chips.

"Two pair showing."
"Call?"
"Check."
"Call?"
"Call." Clink.
"I raise." Clink. Clink.
"See your raise and raise you back." Clink clink clink.
"Call." Clink Clink.
"I'm in." Clink.
"I'm out."
"Let's see 'em."

It was a song to me, a lullaby. Now Daddy went to bed right after the weather   3
and Mama stayed up to see Jack Paar (later she stayed up to see Steve Allen and
Johnny Carson and even Joey Bishop, but not David Letterman). I went to sleep
alone, listening to voices in my memory.

Daddy stopped buying Perry Mason books. Perry was on television and that was   4
so much easier for him, Daddy said, because he could never remember which Perry
Mason books he'd read and was always buying the wrong ones by mistake, then
reading them all the way to the end before he realized he'd already read them.
Television fixed that, he said, because although the stories weren't as good as the
stories in the books, at least he knew he hadn't already read them. But it had been
Daddy and Perry who'd taught me how fine it could be to read something you liked
twice, especially if you didn't know the second time wasn't the first time. My mother
used to laugh at Daddy. She would never buy or read the same book again and
again. She had her own library card. She subscribed to magazines and belonged
to the Book-of-the-Month Club. Also, she hated mystery stories. Her favorite books
were about doctors who found God and women who found doctors. Her most favorite
book ever was *Gone with the Wind,* which she'd read before I was born. Read it
while she vacuumed the floor, she said. Read it while she'd ironed shirts. Read it
while she'd fixed dinner and read it while she'd washed up. Mama sure loved that
book. She dropped Book-of-the-Month after she discovered *As the World Turns.*
Later, she stopped her magazine subscriptions. Except for *TV Guide.* I don't know
what she did with her library card. I know what she didn't do with it.

Mom quit taking me to the movies about this time, not that she'd ever take   5
me to the movies very often after Mr. Disney let Bambi's mother get killed, which
she said showed a lack of imagination. She and Daddy stopped going to movies,

period. Daddy claimed it was because movies weren't as much fun after Martin broke up with Lewis, but that wasn't it. Most movies he cared about seeing would one day show up on television, he said. Maybe even Martin and Lewis movies. All you had to do was wait. And watch.

After a while, we didn't play baseball anymore, my daddy and me. We didn't go to baseball games together, either, but we watched more baseball than ever. That's how Daddy perfected The Art of Dozing to Baseball. He would sit down in his big chair, turn on the game and fall asleep within five minutes. That is, he appeared to be asleep. His eyes were shut. He snored. But if you shook him and said, Daddy, you're asleep, he'd open his eyes and tell you what the score was, who was up and what the pitcher ought to throw next. The Art of Dozing to Baseball. I've worked at it myself, but have never been able to get beyond waking up in time to see the instant replay. Daddy never needed instant replay and, no, I don't know how he did it; he was a talented man and he had his secrets.

Our lives began to seem centered around, and somehow measured by, television. My family believed in television. If it was on TV, it must be so. Calendars were tricky and church bells might fool you, but if you heard Ed Sullivan's voice you knew it was Sunday night. When four men in uniforms sang that they were the men from Texaco who worked from Maine to Mexico, you knew it was Tuesday night. Depending on which verse they were singing, you knew whether it was seven o'clock or eight o'clock on Tuesday night. It was the only night of the week I got to stay up until eight o'clock. My parents allowed this for purely patriotic reasons. If you didn't watch Uncle Milty on Tuesday nights, on Wednesday mornings you might have trouble persuading people you were a real American and not some commie pinko foreigner from Dallas. I wasn't crazy about Milton Berle, but I pretended I was; an extra hour is an extra hour, and if the best way to get your daddy's attention is to watch TV with him, then it was worth every joke Berle could steal.

Television was taking my parents away from me, not all the time, but enough, I believed. When it was on, they didn't see me, I thought. Take holidays. Although I was an only child, there were always grandparents, aunts, uncles, and cousins enough to fill the biggest holiday. They were the best times. White linen and old silver and pretty china. Platters of turkey and ham, bowls of cornbread dressing and sweet potatoes and ambrosia. Homemade rolls. Glass cake stands holding pineapple, coconut, angel food and devil's food cakes, all with good boiled icing. There was apple pie with cheese. There were little silver dishes with dividers for watermelon pickles, black olives, and sliced cranberry jelly. There was all the iced tea you'd ever want. Lord, it was grand. We kids always finished first (we weren't one of those families where they make the kids eat last and you never get a drumstick). After we ate, we'd be excused to go outside, where we'd play. When we decided the grown-ups had spent enough time sitting around the table after they'd already finished eating, which was real boring, we'd go back in and make as much noise as we could, until finally four or five grown-ups would come outside and play with us because it was just easier, that's all. We played hide-and-seek or baseball or football or dodge ball. Sometimes we just played ball. Sometimes we just played. Once in a while, there would be fireworks, which were always exciting ever since the Christmas Uncle Buck shot off a Roman candle and set the neighbor's yard on fire, but that was before we had a television.

Now, holiday dinners began to be timed to accommodate the kickoff, or once   9
in a while the halftime, depending on how many games there were to watch; but
on Thanksgiving or New Year's there were always games so important they absolutely
could not be missed under any circumstances, certainly not for something as inconsequential as being "it" and counting to ten while you pretended not to see six
children climb into the backseat of your car.

> "Ssshhh, not now, Linda Jane. The Aggies have the ball."
> "But you said . . . you promised . . . . "
> "Linda Jane, didn't your daddy just tell you to hush up? We can't hear the television for
> you talking."

■ Reading Comprehension Questions

1. Which of the following would be the best alternative title for this selection?
   a. The Effects of Television on Children
   b. How Television Hurt My Childhood
   c. Television and Reading
   d. Advantages and Disadvantages of Television

2. Which sentence best expresses the main idea of the selection?
   a. After they bought a television set, Ellerbee's parents stopped reading.
   b. The Ellerbees enjoyed a wide variety of television shows.
   c. Holidays at the Ellerbee household were centered on television.
   d. Television changed Ellerbee's family for the worse.

3. Although Ellerbee and her father were baseball fans, after they got a television set they
   a. no longer attended baseball games.
   b. refused to watch baseball on TV.
   c. began to watch Milton Berle instead of baseball.
   d. preferred football to baseball.

4. Ellerbee says she may have learned to edit her thoughts and speak quickly because
   a. the mystery books she read taught her to communicate rapidly.
   b. she often gave short reports on baseball games to her father.
   c. her parents thought children should spend more time reading than talking.
   d. she was allowed to speak freely only during television commercials.

5. After the author's parents bought a TV set, holiday dinners were
   a. no longer fancy meals.
   b. timed according to the football games being broadcast.
   c. delayed until the children were finished playing outside.
   d. times when the children and adults enjoyed lingering at the table together.

6. In paragraph 4, the author implies that
   a. her mother was silly for liking *Gone with the Wind.*
   b. television had tempted her mother away from an activity she had once loved.
   c. her mother often reread books about doctors.
   d. book clubs are a poor source for good books.

7. Ellerbee implies that
   a. her parents bought a TV set in order to spend less time talking together.
   b. television's effects on her family must have been unusual.
   c. once her family had a TV set, her parents paid too little attention to her.
   d. good television shows bring adults and children closer together.

8. Ellerbee implies that television made her family more
   a. efficient.
   b. inactive.
   c. close.
   d. energetic.

9. The word *inconsequential* in "on Thanksgiving or New Year's there were always games so important they absolutely could not be missed . . . , certainly not for something as inconsequential as being 'it'" (paragraph 9) means
   a. unimportant.
   b. serious.
   c. noisy.
   d. physically demanding.

10. The word *cadence* in "From the kitchen I could . . . hear the rolling cadence of their speech, the rising and falling of their voices and the sound of chips. 'Two pair showing.' 'Call?' 'Check.' 'Call?' 'Call.' Clink" (paragraph 2) means
    a. loud anger.
    b. distance.
    c. silence.
    d. rhythmic flow.

■ Discussion Questions

About Content

1. How did television change the Ellerbee family's lives?
2. The reader can learn quite a bit about Ellerbee's parents from the descriptions in her essay. What kind of person do you think Ellerbee's father was? Her mother? Give evidence from the reading to support your points.
3. Ellerbee writes, "Our lives began to seem centered around, and somehow measured by, television" (paragraph 7). In what ways was that so? When, if ever, do you center your life on television?

4. We often think of television as something that children watch too much of, but Ellerbee writes that it was her parents who watched too much TV. As a result, television made Ellerbee's childhood lonely. How might her parents have spent more active time with her without giving up television altogether? What activities did you and your parents share? If you have children, what activities do you and they share?

About Structure

5. "Television Changed My Family Forever" is basically a list of ways in which TV changed the author's family. After the introduction, for instance, paragraph 1 is about how TV changed the Ellerbees' dinnertime. Paragraphs 2–3 are about how TV changed her parents' interaction with each other and with their friends. Below, write what paragraphs 4, 5, and 6 are about.

Paragraph 4 is about _____

Paragraph 5 is about _____

Paragraph 6 is about _____

6. In discussing the changes television made in her life, Ellerbee contrasts what her life was like without television and what her life was like with television. Which two time words does she use in paragraphs 2–3 to contrast those two time periods? Write those words here:

_____   _____

About Style and Tone

7. Irony is an inconsistency between what might be expected to happen and what really happens. How does Ellerbee use irony in the very first sentence of her essay?

8. Ellerbee concludes her essay with some dialogue. How does this dialogue support her thesis?

▪ Writing Assignments

Assignment 1: Writing a Paragraph

Ellerbee writes, "Television was taking my parents away from me." Write a paragraph in which you describe at least three ways parents can make a special effort to spend active time with their children. You can include ways that are suggested by Ellerbee's essay (such as sitting around the table at dinnertime), or any other way that appeals to you, or both.

Assignment 2: Writing a Paragraph

Although Ellerbee's mother and father were once eager readers, they stopped reading when they bought a television set. Unfortunately, watching television has replaced reading in many households. Write a paragraph in which you discuss several ways reading might be encouraged among adults and children.

Assignment 3: Writing an Essay

Ellerbee points out some of the ways in which television can interfere with family communication. However, many people defend television, citing educational children's programs and inexpensive entertainment among its benefits. Make a list of the benefits you see in television. Then write an essay in which you defend television by citing several of its most important benefits. For each positive point you list, explain why it is beneficial and include one or more examples.

Alternatively, you can write an essay in which you criticize television. In preparation, list the disadvantages you see in television. Choose at least three of the most persuasive disadvantages to use in your essay. For each negative point you list, explain why it is a disadvantage and include one or more examples.

The Steel Magnolias

Beth Johnson Ruth

 If you think actresses conform to a type, you'll be pleasantly surprised by the selection that follows. Having watched six film stars swap confidences on a talk show, Beth Johnson Ruth describes striking differences among them. She also describes the sharp contrast between the outward appearance and inner nature of some of these women. Whether you think of yourself as outgoing or shy, you're sure to identify with one of these intriguing personalities and to be fascinated by them all.

Recently, viewers of *The Oprah Winfrey Show* had the opportunity of sitting in on   1
Winfrey's fascinating conversation with six remarkable women: the stars of the
movie *The Steel Magnolias.*

While *Magnolias* garnered only so-so reviews, the film did succeed in bringing together a dazzling cast of top female talent: Sally Field, Julia Roberts, Shirley MacLaine, Dolly Parton, Daryl Hannah, and Olympia Dukakis. Watching these women act and interact in an hour of informal conversation gave the viewer a sense of what made each of them tick. Deliberately or not, the actresses' strengths and weaknesses were on display.

As the interview began, the viewer's attention was drawn to the couch on which sat MacLaine, looking drawn and intense; Roberts, radiating her gorgeous, healthy young animal vitality; and Sally Field. Field was a polished adult version of the perky brunette who grew up before America's eyes as Gidget and the Flying Nun and then went on to win two Oscars. In *Magnolias,* she portrays her "oldest" role, that of the mother of a young bride, Julia Roberts.

Perhaps it is the experience of growing up in the public eye that gives Field her apparently limitless affinity for the camera. She assumed the role of spokeswoman for the group, promptly volunteering lengthy answers to many of Oprah's questions. As she perched there in her blue jeans and casual blazer, her endearingly round chipmunk cheeks, scrubbed all-American good looks, and shiny swinging hair made her appear nearly as youthful and innocent as in her Gidget days. With a childlike self-absorption, she gave a heartfelt account of the anguish she experienced while playing the mother of the dying Roberts. She described, too, the "constant pain" and lack of security she feels in her life and career. Her words were reminiscent of an adolescent who is just discovering her own identity and who feels driven to examine publicly her every thought and emotion. And while the viewer began to feel exasperated at Field's endless stream of talk, it seemed evident that her tendency to self-examination has helped make her the fine actress she is. It is impossible to imagine Field giving herself less than fully to a role, or playing a "quickie" part just for some cash. Judging from her appearance on *Oprah,* when you get Sally Field, you get *all* of Sally Field.

Sitting next to Field on the couch was her film "daughter," young Julia Roberts—earthy, tomboyish, gorgeous, and likeable. Everything about Roberts seems just slightly larger than life. Her endless legs, clad in embroidered blue jeans, were tucked up under her as she sat tailor-fashion on the couch. She continually played with the curling red-brown hair that fell below her shoulders, shoving fistfuls of it atop her head and letting it go again. Her outsize mouth and explosive laughter added to the impression that here was an extrovert who lives life to the full. Stroking MacLaine's back in a moment of compassion, gripping Field's hand as her "mother" described Roberts' funeral scene in the film, tossing a humorous one-liner into the discussion when it needed perking up, Roberts exuded the confidence of a healthy, happy young woman who drives all the boys crazy and is poised optimistically on the brink of a successful career.

Next came Shirley MacLaine, looking her fifty-plus years, except for her nineteen-year-old legs, well exposed under a short green skirt. Her wispy cap of vivid orange hair emphasized the chalk-whiteness of her face. Beside the vibrant Roberts, MacLaine seemed inner-directed, almost withdrawn. Unlike Roberts' or Field's animated remarks and silly jokes, MacLaine's comments were quiet and serious. Her much-publicized otherworldliness was evident in her remarks about working on a movie that was all "feminine energy," or her citing of the somewhat bewildering Oriental advice to "be a bamboo." Like Field, she appears to be deeply involved in self-exploration, but her inward journey seems to have lent her a serenity the younger actress lacks.

Moving around the room, the viewer's eye was next caught by Dolly Parton, who would be hard to miss in any crowd. As usual, she was decked out in an elaborate wig of blond ringlets, false eyelashes, and bright red lips; her absurdly tiny body with its comic-book breasts was packed into a low-cut sequined black dress. Her remark to Oprah that she is "the phoniest-looking person you'll ever meet, but one of the realest people you'll ever know," was revealing. Phony-looking she is indeed, but Miss Dolly seems to have absolutely no questions about who she is inside. Looking Oprah in the eye, she spoke in no-nonsense terms about her own "gentleness," "toughness," and "sensitivity." In contrast to Field's angst-ridden monologues and MacLaine's New Age pronouncements, Parton seemed firmly grounded in the here and now, glad for her success and not about to mess it up through too much navel-gazing. She listened patiently enough to the others' self-exploration, but demonstrated what seemed to be a genuine kindness as well as a distaste for whining by breaking into one of Field's soliloquies to turn Oprah's attention to Daryl Hannah, who had been sitting mutely throughout the interview. Praising "this beautiful sex symbol who was willing to play a nerd" (in *Steel Magnolias*), Parton skillfully brought the apparently very shy woman into the conversation.

Hannah was almost unrecognizable in her dowdy man's T-shirt and baggy black vest, her hair pulled back untidily. Curled up in semifetal position in her chair and scratching herself vigorously through the interview, Hannah shrank from the camera's attention. Her eyes downcast, Hannah admitted in a stumbling monotone what was already evident from her manner: she far prefers playing a role than "being herself." She called the role of a mousy dweeb in *Magnolias* a "great comfort," particularly enjoying the fact that people had failed to recognize her on the set. As Hannah's discomfort at being the center of attention grew, Olympia Dukakis, Parton, and MacLaine all rushed to support her in kind and diplomatic ways, pointing out that Hannah was born to be a character actress rather than, as Hannah said herself, "some sort of ornament." "Being herself," said Dukakis, is a problem for shy Hannah not because she has no self, but because "she has so many selves. . . . That's the richness."

Dukakis said almost as little as Hannah throughout the hour, but the impression she left was not of a shy person but of a sensible woman satisfied to let the others have her share of the spotlight. Handsome in a purple cowl-necked sweater that contrasted with her short white hair, Dukakis generally limited her remarks to praise of the other actresses' performances. She seemed bemused by the discussion of the "pain" of being a creative artist, adding that while she is always concerned about getting a good part and doing her best work, she doesn't understand that pain. Plainly she is a hard-working actress who enjoys her job and doesn't feel in tune with self-aggrandizing "movie star" talk.

Despite their many differences, it was evident throughout the program that 10 these six actresses had thoroughly enjoyed working together and have remained friends. The experience of making *Steel Magnolias* sounded like a combination slumber party and family gathering of several months' duration, and each of the women spoke of the experience with tremendous fondness and some regret that it is over. Their various strengths and weaknesses seem to have intertwined in a way that buoyed up each of them, producing an environment where each felt a genuine freedom and comfort in the company of the others.

■ Reading Comprehension Questions

1. Which of the following would be the best alternative title for this selection?
   a. *The Oprah Winfrey Show*
   b. A Conversation with Six Actresses
   c. Young and Middle-Aged Actresses
   d. *Steel Magnolias*, the Movie

2. Which sentence best expresses the main idea of the selection?
   a. You can learn a lot about people on talk shows.
   b. Sally Field, Roberts' mother in *Steel Magnolias,* was spokeswoman for the group of actresses.
   c. A talk show reveals that the stars of *Steel Magnolias* are six remarkable and different women who worked well together.
   d. Though it didn't get great reviews, *Steel Magnolias* is worth seeing because of its six talented female actresses.

3. According to the selection,
   a. Sally Field was shy about speaking up.
   b. Daryl Hannah prefers character parts.
   c. Dolly Parton is confused about who she is.
   d. Olympia Dukakis finds acting painful.

4. The author found Daryl Hannah to be
   a. vain.
   b. plain-looking.
   c. shy.
   d. competitive.

5. According to the author, Olympia Dukakis
   a. is sensible.
   b. likes to talk about herself.
   c. dislikes the spotlight.
   d. is very shy.

6. In paragraph 4, the author implies that Sally Field
   a. acted better than the others.
   b. is wealthier than the others.
   c. is not very wholesome.
   d. talked too much.

7. The author implies that the actresses are friends because they
   a. are alike.
   b. will do another movie together.
   c. grew to like each other on the set.
   d. had fun together on the *Oprah Winfrey Show.*

8. *True or false?* _____ The author implies that the actresses have been insensitive to each other's needs.

9. The word *exuded* in "Roberts exuded the confidence of a healthy, happy young woman who drives all the boys crazy" (paragraph 5) means
   a. hid.
   b. judged.
   c. gave off.
   d. denied.

10. The word *mutely* in "Daryl Hannah . . . had been sitting mutely throughout the interview . . . Parton skillfully brought [her] . . . into the conversation" (paragraph 7) means
   a. noisily.
   b. straight.
   c. silently.
   d. questioning.

■ **Discussion Questions**

About Content

1. Why do you think there is such a contrast between Dolly Parton's "phony" appearance and her open, direct personality?

2. On the basis of the descriptions that Ruth provides, which of the six actresses do you most admire—and why?

3. As the author suggests, acting holds different attractions for different people. Keeping Ruth's piece in mind, what do you think might be some of these reasons?

About Structure

4. The author uses a few space signals to add coherence to her description. Find two such signals and write them (with their paragraph numbers) in the spaces below:

_____ (paragraph _____)

_____ (paragraph _____)

5. By having her conclusion echo the introduction, the author adds unity to her article. Which paragraphs make up her introduction? What in the introduction is echoed in the conclusion?

6. Ruth writes in her conclusion that there are "many differences" among the six actresses. What support does she offer throughout the article for this statement about differences?

About Style and Tone

7. The author's descriptions often reveal her largely sympathetic, admiring attitude toward the actresses. For example, Ruth's admiration of Roberts' energy and looks is clear in her description of the actress as "radiating" a "gorgeous, healthy young animal vitality" (paragraph 3). Find two other examples of words or phrases that reveal the author's opinion and write them (and their paragraph numbers) in the spaces below:

_____ (paragraph _____)

_____ (paragraph _____)

8. The author uses descriptions of "body language" to reveal something of Roberts' and Hannah's personalities. Find one such description and write it (and its paragraph number) in the spaces below:

_____ (paragraph _____)

■ **Writing Assignments**

Assignment 1: Writing a Paragraph

A writing assignment based on this selection is on page 189.

Assignment 2: Writing a Paragraph

Dolly Parton described herself to Oprah Winfrey as the "phoniest-looking person you'll ever meet, but one of the realest people you'll ever know." Daryl Hannah has an on-screen image as a sex symbol, but in real life she's painfully shy. Clearly, appearances can be at odds with personality. Write a paragraph about someone whose appearance at first fooled you (or someone else). Describe the person's appearance in some detail and contrast it with what you discovered to be the person's underlying character. Like Ruth, use quotations and descriptions of clothing, looks, posture, and movements to support your general statements.

Assignment 3: Writing an Essay

For Sally Field, the value of a particular role may include teaching her something about herself. Think of some "role" you have played—coach, baby-sitter, cashier, girlfriend or boyfriend, or even sympathetic listener. What did you learn about yourself from the experience? Write an essay in which you explain three specific things you learned about yourself from a particular activity or relationship.

Following is an example of a possible thesis statement and a plan of development:

> As a Little League coach, I learned a lot about myself. I learned that I have patience, that I have a talent for encouraging young people, and that I enjoy working with them.

As you plan your essay, think of interesting, persuasive examples for each of your supporting paragraphs. For example, a paragraph about having patience might narrate two or three annoying incidents during games in which you could have lost your temper but instead handled the situation coolly. A paragraph on encouraging young people might explain how you motivated your team and helped a discouraged player feel better about himself or herself.

People Need People

S. Leonard Syme

"People who need people," says the song, "are the luckiest people in the world." Recent studies indicate that they are also among the healthiest. We don't know exactly why strong family and community ties should help the body's immune system fight disease, but the evidence is growing rapidly that they do. In the following article, written for *American Health* magazine, a medical doctor prescribes friendship as the key to a long and healthy life.

1   Between 1970 and 1980, according to the latest United States census, the number of men living alone rose 92.3 percent; the figure for women went up 50.6 percent. Loneliness is apparently becoming a more common aspect of American life, and this may have serious effects on health and well-being.

2   It's long been known, for example, that widowers and widows do not live as long as married men and women. Several investigators, including my own group at the University of California, Berkeley, have been attempting to study this issue in more detail.

3   The latest research has gone beyond the traditional measures of loneliness—such as marital status—to look at the more subtle influence of social networks on health. So far, this work suggests that a society that fosters connectedness to others—such as traditional Japanese society—may be healthier, in a real sense, than a culture as individualistic as our own.

4   A colleague of mine, Lisa Berkman, Ph.D., did a study that shows how all kinds of people can suffer physically from a lack of social support. In 1974 she examined the records of seven thousand people in Alameda County, California, who had been randomly chosen for interviews about their lives and social relationships a decade earlier.

5   Berkman was able to classify these people in terms of their social support networks, ranging from the relatively isolated to those who were extensively involved with others. She then went to the state health department and examined the death rates in this group over nine years. Sure enough, those who were more isolated had death rates two to three times higher during this period than those with more extensive social ties. The more such ties, the lower the death rate. This finding was true for both sexes and all ages, social classes, and races. Further, the findings were independent of such other factors as smoking, alcohol consumption, physical activity, obesity, eating patterns, and use of health services.

Our first thought was that those who were more isolated were sick already and 6
that was the reason they had a higher death rate. But we could find no evidence
that this was true. While I was convinced that prior ill health did not explain the
findings, I nevertheless was anxious for some more supportive evidence. Just a few
months ago that confirmation came through. Data are now in from a ten-year study
at the University of Michigan that followed 2,754 adults in Tecumseh, Michigan,
and asked the question, "Does the social network affect physical health?"

The researchers, James House, Ph.D., and his colleagues, carefully measured 7
the participants' health at the beginning of the study to rule out the possibility that
people might become isolated because they were already sick. They then looked
at their subjects' personal relationships and group activities—and their health—
for a decade. The result: those with the least social contacts had two to four times
the mortality rate of the well-connected.

The Surprising Japanese: Urban, Stressed—and Healthy

Consider these findings along with our research on Japanese immigrants. It is 8
said that many of our health problems are traceable to such modern evils as
industrialization, pollution, and so on. Japan, however, offers a striking exception.
It is highly industrialized, has a high level of technology, is one of the most urbanized
nations in the world, and suffers from urban pollution that is at least equal to ours.
Cigarette smoking and high blood pressure are also common in Japan. And if you've
visited their large cities, you know the pace of life is at least as frantic as ours.

Yet Japan now has the highest life expectancy in the world, with one of the 9
lowest reported rates of heart disease. Why?

The easiest explanation would be that the Japanese have a favorable genetic 10
makeup. This is plausible, but the evidence does not entirely support this idea.
Instead, something about their life-style seems to hold the key. When Japanese
move to California, those who adopt Western ways exhibit a disease pattern very
much like that of other Westerners. Those who retain Japanese ways have lower
disease rates, as if they were still in Japan. Because Hawaii is not as Westernized
as California, Japanese there generally remained healthier than those on the main-
land—though not as healthy as those in Japan.

We did a study of twelve thousand Japanese men, some in the San Francisco 11
Bay Area, some in Hawaii, and some in the southwestern area of Japan, from which
most of the Japanese immigrants came. My colleague Michael Marmot, Ph.D., found
very low rates of heart disease among Japanese in the Bay Area who grew up in
Japanese neighborhoods, whose childhood friends were Japanese, who attended
Japanese-language schools in addition to English-language schools, and who returned to Japan for more schooling. He also found low disease rates among those
who, as adults, kept their ties to the Japanese community.

In contrast, those Japanese who became Westernized—both as children and   12
as adults—had coronary heart disease rates five times higher, even after we had
taken into account the usual risk factors of diet, serum cholesterol, smoking, and
blood pressure. The Japanese who retained their community ties—and their health—
often ate Western foods, had high serum cholesterol levels, smoked cigarettes,
and had high blood pressure. It is possible that their intimate community bonds
protected them.

It is one thing to talk about staying involved with the Japanese community. It   13
is another to explain precisely what this means. I now believe that the special
characteristic of Japanese culture is the importance of social ties and social
supports.

To the Japanese one's very identity is bound up with one's group. In Western   14
society individualism is far more predominant. The American hero is the cowboy
who stands alone and follows his convictions no matter what others think and no
matter what the cost. John F. Kennedy's book *Profiles in Courage* tells the stories
of eight American public figures who stood up for their beliefs, even though others
thought they were wrong and tried to pressure them to change their minds. A
Japanese colleague told me that in Japan these heroes would be considered mentally ill.

In Japan, people often go through school with the same friends, graduate   15
together, and work together in the same company for much of their lives. They value
their social networks so highly that, whenever possible, employers try to move work
groups together. The famous Quality Control Circle, considered the key to Japan's
incredible productivity, is a stable working team.

Why Moss Can Be Beautiful

Another important feature of Japanese life is the concept of the native place—a   16
place you come from and a place to which you will return after you retire. You *can*
go home again. It is a place to which you return all your life and where people know
you and keep track of you.

How many Americans have a native place? Perhaps the simplest way to describe   17
the difference in the Japanese and American approaches to life is in terms of the
Japanese saying, "A rolling stone gathers no moss." Since moss is a beautiful and
treasured thing, a stone without moss is not much of a stone. To acquire moss,
you must have the patience to stay put.

In the United States this saying is meant in exactly the opposite way—it's best   18
to keep moving on, so that moss doesn't dirty your slick surface. Moss is a sure
sign that you're not a go-getter.

But moving on breaks old ties and exacts a high cost. From these studies it   19
seems that, for reasons not yet understood, people with more stable social bonds
have better health than those who are more isolated. Social ties seem to buffer us
from the effects of disease risk factors.

Disease rates go up with certain changes in life—particularly events that cause   20
social disruption, such as the death of a spouse or some other loved one, job
changes, loss of a job, and moving. When social ties are interrupted or broken, the
rates of many diseases rise: coronary heart disease, cancer, arthritis, strokes,
accidents, mental illness, upper respiratory ailments, infections of wisdom teeth,
and so on. Since the effects are so wide-ranging, it seems that interrupted social
ties affect the body's defense systems, so that a person becomes more susceptible
to a number of conditions. The particular disease one gets may be tied to such
specific risk factors as serum cholesterol, blood pressure, smoking, viruses, and
air pollution.

What we are seeing, in effect, is that loneliness is a health hazard. The idea   21
is not a new one, but the data have never been as persuasive as they are now.
The evidence forces us to look for positive ways to fight loneliness—and illness.

Yes, married people have lower rates of disease than those who are widowed,   22
divorced, or single. We cannot explain this in terms of clear physical differences—
in age, weight, physical activity, or standard heart disease risk factors—between
the single and the wed.

Even owning a pet—an easy remedy for loneliness—can have an effect on   23
health. Pet owners, according to one study, have better survival rates after heart
attacks than those who don't own an animal.

Hard Times Make Fast Friends

Human companionship can be more important than comfort, safety, or affluence in   24
determining the quality of a person's life. For years people have told me that the
best times in their lives were when they were involved closely with others. And it
does not seem to matter whether the situation was pleasant or miserable.

Linda Nilson, Ph.D., a sociologist at UCLA, reports that residents in communities   25
struck by natural disasters (tornadoes, hurricanes, floods, earthquakes) do *not*
panic, loot, and suffer psychological breakdowns. They generally keep their heads,
care for one another, share scarce resources, and reach an emotional high as they
pull together to face the common challenges of survival and rebuilding.

Many people actually feel better about themselves and their neighbors, she   26
adds, after going through a disaster. They are proud of the way they handled the
crisis and touched by the generosity of others, and they look on their part in the
common recovery effort as the most meaningful work of their lives. Nilson notes
that in no case on record in the United States have authorities had to declare
martial law in a natural disaster area—and she has analyzed more than one hundred
reports of responses to such disasters over the past sixty years.

■

Well, what shall we make of all this? What are the practical implications for how   27
we live our lives to preserve our health? Exhortations to "be friendly" or "smile"
won't be enough, and neither will singing forty choruses of "Up with People." But
it should certainly be possible to make it easier for people to work together and be
together if they choose to.

Educational campaigns should not just teach people to look for the seven signs 28 of cancer, but also give them information they can use to make healthy decisions for themselves and their families: Is this move necessary? What are the real costs of this promotion? What groups can I join that will share my interests and generate intellectual and social excitement?

More and more, people are coming together voluntarily to support one another, 29 almost in opposition to social and institutional trends. The results achieved by self-help groups, such as Alcoholics Anonymous and Gamblers Anonymous, are impressive; so are those of the support groups for people in particular situations, such as those recovering from cancer operations, going through divorce, or moving to a new city. It seems that, whatever the self-help group's philosophy, being in a group is itself therapeutic.

All of us could learn from these examples. But it shouldn't take a common 30 problem like alcoholism or gambling—or a natural disaster—to draw people together. We need to recognize the importance of community, of touching other people, in our daily existence. Our health, our lives, may depend on it.

■ Reading Comprehension Questions

1. Which of the following would be the best alternative title for this selection?
   a. Living Longer in the United States
   b. The Value of Human Companionship
   c. The Self-Help Group
   d. Aging in Japanese Society

2. Which sentence best expresses the main idea of the selection?
   a. Many of our health problems are caused by industrialization and pollution.
   b. People live longer when they have good social contacts.
   c. The Japanese have a genetic makeup that helps them live longer.
   d. Disease rates increase when people make changes in their lives.

3. Researchers found that people in areas hit by natural disasters
   a. helped each other.
   b. panicked immediately.
   c. usually resorted to looting.
   d. often isolated themselves from other people.

4. *True or false?* _____ Married people have lower rates of disease than those who are widowed, divorced, or single.

5. People who live alone
   a. are usually unemployed, divorced women.
   b. have lower serum cholesterol levels.
   c. have higher death rates.
   d. eat and smoke more than married people.

6. The author implies that
   a. a person's health does not suffer because he or she has few social contacts.
   b. sickness isolates people from other people.
   c. in Japan, the individual's rights are not as important as the group's.
   d. cigarette smoking and high blood pressures are uncommon in Japan.

7. The author implies that
   a. Japan has less pollution and industrialization than the United States.
   b. the pace of life is slower in Japan than in the United States.
   c. Hawaii's climate is healthier for the Japanese than Japan's climate.
   d. the Japanese do not consider the American cowboy as their kind of hero.

8. *True or false?* _____ The author implies that many Americans do not have the concept of a native place.

9. The word *buffer* in "Social ties seem to buffer us from ... disease risk factors" (paragraph 19) means
   a. free.
   b. weaken.
   c. frighten.
   d. protect.

10. The word *therapeutic* in "being in a group is itself therapeutic" (paragraph 29) means
    a. necessary.
    b. harmful.
    c. healing.
    d. unusual.

■ Discussion Questions

About Content

1. What characteristics of Japanese society prevent loneliness?

2. Why do disasters and hard times cause people to "reach an emotional high" (paragraph 25)? Why do many people feel better about each other after such times?

3. Do you think that college students generally have a strong sense of connectedness to others? When do you feel most lonely? What techniques have you learned to combat this feeling?

About Structure

4. Besides paragraph 1, locate two other paragraphs where the author uses statistics to make a point:

    _____   _____

5. Find three change-of-direction signals used in paragraphs 8–12 and write them below:

    _____

    _____

    _____

6. This essay contrasts American isolation with the Japanese sense of community. In paragraphs 8 to 18, does Syme use mainly a point-by-point or a one-side-at-a-time contrast?

About Style and Tone

7. Why does Syme use questions to begin the concluding section of the essay (paragraphs 27–30)? What is his persuasive purpose in his concluding paragraphs?

8. For what audience might this essay have been intended: scholars, psychologists, teachers, students, or the general public? How can you tell?

■ Writing Assignments

Assignment 1: Writing a Paragraph

A writing assignment based on this selection is on page 164.

Assignment 2: Writing a Paragraph

The Japanese have a concept of "native place," a place where each person is from and where he or she feels truly at home. In a less formal way, most of us also have a place where we feel "at home." We can turn to such a place to replenish ourselves and restore our peace of mind. In a paragraph, identify your special place and describe it in detail. Your topic sentence might read "_____ is a special place where I feel relaxed and at home." Use only those details that add to the dominant impression of comfort and ease.

Assignment 3: Writing an Essay

While Americans may not often belong to large, stable communities, our personal relationships can keep us from feeling isolated. What do you especially value about the people who are close to you? You may prefer such time-honored qualities as loyalty and openness. You may also delight in more unusual traits, like a wacky sense of humor, a shared interest in an unusual pastime, or a love of friendly arguments. Examine your friends and families to determine which aspects of their personalities you particularly enjoy. Then write an essay describing three of the qualities you most appreciate in your personal relationships.

Remember to list in your thesis statement the three qualities you select. Each characteristic, in turn, will provide the subject for one of your three topic sentences. Use examples from your friends, your family, or both to support your topic sentences.

Here is one student's outline for this essay.

Thesis: Three of the qualities I most appreciate in my personal relationships are shared interests, honesty, and a sense of humor.

Topic sentence 1: Sharing special interests with my friends and family has been one source of great pleasure for me.
a. My friend Jon and I have listened to rock music together for years.
b. My father and I love going to baseball games together.
c. Lately, a couple of friends and I have enjoyed discussing Stephen King's books.

Topic sentence 2: I also highly value honesty in my personal relationships.
a. I know I can count on my sister to give me honest evaluations of outfits I wear.
b. I hope that my friends will speak about their true preferences for how to spend an evening.
c. I am pleased that my good friends and my family do not agree with my opinions just to be polite.

Topic sentence 3: Finally, I especially value humor in my personal relationships.
a. I like to be able to laugh with my friends after a hard day of work.
b. I look forward to my friend Nelson's practical jokes.
c. My sister and I are better friends than we would be if we could not tease each other.

What It Means to Be Young Today

Vance Packard

The childhood years, we have been told, are the golden years—filled with play and innocent happiness, free of worry or adult responsibility. Not so, says Vance Packard, in the following chapter from his book *Our Endangered Children*. Packard suggests that an increasing number of today's children are living lives fraught with fear and loneliness. And he feels that many of today's adults are doing little or nothing to reverse this trend.

Children today are confronting some modern forms of damnation. What are the forms? Who are the children? 1

Millions of children are barely involved at all. They are being well raised in stimulating, concerned communities. Perhaps they have stresses, lots of them. But they enjoy their parents. Life is an engrossing, frequently delightful experience. 2

For more millions, however, life in much of the Western world provides a scarcity of delights for youngsters and many blighting and bruising experiences. For the *majority* of today's children, being young may mean the following things, among others. 3

Wondering if your parents are going to split—or, if they have, living in a one-parent home. The rise in the breakup of homes in the past dozen years has been stunningly swift by historical standards. Largely as a result, nearly half the children born in the last few years will spend a portion of their lives living in a one-parent household before reaching age eighteen, according to projections based on figures from the United States Bureau of the Census. This assumes that present trends in marital disruption (and illegitimacy) continue. 4

At many American elementary schools more than 40 percent of the students come from disrupted homes. In such situations a youngster, after listening to classmates from such homes, may start wondering and worrying, even though his or her own mom and dad seem to be getting along OK. 5

A girl at a Lexington, Massachusetts, school recalled what it was like as the split-up of her parents began: "You hear your parents fighting about you all the time. I had to watch my parents fight over the dumbest little things. It makes you feel really guilty. It makes you feel bad, very small, and inferior." 6

Approximately a third of all American youngsters no longer live with both their natural parents. The historian Christopher Lasch suggests that "the absence of the father impresses many observers as the most striking fact about the contemporary family." 7

Being lonely a lot of the time. There are many indicators of a new loneliness   8
among children. The new sprawling metropolitan areas tend to be antichild. It is
hard to find decent places to play; the child learns: You have to be wary of strangers.
You are likely to be alone a lot at home or feel alone at school (vast school facilities
discourage intimacy; if you live in a high-rise, fewer friends visit you; if you are one
of the twelve million youngsters who now move every year, you have to wait for
overtures of friendship from new neighbors and classmates who are appraising you).

I have met children of corporate nomads who by the age of eleven have moved   9
nine times, often to distant places. A mother in Darien, Connecticut, where many
corporate families move in and out every year, told me of the traumatic effect their
latest move had on their shy fourteen-year-old daughter. She had reached the age
where being in a peer group and dating had suddenly become very important. This
girl went to the refrigerator and gained forty pounds within a year. An assistant
school principal in Darien commented: "We often see a newcomer looking lonely
and miserable."

Seeing a lot of "No Children" signs on apartment houses while on your way   10
to school. Nationwide, a large majority of all apartment house owners now put
restrictions of some kind on tenants who have children. Often it is an outright ban.
In several major cities children are banned from almost all the nice new apartment
complexes being built. Youngsters are learning early how it feels to be a liability to
their parents.

Some of the signs on apartment buildings indicate that pets are acceptable   11
but not children. Many children sent away to boarding school know that one reason
is that it was the only way their parents could keep their home in an apartment or
condominium.

If you are small, having a strong possibility of being left every weekday with   12
some kind of caretaker (or caretakers), usually outside your home. A large number
of preschool children today have mothers who at some point will take outside jobs.
Presently, at least a fourth of American infants and toddlers under age three have
mothers who hold down some sort of an outside job; among all preschoolers, the
mothers of almost half have jobs.

As mothers have surged into the labor force—a 200 percent increase in twelve   13
years—American society is still fumbling with the challenge of ensuring good care
for their children. Only beginnings are being made by employers to provide flexible
arrangements to ease the new difficulties of parenting. There are no licensed facilities available for three-quarters of the children whose mothers work.

The result is that quite a few million children today are being shortchanged on   14
good care in their early years. Many, in fact, are placed in what are essentially
warehouses for children—from eight to ten hours a day.

Being home a lot in an empty house. It is estimated that about twenty thousand   15
small children under the age of six stay in the home all day alone, usually with a
television set left on. Their desperate working mothers haven't been able to make
any other arrangement. A Chicago boy, age three, was found making his own lunch.
The main problem was climbing up on chairs to get to cabinet doors.

After school, the number of young school-age children home alone soars. In 16
the United States there are by conservative estimates two million "latchkey" children. The YMCA puts the figure closer to ten million. Most let themselves into empty
homes with their own key, sometimes hung around their necks. Many hate it.

In State College, Pennsylvania, a community organization became concerned 17
because increasing numbers of elementary school children had to fend for themselves in an empty house after school. The group set up a "Phone Friend" service
to act as a mother's assistant in providing information and advice. It receives about
thirty to forty calls a week from children. The overwhelming proportion of the calls,
according to a Penn State University professor, Louise Guerney, are "because of
loneliness and fear—usually from noises or because parents, sitters, or older sibs
fail to arrive home when expected."

Another Penn State specialist in human development, James Garbarino, says 18
we have been seeing "a general emptying of the social environment of children."

Having little real contact with adults. Most of the adults on a child's block go 19
away to a kind of work he or she only vaguely understands. There is little chance
to work alongside interesting adults on interesting projects.

A study by Herbert Wright and associates at the University of Kansas found 20
that children growing up where there is a real community, as in a small town, get
to know *well* a considerably greater number of adults in various walks of life than
do their urban age-mates. And they are more apt to be active participants in the
adult settings.

Children today even have less interactive contact with their own parents, who, 21
on average, spend less time in the home area than they did previously. One study
of fathers found they typically spent less than a minute a day in warm, close
interaction with their infant children.

Feeling you are a burden and being given few ways to make yourself useful. 22
A youngster knows that the reason for living in a crummy neighborhood is so that
he and his sister can each have a separate bedroom. In most of the urban United
States the cost of a three-bedroom home in a good neighborhood is beyond the
means of the typical family. Youngsters wonder if they will be able to go to college
because already it would cost nearly a third of the family income. In many millions
of families the only way offered for youngsters to demonstrate responsibility is to
do nonproductive maintenance chores around the house.

More traditional societies have usually viewed children as treasured assets. 23

Living in a neighborhood that makes you apprehensive. The Foundation for 24
Child Development, in a nationwide survey of 2,300 youngsters aged seven to
eleven, reported that its "most disturbing discovery" was the high level of apprehen-
siveness among the children. More than two-thirds said they felt afraid "that somebody might get into their home." And a quarter of the children said "yes" to the
question "When you go outside, are you afraid someone might hurt you?"

Some of the apprehension might be based on a generalized anxiety about life,   25
aggravated in many cases by watching too much violence on television. But most
of the youngsters could report disturbing experiences. About a fourth of them lived
in areas where crime was commonplace or where "undesirable" people were likely
to be on the streets or in the parks and playgrounds.

Adjusting to newcomers in your home. If Mom has gone through divorce, it   26
means that in a matter of months new men will probably be coming into the house.
One who becomes special may leave around dawn, or stay for breakfast. In most
cases both parents will eventually remarry. About one youngster in eight now has
a parent who is not a biological parent. For a child, the parents' remarrying can
become confusing.

Rutgers behaviorist Lionel Tiger vividly put it this way: 27

*Many people are married to people who have been married to other people who are now
married to still others to whom the first partners may not have been married but to
whom somebody has likely been married.*

In that scramble, where are the child's two natural parents? We have been   28
seeing a breaking up and regrouping of parental affiliations unprecedented in history.

Eating a lot of food that has been left for you—or food you must go out and   29
get at some fast-food place. Eating together has been called the oldest human
ritual. The tradition of families eating their meals at home together around a table
and discussing the triumphs and problems of the day is a long one in many countries.
Now such family dining is becoming a fading custom in the United States.

First the family lunch disappeared as members began traveling beyond their   30
neighborhood for work or school. Then the family breakfast disappeared as everyone,
including mother, became in a hurry to depart on differing schedules. Now only a
minority of families eat a supper together around a table at home. About half of all
parents who still eat supper with their children do so in a darkened room eating off
trays grouped around the television set, according to a communications study made
at the University of Pennsylvania. The food has often been brought in from nearby
fast-food outlets in paper containers. If family members arrive home at different
hours, the child may eat alone, often in front of the TV set in his or her own room.

Having most of the talk you hear come from machines rather than from people   31
you know. In one generation the circumstances of growing up in the United States
have been profoundly changed by television and radio.

Millions of young children are put down in front of television, the great baby-   32
sitter and pacifier, and left there for hours at a stretch. Mary Jo Bane, a Harvard
authority on children, states: "Television is by far the most important new child-
care arrangement of this century." Preschool children—most of them unable to
distinguish commercials from programming—listen to the TV voices nearly four
hours a day. Older youngsters, despite time spent at school, spend almost as many
hours watching TV. In addition, those over ten years old hear, for about two hours
a day, voices—often throbbing or raucous voices—coming from their radios or tape
decks. Often these voices are coming at them as they do homework.

Often coping with parents who are pretty self-absorbed, or uncertain about 33
their proper role in life. The noted polling firm headed by Daniel Yankelovich made a study of the changing American family. Its principal finding was that a "new breed" of parent was emerging, much less family-oriented than traditionally. It found 43 percent of the parents surveyed to be of this new breed. They put self-fulfillment over worldly success and duty to self over duty to others, including their own children. In effect they say to their children: "I want to be free, so why shouldn't you children be free? We will not sacrifice for you, because we have our own life to lead. But when you are grown, you owe us nothing."

Many employed mothers of small children relish the work experience. And both 34
parents appreciate the extra income. Still, many such mothers are torn emotionally. They wonder if they are short-changing their children on nurturance. Many young fathers, too, are confused about their changing role. They know that with their wife working they should be pitching in as a partner in child and household care. They espouse the egalitarian ideal, but often do more talking than acting.

■

I have noted in a dozen different ways what it is likely to mean to be young today. 35
And I could go on.

These meanings add up to a new kind of adversity for millions of children. They 36
promote a sense of insecurity that may lie behind a seemingly cheerful countenance. They often add up to a poor foundation for adult life.

Many of these new kinds of stresses and possible blighting factors can be 37
counteracted by wise parenting and good community situations. But these meanings of being young today do present a challenge to parents and to our society.

■ Reading Comprehension Questions

1. Which of the following would be the best alternative title for this selection?
   a. Warning: Childhood in Danger
   b. Today's Children
   c. The Threat of Divorce
   d. The Problems of Working Parents

2. Which sentence best summarizes the article's main point?
   a. Working mothers disrupt family stability.
   b. American families cannot cope with divorce.
   c. Our society does not value children enough.
   d. Children are more sophisticated than they used to be.

3. A "latchkey child" is a child who
   a. is home alone all day.
   b. cannot be trusted with a house key.
   c. comes home to an empty house.
   d. lives in an unsafe neighborhood.

4. According to one study, many fathers spent less than _____ a day in close interactions with their infants.
   a. one minute
   b. a half hour
   c. one hour
   d. two hours

5. According to the article, perhaps the most important child-care arrangement of this century is
   a. the licensed day-care facility.
   b. extended school hours.
   c. the paid baby-sitter.
   d. television.

6. Who or what does Packard imply is mainly to blame for stresses on children?
   a. "modern" experts on child-raising
   b. parents
   c. teachers
   d. television

7. The author implies that unhappy childhood years can
   a. prepare people to be better parents.
   b. result in adult criminal behavior.
   c. make a person not want to have any children.
   d. have harmful long-term emotional effects.

8. The article suggests that family togetherness improves when members
   a. eat meals together.
   b. watch TV together.
   c. move to a new home.
   d. have a lot of company.

9. The word *appraising* in "you have to wait for overtures of friendship from new neighbors and classmates who are appraising you" (paragraph 8) means
   a. criticizing.
   b. rejecting.
   c. welcoming.
   d. evaluating.

10. The word *adversity* in "These meanings add up to a new kind of adversity for millions of children" (paragraph 36) means
    a. opportunity.
    b. fantasy.
    c. situation.
    d. hardship.

■ **Discussion Questions**

About Content

1. How are many of today's children cut off from other children? How are they isolated from their parents and from other meaningful adults?
2. What fears beset a number of children today, according to Packard? Are all these fears realistic, do you think, or are some of them childish exaggerations?
3. What is the "new breed" of parents like, as Packard describes them? Do you agree that they are likely to be poor parents?
4. Packard suggests that many children today are very unhappy because of the twelve stresses he outlines. Do you agree with his point of view, or do you think that he is being overly negative?

About Structure

5. Packard has sequenced his twelve criticisms of children's lives today in a random order. If they had been arranged in order of importance, which three do you think might be considered least important? Which three might be considered most important?
6. To support his points, Packard provides several kinds of evidence. Which of the following is the only evidence he does *not* use?
   a. statistics
   b. research studies
   c. opinions of authorities
   d. his own childhood experiences
7. Analyze the two-paragraph section on "Eating a lot of food . . ." (paragraphs 29–30). What is the topic sentence for these two paragraphs? What are three time signals that Packard uses to develop his idea?

   Topic sentence: _____

   _____

   Time signals: _____   _____   _____

About Style and Tone

8. Packard conveys his strongly negative attitude by using some judgmental words and phrases. For example, in paragraph 14, he calls day-care centers "warehouses for children." Find two other places where he uses such judgments, and write the words below:

   _____   _____

■ Writing Assignments

Assignment 1: Writing a Paragraph

A writing assignment based on this selection is on page 135.

Assignment 2: Writing a Paragraph

Suppose that you are a counselor in an elementary school. A child has been referred to you because of one of the problems in "What It Means to Be Young Today." Select one of the problems from the article that you are especially interested in, and make up a detailed list of possible solutions to the problem. Then write a paragraph in which you suggest three of these solutions to the child's parent or parents. Be specific about what the parents can and should do and why.

Typical topic sentences might be:

Although you work full time, there are several actions you can take to cut down on the time Karen spends at home alone.

There are several important ways you can help Elena adjust to not having her father at home anymore.

You may be able to calm Michael's fears about your new neighborhood in one or more of the following ways.

Assignment 3: Writing an Essay

As a child, did you experience some of the problems Vance Packard describes? Or, if you are a parent, have your own children encountered some of these problems? Write an essay describing how three of those problems affected your growing up or how they are affecting your children's growing up. You may also want to describe how your family was or was not successful in dealing with the problems.

In your introductory paragraph, you might use a thesis statement similar to one of the following:

After my parents divorced, my life changed in three important ways: (*list the changes you will discuss in the next three paragraphs*).

When my wife went back to work full time, we had to deal with the following problems: (*list the three problems you will discuss*).

As my sister and I grew up, my parents eliminated some of the worst effects of television by making us eat at the kitchen table, by limiting our TV hours, and by providing us with alternative activities.

Before starting your essay, you should read over the guidelines on essay writing presented on pages 207–228.

Will You Go Out with Me?

Laura Ullman

If you are a man, have you ever been asked out on a date by a woman? If you are a woman, do you feel that you have to wait for a man to ask you out? And once a date is set, do you wonder who should pay? Previous generations of daters had few choices—the man asked, and the man paid. And dates were often formal, up-tight events. Today, the rules of dating are more flexible, but has that made dating easier? In this article from *Newsweek,* a college student, Laura Ullman, shares some of her thoughts on playing the new dating game.

1   Every day I anxiously wait for you to get to class. I can't wait for us to smile at each other and say good morning. Some days, when you arrive only seconds before the lecture begins, I'm incredibly impatient. Instead of reading the *Daily Cal,* I anticipate your footsteps from behind and listen for your voice. Today is one of your late days. But I don't mind, because after a month of desperately desiring to ask you out, today I'm going to. Encourage me, because letting you know I like you seems as risky to me as skydiving into the sea.

2   I know that dating has changed dramatically in the past few years, and for many women, asking men out is not at all daring. But I was raised in a traditional European household where simply the thought of my asking you out spells naughty. Growing up, I learned that men call, ask, and pay for the date. During my three years at Berkeley, I have learned otherwise. Many Berkeley women have brightened their social lives by taking the initiative with men. My girlfriends insist that it's essential for women to participate more in the dating process. "I can't sit around and wait anymore," my former roommate once blurted out. "Hard as it is, I have to ask guys out—if I want to date at all!" Wonderful. More women are inviting men out, and men say they are delighted, often relieved, that dating no longer solely depends on their willingness and courage to take the first step. Then why am I digging my nails into my hand trying to muster up courage?

3   I keep telling myself to relax, since dating is less stereotypical and more casual today. A college date means anything from studying together to sex. Most of my peers prefer casual dating anyway because it's cheaper and more comfortable. Students have fewer anxiety attacks when they ask somebody to play tennis than when they plan a formal dinner date. They enjoy last-minute "let's make dinner together" dates because they not only avoid hassling with attire and transportation but also don't have time to agonize.

4   Casual dating also encourages people to form healthy friendships prior to starting relationships. My roommate and her boyfriend were friends for four months before their chemistries clicked. They went to movies and meals and often got together with mutual friends. They alternated paying the dinner check. "He was like a girlfriend," my roommate once laughed—blushing. Men and women relax and get to know each other more easily through such friendships. Another friend of mine believes that casual dating is improving people's social lives. When she wants to let a guy know she is interested, she'll say, "Hey, let's go get a yogurt."

Who pays for it? My past dates have taught me some things: you don't know   5
if I'll get the wrong idea if you treat me for dinner, and I don't know if I'll deny you
pleasure or offend you by insisting on paying for myself. John whipped out his wallet
on our first date before I could suggest we go Dutch. During our after-dinner stroll
he told me he was interested in dating me on a steady basis. After I explained I
was more interested in a friendship, he told me he would have understood had I
paid for my dinner. "I've practically stopped treating women on dates," he said
defensively. "It's safer and more comfortable when we each pay for ourselves."
John had assumed that because I graciously accepted his treat, I was in love. He
was mad at himself for treating me, and I regretted allowing him to.

Larry, on the other hand, blushed when I offered to pay for my meal on our first   6
date. I unzipped my purse and flung out my wallet, and he looked at me as if I had
addressed him in a foreign language. Hesitant, I asked politely, "How much do I
owe you?" Larry muttered, "Uh, uh, you really don't owe me anything, but if you
insist . . ." Insist, I thought, I only offered. To Larry, my gesture was a suggestion
of rejection.

Men and women alike are confused about who should ask whom out and   7
who should pay. While I treasure my femininity, adore gentlemen, and delight in a
traditional formal date, I also believe in equality. I am grateful for casual dating
because it has improved my social life immensely by making me an active participant
in the process. Now I can not only receive roses but can also give them. Casual
dating is a worthwhile adventure because it works. No magic formula guarantees
"he" will say yes. I just have to relax, be Laura, and ask him out in an unthreatening
manner. If my friends are right, he'll be flattered.

Sliding into his desk, he taps my shoulder and says, "Hi, Laura, what's up?"   8

"Good morning," I answer with nervous chills. "Hey, how would you like to have   9
lunch after class on Friday?"

"You mean after the midterm?" he says encouragingly. "I'd love to go to lunch   10
with you."

"We have a date," I smile.   11

■ Reading Comprehension Questions

1. Which of the following would be the best alternative title for this selection?
   a. Relations between Men and Women
   b. Dating: Who Pays?
   c. The Risks of Dating
   d. Modern Dating—A Casual Approach

2. Which sentence best expresses the article's main point?
   a. Asking men out is hard for traditional women.
   b. Casual dating may improve people's social lives.
   c. While today's casual dating style is confusing, it has great advantages.
   d. Men and women are confused about who should pay for dates and why.

3. The author's peers prefer casual dating because it is
   a. less confusing than formal dating.
   b. cheaper and more comfortable.
   c. more likely to leap quickly to deep romance.
   d. all of the above.

4. Which sentence best expresses the main idea of paragraphs 5 and 6?
   a. Ullman has no luck with men.
   b. Dating requires taking risks.
   c. Casual dating can still cause confusion and misunderstanding.
   d. Casual dating is to be preferred over formal dating.

5. *True or false?* _____ The author enjoys going on a traditional formal date.

6. We can conclude that the main reason it takes courage to ask someone out is the
   a. expense of a date.
   b. risk of rejection.
   c. risk of offending traditional parents.
   d. possibility that the person may misinterpret your intentions.

7. The author implies that *both* John and Larry
   a. were hurt by Laura's behavior.
   b. preferred that Laura always pay her share.
   c. felt men should always pay for a woman's dinner.
   d. saw paying for dinner as an indication of a serious commitment.

8. The author implies that her classmate responded to her invitation to go to lunch
   a. as if he had expected it.
   b. with obvious embarrassment.
   c. exactly as she hoped he would.
   d. with guilt that he had not asked her out first.

9. The word *initiative* in "Many Berkeley women have brightened their social lives by taking the initiative with men" (paragraph 2) means
   a. romance.
   b. first step.
   c. a ride.
   d. shy approach.

10. The words *muster up* in "Then why am I digging my nails into my hand trying to muster up courage?" (paragraph 2) mean
    a. avoid.
    b. gather.
    c. believe.
    d. twist.

■ Discussion Questions

About Content

1. According to Ullman, what do young people prefer about a casual date as contrasted with a formal dinner date? And what do they like about last-minute dates?

2. From a woman's point of view, what advantages are there to being able to ask a man out?

3. The author claims that "for many women, asking men out is not at all daring." Why then do you think *she* is so nervous about inviting a young man for a date? Do any of the young women you know ask men out on dates? If so, what have their experiences been like?

4. "Casual dating," writes Ullman, ". . . encourages people to form healthy friendships prior to starting relationships" (paragraph 4). What do you think she means by "healthy friendships"? Do you agree with this view of casual dating?

About Structure

5. To whom does the author address her first paragraph? Do you think this approach helps make her essay more effective or less effective? Why?

6. What is the relationship between the first two paragraphs and the last paragraph? How does that relationship add to the essay?

About Style and Tone

7. Ullman emphasizes her points and enlivens her essay by being generous with examples. Below, cite one of her examples and explain what general point it illustrates.

_____

_____

_____

_____

_____

_____

_____

8. In paragraph 5, Ullman uses time signals to clarify the narrative. Find three time signals in that paragraph, and write them here:

_____

_____

_____

■ Writing Assignments

Assignment 1: Writing a Paragraph

When, if ever, should a woman pay her own way on a date? Express your opinion in a paragraph that begins with one of the following topic sentences:

A woman should never pay her own way on a date.

There are some occasions when a woman should pay her own way on a date.

A woman should always pay her own way on a date.

If you choose the first or third topic sentence, develop your paragraph with two or three reasons that support your opinion. If you choose the second topic sentence, support it by discussing two or three occasions on which it would be appropriate for a woman to pay her own way.

Assignment 2: Writing a Paragraph

Ullman's problem of getting up the courage to ask someone out is common among both men and women. If you've experienced this kind of hesitation and uncertainty, explain how you tried to overcome your anxiety and make your move.

An alternative is to explain how you tried to solve another typical dating problem. Here are a few examples of problems you might want to write about:

Setting down rules (sexual, social, or otherwise) that both of you can live with

Asking your partner to change inappropriate behavior

Telling your partner you want more out of the relationship

Explaining that you'd also like to date others

Getting out of a relationship

Coping with the end of a relationship

State the problem in an opening sentence and then go on to develop and detail your solution in the rest of the paragraph.

Assignment 3: Writing an Essay

Ullman writes, "Casual dating . . . encourages people to form healthy friendships prior to starting relationships." What's your idea of a "healthy friendship"? Think about the nature of strong friendships you've enjoyed, and find several qualities that made them especially important to you. Then write an essay in which you describe three of those qualities. To clarify and enliven your writing, include a generous number of examples based on people you know. Your thesis statement will be similar to this one: "My idea of a healthy friendship includes three special qualities: _____, _____, and _____." (The list of qualities will show your plan of development.)

Here are some qualities you may wish to consider:

Having interests similar to your own
Ability to accept your faults as well as your good points
Willingness to be helpful at times of need
Having the interest and patience to be a good listener
Having your best interests at heart
Willingness to share (cash, a car, food) when necessary

Alternatively, consider the qualities that can characterize an *unhealthy* friendship. Using examples drawn from your own experience or your observation of other people's relationships, write an essay in which you describe three qualities of an unhealthy friendship. Use a thesis statement similar to this one: "There are three qualities that warn me that a friendship is unhealthy: _____, _____, and _____." (The list of qualities will show your plan of development.)

These are some qualities you might consider for your essay:

Insistence on agreement on all matters
Tendency for one person to do all or most of the emotional giving
Tendency for one person to make all or most of the financial decisions
Unwillingness to share problems
Inability to "be oneself" in the relationship
Need to exclude other people from the relationship
Encouragement of unhealthy or harmful behavior

A Drunken Ride, a Tragic Aftermath

Theresa Conroy and Christine M. Johnson

 Have you ever sat behind the wheel of your car after drinking? Have you ever assured yourself, "I haven't had too much. I'm still in control"? If you have, you're not alone. The large number of arrests for drunk driving proves that plenty of drivers who have been drinking thought they were capable of getting home safely. After all, who would get into a car with the intention of killing himself or herself or others? Yet killing is exactly what many drunk drivers do. If all drivers could read the following selection— a newspaper report on one tragic accident—perhaps the frequent cautions about drinking and driving would have some impact. Read the article and see if you agree.

When Tyson Baxter awoke after that drunken, tragic night—with a bloodied head, broken arm, and battered face—he knew that he had killed his friends. 1

"I knew everyone had died," Baxter, eighteen, recalled. "I knew it before anybody told me. Somehow, I knew." 2

Baxter was talking about the night of Friday, September 13, the night he and seven friends piled into his Chevrolet Blazer after a beer-drinking party. On Street Road in Upper Southampton, he lost control, rear-ended a car, and smashed into two telephone poles. The Blazer's cab top shattered, and the truck spun several times, ejecting all but one passenger. 3

Four young men were killed. 4

Tests would show that Baxter and the four youths who died were legally intoxicated. 5

Baxter says he thinks about his dead friends on many sleepless nights at the Abraxas Drug and Alcohol Rehabilitation Center near Pittsburgh, where, on December 20, he was sentenced to be held after being found delinquent on charges of vehicular homicide. 6

"I drove them where they wanted to go, and I was responsible for their lives," Baxter said recently from the center, where he is undergoing psychological treatment. "I had the keys in my hand, and I blew it." 7

The story of September 13 is a story about the kind of horrors that drinking and driving is spawning among high school students almost everywhere, . . . about parents who lost their children in a flash and have filled the emptiness with hatred, . . . about a youth whose life is burdened with grief and guilt because he happened to be behind the wheel. 8

It is a story that the Baxter family and the dead boys' parents agreed to tell in the hope that it would inspire high school students to remain sober during this week of graduation festivities—a week that customarily includes a ritual night of drunkenness.   9

It is a story of the times.   10

■

The evening of September 13 began in high spirits as Baxter, behind the wheel of his gold Blazer, picked up seven high school chums for a drinking party for William Tennent High School students and graduates at the home of a classmate. Using false identification, according to police, the boys purchased one six-pack of beer each from a Warminster Township bar.   11

The unchaperoned party, attended by about fifty teenagers, ended about 10:30 P.M. when someone knocked over and broke a glass china cabinet. Baxter and his friends decided to head for a fast-food restaurant. As Baxter turned onto Street Road, he was trailed by a line of cars carrying other partygoers.   12

Baxter recalled that several passengers were swaying and rocking the high-suspension vehicle. Police were unable to determine the vehicle's exact speed, but, on the basis of the accounts of witnesses, they estimated it at fifty-five miles per hour—ten miles per hour over the limit.   13

"I thought I was in control," Baxter said. "I wasn't driving like a nut; I was just . . . driving. There was a bunch of noise, just a bunch of noise. The truck was really bouncing.   14

"I remember passing two [cars]. That's the last I remember. I remember a big flash, and that's it."   15

Killed in that flash were: Morris "Marty" Freedenberg, sixteen, who landed near a telephone pole about thirty feet from the truck, his face ripped from his skull; Robert Schweiss, eighteen, a Bucks County Community College student, whose internal organs were crushed when he hit the pavement about thirty feet from the truck; Brian Ball, seventeen, who landed near Schweiss, his six-foot-seven-inch frame stretched three inches when his spine was severed; and Christopher Avram, seventeen, a premedical student at Temple University, who landed near the curb about ten feet from the truck.   16

Michael Serratore, eighteen, was thrown fifteen feet from the truck and landed on the lawn of the CHI Institute with his right leg shattered. Baxter, who sailed about ten feet after crashing through the windshield of the Blazer, lost consciousness after hitting the street near the center lane. About five yards away, Paul Gee Jr., eighteen, lapsed into a coma from severe head injuries.   17

John Gahan, seventeen, the only passenger left in the Blazer, suffered a broken ankle.   18

Brett Walker, seventeen, one of several Tennent students who saw the carnage after the accident, would recall later in a speech to fellow students: "I ran over [to the scene]. These were the kids I would go out with every weekend.   19

"My one friend [Freedenberg], I couldn't even tell it was him except for his eyes. He had real big, blue eyes. He was torn apart so bad. . . ."   20

■

Francis Schweiss was waiting up for his son, Robert, when he received a telephone call from his daughter, Lisa. She was already at Warminster General Hospital.   21

"She said Robbie and his friends were in a bad accident and Robbie was not here" at the hospital, Schweiss said. "I got in my car with my wife; we went to the scene of the accident."   22

There, police officers told Francis and Frances Schweiss that several boys had been killed and that the bodies, as well as survivors, had been taken to Warminster General Hospital.   23

"My head was frying by then," Francis Schweiss said. "I can't even describe it. I almost knew the worst was to be. I felt as though I were living a nightmare. I thought, 'I'll wake up. This just can't be.'"   24

In the emergency room, Francis Schweiss recalled, nurses and doctors were scrambling to aid the injured and identify the dead—a difficult task because some bodies were disfigured and because all the boys had been carrying fake drivers' licenses.   25

A police officer from Upper Southampton was trying to question friends of the dead and injured—many of whom were sobbing and screaming—in an attempt to match clothing with identities.   26

■

When the phone rang in the Freedenberg home, Robert Sr. and his wife, Bobbi, had just gone upstairs to bed; their son Robert Jr. was downstairs watching a movie on television.   27

Bobbi Freedenberg and her son picked up the receiver at the same time. It was from Warminster General. . . . There had been a bad accident. . . . The family should get to the hospital quickly.   28

Outside the morgue about twenty minutes later, a deputy county coroner told Rob Jr., twenty-two, that his brother was dead and severely disfigured; Rob decided to spare his parents additional grief by identifying the body himself.   29

Freedenberg was led into a cinderblock room containing large drawers resembling filing cabinets. In one of the drawers was his brother, Marty, identifiable only by his new high-top sneakers.   30

"It was kind of like being taken through a nightmare," Rob Jr. said. "That's something I think about every night before I go to sleep. That's hell. . . . That whole night is what hell is all about for me."   31

■

As was his custom, Morris Ball started calling the parents of his son's friends after Brian missed his 11:00 P.M. curfew.   32

The first call was to the Baxters' house, where the Baxters' sixteen-year-old daughter, Amber, told him about the accident.   33

At the hospital, Morris Ball demanded that doctors and nurses take him to his son. The hospital staff had been unable to identify Brian—until Ball told them that his son wore size fourteen shoes.   34

Brian Ball was in the morgue. Lower left drawer.   35

"He was six foot seven, but after the accident he measured six foot ten, because 36
of what happened to him," Ball said. "He had a severed spinal cord at the neck.
His buttocks were practically ripped off, but he was lying down and we couldn't see
that. He was peaceful and asleep.

"He was my son and my baby. I just can't believe it sometimes. I still can't 37
believe it. I still wait for him to come home."

∎

Lynne Pancoast had just finished watching the 11:00 P.M. news and was curled up 38
in her bed dozing with a book in her lap when the doorbell rang. She assumed that
one of her sons had forgotten his key, and she went downstairs to let him in.

A police light was flashing through the window and reflecting against her living 39
room wall; Pancoast thought that there must be a fire in the neighborhood and that
the police were evacuating homes.

Instead, police officers told her there had been a serious accident involving 40
her son, Christopher Avram, and that she should go to the emergency room at
Warminster General.

At the hospital she was taken to an empty room and told that her son was dead. 41

∎

Patricia Baxter was asleep when a Warminster police officer came to the house and 42
informed her that her son had been in an accident.

At the hospital, she could not immediately recognize her own son lying on a 43
bed in the emergency room. His brown eyes were swollen shut, and his straight
brown hair was matted with blood that had poured from a deep gash in his forehead.

While she was staring at his battered face, a police officer rushed into the room 44
and pushed her onto the floor—protection against the hysterical father of a dead
youth who was racing through the halls, proclaiming that he had a gun and shouting,
"Where is she? I'm going to kill her. I'm going to kill him. I'm going to kill his mother."

The man, who did not have a gun, was subdued by a Warminster police officer 45
and was not charged.

Amid the commotion, Robert Baxter, a Lower Southampton highway patrol offi- 46
cer, arrived at the hospital and found his wife and son.

"When he came into the room, he kept going like this," Patricia Baxter said, 47
holding up four fingers. At first, she said, she did not understand that her husband
was signaling that four boys had been killed in the accident.

After Tyson regained consciousness, his father told him about the deaths. 48

"All I can remember is just tensing up and just saying something," Tyson Baxter 49
said. "I can remember saying, 'I know.'

"I can remember going nuts." 50

∎

In the days after the accident, as the dead were buried in services that Tyson Baxter 51
was barred by the parents of the victims from attending, Baxter's parents waited
for him to react to the tragedy and release his grief.

"In the hospital he was nonresponsive," Patricia Baxter said. "He was home 52
for a month, and he was nonresponsive.

"We never used to do this, but we would be upstairs and listen to see if Ty responded when his friends came to visit," she said. "But the boy would be silent. That's the grief that I felt. The other kids showed a reaction. My son didn't." 53

Baxter said, however, that he felt grief from the first, that he would cry in the quiet darkness of his hospital room and, later, alone in the darkness of his bedroom. During the day, he said, he blocked his emotions. 54

"It was *just* at night. I thought about it all the time. It's still like that." 55

At his parents' urging, Baxter returned to school on September 30. 56

"I don't remember a thing," he said of his return. "I just remember walking around. I didn't say anything to anybody. It didn't really sink in." 57

Lynne Pancoast, the mother of Chris Avram, thought it was wrong for Baxter to be in school, and wrong that her other son, Joel, a junior at William Tennent, had to walk through the school halls and pass the boy who "killed his brother." 58

Morris Ball said he was appalled that Baxter "went to a football game while my son lay buried in a grave." 59

Some William Tennent students said they were uncertain about how they should treat Baxter. Several said they went out of their way to treat him normally, others said they tried to avoid him, and others declined to be interviewed on the subject. 60

The tragedy unified the senior class, according to the school principal, Kenneth Kastle. He said that after the accident, many students who were friends of the victims joined the school's Students Against Driving Drunk chapter. 61

Matthew Weintraub, seventeen, a basketball player who witnessed the bloody accident scene, wrote to President Reagan and detailed the grief among the student body. He said, however, that he experienced a catharsis after reading the letter at a student assembly and, as a result, did not mail it. 62

"And after we got over the initial shock of the news, we felt as though we owed somebody something," Weintraub wrote. "It could have been us and maybe we could have stopped it, and now it's too late. . . ." 63

"We took these impressions with us as we then visited our friends who had been lucky enough to live. One of them was responsible for the accident; he was the driver. He would forever hold the deaths of four young men on his conscience. Compared with our own feelings of guilt, [we] could not begin to fathom this boy's emotions. He looked as if he had a heavy weight upon his head and it would remain there forever." 64

About three weeks after the accident, Senator H. Craig Lewis (D., Bucks) launched a series of public forums to formulate bills targeting underage drinking. Proposals developed through the meetings include outlawing alcohol ads on radio and television, requiring police to notify parents of underage drinkers, and creating a tamperproof driver's license. 65

The parents of players on William Tennent's 1985–1986 boys' basketball team, which lost Ball and Baxter because of the accident, formed the Caring Parents of William Tennent High School Students to help dissuade students from drinking. 66

Several William Tennent students, interviewed on the condition that their names not be published, said that, because of the accident, they would not drive after drinking during senior week, which will be held in Wildwood, N.J., after graduation June 13. 67

But they scoffed at the suggestion that they curtail their drinking during the celebrations.   68

"We just walk [after driving to Wildwood]," said one youth. "Stagger is more like it."   69

"What else are we going to do, go out roller skating?" an eighteen-year-old student asked.   70

"You telling us we're not going to drink?" one boy asked. "We're going to drink very heavily. I want to come home retarded. That's senior week. I'm going to drink every day. Everybody's going to drink every day."   71

■

Tyson Baxter sat at the front table of the Bucks County courtroom on December 20, his arm in a sling, his head lowered and his eyes dry. He faced twenty counts of vehicular homicide, four counts of involuntary manslaughter, and two counts of driving under the influence of alcohol.   72

Patricia Ball said she told the closed hearing that "it was Tyson Baxter who killed our son. They used the car as a weapon. We know they killed our children as if it were a gun. They killed our son."   73

"I really could have felt justice [was served] if Tyson Baxter was the only one who died in that car," she said in an interview, "because he didn't take care of our boys."   74

Police officers testified before Bucks County President Judge Isaac S. Garb that tests revealed that the blood-alcohol levels of Baxter and the four dead boys were above the 0.10 percent limit used in Pennsylvania to establish intoxication.   75

Baxter's blood-alcohol level was 0.14 percent, Ball's 0.19 percent, Schweiss's 0.11 percent, Avram's 0.12 percent, and Freedenberg's 0.38 percent. Baxter's level indicated that he had had eight or nine drinks—enough to cause abnormal bodily functions such as exaggerated gestures and to impair his mental faculties, according to the police report.   76

After the case was presented, Garb invited family members of the dead teens to speak.   77

In a nine-page statement, Bobbi Freedenberg urged Garb to render a decision that would "punish, rehabilitate, and deter others from this act."   78

The parents asked Garb to give Baxter the maximum sentence, to prohibit him from graduating, and to incarcerate him before Christmas day. (Although he will not attend formal ceremonies, Baxter will receive a diploma from William Tennent this week.)   79

After hearing from the parents, Garb called Baxter to the stand.   80

"I just said that all I could say was, 'I'm sorry; I know I'm totally responsible for what happened,' " Baxter recalled. "It wasn't long, but it was to the point."   81

Garb found Baxter delinquent and sentenced him to a stay at Abraxas Rehabilitation Center—for an unspecified period beginning December 23—and community service upon his return. Baxter's driver's license was suspended by the judge for an unspecified period, and he was placed under Garb's jurisdiction until age twenty-one.   82

Baxter is one of fifty-two Pennsylvania youths found responsible for fatal drunken-   83
driving accidents in the state in 1985.

Reflecting on the hearing, Morris Ball said there was no legal punishment that   84
would have satisfied his longings.

"They can't bring my son back," he said, "and they can't kill Tyson Baxter."   85

■

Grief has forged friendships among the dead boys' parents, all of whom blame   86
Tyson Baxter for their sons' death. Every month they meet at each other's homes,
but they seldom talk about the accident.

Several have joined support groups to help them deal with their losses. Some   87
said they feel comfortable only with other parents whose children are dead.

Bobbi Freedenberg said her attitude had worsened with the passage of time.   88
"It seems as if it just gets harder," she said. "It seems to get worse."

Freedenberg, Schweiss, and Pancoast said they talk publicly about their sons'   89
deaths in hopes that the experience will help deter other teenagers from drunken
driving.

Schweiss speaks each month to the Warminster Youth Aid Panel—a group of   90
teenagers who, through drug use, alcohol abuse, or minor offenses, have run afoul
of the law.

"When I talk to the teens, I bring a picture of Robbie and pass it along to   91
everyone," Schweiss said, wiping the tears from his cheeks. "I say, 'He was with
us last year.' I get emotional and I cry. . . .

"But I know that my son helps me. I firmly believe that every time I speak, he's   92
right on my shoulder."

When Pancoast speaks to a group of area high school students, she drapes   93
her son's football jersey over the podium, and displays his graduation picture.

"Every time I speak to a group, I make them go through the whole thing vicari-   94
ously," Pancoast said. "It's helpful to get out and talk to kids. It sort of helps keep
Chris alive. . . . When you talk, you don't think."

■

At Abraxas, Baxter attended high school classes until Friday. He is one of three   95
youths there who supervise fellow residents, who keep track of residents'
whereabouts, attendance at programs, and adherence to the center's rules and
regulations.

Established in Pittsburgh in 1973, the Abraxas Foundation provides an alterna-   96
tive to imprisonment for offenders between sixteen and twenty-five years old whose
drug and alcohol use has led them to commit crimes.

Licensed and partially subsidized by the Pennsylvania Department of Health,   97
the program includes work experience, high school education, and prevocational
training. Counselors conduct individual therapy sessions, and the residents engage
in peer-group confrontational therapy sessions.

Baxter said his personality had changed from an "egotistical, arrogant" teenager   98
to someone who is "mellow" and mature.

"I don't have quite the chip on my shoulder. I don't really have a right to be   99
cocky anymore," he said.

Baxter said not a day went by that he didn't remember his dead friends.   100

"I don't get sad. I just get thinking about them," he said. "Pictures pop into my   101
mind. A tree or something reminds me of the time. . . . Sometimes I laugh. . . .
Then I go to my room and reevaluate it like a nut," he said.

Baxter said his deepest longing was to stand beside the graves of his four   102
friends.

More than anything, Baxter said, he wants to say good-bye.   103

"I just feel it's something I *have* to do, . . . just to talk," Baxter said, averting   104
his eyes to hide welling tears. "Deep down I think I'll be hit with it when I see the
graves. I know they're gone, but they're not gone."

■ Reading Comprehension Questions

1. Which of the following would be the best alternative title for this selection?
    a. The Night of September 13
    b. A Fatal Mistake: Teenage Drinking and Driving
    c. The Agony of Parents
    d. High School Drinking Problems

2. Which sentence best expresses the main idea of the selection?
    a. Teenagers must understand the dangers and consequences of drinking
        and driving.
    b. Tyson Baxter was too drunk to drive that night.
    c. The Abraxas Foundation is a model alternative program to imprisonment
        for teenagers.
    d. Teenagers are drinking more than ever before.

3. The hospital had trouble identifying the boys because
    a. officials could not find their families.
    b. the boys all had false licenses and some of their bodies were mutilated.
    c. there weren't enough staff members on duty at the hospital that night.
    d. everyone was withholding information.

4. Tyson Baxter feels that
    a. the judge's sentence was unfair.
    b. he will never graduate from high school.
    c. he is responsible for the whole accident.
    d. he should not be blamed for the accident.

5. *True or false?* _____ Because of the accident, all the seniors promised that
    they would not drink during senior week.

6. The authors imply that the parents of the dead boys felt that
   a. Tyson should not be punished.
   b. their boys shared no blame for the accident.
   c. Tyson should have come to the boys' funerals.
   d. Tyson should be allowed to attend graduation.

7. The authors imply that most of the parents' anger has been toward
   a. school officials.
   b. Senator H. Craig Lewis.
   c. their local police.
   d. Tyson Baxter.

8. The authors imply that Tyson
   a. behaved normally after the accident.
   b. will always have a problem with alcohol.
   c. no longer thinks about his dead friends.
   d. is benefiting from his time at Abraxas.

9. The word *fathom* in "Compared with our own feelings of guilt, [we] could not begin to fathom this boy's emotions" (paragraph 64) means
   a. choose.
   b. understand.
   c. mistake.
   d. protest.

10. The word *dissuade* in "The parents . . . formed the Caring Parents of William Tennent High School Students to help dissuade students from drinking" (paragraph 66) means
    a. discourage.
    b. delay.
    c. organize.
    d. frighten.

■ Discussion Questions

About Content

1. Why do the authors call their narrative "a story of the times"?

2. Exactly why did four teenagers die in the accident? To what extent were their deaths the driver's fault? Their own fault? Society's fault?

3. What effect has the accident had on other Tennent students? In view of the tragedy, can you explain the reluctance of the Tennent students to give up drinking during "senior week"?

4. How would you describe the attitude of Tyson Baxter after the accident? How would you characterize the attitude of the parents? Whose attitude, if any, seems more appropriate under the circumstances?

About Structure

5. The lead paragraphs in a newspaper article such as this one are supposed to answer questions known as the *five W's:* who, what, where, when, and why.

    Which paragraphs in the article answer these questions? _____

6. The authors *do not* use transitional words to move from one section of their article to the next. How, then, do they manage to keep their narrative organized and clear?

About Style and Tone

7. Why do the authors use so many direct quotations in their account of the accident? How do these quotations add to the effectiveness of the article?

8. What seems to be the authors' attitude toward Tyson Baxter at the end of the piece? Why do you think they end with Tyson's desire to visit his dead friends' graves? What would have been the effect of ending with Lynne Pancoast's words in paragraph 94?

■ **Writing Assignments**

Assignment 1: Writing a Paragraph

While drunk drivers come in all ages, a large percentage of them are young. Write a paragraph explaining what you think would be one or more *effective* ways of dramatizing to young people the dangers of drunk driving. Keep in mind that the young are being cautioned all the time, and that some of the warnings are so familiar that they probably don't have any impact.

What kind of caution or cautions would make young people take notice? Develop one approach in great detail or suggest several approaches for demonstrating the dangers of drunk driving to the young.

Assignment 2: Writing a Paragraph

Tyson Baxter's friends might still be alive if he had not been drunk when he drove. But there is another way their deaths could have been avoided—they might have refused to get into the car. Such a refusal would not have been easy; one does not, after all, want to embarrass a person who has given you a ride to some event. At the same time, it may be absolutely necessary to make such a refusal. Write a paragraph suggesting one or more ways to turn down a ride from a driver who may be drunk.

Assignment 3: Writing an Essay

A number of letters to the editor followed the appearance of "A Drunken Ride, a Tragic Aftermath." Here are some of them:

To the Editor:

I am deeply concerned by the June 8 article, "A Drunken Ride, a Tragic Aftermath," not because of the tragedy it unfolds, but because of the tragedy that is occurring as a result.

It is an injustice on the part of the parents whose children died to blame Tyson Baxter so vehemently for those deaths. (I lost my best friend in a similar accident eight years ago, and I haven't forgotten the pain or the need to blame.) All the youths were legally intoxicated. None of them refused to go with Mr. Baxter, and I submit that he did not force them to ride with him.

Yes, Mr. Baxter is guilty of drunk driving, but I would like the other parents to replace Mr. Baxter with their sons and their cars and ask themselves again where the blame lies.

Tyson Baxter did not have the intent to kill, and his car was not the weapon. All these boys were Mr. Baxter's friends. The weapon used to kill them was alcohol, and in a way each boy used it on himself.

If we are to assign blame it goes far beyond one drunk eighteen-year-old.

The answer lies in our society and its laws—laws about drinking and driving, and laws of parenting, friendship, and responsibility. Why, for instance, didn't the other youths call someone to come get them, or call a taxi, rather than choose to take that fatal ride?

These parents *should* be angry and they *should* fight against drunk driving by making people aware. But, they shouldn't continue to destroy the life of one boy whose punishment is the fact that he survived.

Elizabeth Bowen
Philadelphia

To the Editor:

I could not believe the attitude of the parents of the boys who were killed in the accident described in the June 8 article "A Drunken Ride, a Tragic Aftermath." Would they really feel that justice was done if Tyson Baxter were dead, too?

Tyson Baxter is not the only guilty person. All the boys who got into the vehicle were guilty, as well as all the kids at the party who let them go. Did any of the parents question their children earlier that fateful night as to who would be the "designated driver" (or did they think their sons would never go out drinking)?

How would those parents feel if their son happened to be the one behind the wheel?

I do not want to lessen the fact that Tyson Baxter was guilty (a guilt he readily admits to and will carry with him for a lifetime). However, should he have to carry his own guilt and be burdened with everyone else's guilt as well?

Andrea D. Colantti
Philadelphia

To the Editor:

Reading the June 8 article about the tragic aftermath of the drunken-driving accident in which high school students were killed and injured, I was aware of a major missing element. That element is the role of individual responsibility.

While we cannot control everything that happens to us, we can still manage many of the events of our lives. Individual responsibility operates at two levels. First is the accountability each person has for his own actions. To drink, or not to drink. To drink to excess, or to remain sober. To ride with someone who has been drinking, or to find another ride.

Second is the responsibility to confront those who are drinking or using drugs and planning to drive. To talk to them about their alcohol or drug consumption, to take their keys, call a cab, or do whatever else a friend would do.

The toughest, most punitive laws will not prevent people from drinking and driving, nor will they rectify the results of an accident. The only things we can actually control are our personal choices and our responses.

Don't drink and drive. Don't ride with those that do. Use your resources to stop those who try.

Gregory A. Gast
Willow Grove

To the Editor:

After reading the June 8 article about the tragic accident involving the students from William Tennent High School, my heart goes out to the parents of the boys who lost their lives. I know I can't begin to understand the loss they feel. However, even more so, my heart goes out to them for their inability to forgive the driver and their ability to wish him dead.

I certainly am not condoning drunk driving; in fact, I feel the law should be tougher.

But how can they be so quick to judge and hate this boy, when all their sons were also legally drunk, some more so than the driver, and any one of them could have easily been the driver himself? They all got into the car knowingly drunk and were noisily rocking the vehicle. They were all teenagers, out for a night of fun, never thinking of the consequences of drunk driving.

I would view this differently had the four dead boys been in another car, sober, and hit by a drunk driver. However, when you knowingly enter a car driven by someone who is drunk and are drunk yourself, you are responsible for what happens to you.

Tyson Baxter, the driver, needs rehabilitation and counseling. He will live with this for the rest of his life. The parents of the four boys who died need to learn about God, who is forgiving, and apply that forgiveness to a boy who desperately needs it. He could have easily been one of their sons.

Debbie Jones
Wilmington

To the Editor:

The June 8 article "A Drunken Ride, a Tragic Aftermath" missed an important point. The multiple tragedy was a double—a perhaps needless—tragedy because the young men were not belted into their seats when the Blazer crashed.

All of those who were killed and severely injured had been thrown out of the vehicle; the only one left inside suffered a broken ankle. Had all been properly belted, all or most would probably have survived with similar minor injuries.

As much as this article points up the dangers of drunken driving, it also points up the absolute need for a mandatory seat-belt law strictly enforced. Two other points reinforce this. With eight people, the Blazer was overloaded by a factor of two. Also, Tyson Baxter, the driver, stated that his passengers were bouncing about and making the vehicle rock, a dangerous situation even when the driver is stone cold sober; being belted in puts a real damper on this sort of thing.

Roy West
Philadelphia

These letters make apparent a difference of opinion about how severely Tyson Baxter should be punished. Write an essay in which, in an introductory paragraph, you advance your judgment about the appropriate punishment for Tyson Baxter. Then provide three supporting paragraphs in which you argue and defend your opinion. You may use or add to ideas stated in the article or the letters, but think through the ideas yourself and put them into your own words.

ACKNOWLEDGMENTS

Sheila Akers, "Power Learning." Copyright © 1986. Reprinted by permission of the author.

Maya Angelou, "Adolescent Confusion" (editor's title), from *I Know Why the Caged Bird Sings.* Copyright © 1969 by Maya Angelou. Reprinted by permission of Random House, Inc.

Katherine Barrett, "Old Before Her Time," from *Ladies' Home Journal* magazine. Copyright © 1983 by Meredith Corporation. All rights reserved.

Theresa Conroy and Christine Johnson, "A Drunken Ride, a Tragic Aftermath," from *The Philadelphia Inquirer.* Copyright © 1986, The Philadelphia Inquirer. Reprinted by permission.

Delores Curran, "What Good Families Are Doing Right," from *McCall's* (March 1983). Reprinted by permission.

Linda Ellerbee, "Television Changed My Family Forever," from *Move On.* Copyright © 1991 by Linda Ellerbee. Reprinted by permission of the Putnam Publishing Group.

Anita Garland, "Let's Really Reform Our Schools." Copyright © 1994. Reprinted by permission of the author.

Bob Greene, "The Tryout" and "Sequel." Copyright © 1986 by John Deadline Enterprises, Inc. First appeared in *Esquire:* (1) March 1986, (2) August 1986.

Ann McClintock, "Finding a Career and a Job: A No-Nonsense Guide." Copyright © 1987. Reprinted by permission of the author.

Vance Packard, "What It Means to Be Young Today," from *Our Endangered Children.* Copyright © 1977 by Vance Packard. Reprinted with permission of Little, Brown and Company.

Beth Johnson Ruth, "The Steel Magnolias." Reprinted by permission.

Michael Ryan, "They Call Him a Miracle Worker," from *Parade* (December 25, 1988). Reprinted by permission.

S. Leonard Syme, "People Need People," from *American Health* (July-August 1982). Reprinted by permission of S. Leonard Syme.

Earl Ubell, "How to Think Clearly," from *Parade* (October 7, 1984). Reprinted by permission.

Laura Ullman, "Will You Go Out with Me?" Reprinted by permission.

570

APPENDIX

ANSWERS AND CHARTS

PREVIEW

This Appendix provides answers for the Introductory Projects in Part Four. It also provides four useful charts: an assignment chart, a spelling list to be filled in by the student, a general form for planning a paragraph, and a reading comprehension chart.

ANSWERS TO INTRODUCTORY PROJECTS

Sentence Fragments (page 236)

1. verb
2. subject
3. subject . . . verb
4. express a complete thought

Run-Ons (page 253)

1. period
2. *but*
3. semicolon
4. *When*

Standard English Verbs (page 268)

enjoyed . . . enjoys; started . . . starts;
cooked . . . cooks
1. past . . . *-ed*
2. present . . . *-s*

Irregular Verbs (page 277)

1. crawled, crawled (regular)
2. brought, brought (irregular)
3. used, used (regular)
4. did, done (irregular)
5. gave, given (irregular)
6. laughed, laughed (regular)
7. went, gone (irregular)
8. scared, scared (regular)
9. dressed, dressed (regular)
10. saw, seen (irregular)

Subject-Verb Agreement (page 285)

The second sentence in each pair is correct.

Consistent Verb Tense (page 290)

discovered . . . remembered

Pronoun Agreement, Reference, and Point of View (page 294)

The second sentence in each pair is correct.

Misplaced Modifiers (page 313)

1. Intended: A young man with references is wanted to open oysters.
   Unintended: The oysters have references.
2. Intended: On their wedding day, Clyde and Charlotte decided they would have two childen.
   Unintended: Clyde and Charlotte decided to have two children who would magically appear on the day of their wedding.
3. Intended: The students who failed the test no longer like the math instructor.
   Unintended: The math instructor failed the test.

Dangling Modifiers (page 317)

1. Intended: My dog sat with me as I smoked a pipe.
   Unintended: My dog smoked a pipe.
2. Intended: He looked at a leather-skirted woman.
   Unintended: His sports car looked at a leather-skirted woman.
3. Intended: A beef pie baked for several hours.
   Unintended: Grandmother baked for several hours.

Faulty Parallelism (page 322)

The second sentence in each pair reads more smoothly and clearly.

Capital Letters (page 331)

All the answers to questions 1 to 13 should be in capital letters.

14. The   15. I   16. ''That . . .''

Apostrophe (page 344)

1. The purpose of the 's is to show possession (that Larry owned the motorcycle, the boyfriend belonged to the sister, Grandmother owned the shotgun, and so on).
2. The purpose of the apostrophe is to show the omission of one or more letters in the contractions — two words shortened to form one word.
3. The 's shows possession in each of the second sentences: the body of the vampire; the center of the baked potato. In each first sentence, the s is used to form simple plurals: more than one vampire; more than one potato.

Quotation Marks (page 353)

1. The purpose of quotation marks is to set off the exact words of a speaker. (The words that the young man actually spoke aloud are set off with quotation marks, as are the words that the old woman spoke aloud.)
2. Commas and periods go inside quotation marks.

Comma (page 361)

1. a. Frank's interests are Maria, television, and sports.
    b. My mother put her feet up, sipped some iced tea, and opened the newspaper.
2. a. Although the Lone Ranger used lots of silver bullets, he never ran out of ammunition.
    b. To open the cap of the aspirin bottle, you must first press down on it.
3. a. Kitty Litter and Dredge Rivers, Hollywood's leading romantic stars, have made several movies together.
    b. Sarah, who is my next-door neighbor, just entered the hospital with an intestinal infection.
4. a. The wedding was scheduled for four o'clock, but the bride changed her mind at two.
    b. Verna took three coffee breaks before lunch, and then she went on a two-hour lunch break.
5. a. Lola's mother asked her, "What time do you expect to get home?"
    b. "Don't bend over to pat the dog," I warned, "or he'll bite you."
6. a. Roy ate seventeen hamburgers on July 29, 1992, and lived to tell about it.
    b. Roy lives at 817 Cresson Street, Detroit, Michigan.

Other Punctuation Marks (page 371)

1. pets: holly
2. freeze-dried
3. Shakespeare (1564–1616)
4. Earth; no
5. proudly—with

Commonly Confused Words (page 396)

Your mind and body . . . . *There* is a lot of evidence . . . .
then it will . . . said *to* have . . . *It's* not clear

Effective Word Choice (page 408)

1. *Flipped out* is slang.
2. *Few and far between* is a cliché.
3. *Ascertained* is a pretentious word.
4. The first sentence here is wordy.

CHARTS

ASSIGNMENT CHART

Use this chart to record daily or weekly assignments in your composition class. You might want to print writing assignments and their due dates in capital letters so that they stand out clearly.

Date Given	Assignment	Date Due

Date Given	Assignment	Date Due

SPELLING LIST

Enter here the words that you misspelled in your papers (note the examples). If you add to and study this list regularly, you will not repeat the same mistakes in your writing.

Incorrect Spelling	Correct Spelling	Points to Remember
alright	all right	two words
ocasion	occasion	two "c"s

FORM FOR PLANNING A PARAGRAPH

To write an effective paragraph, first prepare an outline. Often (though not always) you may be able to use a form like the one below.

Topic sentence: _____

_____

_____

Support (1): _____

_____

Details:

Support (2): _____

_____

Details:

Support (3): _____

_____

Details:

READING COMPREHENSION CHART

Write an X through the numbers of any questions you missed while answering the comprehension questions for each selection in Part Five, Fifteen Reading Selections. Then write in your comprehension score. (To calculate your score for each reading, give yourself 10 points for each item that is *not* X'd out.) The chart will make clear any skill question you get wrong repeatedly, so that you can pay special attention to that skill in the future.

Selection	Subject or Title	Thesis or Main Idea	Key Details			Inferences				Vocabulary in Context		Comprehension Score
Greene	1	2	3	4	5	6	7	8		9	10	%
Ryan	1	2	3	4	5	6	7	8		9	10	%
Curran	1	2	3	4	5	6	7	8		9	10	%
Angelou	1	2	3	4	5	6	7	8		9	10	%
Garland	1	2	3	4	5	6	7	8	9	10	%
Akers	1	2	3	4	5	6	7	8		9	10	%
Barrett	1	2	3	4	5	6	7	8	9	10	%
McClintock	1	2	3	4	5	6	7	8		9	10	%
Ubell	1	2	3	4	5	6	7	8		9	10	%
Ellerbee	1	2	3	4	5	6	7	8		9	10	%
Ruth	1	2	3	4	5	6	7	8		9	10	%

Selection	Subject or Title	Thesis or Main Idea	Key Details			Inferences			Vocabulary in Context		Comprehension Score
Syme	1	2	3	4	5	6	7	8	9	10	%
Packard	1	2	3	4	5	6	7	8	9	10	%
Ullman	1	2	3	4	5	6	7	8	9	10	%
Conroy and Johnson	1	2	3	4	5	6	7	8	9	10	%

INDEX